John Dewey

John Dewey

A Reader for Teachers and Education Students

Edited by

DAVID A. GRANGER

Cover credit: Photo of John Dewey by Robert Norwood. Photo courtesy of the Special Collections Research Center, Southern Illinois University Carbondale. Used with permission.

Published by State University of New York Press, Albany

© *The Collected Works of John Dewey, 1882–1953*, edited by Jo Ann Boydston

© 2025 State University of New York

All rights reserved

Printed in the United States of America

No part of this book may be used or reproduced in any manner whatsoever without written permission. No part of this book may be stored in a retrieval system or transmitted in any form or by any means including electronic, electrostatic, magnetic tape, mechanical, photocopying, recording, or otherwise without the prior permission in writing of the publisher.

Links to third-party websites are provided as a convenience and for informational purposes only. They do not constitute an endorsement or an approval of any of the products, services, or opinions of the organization, companies, or individuals. SUNY Press bears no responsibility for the accuracy, legality, or content of a URL, the external website, or for that of subsequent websites.

EU GPSR Authorised Representative:
Logos Europe, 9 rue Nicolas Poussin, 17000, La Rochelle, France
contact@logoseurope.eu

For information, contact State University of New York Press, Albany, NY
www.sunypress.edu

The author expresses gratitude for permission to use material from the following: *The Collected Works of John Dewey*, edited by Jo Ann Boydston. Carbondale, IL: Southern Illinois University Press, 1969–1991.

Library of Congress Cataloging-in-Publication Data

Names: Dewey, John, 1859–1952, author. | Granger, David A. editor.
Title: John Dewey : a reader for teachers and education students / [John Dewey] ; edited by David Granger.
Description: Albany : State University of New York Press, [2025] | Includes bibliographical references and index.
Identifiers: LCCN 2024029390 | ISBN 9798855801408 (hardcover : alk. paper) | ISBN 9798855801415 (ebook) | ISBN 9798855801392 (pbk. : alk. paper)
Subjects: LCSH: Dewey, John, 1859–1952—Knowledge—Education. | Dewey, John, 1859–1952—Philosophy. | Education—Philosophy. | Education—Social aspects. | Experiential learning. | Progressive education.
Classification: LCC LB875.D5 D477 2025 | DDC 370.1/2—dc23/eng/20241211
LC record available at https://lccn.loc.gov/2024029390

*Dedicated to the Faculty, Staff, and Students of the
Ella Cline Shear School of Education at SUNY Geneseo*

Contents

Acknowledgments — xi

Previous Publication Details — xiii

Glossary of Deweyan Terms — xvii

Introduction: John Dewey: The Education of a Lifelong Learner — 1

I. The Nature of Learning

1. What Psychology Can Do for the Teacher (1895) — 19
2. Education, Direct and Indirect (1904) — 33
3. From *How We Think* (1933) — 41
   What Is Thinking? — 42
   Analysis of Reflective Thinking — 51

II. The Nature of Method

4. Method in Science Teaching (1916) — 67
5. The Classroom Teacher (1923) — 75
6. From *Experience and Education* (1938) — 85
   The Need of a Theory of Experience — 86
   Criteria of Experience — 90

III. The Nature of Subject-Matter and Curriculum

7	*The Child and the Curriculum* (1902)	105
8	From *Democracy and Education* (1916)	123
	The Nature of Subject Matter	124
9	From *The Way Out of Educational Confusion* (1931)	137

IV. Theory and Practice in Education

10	The Relation of Theory to Practice in Education (1904)	145
11	From *The Sources of a Science of Education*, Part 1 (1929)	163
	Part I: Education as a Science	163
	Education as an Art	166
12	The Need for a Philosophy of Education (1934)	173

V. The Individual and Society in Democratic Education

13	Individuality in Education (1922)	185
14	Education and Social Change (1937)	195
15	Democracy and Education in the World of Today (1938)	205

VI. Morals, Ethics, and the Education of Habit

16	From *Moral Principles in Education* (1909)	219
	The Moral Training Given by the School Community	220
	The Moral Training from Methods of Instruction	224
	The Social Nature of the Course of Study	227

17	From *Human Nature and Conduct* (1922)	233
	Introduction	234
	Part One: The Place of Habit in Conduct	241
	Part Two: The Place of Impulse in Conduct	246
	Part Three: The Place of Intelligence in Conduct	249

VII. The Arts and Aesthetic Education

18	Individuality and Experience (1926)	257
19	Experience, Nature, and Art (1925)	265
20	From *Art as Experience* (1934)	273
	Art and Civilization	273

VIII. Vocational Education and Policy

21	Some Dangers in the Present Movement for Industrial Education (1913)	297
22	Learning to Earn: The Place of Vocational Education in a Comprehensive Scheme of Public Education (1917)	303

IX. The Profession of Teaching

23	*My Pedagogic Creed* (1897)	313
	Article One. What Education Is	313
	Article Two. What the School Is	316
	Article Three. The Subject-Matter of Education	318
	Article Four. The Nature of Method	320
	Article Five. The School and Social Progress	321
24	Toward a National System of Education (1935)	325
25	Those Who Aspire to the Profession of Teaching (1938)	331
Reader Bibliography		337
Selective Annotated Bibliography		339
Index		345

Acknowledgments

I am deeply grateful to the many individuals who generously provided support and assistance as I navigated my way through this rewarding project. I mention just a few here.

Richard Carlin, at the State University of New York Press, approached me with a unique vision for a Dewey reader for teachers. I immediately saw the great potential of the project; indeed, of the very real need for a book of this kind. While I had some previous experience as a journal editor, this venture was largely unfamiliar terrain. Richard's confidence in me was very reassuring, and his guidance throughout was a significant contributor to the successful completion of the book.

Longtime friends Jim Garrison and Larry Hickman provided feedback on an early draft of the introduction and shared my enthusiasm for the project.

I likewise benefited from the knowledge and expertise of my valued colleagues at SUNY Geneseo. Dennis Showers pointed out the need for greater clarity in the summary material on Dewey and science education. Annmarie Urso offered advice on scholarly resources for the material on Dewey and disability. Tactfully (in most cases), my teacher education students continue to keep me grounded in "real world" issues and concerns when my theoretical musings run too far afield of the subject matter at hand. I have been assured that this is no easy assignment. I am grateful as well to several anonymous reviewers from State University of New York Press for their edifying words and timely advice. As always, I accept full responsibility for any shortcomings remaining in the text.

A big thank you as well to Southern Illinois University Press for giving me permission to use a substantial amount of material from the award-winning *Collected Works* edition of Dewey's writings. These estimable volumes have been a constant companion since my early graduate school days.

Finally, I owe a debt of gratitude to my wife, Amy, and daughter, Isabel, a newly minted college graduate ("Go Brewers!"), for not holding me to my word when I announced that I was done writing books a mere six months before taking on this project. The fact that Dewey had already completed most of the work was, of course, largely beside the point.

Previous Publication Details

1. "What Psychology Can Do for the Teacher" appeared originally in a book by John Dewey and James A. McLellan, *The Psychology of Number*, 1895.

2. "Education, Direct and Indirect" was delivered as an address at the Francis W. Parker School, Chicago, January 1904. Published in *Progressive Journal of Education* 2 (1909): 31–38.

3. *How We Think: A Restatement of the Relation of Reflective Thinking to the Educative Process* was published by D.C. Heath and Company, Lexington, MA, 1933.

4. "Method in Science Teaching" was delivered as an address before the Science Section of the National Education Association in New York, July 1916. First published in *General Science Quarterly* 1 (1916): 3–9.

5. "The Classroom Teacher" was delivered as an address at the State Conference of Normal School Instructors at Bridgewater, MA, September 5, 1922. First published in *General Science Quarterly* 7 (1924): 463–72.

6. *Experience and Education* was delivered as the Kappa Delta Pi Lecture, 1938. It was published the same year by Kappa Delta Pi, West Lafayette, IN.

7. *The Child and the Curriculum*, University of Chicago Press, Chicago, 1900.

8. *Democracy and Education*, Macmillan Co., New York, 1916.

9. *The Way Out of Educational Confusion* is from the Inglis Lecture on Secondary Education at Harvard University, March 11, 1931. Published by Harvard University Press, Cambridge, MA, 1931.

10. "The Relation of Theory to Practice in Education" was published in *Third Yearbook* of the National Society for the Scientific Study of Education, University of Chicago Press, 1904.

11. *The Sources of a Science of Education* was delivered as the Kappa Delta Pi Lecture, 1929. It was published that same year by Horace Liveright, New York.

12. "The Need for a Philosophy of Education" was first published in *New Era in Home and School* 15 (November 1934): 211–14, from an address to the South African Education Conference in Capetown and Johannesburg, July 1934.

13. "Individuality in Education" was delivered as an address at the State Conference of Normal School Instructors at Bridgewater, MA, September 5, 1922. First published in *General Science Quarterly* 7 (1924): 157–66.

14. "Education and Social Change" was first published in *Social Frontier* 3 (May 1937): 235–38.

15. "Democracy and Education in the World of Today" was first published as a pamphlet by the Society for Ethical Culture, New York, 1938, fifteen pages.

16. *Moral Principles in Education*, the Riverside Press (part of Houghton Mifflin Company), Cambridge, MA, 1909.

17. *Human Nature and Conduct: An Introduction to Social Psychology* was published by the Modern Library, New York, 1922.

18. "Individuality and Experience" appeared originally in the *Journal of the Barnes Foundation*, 1926.

19. "Experience, Nature and Art" appeared originally in the *Journal of the Barnes Foundation*, 1925.

20. *Art as Experience* is based on the William James Lecture at Harvard University, 1932, published by Minton, Balch & Company, New York, 1934.

21. "Some Dangers in the Present Movement for Industrial Education" was first published as "An Undemocratic Proposal" in *American Teacher* 2 (1913): 2–4. Revised and reprinted in *Child Labor Bulletin* 1 (1913): 69–74.

22. "Learning to Earn: The Place of Vocational Education in a Comprehensive Scheme of Public Education" was delivered as an address at the annual meeting of the Public Education Association, Hotel Biltmore, February 20, 1917. First published in *School and Society* 5 (1917): 331–35. Republished in *Education Today*, ed. Joseph Ratner (New York: G.P. Putnam's Sons, 1940), 126–32.

23. *My Pedagogic Creed* was first published in *School Journal LIV* (January 1897), 77–80.

24. "Toward a National System of Education" was first published in *Social Frontier* 1 (June 1935): 9–10, as "John Dewey's Page."

25. "To Those Who Aspire to the Profession of Teaching" was first published in *My Vocation, by Eminent Americans: Or What Eminent Americans Think of Their Callings*, comp. Earl Granger Lockhart (New York: H.W. Wilson Co., 1938), 325–34.

Glossary of Deweyan Terms

Art: Dewey dismisses the popular idea that the arts transport us to an alternative reality of some kind. Instead, he contends that the arts originate from, and remain rooted in, the naturally occurring aesthetic qualities of everyday experience (e.g., qualities such as elegance, sublimity, rhythm, and novelty). More specifically, the arts accentuate, enhance, and preserve the meaning and value of these aesthetic qualities. Rather than representing the world through imitation, the arts re-present it to us in new, and often unusual, ways. (The subarea of philosophy that explores the nature of the arts is called aesthetics or, in Dewey's preferred spelling, esthetics.)

Culture: Culture is an essential concept for Dewey. Broadly speaking, culture is an expression of the way people live and interact meaningfully together in a particular shared environment or set of conditions. It is also a potential of nature, since human beings, the creators of culture, are part of the natural world. Culture includes the fine arts, but it also encompasses the practical arts, popular culture, disability culture, and, ultimately, the creative products of myriad forms of human experience and endeavor (e.g., customs and language). Relatively late in life, Dewey came to believe that the overall quality of a culture can be determined by the variety and vitality of art it produces.

Democracy: In Dewey's view, democracy is not simply a set of abstract rights and privileges or governmental processes. Rather, democracy is a way of life. As such it requires the creation of democratic habits of thought and action, along with free and open communication, and a core of shared norms and values enriched by diverse perspectives. This means that democracy is always in the making, a never-ending experiment in associated living. Nor is democracy strictly a political concept: it also extends to socioeconomic arrangements and issues related to things like equal educational opportunity, access to health care, and equitable working conditions. For Dewey, democracy is the way of life most capable of maximizing the potential of every human being for meaningful experience and a purposeful existence.

Empiricism: A product of the Enlightenment, empiricism is the theory that all knowledge is ultimately derived from sense-experience. (There are no innate ideas.) Dewey, as an empiricist, focuses his inquiries on objects and events open to observation (direct or indirect) and reflection. He is, moreover, a "radical empiricist," believing that prereflective experience is nondualistic in nature. This means that, prior to reflection, self and world, and the relations between them, comprise an experiential whole. The same is true of mind and body, reason and emotion, art and science, and other prominent dualisms. Though often treated as preexisting or a priori, these dualisms are actually conceptual tools constructed for specific, and limited, intellectual purposes. For Dewey, then, there is a direct relationship between *how* we experience and *what* we experience.

Experience: Experience, according to Dewey, derives from the interaction (or, in later writings, transaction) between human beings and their environments. This self-world interaction takes the form of a coordinated circuit of give and take, doing and undergoing, from simple breathing and eating to the most complex human activity. The content and quality of experience are determined by the things that contribute to this interaction, be they human, material, or ideational. Every experience is consequently unique. Experience is also continuous (we are never outside it), though some experiences feel unified and complete, with a discernible beginning, middle, and end. (Dewey calls this "*an* experience.") Experience additionally has cognitive (thinking) and noncognitive (feeling) dimensions, often in some combination. The source of all human learning, experience can be educative as well as noneducative or (in Dewey's term) mis-educative.

Expression: Expression, according to Dewey, is more than a mere outpouring of emotion. The impulse to express something and the emotion that sustains it (e.g., in trying to find just the right word for a speech or color of paint for a picture) must lead to thoughtful activity for an authentic act of expression. More specifically, the "inner" experiential dimension of expression, including some initiating idea or inspiration, is infused with meaning only as it is connected with some "outer" raw material, namely, a medium such as words, paint, or sound. This enhanced meaning requires that we arrange the material and make it articulate in a way that fuses emotion, action, and meaning into a coherent whole. When successful, this fusion transforms and enriches the original idea or inspiration.

Fact: Dewey dismisses the centuries-old idea that the world is made up of preexisting facts or bits of sensory data, waiting to be discovered and pieced together like an elaborate jigsaw puzzle. Rather, facts are arti-facts of inquiry: they are constructions of meaning conceived for specific purposes within particular situations. Nor are facts completely value-free or value-neutral. Like inquiry itself, facts always reflect particular beliefs, values, interests, and purposes.

Freedom: Dewey embraces what is often called "positive" freedom, or freedom *for*, as opposed to "negative" freedom, or freedom *from*. The latter concept emphasizes freedom from constraint or restriction, being able to do as you wish, at least in the abstract. Dewey notes, however, that this form of freedom is empty and meaningless without structures or boundaries of some kind. Absent these, freedom inevitably devolves into randomness, chaos, and isolation. (Imagine a game without any rules.) Freedom is also empty without the educational, financial, and other resources necessary for meaningful, realistic choices in life. This is freedom *for* or positive freedom.

Habit: Habits are the basic structures of human behavior. They take a virtually endless variety of forms incorporating both mind and body. Our various habits, in combination, make up our character or personality, while the shared habits of a social group constitute its customs or culture. These habits are actuated by natural impulses and constructed, and reconstructed, through all manner of creative problem-solving activity. Habits are also shaped by the living spaces we in-habit, especially when we are young. (We call this socialization or enculturation.) The more intelligent, flexible, and varied our habits, according to Dewey, the greater our ability to find and create meaning in experience. These habits represent growth and increased sensitivity to the environment, and thus contribute to our general well-being. On the other hand, nonintelligent habits, or those resulting from experiential confinement or restraint, can be very rigid and restrictive. They tend to limit or arrest growth.

Idealism: Idealism is the theory that what we experience as reality is ultimately determined by the mind. Nor is reality reducible to the material world. This is because ideas are considered superior to, or more real than, the material world. Absolute idealism, like that of philosopher G. W. F. Hegel, maintains that some infinite universal mind or consciousness (e.g., God or Absolute Spirit) unites the universe in an all-inclusive, enveloping whole. Dewey was drawn to Hegelian idealism early in his career and aspects of it remain, in naturalized form, in his later philosophy. (The subarea of philosophy that addresses questions about the general nature of reality is called metaphysics. Ontology, a narrower term, is the study of forms of being.)

Imagination: Imagination is commonly viewed as a special mental power used only in certain situations—for example, when we are creating or experiencing art. Dewey, however, argues that all conscious experience contains some element of imagination: It is a fundamental part of the ongoing drama of our everyday lives. Imagination pulls together past, present, and future, giving our experiences a sense of anticipation and, with the aid of memory, a narrative or story-like structure. As a principal means of expanding our intellectual horizons, imagination also allows ideas and meanings to move outside their origins in particular times and places. Imagination, then, differs from fantasy in that it is purposeful and goal directed rather than arbitrary and aloof.

Impulse: Human impulses are rooted in our biology and enable us to learn, adapt, and survive. (Like other biological organisms, if we don't learn and adapt, we don't survive.) More specifically, impulses provide the internal stimulus to act in certain predetermined but very general ways. They serve as forces for change, while habits are mechanisms of growth and conservation. Dewey identifies four basic impulses in children: the impulses to inquire, to construct, to communicate, and to express. The role of teachers and other adults is to help nurture and guide these natural impulses in productive ways so they develop into fruitful, intelligent habits. Stifling or corrupting them, on the other hand, is a harmful form of miseducation.

Individual/individualism: Dewey rejects the possibility of a presocial individual. He is also critical of forms of individualism that view humans as self-sufficient or self-realizing beings. On the contrary, Dewey stresses that we are naturally social creatures from birth (we would not survive otherwise); and the social world makes possible even our most basic forms of meaning-making and understanding. The role of education is to provide us with the constructive habits necessary for self-realization and autonomy. Genuine individuality—having not just a mind, but an *individual* mind—is essential to this process. It requires that we actively assimilate, in our own unique ways, the various intellectual resources (e.g., ideas and beliefs) in our social and cultural surroundings. Individuality is thus an achievement, not a given.

Intelligence: Intelligence, like imagination, is typically viewed as a power humans possess in different amounts. (Thus it can supposedly be quantified and measured.) For Dewey, however, intelligence is less a power we hold and more a way of doing things: it is a method of addressing problems that allows us to understand and thoughtfully modify experiential conditions. To do this effectively, the intellect must be forward looking; it has to anticipate future problems and possibilities. This requires effective habits of evaluation, judgment, and action. (Note that the noun "intelligence" functions here as the adverb "intelligently.") The "method of intelligence" is not perfectible, according to Dewey, but it can always be improved.

Knowledge: Dewey denies that knowledge is an autonomous possession, something that can be passed unchanged from person to person. He is more interested in the process of knowing, that is, with our ability to effectively use the problem-solving tools (i.e., active "know-how") we have acquired from past experience. Through this process, we regularly adjust or discard old, inadequate habits, beliefs, and understandings, and acquire new, more effective ones. This means that knowledge is fluid: it reflects our ever-changing relationships with the things that make up our ever-evolving world. Dewey also maintains that the goal of education is not simply to acquire knowledge: Knowledge is not the "be-all, end-all" of human experience. There are other richer and more directly meaningful forms of experience, like those fostered by encounters with the arts. Knowledge can assist us in making the most out of these encounters, but it is not an end-in-itself. (The subarea of philosophy that addresses the nature of knowledge and knowing is called epistemology.)

Language: Dewey refuses the popular idea that language provides a mirror image of the world. Nor do individual words tell us about things like labels on a tin can. (As human beings, we stand to the world in innumerable ways.) Language is rather a tool of practical, collective activity, and a singularly effective one. (Dewey calls it "the tool of tools.") Its basic purpose is communication: creating participation in shared endeavors. More specifically, language provides us with rules for using and interpreting things, in essence putting us on the same page so we can live and work effectively together. A failure of understanding is really a failure to come to agreement in action.

Means and ends: Means and ends are relational concepts for Dewey. They denote two parts of a single process, a means-ends continuum. Means and ends are also mutually informing. Ends serve as aims or goals and help determine the means to achieve them. If the necessary means are not available, we must adjust our ends. Means also provide intermediate goals or what Dewey calls "ends-in-view." Ends-in-view keep us on track in pursuing our ultimate ends and help us make any course corrections along the way. Intermediate goals can also provide their own sense of accomplishment. As we mature, we learn to strive for aims or goals that require many intermediate steps or ends-in-view. These additional steps can increase our sense of satisfaction once our ultimate ends are achieved. Play, in contrast, marks the coalescence of means and ends in that play is its own end or reward.

Mind: Dewey's conception of human learning is premised on the idea that the mind is active rather than passive: it is a dynamic system of meanings and purposes, and always functions in conjunction with our bodies. Our minds reach out into the world. Thus, we "mind" our elders and teachers "mind" their students. In short, mind denotes our interest in, and concern for, all the things that add meaning and value to our lives: practical, intellectual, and emotional.

Naturalism: Naturalism is a form of realism that accepts the priority of the common-sense world, including natural forces and laws. For Dewey, so-called subjective things, like feelings and values, are also part of this common-sense world. The results of scientific inquiry must continually be tested against everyday lived experience. We are not outside observers of a static world, but active participants in a universe where change is ongoing. Consequently, there is no such thing as certain knowledge or absolute truth. Naturalists likewise reject the transcendent or supernatural, as well as forms of scientific reductionism that devalue the common-sense world. Dewey was a Darwinian naturalist for most of his life.

New psychology/constructivism: New psychology, or constructivism, theorizes that we make sense of things, and construct meaning and knowledge, through active engagement with our surroundings. (Learners are proactive participants in experience.) Since intellectual and moral growth take place over time, we naturally draw on and adapt what we learned in the past in constructing new meanings. This should not be interpreted as a form of relativism: if these constructions are to serve our purposes, they must accommodate objective conditions. Some constructions consequently have more practical value than others. Moreover, because Dewey emphasizes the social nature of human beings and their surroundings, he is often considered a "social constructivist." This term reflects the shared construction of meaning and knowledge by distinct individuals working together within communities of inquiry, like discussion groups or research teams. Finally, these constructions are always subject to critique and revision.

Old psychology/faculty psychology: "Old" or faculty psychology predates constructivism and differs from it significantly. It originated in the eighteenth century and was derived largely from speculation. Faculty psychology emphasizes passive absorption of material to be learned, often through rote memorization, and conceives the mind as a fixed array of faculties (e.g., memory, reason, and imagination). Unlike constructivism, subject matter in faculty psychology must retain the form in which it is presented via lectures and textbooks, facilitating assessment through standardized tests. (Learners are passive receptacles of experience.) In addition, faculty psychology separates mind and body, typically educating them independently. It also views learners as autonomous individuals rather than social beings, and considers effort more essential in the learning process than interest. Dewey was a vocal critic of this theory of learning.

Pedagogy: Pedagogy is the Greek word for the theory and practice of teaching or, more concisely, the methodology of education. Theory and practice, for Dewey, are two parts of a single, ongoing process. Each should inform and add meaning to the other, promoting deeper understanding and enhanced professional judgment.

Perception: Dewey views perception as a temporally developing, exploratory process. (Recognition, in contrast, is often immediate.) To perceive is to attend to the distinctive features of objects, events, or people as they exist and function in the "here and now." This form of attending takes work. Its potential rewards, however, allow us to reconstruct and revitalize our habitual modes of experience and sense-making. Doing so can reveal a thing's hidden or alternative meaning and significance. Perception consequently engages all of the senses, not just our visual organs.

Philosophy: Like the ancient Greeks, Dewey views philosophy as a form of wisdom. In fact, he honorifically dubs it "the general theory of education." Philosophy's chief educational aim is to promote a better, more just, and more equitable world through systematic social and cultural critique. Doing so requires intelligent application of empirical methods, with inquiry that both begins and ends at the level of everyday lived experience. Central to this broad-based critique is the question of values. What kinds of things do we value and why? Which of these things are actually worth pursuing, or valuable, when we consider their costs and consequences? Variants of these questions can be found in the American philosophical movement known as pragmatism, with which Dewey is often associated.

Science: Science, like art, is an artifact or by-product of everyday lived experience. Both are purposeful, creative responses to the human condition. They facilitate our efforts to live wisely and well, and take a potentially infinite number of forms. For this reason, Dewey refers to science very broadly as "the method of intelligence." This includes the formal scientific method, but many other less formal kinds of inquiry and problem-solving as well. Dewey also asserts that science can be an art when its forms and instrumentalities (e.g., mathematical equations or molecular structures) are objects of immediately enjoyed perception.

Situation: Situations are dynamic combinations of objects, ideas, people, and activities that define and shape our everyday experiences. They provide a kind of experiential choreography, regulating, through habituation, how we think, feel, and act, in different environments (e.g., at a school athletic event vs. in a classroom). When situations are unfamiliar or become confused, creating an immediately felt difficulty, we have to locate, define, and address the problem(s) for our activities to resume. In this way, situations are the dramatic settings of our everyday lives: they are what we live in and for, giving our experiences meaning, value, and a sense of purpose.

Truth: Truth, Dewey argues, is neither timeless nor absolute. The universe is constantly evolving, as is our place in it, and no human being is infallible. Dewey consequently prefers to speak of "warranted assertions";

that is, working, temporary truths constructed over time through systematic inquiry. From this perspective truths serve as "regulative principles," verified through inquiry, and are always open to revision based on future inquiries. This means that objectivity is arrived at through intersubjective agreement rather than individual insight or divine inspiration.

Value/evaluation: Values are often viewed as nonrational personal preferences. Dewey, however, argues that values are human constructions and, as such, are amenable to rational processes of evaluation. Value-qualities, or direct satisfactions, are not normally subject to any form of evaluation (e.g., with regard to our fondness for certain types of food). Yet it is possible to examine the conditions that produce these value-qualities and the consequences of pursuing and attaining them (e.g., recognizing that these foods are unhealthy, perhaps, or deplete the environment of something of greater value). As a result, we might modify our tastes, attitudes, or practices accordingly. (The subarea of philosophy that considers the nature of values is called axiology.)

Introduction

John Dewey: The Education of a Lifelong Learner

This John Dewey reader was designed specifically for teachers, teacher educators, and education students. Using carefully selected articles, lectures, book chapters, and other miscellaneous writings from Dewey's collected works, it covers major concepts and ideas from this esteemed thinker's extensive research and reflections on teaching and learning.[1] The twenty-five readings were carefully chosen for their accessibility and their continuing relevance to the work of classroom teachers and other school-based practitioners. Though the pieces date back to the 1890s, readers will find that they can still speak, with considerable wisdom and insight, to many aspects of education and issues surrounding teaching and learning today. To further enhance its usefulness, the book contains a Glossary of Deweyan Terms, a scene-setting summary of each reading, a Selective Annotated Bibliography, and an index. Thus instead of merely encountering Dewey's views secondhand, this book empowers readers to access and explore primary sources in a user-friendly way as a preliminary to consulting the interpretations and opinions of others.

Readers should not feel pressed to agree with Dewey on every point. Any earnest critique must accept the prospect of revising or dismissing Dewey's thinking on whatever the topic at hand. This is a practice Dewey himself, as a fallibilist who recognized the limitations of his personal experience and perspective, openly encouraged. Indeed, Dewey was deeply attuned to the social and historical currents that actively shaped both his private life and his public work. Writing across multiple disciplines to varied audiences in numerous forums, he was a model public intellectual.

By any measure, Dewey enjoyed a very long and productive life. He was born to Archibald and Lucinia Rich Dewey in Burlington, Vermont, in 1859, as the country was edging ever closer to the Civil War. He died, still actively writing, at age ninety-two in 1952, during the first phase of the Cold War. To fully appreciate the scope and substance of Dewey's thinking about education, readers need to bear in mind the radical changes and momentous events that occurred in the US and the world during this time.

As cliché as it sounds, the only constant in Dewey's day was change. Perhaps most consequential were the cataclysms of the Civil War and two world wars, prompting the abolition of slavery in 1865 and the establishment of the League of Nations (1920) and the United Nations (1945). Dewey also witnessed disruptions in society and urban life wrought by recurring waves of immigrants from many parts of the world. This included places he would later visit during his extensive travels in Europe, Asia, and Mexico. The population of New York City, where Dewey lived much of his life, increased from 1.5 million in 1870 to 12.3 million in 1955 and fifteen states were added to the union. Noteworthy, too, the Great Depression cast a dark pall over the interwar 1930s, drawing Dewey into the contentious world of political debate, where he soberly resisted the lure of ideological extremes. Dewey additionally experienced several revolutionary developments in transportation, most notably automobiles and airplanes, as well as communication, with the invention of the telephone and expanded mail service. US railroad trackage grew from a mere 9,000 miles in 1850 to over 250,000 by 1950. Advances in oil and coal technologies, and later atomic science, also made possible the electrification of homes, businesses, and schools, as well as the growth of industry and establishment of the factory system. This led to mass production on an unprecedented scale and, with deteriorating working conditions, organized labor, a cause Dewey staunchly supported.

As his public engagement evolved, Dewey advocated increasingly for greater equity for girls and women (including schoolteachers) and people of color, especially in the social, political, and educational realms.[2] This activist mentality was instilled in Dewey by a trio of dynamic women: his mother, Lucinia Dewey, an evangelical philanthropist; his first wife, Alice Chipman, a lifelong reformer; and Jane Addams, a pioneer in the settlement house movement. In fact, the progressive reforms of the early twentieth century, catalyzed by the fledgling social sciences, took on many increasingly pressing issues of the day. This included more informed and humanitarian approaches to poverty, alcoholism, disease, mental illness, and the education and assimilation of immigrants and indigenous peoples. This initiated a brief period of utopianism, sometimes associated with

Dewey, that would not survive the horrors of World War I, a conflict that failed utterly in its bid to make the world safe for democracy. Dewey would ultimately describe himself as a meliorist, holding that progress is never inevitable and requires sustained human effort.

Dewey's writings attest to his extensive interest in the educational significance of these historic changes and events. This is especially the case with the aims and practices of formal schools, which were still legally segregated until 1954, two years after Dewey's death. It confirms as well that Dewey's views on human nature and learning were profoundly influenced by Charles Darwin's *Origin of Species* (1859) and the rapidly advancing science of evolution. In addition, Dewey's works demonstrate his resolute belief that democracy alone can provide the political and social arrangements necessary to maximize the potential of all people for meaningful experience and a life well lived. Democracy, in Dewey's view, is an ever-evolving way of being, not simply a collection of rights and procedures or winner-take-all majority rule.

Dewey's attraction to philosophy gradually emerged during his undergraduate education at the University of Vermont (1875–1879). Initially seeking his intellectual path through independent reading, Dewey's formal studies began in earnest his junior year in coursework on evolutionary biology, most notably T. H. Huxley's newly published *Elements of Physiology* (1878). This Darwinian introduction to the organic character of human life held great appeal for Dewey. It was soon supplemented his senior year by the revolutionary thinking of German philosopher Immanuel Kant. This eighteenth-century polymath argued that human experience provides us only limited knowledge about the world, and he spoke of an independent and unknowable realm of eternal ideas on which the processes of human reason ultimately depend. Not surprisingly, this move beyond the confines of traditional empiricism attracted many New England Transcendentalists, including one of Dewey's favorite professors, H. A. P. Torrey. Another important factor was the Kantian theology of Samuel Taylor Coleridge's *Aids to Reflection* (1825). Popularized by former University of Vermont president James Marsh, Coleridge's creative interpretation of Kant seemed to permit a form of empirical naturalism (even, perhaps, evolutionary science) that still made room for the supernatural. It was believed that each reality, though perhaps distinct, might have its own place and role in human experience.

Directly after graduation in 1879, and still painfully shy at age twenty, Dewey spent several unsatisfying years as a high school teacher. Feeling experientially overmatched and intellectually understimulated, he immersed himself in reading and writing philosophy whenever time permitted. This led eventually to Dewey's first scholarly article, "The Metaphysical Assumptions of Materialism" (1882), a highly theoretical piece, reflecting his studies at Vermont, published in the *Journal of Speculative Philosophy*. Also during this time Dewey had what he termed a "mystical experience," an indelible sense of being at one with the universe that resonated with his reading in Coleridge. It was an experience he would never forget.

Dewey's desire to return to academia prompted him in 1882 to enroll as a graduate student at Johns Hopkins University in Baltimore. Here, at a cutting-edge institution dedicated to scientific research, Dewey entered the final phase of his intellectual awakening. In just two short years his thinking would evolve remarkably.

Contrary to Johns Hopkins' focus on the sciences, Dewey became enamored with the absolute idealism of another innovative German philosopher, G. W. F. Hegel. Under the tutelage of professor G. S. Morris, Dewey found in Hegel a thinker who promised to move beyond Kantian dualisms and unite, through infinite, universal mind or consciousness (i.e., God or Absolute Spirit), diverse kinds of existences. This Hegelian form of self-realization encompassed the physical and mental, the secular and spiritual, the natural and supernatural, and the individual and social, as well as the finite minds of individual human beings. In this way, as Dewey saw it, Hegel provided a philosophical vision of a thoroughly interconnected universe, an organic whole of interdependent parts—one, moreover, that could seemingly accommodate the Christian worldview of his upbringing.

Despite some initial reservations, Dewey was also drawn to the emerging science of experimental psychology. Through professor G. Stanley Hall, a devoted empiricist who spurned the idealism of Hegel, Dewey encountered what was at the time called the "new" psychology. Another import from Germany, its main objective was to embed psychology in the study of human physiology using the tools of laboratory science. From the perspective of evolutionary biology, this new psychology defied convention in rejecting the passive, disembodied view of mind of "faculty psychology" (or the "old" psychology), with its reliance on rote memorization and recitation and a spectator model of knowing. In time, it would become the cornerstone of Dewey's rich conception of education and human learning. However, given the heady draft of Hegelianism he had already imbibed at Johns Hopkins, the young philosopher was, much to Hall's chagrin, more interested in trying to reconcile the new psychology with Hegel's absolute idealism, hoping the two might be made compatible. Specifically, Dewey suggested that advocates of the new psychology ennoble their empirical findings in the higher reality of the absolute (i.e., with the human body as the organ of the soul). Hegelians, meanwhile, could employ the new psychology to ground this absolute not in abstract structures of logic, but in the diversity-in-unity of an organic universe (i.e., with the soul realizing itself through the human body). Such, perhaps, might make a science of idealism. In the end, though, as we will see, this brand of Hegelianism could not satisfy even Dewey.

An existential crisis in Dewey's personal life helps explain his early receptivity to these particular thinkers and ideas. As he later wrote in his brief memoir "From Absolutism to Experimentalism" (1930), growing up in an evangelical household in New England had left Dewey's psyche with what he described as an "inward laceration."[3] This wound, which emerged (predictably enough) in Dewey's adolescence, stemmed from a rift between his physical impulses as a biological being and the austere beliefs and principles he was obligated to uphold as an evangelical Christian. Both were integral parts of his life, yet they seemed to pull in different and incompatible directions. This fostered both irritation and guilt, furthering his sense of isolation of self from world, body from soul, and nature from God. It also suggests that Dewey's crisis arose out of personal experience, coming of age in an environment of confusion and conflict, and not in any specific philosophical beliefs. However, Dewey's longing to soothe or heal this wound, in its emotional and its intellectual dimensions, naturally drew him in certain directions philosophically.

That process began in college with Dewey's introduction to Huxley's evolutionary biology. In the moving organic wholes of Huxley's naturalism, Dewey tells us, he found "a sense of interdependence and interrelated unity that gave form to intellectual stirrings that had been previously [nebulous], and created a . . . model . . . to which material in any field ought to conform."[4] This organicist model furnished Dewey with a philosophical template that he would regularly revisit and revise. Kant's challenge to conventional empiricism, on the other hand, initiated the move toward a more active conception of the human mind. This also made sense to Dewey and, in hindsight, cohered with aspects of the new psychology he would later study at Johns Hopkins. Yet Kant's unknowable realm of eternal ideas still left the young philosopher with an unbridgeable gap between self and world. Coleridge's *Aids to Reflection* looked to close that gap by conceiving both spirit and human reason in terms of direct experience, actual living, freed from abstract theological doctrines and philosophical systems. This idea, too, Dewey would repeatedly draw from and amend over the years. Finally, Dewey recalled that Hegel "supplied a demand for unification that was doubtless an intense emotional craving. . . . Hegel's treatment of human culture, of institutions and the arts, involved [a] dissolution of hard-and-fast dividing walls, and had a special attraction for me."[5] When he left Johns Hopkins, Dewey had yet to accept evolutionary biology and the new psychology as intellectually sufficient without the higher unity of Hegel's universal mind, including its implicit promise of social progress. In other words, he had not made the move from an organic idealism to an organic naturalism, or, as he later put it, "from absolutism to experimentalism." That said, Dewey was poised to begin a lifelong effort to reconceive, and move beyond, a host of dualisms he found intellectually dubious and destructive educationally. In doing so, as we will see, he often replaced the binary logic of either/or with the more holistic logic of both-and.

Dewey's first academic appointment took him in 1884 to the University of Michigan. Joined on the faculty by his Johns Hopkins' mentor G. S. Morris, Dewey's teaching and writing continued to stress the social dimensions of his Hegelian idealism. Dewey's Christian upbringing also remained intact and he became an active member of the First Congregational Church of Ann Arbor, where he regularly donated his time as a Sunday school teacher. Then, as well, Dewey met his first love and future wife, Alice Chipman. A gifted philosophy student and an avid reader, she happened to be living in the same boardinghouse as Dewey. Alice evidently enjoyed his classes, and they discussed philosophy and experimental psychology together in the evenings around the dinner table. It soon became obvious, however, that Alice was very much a doer, concerned with the quality of people's everyday lives, while Dewey's work was still largely steeped in theory. Over the next several years, she encouraged Dewey to wean himself from the abstractions of Hegel along with the formal trappings of institutionalized religion. As an alternative, Alice urged Dewey to ground more of his work in science-based educational reform and the cause of feminism. This transition alleviated Dewey's inward laceration and soon bore fruit in two articles written for popular science journals, "Education and the Health of Women" (1885) and "Health and Sex in Higher Education" (1886). Using empirical data, these short pieces added to a growing body of research dispelling the age-old myth that intellectual activity and formal university studies are constitutionally unhealthy for women. Alice married Dewey in 1886.

After a brief detour to the University of Minnesota (1888–1889), Dewey decamped again to Michigan and remained there until 1894. He and Alice decided to start a family as well. Dewey's natural affection for children was immediately obvious and, happily, never waned; and he began eagerly observing and documenting their growth and development. Dewey was also now devoting more attention to the psychology of teaching, especially issues related to student engagement and intellectual freedom, and he started interpreting democracy in ethical terms across a range of human activities (e.g., industrial democracy and cultural democracy). By the fall of 1894, the sharper focus and increased vitality of Dewey's research agenda saw him recruited by another major research institution, the newly founded University of Chicago. All of these events virtually guaranteed Dewey's deeper immersion in the new psychology and the inner workings of the teaching and learning process. The tangible reality of children was pulling him ever farther from the intangible world of the absolute. Dewey was offered and readily accepted joint appointments at Chicago in philosophy, psychology, and pedagogy, or the theory and practice of teaching. Dewey's star was clearly on the rise. Alice later joined him in this diverse and dynamic mecca of the Midwest with their three young children in tow.

The Deweys' decade in Chicago from 1894 to 1904 was particularly eventful and left a lasting mark on the entire family. Certainly one highlight was the founding of the University of Chicago Laboratory School in 1896.[6] The Deweys conceived this unique institution as both a proper school and a laboratory for creative application and firsthand study of the new psychology. In other words, its purpose was largely experimental, to integrate theory and practice; it was not intended as a model or demonstration school. And like any democratic community, in Dewey's view, its social bonds had to be continuously renewed through cooperative relationships and meaningful shared experience. Alice served in several positions, among them teacher and school principal. Most of the students were from the immediate university area, the offspring of local professionals, including the Dewey children. The school was staffed by a small cadre of talented, forward-thinking teachers and profited from the intellectual resources of the university.[7] Such an arrangement, Dewey believed, offered a unique opportunity to discard many of the dualistic attitudes and practices of faculty psychology that plagued conventional schooling. Most importantly, Dewey's expanding organic naturalism precipitated a new, more integrative and holistic model of human learning and growth, drawing on concepts from biology and evolutionary theory. Following this model, human beings are both *in* and *of* the natural world, not armchair observers on the outside looking in.

Dewey's take on the new psychology was first outlined in his landmark essay "The Reflex Arc Concept in Psychology" (1896).[8] In a nutshell, it argued that human relations with the world—the source of what we call "experience"—are not, as commonly believed, a series of intermittent reflex responses. Rather, our experience comprises an organic unity of ongoing, purposeful interactions with our environment, from the simplest activity (e.g., breathing or eating) to the most complex (e.g., doing brain surgery or painting a picture), and it involves the entire human being. Nor do we ever exist outside experience; it is our one and only medium of living and learning. Problems arise in experience when an existing pattern of interaction—typically, a habit derived from past experience—is disrupted or inadequate for some new and unfamiliar situation, causing disunity. The novel situation does not make sense, creating an immediately felt difficulty. Our activity, whatever its nature, is consequently blocked. Some kind of intelligent problem-solving, drawing on available resources (human, material, or ideational), is necessary for the activity previously underway to resume. This entails experimenting with possible solutions, both tangibly and through the exercise of imagination. (At times this might result in a change in the aim or goal of the activity.) If the process is successful, learning and growth occur as a new, more effective habit is created and some aspect(s) of the situation are modified. The blockage to our activity is removed and the now more-manageable situation again makes sense.

Students in the University Laboratory School often experienced this process through group activities based on "real world" occupations, some of which once occurred in the home or neighborhood shops, prior to industrialization, to meet domestic needs concerning food, clothing, and shelter. These purposeful, social activities entailed much more than amassing facts. Dewey believed that meaning in experience is a function of connections and relationships among ideas, objects, and people. Isolated facts, he argued, are mostly meaningless and consequently hard to remember. But the hands-on, social-centered activities at the Lab School offered subject matter for a rich, integrated curriculum, one that readily engaged students' interests and fostered what we now call "teachable moments," enlivened by the direct experience of meaning and growth. These student interests were guided by the teachers utilizing four natural impulses essential to learning but hindered by the strictures of faculty psychology: the impulses to inquire, to construct, to communicate, and to express.

For example, one year the Lab School students recognized the need for a dedicated space where student clubs could meet: a clubhouse. This problematic situation was not imposed on the students: it was a genuine felt need arising from their own firsthand experience. The situation evoked further thought, leading to consultation with teachers, who, once approving the project, had to determine their own form and degree of participation. Over the course of the project both teachers and students acquired new knowledge (e.g., regarding building design, cost of materials, and community impact) and hands-on skills (e.g., drawing, measuring, and using tools). Field trips to other building sites and research in geography, geology, and health and safety contributed as well. The project also required that students develop democratic social habits through negotiating and taking on different roles based on their ages, abilities, and interests. Further problematic situations naturally arose in the completion of the clubhouse, requiring teacher guidance and the creation of additional new knowledge and skills. With each step, the students' array of habits was expanding, the new and improved habits becoming, in a very real sense, part of the students' lived word or habitat.[9]

Reformer and activist Jane Addams also contributed to Dewey's education in Chicago. Her social work in and around Hull House pulled Dewey out of the university's ivory tower and into the larger reality of city life. Cofounded by Addams and Ellen Gates Starr in 1889, Hull House was the first fully inclusive settlement house in the United States. As such it provided community services, education, and arts programming for immigrants from diverse backgrounds. Its patrons were overwhelmingly poor: many worked for a pittance in factories or stockyards where labor laws were few and, amid political corruption, largely unenforced. Inadequate sanitation and a lack of clean water fostered numerous health problems. Moreover, there were far too few schools for the growing masses of immigrant children. Addams's and Dewey's complementary efforts to mitigate these problems brought out the best in each other. They often reversed roles as student and teacher: while Dewey served as a board member and frequent speaker at Hull House, Addams's support for the expanding immigrant population boosted Dewey's efforts, prompted by Alice, to immerse himself in public life and practical activism. The intercultural nature of Hull House also called for a high degree of attunement with the local knowledge and culture of its patrons. In this democratic community, paternalism was expressly avoided: everybody potentially had something valuable to share or teach, be it across generations or across cultures. In this way Hull House was both a trustee of the people's interests and a student of their experiences. It is not surprising, then, that the Deweys drew liberally on Hull House as a working model for their vision of the Lab School as a democratic social center. It, too, was a dynamic organic unity wherein individual community members developed their unique talents and interests while contributing to the larger social whole.

Dewey's time in Chicago also marked his formal break with the church. Alice, who had long encouraged him to end his affiliation, no doubt approved. Dewey would nonetheless continue to clarify his ideas about the nature and value of religious experience, especially in the context of democratic life and community. As well, by 1900 the Dewey family had expanded with three additional children. Tragically, however, two sons were lost to illness while traveling in Europe, a trauma from which their parents would never fully recover.[10] Several of Dewey's best-known educational writings come from this period. In *My Pedagogic Creed* (1897), Dewey offered a series of statements, followed by brief explanations, outlining his beliefs on the psychological and social dimensions of teaching and learning. *The School and Society* (1899) and *The Child and the Curriculum* (1902), two of Dewey's most popular books, chronicled the implementation of the new psychology at the Lab School, emphasizing the social and historical dimensions of students' learning. They additionally provided a glimpse of developments in the experimental school over its first several years.

Alas, the Lab School also figured prominently in the Deweys' eventual decision to leave Chicago. Dewey's relationship with university president William Rainey Harper had become strained over the years, and a merger with the progressive Francis Parker School was the proverbial straw that broke the camel's back. Alice would presumably carry on as principal of the new, larger school, but this arrangement ruffled feathers among the Parker school staff and Alice's principalship was slated to be, as the Deweys saw it, unjustly terminated.

Again Dewey's reputation as a philosopher and educator ensured that a new academic post would soon materialize. This time it was New York City's crown jewel Columbia University, established in 1754, and its younger affiliate, Teachers College (1887). Significantly, Dewey would no longer benefit from the hands-on research and organic synthesis of theory and practice he enjoyed at the Chicago Lab School. (On the plus side, he was freed from time-consuming administrative duties.) Dewey would continue, however, to explore the relationship between empirical science and education at every opportunity. Yet without the experimental proving ground of the Lab School, Dewey's thinking was increasingly appropriated by other educators and pushed to extremes, even among his professed supporters. The main culprit was popularly called "child-centered" pedagogy. It often promoted an exaggerated "hands-off" form of teaching that, Dewey worried, fostered aimless indulgence and intellectual indifference in students. In reality, he explained, teachers retained the responsibility as adults to use their wisdom and experience in guiding students' learning utilizing meaningful subject matter. The teacher's role was in fact more demanding with the new psychology, not less.[11]

This distortion of his ideas notwithstanding, Dewey was undaunted in seeking further opportunities to expand his experiential horizons as a lifelong learner. He eagerly cultivated personal and professional relationships with leading thinkers from diverse disciplines, among them anthropology, political science, physics, and the arts. This culminated in a number of Dewey's best-known and most respected works, many published after his retirement in 1930. Some of the intellectual themes Dewey developed in Chicago were now augmented significantly. In other cases, the themes were applied to new subjects.

Looking first at Dewey's major philosophical works, *Experience and Nature* (1925) argued that language evolved principally as a means of creating participation in shared experience and activity, while knowledge, as a form of belief, is an instrument or tool of problem-solving; *Ethics* (1908/1932) rejected the abstract idealism of Kantian ethics and the hedonism of utilitarianism, proposing instead an ethics of "intelligent sympathy" attuned to the welfare of others; *The Quest for Certainty* (1929) reconceived truth pragmatically as a "regulative principle" verified through inquiry and always open to change in light of future inquiries; *Individualism, Old and New* (1930) rejected the myth of the presocial individual, arguing that genuine individuality arises only from the creative assimilation of social and cultural life; *Logic: The Theory of Inquiry* (1938) looked to align the formal truths of logical theory with the provisional truths of scientific practice and evolutionary processes; and *Theory of Valuation* (1939) urged that values not be conceived as nonrational personal preferences, but rather as genuine existences amenable to rational processes of evaluation.

Of notable works in new subject areas for Dewey, *The Public and Its Problems* (1927) offered a spirited defense of participatory democracy at a time of increasing skepticism in the US, emphasizing the need for public forms of association; *Art as Experience* (1934) discarded elitist attitudes and insular conventions in the artworld using a naturalistic aesthetics that rooted the arts in everyday experience and events; and *A Common Faith* (1934) looked to free the religious quality of experience from the dogmatisms of institutionalized religion, proposing instead democratic life as a worthy religious ideal coupled with a secular natural supernaturalism.

Turning to Dewey's popular texts on education during this period, *Moral Principles in Education* (1909) argued that schooling inevitably has a moral impact on students, intentional or collateral, or both, the critical issue being the kind of impact; *Interest and Effort in Education* (1913) rejected yet another popular dualism in maintaining that student interest and effort are naturally complementary and must work together in experience for optimal learning; *Democracy and Education* (1916) explored the consequences of Dewey's belief that education be embedded in the direct experience of democratic living (i.e., learning through living), and not treated merely as preparation for an abstract and remote future; *Human Nature and Conduct* (1922) built on the organic naturalism of Dewey's reflex arc paper, examining its broader implications for social psychology, morals, and ethics; *How We Think* (1910/1933) analyzed the process of reflective thinking, in its myriad forms and dimensions, as both a means and an end of learning; and, finally, *Experience and Education* (1938) exposed the faulty premises of the child-centered vs. curriculum-centered education debate, and defined mis-educative experiences as those that curtail future learning and growth, while genuinely educative experiences provide a catalyst.

Predictably, Dewey did not only pursue his scholarly interests through bookish means during this intellectually stimulating period. He also traveled a great deal. As a self-styled fortune hunter of democracy, Dewey was continually seeking evidence of democratic forms of life among diverse peoples and cultures. Columbia president Nicholas Murray Butler, to his credit, generously supported these endeavors, allowing Dewey to live and work abroad for months at a time. As compensation, Dewey wrote extensively about his experiences overseas, sharing his impressions of life in parts of the world undergoing substantial social, political, and cultural change. Other new encounters were more personal but no less educational.

While vacationing in Italy in 1905, the Deweys met and adopted a young boy, Sabino, who had contracted bone tuberculosis of the knee. While the Deweys enjoyed all the social benefits of power and privilege, and successful surgery greatly improved Sabino's mobility, they struggled to place him in a conventional school and classroom. In response, the Deweys began campaigning for greater equity for the disabled and spoke out publicly against budget cuts to special education. In addition, Dewey developed a close friendship with Philadelphia philanthropist and art collector Albert C. Barnes in the 1920s. After spending many hours together sharing ideas about the arts and education, Dewey agreed to serve as the first director of education at the innovative Barnes Foundation and gallery. Barnes later reciprocated by taking the Deweys on several trips abroad to experience firsthand the artistic masterpieces of European museums and churches. These excursions, along with Barnes's exquisite art collection, proved invaluable for Dewey in writing *Art as Experience*.

Dewey also spent considerable time in the Far East. A short trip to Japan with Alice in 1919 subsequently led to a two-year sabbatical in China (1919–1921), where Dewey was warmly received as the "philosopher of democracy." While in Japan, Dewey was granted the opportunity to lecture at the University of Tokyo. Yet he later wrote of his dismay at the many overt signs of Japanese imperialism and its clear prohibition on anything, such as free speech, that might promote democratic ends. Dewey's sojourn in China was much more satisfying. Chinese progressives at the time were embittered by Japanese subjugation and the blatant governmental corruption that succeeded the ouster of the Manchu dynasty. Student dissenters, in particular, were eager to discuss and debate Dewey's pragmatic social and political theory and his vision of cultural democracy. Dewey was similarly well received in Turkey. In 1924, the Turkish government invited him to review the country's education system and make suggestions for its expansion and democratization. This was part of a larger reform agenda affirming Turkish independence and recognizing the rich heritage of its people. Dewey's well-received proposals envisioned Turkish day schools as centers of democratic habits and integral parts of local community life. Unfortunately, Alice would suffer a series of strokes soon after the Deweys returned to New York; she passed away on July 14, 1927.[12]

Dewey's much-publicized trip to Soviet Russia in 1928 focused similarly on the education and workaday lives of ordinary citizens. His initial observations suggested that the Russian Revolution (1917–1923) had done much to free the people's creative energies, as evidenced by popular culture infused with the arts and promising new educational initiatives. However, Dewey also sensed many institutionalized sources of repression. These included the omnipresent secret police, frequent arrests and deportations of political adversaries, and the ideological myopia of communist propaganda, particularly as it targeted Russian youth. These "Impressions of Soviet Russia" did, nonetheless, help prepare Dewey in 1937 to chair what was informally dubbed the "Dewey Commission." This unofficial commission was tasked by a group of American leftist intellectuals with evaluating Stalin's charges of treason against political foe Leon Trotsky in the famous Moscow purge trials. The commission convened in Mexico City, where Trotsky had found refuge in the home of partisan artists Diego Rivera and Frida Kahlo. Dewey, then seventy-eight, served admirably in his role as chair, working to ensure the fairness of the proceedings while overtly wearing his equanimity on his sleeve. Trotsky was symbolically exonerated by the commission in 1937, though he and Dewey, who disavowed Communism, remained at odds concerning the wisdom and propriety of far-left politics. This unique venture in Mexico was, according to Dewey, the most interesting experience of his life.

Dewey would live and work productively for another fifteen years, eventually succumbing to pneumonia on June 1, 1952. His legacy as a public intellectual, and the nature and degree of his influence on education in the US and elsewhere, remain subjects of considerable deliberation and debate. Revered by many and maligned by others, appraisals of Dewey continue to evolve with the shifting political winds and the pendulum swing of educational reform. That said, there is more scholarship sympathetic to Dewey appearing today than ever before.

This introduction would be incomplete without a few words on Dewey's habits and purposes as a writer. As many people have pointed out, Dewey's voice is rather detached and removed in his formal writings; he can come off sounding somewhat cold and aloof, though he was in fact very personable and attentive. This can take some getting used to.[13] Some readers also find Dewey's ideas and train of thought difficult to follow at times. This is often traceable to Dewey's unique interpretation of many of his key terms (even though he avoided technical jargon). The meanings of ordinary words like "experience," "situation," "habit," "mind," "fact," "truth," and "art" undergo significant modification in Dewey's vocabulary. These modifications, he tells us, resulted from his efforts to be true to "the concrete diversity of experienced things" with an "intellectual honesty" and integrity that, he admits, made writing "hard work" at times.[14] As we saw earlier, Dewey often rejected either/or dualisms and other common linguistic forms that treat abstractions as immutable realities. Instead, he developed a more contextualized, holistic vocabulary, one less direct and readily grasped than one might perhaps like, but also more responsive to the moving, richly textured fabric of everyday experience. For readers who take the time to acclimate to Dewey's habits and purposes as a writer, the alternative perspective he offers can shed valuable light on the conditions necessary for enriched human experience and lifelong learning.

Notes

1. Citations of Dewey's writings (Southern Illinois University Press, *Collected Works* edition) are given in standard form, consisting of initials representing the set (*EW*, *MW*, and *LW* for *Early Works*, *Middle Works*, and *Later Works*, respectively), the volume number, and the page number.

2. Dewey participated in the National Negro Conference in 1909, which called for the founding of the NAACP (1910), of which he then became a charter member. Dewey also helped establish the American Civil Liberties Union (1920), the American Association of University Professors (1915), the American Federation of Teachers (1916), and the New York City Teachers Guild (1935), which later became the United Federation of Teachers (1960). That said, readers will encounter in Dewey language they might find jarring regarding race, ethnicity, and gender. This includes anachronisms like "Hindoo," "Bushman," and "Oriental," as well as the linear historicism of "savage" and "primitive." Then again, Dewey often acknowledged the achievements of non-Western cultures (e.g., in philosophy and the arts), and he affirmed at the National Negro Conference that "there is no inferior race, and the members of a race so-called should each have the same opportunities of social environment and personality as those of the more favored race." See John Dewey, "Address to National Negro Conference," in *John Dewey: The Middle Works, Vol. 4*, ed. Jo Ann Boydston (Carbondale: Southern Illinois University Press, 1977), 157. Like the vast majority of people in his day, Dewey also regularly used masculine pronouns (e.g., he, him, his).

3. John Dewey, "From Absolutism to Experimentalism," in *John Dewey: The Later Works, Vol. 5*, ed. Jo Ann Boydston (Carbondale: Southern Illinois University Press, 1984), 153.

4. Dewey, "From Absolutism to Experimentalism," 147.

5. Dewey, "From Absolutism to Experimentalism," 153.

6. The initial enrollment of the Laboratory School was only fifteen, but it eventually grew to 140 students by 1904. Today, it is also commonly known

as the Dewey School and serves around 2,000 students grades pre-K to12. This includes approximately 50 percent students of color, while 37 percent identify as part of the LGBTQ+ community. You can learn more here: https://www.ucls.uchicago.edu/about-lab.

7. Perhaps the best example is friend and colleague George Herbert Mead, whom Dewey credits with deepening his appreciation for the social nature of mind and identity. See Mead's lectures published posthumously in *Mind, Self, and Society* (Chicago: University of Chicago Press, 1934).

8. John Dewey, "The Reflex Arc Concept in Psychology," in *John Dewey: The Early Works, Vol. 5*, ed. Jo Ann Boydston (Carbondale: Southern Illinois University Press, 1972), 96–109.

9. This is an example of what today is commonly termed constructivism or, with Dewey, social constructivism. Note that it is not a form of relativism. To serve our purposes, constructions of meaning and knowledge must accommodate objective conditions. Moreover, as demonstrated by the clubhouse project, these are shared constructions, conceived by distinct individuals working together within communities of inquiry. The constructions are likewise always subject to critique and revision. For more on the Lab School clubhouse project, see Katherine Camp Mayhew and Anna Camp Edwards, *The Dewey School: The Laboratory School of the University of Chicago 1896–1903* (New Brunswick, NJ: Aldine Transaction Publishers, 1965), 228–33.

10. Morris Dewey died of diphtheria in 1895 and Gordon succumbed to typhoid in 1904. Morris was named after G. S. Morris and daughter Jane, the youngest of the Dewey children (and a future world-class physicist), after Jane Addams.

11. Though Dewey is often identified with "progressive education," in reality he had an uneasy relationship with the Progressive Education Association, in part due to its endorsement of child-centered pedagogy. Dewey also rejected the opposite extreme: the rigidity and experiential detachment of curriculum-centered pedagogy.

12. Dewey subsequently married longtime acquaintance Roberta Lowitz Grant in 1946, and the couple adopted two children from Halifax, Nova Scotia.

13. Evidence from some of Dewey's former university students suggests parallels in his demeanor as a classroom teacher. As these witnesses recall, Dewey typically sat the entire period, with crumpled notes in hand. He spoke slowly and in a monotone, pausing seemingly at random, while looking abstractedly out the window. Yet those who learned to pay attention during his lectures came to value the opportunity to hear what was, in effect, Dewey problem-solving out loud. For more on this subject, see Philip W. Jackson, *John Dewey and the Lessons of Art* (New Haven: Yale University Press, 1998), 182–86.

14. Dewey, "From Absolutism to Experimentalism, 151.

I
THE NATURE OF LEARNING

1

What Psychology Can Do for the Teacher (1895)

We begin section one with a lesser-known but illuminating piece entitled "What Psychology Can Do for the Teacher." It first appeared in Dewey and James A. McLellan's book *The Psychology of Number*. (This was just prior to the publication of Dewey's historic paper on the reflex-arc concept in psychology, a critical piece of his constructivist learning theory; for more on this topic, see the introduction.) In this chapter, Dewey discusses some of the psychological factors that make teaching a unique and challenging profession. He underscores the fact that it requires an appreciation for the natural impulses of children, the internal stimulus to meaning-making and growth, along with a working knowledge of child development. Though a variety of instructional supports might be available to the classroom teacher, Dewey encourages intelligent use of research in the psychology of learning supplemented by reflective practice. This approach underscores the importance of the teacher's ability to develop and utilize appropriate learning materials and pedagogical methods.

The value of any fact or theory as bearing on human activity is, in the long run, determined by practical application—that is, by using it for accomplishing some definite purpose. If it works well—if it removes friction, frees activity, economizes effort, makes for richer results—it is valuable as contributing to a perfect adjustment of means to end. If it makes no such contribution it is practically useless, no matter what claims may be theoretically urged in its behalf. To this the question of the relation between psychology and education presents no exception. The value of a knowledge of psychology in general, or of the psychology of a particular subject, will be best made known by its fruits. No amount of argument can settle the question once for all and in advance of any experimental work. But, since education is a rational process, that is a process in harmony with the laws of psychical development, it is plain that the educator need not and should not depend upon vague inductions from a practice not grounded upon principles. Psychology can not dispense with experience, nor can experience, if it is to be rational, dispense with psychology. It is possible to make actual practice less a matter of mere experiment and more a matter of reason; to make it contribute directly and economically to a rich and ripe, because rational, experience. And this the educational psychologist attempts to do by indicating in what directions help is likely to be found; by indicating what kind of psychology is likely to help and what is not likely; and, finally, by indicating what valid reasons there are for anticipating any help at all.

I. As to the last point suggested, that psychology *ought* to help the educator, there can be no disagreement. In the *first place* the study of psychology has a high *disciplinary* value for the teacher. It develops the power of connected thinking and trains to logical habits of mind. These qualities, essential though they are in thorough teaching, there is a tendency to undervalue in educational methods of the present time when so much is made of the accumulation of facts and so little of their organization. In our eager advocacy of "facts and things" we are apparently forgetting that these are comparatively worthless, either as stored knowledge or for developing power, till they have been subjected to the discriminating and formative energy of the intelligence. Unrelated facts are not knowledge any more than the words of a dictionary are connected thoughts. And so the work of getting "things" may be carried to such an extent as to burden the mind and check the growth of its higher powers. There may be a surfeit of things with the usual consequence of an impaired mental digestion. It is pretty generally conceded that the number of facts memorized is by no means a measure of the amount of power developed; indeed, unless reflection has been exercised step by step with observation, the mass of power gained may turn out to be inversely proportional to the multitude of facts. This does not mean that there is any opposition between reflection and true observation. There can not be observation in the best sense of the word without reflection, nor can reflection fail to be an effective preparation for observation.

It will be readily admitted that this tendency to exalt facts unduly may be checked by the study of psychology. Here, in a comparatively abstract science, there *must* be reflection—abstraction and generalization. In nature study we gather the facts, and we *may* reflect upon the facts: in mind study we must reflect in order to get the facts. To observe the subtle and complex facts of mind, to discriminate the elements of a consciousness never the same for two successive moments, to give unity of meaning to these abstract mental phenomena, demands such concentration of attention as must secure the growth of mental power—power to master, and not be mastered by, the facts and ideas of whatever kind which may be crowding in upon the mind; to resolve a complex subject into its component parts, seizing upon the most important and holding them clearly defined and related in consciousness; to take, in a word, any "chaos" of experience and reduce it to harmony and system. This analytic and relating power, which is an essential mark of the clear thinker, is the prime qualification of the clear teacher.

But, in the *second place,* the study of psychology is of still more value to the teacher in its bearing upon his *practical* or strictly professional training.

Every one grants that the primary aim of education is the training of the powers of intelligence and will—that the object to be attained is a certain quality of character. To say that the purpose of education is "an increase of the powers of the mind rather than an enlargement of its possessions"; that education is a science, the science of the formation of character; that character means a measure of mental power, mastery of truths and laws, love of beauty in nature and in art, strong human sympathy, and unswerving moral rectitude; that the teacher is a trainer of mind, a former of character; that he is an artist above nature, yet in harmony with nature, who applies the science of education to help another to the full realization of his personality in a character of strength, beauty, freedom—to say this is simply to proclaim that the problem of education is essentially an ethical and psychological problem. This problem can be solved only as we know the true nature and destination of man as a rational being, and the rational methods by which the perfection of his nature may be realized. Every aim proposed by the educator which is not in harmony with the intrinsic aim of human nature itself, every method or device employed by the teacher that is not in perfect accord with the mind's own workings, not only wastes time and energy, but results in positive and permanent harm; running counter to the true activities of the mind, it certainly distorts and may possibly destroy them. To the educator, therefore, the only solid ground of assurance that he is not setting up impossible or artificial aims, that he is not using ineffective and perverting methods, is a clear and definite knowledge of the normal end and the normal forms of mental action. To know these things is to be a true psychologist and a true moralist, and to have the essential qualifications of the true educationist. Briefly, only psychology and ethics can take education out of its purely empirical and rule-of-thumb stage. Just as a knowledge of mathematics and mechanics have wrought marvelous improvements in all the arts of construction; just as a knowledge of steam and electricity has made a revolution in modes of communication, travel, and transportation of commodities; just as a knowledge of anatomy, physiology, pathology has transformed medicine from empiricism to applied science, so a knowledge of the structure and functions of the human being can alone elevate the school from the position of a mere workshop, a more or less cumbrous, uncertain, and even baneful institution, to that of a vital, certain, and effective instrument in the greatest of all constructions—the building of a free and powerful character.

Without the assured methods and results of science there are just three resources available in the work of education.

1. The first is *native tact and skill,* the intuitive power that comes mainly from sympathy. For this personal power there is absolutely no substitute. "Any one can keep school," perhaps, but not every one can teach school any more than every one can become a capable painter, or an able engineer, or a skilled artist in any direction. To ignore native aptitude, and to depend wholly, or even chiefly, upon the knowledge and use of "methods," is an error fatal to the best interests of education; and there can be no question that many schools are suffering frightfully from ignoring or undervaluing this paramount qualification of the true teacher. But in urging the need of psychology in the preparation of the teacher there is no question of ignoring personal power or of finding a substitute for personal magnetism. It is only a question of providing the best opportunities for the exercise of native capacity—for the fullest development and most fruitful application of endowments of heart and brain. Training and native outfit, culture and nature, are never opposed to each other. It is always a question, not of suppressing or superseding, but of cultivating native

instinct, of training natural equipment to its ripest development and its richest use. A Pheidias does not despise learning the principles necessary to the mastery of his art, nor a Beethoven disregard the knowledge requisite for the complete technical skill through which he gives expression to his genius. In a sense it is true that the great artist is born, not made; but it is equally true that a scientific insight into the technics of his art *helps* to make him. And so it is with the artist teacher. The greater and more scientific his knowledge of human nature, the more ready and skillful will be his application of principles to varying circumstances, and the larger and more perfect will be the product of his artistic skill.

But the genius in education is as rare as the genius in other realms of human activity. Education is, and forever will be, in the hands of ordinary men and women; and if psychology—as the basis of scientific insight into human nature—is of high value to the few who possess genius, it is indispensable to the many who have not genius. Fortunately for the race, most persons, though not "born" teachers, are endowed with some "genial impulse," some native instinct and skill for education; for the cardinal requisite in this endowment is, after all, sympathy with human life and its aspirations. We are all born to be educators, to be parents, as we are not born to be engineers, or sculptors, or musicians, or painters. Native capacity for education is therefore much more common than native capacity for any other calling. Were it not so, human society could not hold together at all. But in most people this native sympathy is either dormant or blind and irregular in its action; it needs to be awakened, to be cultivated, and above all to be intelligently directed. The instinct to walk, to speak, and the like are imperious instincts, and yet they are not wholly left to "nature"; we do not assume that they will take care of themselves; we stimulate a guide, we supply them with proper conditions and material for their development. So it must be with this instinct, so common yet at present so comparatively ineffective, which lies at the heart of all educational efforts, the instinct to help others in their struggle for self-mastery and self-expression. The very fact that this instinct is so strong, and all but universal, and that the happiness of the individual and of the race so largely depends upon its development and intelligent guidance, gives greater force to the demand that its growth may be fostered by favourable conditions; and that it may be made certain and reasonable in its action, instead of being left blind and faltering, as it surely will be without rational cultivation.

To this it may be added that native endowment can work itself out in the best possible results only when it works under right conditions.

Even if scientific insight were not a necessity for the true educator himself, it would still remain a necessity for others in order that they might not obstruct and possibly drive from the profession the teacher possessed of the inborn divine light, and restrict or paralyze the efforts of the teacher less richly endowed. It is the mediocre and the bungler who can most readily accommodate himself to the conditions imposed by ignorance and routine, it is the higher type of mind and heart which suffers most from its encounter with incapacity and ignorance. One of the greatest hindrances to true educational progress is the reluctance of the best class of minds to engage in educational work precisely because the general standard of ethical and psychological knowledge is so low that too often high ideals are belittled and efforts to realize them even vigorously opposed. The educational genius, the earnest teacher of any class, has little to expect from an indifference, or a stolidity, which is proof alike against the facts of experience and the demonstrations of science.

2. The Second Resource is *experience*. This, again, is necessary. Psychology is not a short and easy path that renders personal experience superfluous. The real question is: What kind of experience shall it be? It is in a way perfectly true that only by teaching can one become a teacher. But not any and every sort of thing which passes for teaching or for "experience" will make a teacher any more than simply sawing a bow across violin strings will make a violinist. It is a certain quality of practice, not mere practice, which produces the expert and the artist. Unless the practice is based upon rational principles, upon insight into facts and their meaning, "experience" simply fixes incorrect acts into wrong habits. Nonscientific practice, even if it finally reaches sane and reasonable results—which is very unlikely—does so by unnecessarily long and circuitous routes; time and energy are wasted that might easily be saved by wise insight and direction at the outset.

The worst thing about empiricism in every department of human activity is that it leads to a blind observance of rule and routine. The mark of the empiric is that he is helpless in the face of new circumstances; the mark of the scientific worker is that he has power in grappling with the new and the untried; he is master of principles which he can effectively apply under novel conditions. The one is a slave of the past, the other is a director of the future. This attachment to routine, this subservience to empiric formula, always reacts into the character of the empiric; he becomes hour by hour more and more a mere routinist and less and less an artist. Even that which he has once learned and applied with some interest and intelligence tends to become more and more mechanical, and its application more and more an unintelligent and unemotional procedure. It is never brightened and quickened by adaptation to new ends. The machine teacher, like the empiric in every profession, thus becomes a stupefying and corrupting influence in his surroundings; he himself becomes a mere tradesman, and makes his school a mere machine shop.

3. The Third Resource is *authoritative instruction in methods and devices*. At present, the real opposition is not between native skill and experience on the one side, and psychological methods on the other; it is rather between devices picked up no one knows how, methods inherited from a crude past, or else invented, *ad hoc,* by educational quackery—and methods which can be rationally justified—devices which are the natural fruit of knowing the mind's powers and the ways in which it works and grows in assimilating its proper nutriment. The mere fact that there are so many methods current, and constantly pressed upon the teacher as the acme of the educational experience of the past, or as the latest and best discovery in pedagogy, makes an absolute demand for some standard by which they may be tested. Only knowledge of the principles upon which all methods are based can free the teacher from dependence upon the educational nostrums which are recommended like patent medicines, as panaceas for all educational ills. If a teacher is one fairly initiated into the real workings of the mind, if he realizes its normal aims and methods, false devices and schemes can have no attraction for him; he will not swallow them "as silly people swallow empirics' pills"; he will reject them as if by instinct. All new suggestions, new methods, he will submit to the infallible test of science; and those which will further his work he can adopt and rationally apply, seeing clearly their place and bearings, and the conditions under which they can be most effectively employed. The difference between being overpowered and used by machinery and being able to use the machinery is precisely the difference between methods externally inculcated and methods freely adopted, because of insight into the psychological principles from which they spring.

Summing up, we may say that the teacher requires a sound knowledge of ethical and psychological principles—first, because such knowledge, besides its indirect value as forming logical habits of mind, is necessary to secure the full use of native skill; secondly, because it is necessary in order to attain a perfected experience with the least expenditure of time and energy; and thirdly, in order that the educator may not be at the mercy of every sort of doctrine and device, but may have his own standard by which to test the many methods and expedients constantly urged upon him, selecting those which stand the test and rejecting those which do not, no matter by what authority or influence they may be supported.

II. We may now consider more positively how psychology is to perform this function of developing and directing native skill, making experience rational and hence prolific of the best results, and providing a criterion for suggested devices.

Education has two main phases which are never separated from each other, but which it is convenient to distinguish. One is concerned with the organization and workings of the school as part of an organic whole; the other, with the adaptation of this school structure to the individual pupil. This difference may be illustrated by the difference in the attitude of the school board or minister of education or superintendent, whether state, county, or local, to the school, and that of the individual teacher within the school. The former (the administrators of an organized system) are concerned more with the constitution of the school as a whole; their survey takes in a wide field, extending in some cases from the kindergarten to the university throughout an entire country, in other cases from the primary school to the high or academic school in a given town or city. Their chief business is with the organization and management of the school, or system of schools, upon certain general principles. What shall be the end and means of the entire institution? What subjects shall be studied? At what stage shall they be introduced, and in what sequence shall they follow one another—that is, what shall be the arrangement of the school as to its various parts in time? Again, what shall be the correlation of studies and methods at every period? Shall they be taught as different subjects? in departments? or shall methods be sought which shall work them into an organic whole? All this lies, in a large measure, outside the purview of the individual teacher; once within the institution he finds its purpose, its general lines of work, its constitutional structure, as it were, fixed for him. An individual may choose to live in France, or Great Britain, or the United States, or Canada; but after he has made his choice, the general conditions under which he shall exercise his citizenship are decided for him. So it is, in the main, with the individual teacher.

But the citizen who lives within a given system of institutions and laws finds himself constantly called upon to act. He must adjust his interests and activities to those of others in the same country. There is, at the same time, scope for purely individual selection and application of means to ends, for unfettered action of strong personality, as well as opportunity and stimulus for the free play and realization of individual equipment and acquisition. The better the constitution, the system which he can not directly control, the wider and freer and more potent will be this sphere of individual action. Now, the individual teacher finds his duties within the school as an entire institution; he has to adapt this organism, the subjects taught, the modes of discipline, etc., to the individual pupil. Apart from this personal adaptation on the part of the individual teacher, and the personal assimilation on the part of the individual pupil, the general arrangement of the school is purely meaningless; it has its object and its justification in this individual realm. Geography, arithmetic, literature, etc., may be provided in the curriculum, and their order, both of sequence and coexistence, laid down; but this is all dead and formal until it comes to the intelligence and character of the individual pupil, and the individual teacher is *the medium through which it comes*.

Now, the bearing of this upon the point in hand is that psychology and ethics have to subserve these two functions. These functions, as already intimated, can not be separated from each other; they are simply the general and the individual aspects of school life; but for purposes of study, it is convenient and even important to distinguish them. We may consider psychology and ethics from the standpoint of the light they throw upon the organization of the school as a whole—its end, its chief methods, the order and correlation of studies—and we may consider from the standpoint of the service they can perform for the individual teacher in qualifying him to use the prescribed studies and methods intelligently and efficiently, the insight they can give him into the workings of the individual mind, and the relation of any given subject to that mind.

Next to positive doctrinal error within the pedagogy itself, it may be said that the chief reason why so much of current pedagogy has been either practically useless or even practically harmful is the failure to distinguish these two functions of psychology. Considerations, principles, and maxims that derive their meaning, so far as they have any meaning, from their reference to the organization of the whole institution, have been presented as if somehow the individual teacher might derive from them specific information and direction as to how to teach particular subjects to particular pupils; on the other hand, methods that have their value (if any) as simple suggestions to the individual teacher as to how to accomplish temporary ends at a particular time have been presented as if they were eternal and universal laws of educational polity. As a result the teacher is confused; he finds himself expected to draw particular practical conclusions from very vague and theoretical educational maxims (e.g., proceed from the whole to the part, from the concrete to the abstract), or he finds himself expected to adopt as rational principles what are mere temporary expedients. It is, indeed, advisable that the teacher should understand, and even be able to criticise, the general principles upon which the whole educational system is formed and administered. He is not like a private soldier in an army, expected merely to obey, or like a cog in a wheel, expected merely to respond to and transmit external energy; he must be an intelligent medium of action. But only confusion can result from trying to get principles or devices to do what they are not intended to do—to adapt them to purposes for which they have no fitness.

In other words, the existing evils in pedagogy, the prevalence of merely vague principles upon one side and of altogether too specific and detailed methods (expedients) upon the other, are really due to failure to ask what psychology is called upon to do, and upon failure to present it in such a form as will give it undoubted value in practical applications.

III. This brings us to the positive question: In what forms can psychology best do the work which it ought to do?

1. *The Psychical Functions Mature in a Certain Order.*—When development is normal the appearance of a certain impulse or instinct, the ripening of a certain interest, always prepares the way for another. A child spends the first six months of his life in learning a few simple adjustments; his instincts to reach, to see, to sit erect assert themselves, and are worked out. These at once become tools for further activities; the child has now to use these acquired powers as means for further acquisitions. Being able, in a rough way, to control the eye, the arm, the hand, and the body in certain positions in relation to one another, he now inspects, touches, handles, throws what comes within reach; and thus getting a certain amount of physical control, he builds up for himself a simple world of objects.

But his instinctive bodily control goes on asserting itself; he continues to gain in ability to balance himself, to coordinate, and thus control, the movements of his body. He learns to manage the body, not only at rest, but also in motion—to creep and to walk. Thus he gets a further means of growth; he extends his acquaintance with things, daily widening his little world. He also, through moving about, goes from one thing to another—that is, makes simple and crude *connections* of objects, which become the basis of subsequent relating and generalizing activities. This carries the child to the age of twelve or fifteen months. Then another instinct, already in occasional operation, ripens and takes the lead—that of imitation. In other words, there is now the attempt to adjust the activities which the child has already mastered to the activities which he sees exercised by others. He now endeavours to make the simple movements of hand, of vocal organs, etc., already in his possession the instruments of reproducing what his eye and his ear report to him of the world about him. Thus he learns to talk and to repeat many of the simple acts of others. This period lasts (roughly) till about the thirtieth month. These attainments, in turn, become the instruments of others. The child has now control of all his organs, motor and sensory. The next step, therefore, is to relate these activities to one another consciously, and not simply unconsciously as he has hitherto done. When, for example, he sees a block, he now sees in it the possibility of a whole series of activities, of throwing, building a house, etc. The head of a broken doll is no longer to him the mere thing directly before his senses. It symbolizes "some fragment of his dream of human life." It arouses in consciousness an entire group of related actions; the child strokes it, talks to it, sings it to sleep, treats it, in a word, as if it were the perfect doll. When this stage is reached, that of ability to see in a partial activity or in a single perception, a whole system or circuit of relevant actions and qualities, the imagination is in active operation; the period of symbolism, of recognition of meaning, of significance, has dawned.

But the same general process continues. Each function as it matures, and is vigorously exercised, prepares the way for a more comprehensive and a deeper conscious activity. All education consists in seizing upon the dawning activity and in presenting the material, the conditions, for promoting its best growth—in making it work freely and fully towards its proper end. Now, even in the first stages, the wise foresight and direction of the parent accomplish much, far more indeed than most parents are ever conscious of; yet the activities at this stage are so simple and so imperious that, given any chance at all, they work themselves out in some fashion or other. But when the stage of conscious recognition of meaning, of conscious direction of action, is reached, the process of development is much more complicated; many more possibilities are opened to the parent and the teacher, and so the demand for proper conditions and direction becomes indefinitely greater. Unless the right conditions and direction are supplied, the activities do not freely express themselves; the weaker are thwarted and die out; among the stronger an unhappy conflict wages and results in abnormal growth; some one impulse, naturally stronger than others, asserts itself out of all proportion, and the person "runs wild," becomes willful, capricious, irresponsible in action, and unbalanced and irregular in his intellectual operations.

Only knowledge of the order and connection of the stages in the development of the psychical functions can, negatively, guard against these evils, or, positively, insure the full meaning and free, yet orderly or law-abiding, exercise of the psychical powers. In a word, education itself is precisely the work of supplying the conditions which will enable the psychical functions, as they successively arise, to mature and pass into higher functions in the freest and fullest manner, and this result can be secured only by knowledge of the process—that is, only by a knowledge of psychology.

The so-called psychology, or pedagogical psychology, which fails to give this insight, evidently fails of its value for educational purposes. This failure is apt to occur for one or the other of two reasons: either because the psychology is too vague and general, not bearing directly upon the actual evolution of psychical life, or because, at the other extreme, it gives a mass of crude, particular, undigested facts, with no indicated bearing or interpretations:

1. The psychology based upon a doctrine of "faculties" of the soul is a typical representative of the first sort, and educational applications based upon it are necessarily mechanical and formal; they are generally but plausible abstractions, having little or no direct application to the practical work of the classroom. The mind having been considered as split up into a number of independent powers, pedagogy is reduced to a set of precepts about the "cultivation" of these powers. These precepts are useless, in the first place, because the teacher is confronted not with abstract faculties, but with living individuals. Even when the psychology teaches that there is a unity binding together the various faculties, and that they are not really separate, this unity is presented in a purely external way. It is not shown in what way the various so-called faculties are the expressions of one and the same fundamental process. But, in the second place, this "faculty" psychology is not merely negatively useless for the educator, it is positively false, and therefore harmful in its effects. The psychical reality is that continuous growth, that unfolding of a single functional principle already referred to. While perception, memory, imagination and judgment are not present in complete form from the first, one physical activity is present, which, as it becomes more developed and complex, manifests itself in these processes as stages of its growth. What the educator requires, therefore, is not vague information about these mental powers in general,

but a clear knowledge of the underlying single activity and of the conditions under which it differentiates into these powers.

2. The value for educational purposes of the mere presentation of unrelated facts, of anecdotes of child life, or even of particular investigations into certain details, may be greatly exaggerated. A great deal of material which, even if intelligently collected, is simply data for the scientific specialist, is often presented as if educational practice could be guided by it. Only *interpreted* material, that which reveals general principles or suggests the lines of growth to which the educator has to adapt himself, can be of much practical avail; and the interpreter of the facts of the child mind must begin with knowing the facts of the adult mind. Equally in mental evolution as in physical, nature makes no leaps. "The child is father of the man" is the poetic statement of a psychologic fact.

3. *Every Subject Has Its Own Psychological Place and Method.*—Every special subject, geography, for instance, represents a certain grouping of facts, classified on the basis of *the mind's attitude towards these facts.* In the thing itself, in the actual world, there is organic unity; there is no division in the facts of geology, geography, zoology, and botany. These facts are not externally sorted out into different compartments. They are all bound up together; the facts are many, but the thing is *one*. It is simply some interest, some urgent need of man's activities, which discriminates the facts and unifies them under different heads. *Unless the fundamental interest and purpose which underlie this classification are discovered and appealed to, the subject which deals with it can not be presented along the lines of least resistance and in the most fruitful way.* This discovery is the work of psychology. In geography, for example, we deal with certain classes of facts, not merely in themselves, but from the standpoint of their influence in the development and modification of human activities. A mountain range or a river, treated simply as mountain range or river, gives us geology; treated in relation to the distribution of genera of plants and animals, it has a biological interpretation; treated as furnishing conditions which have entered into and modified human activities—grazing, transportation of commodities, fixing political boundaries, etc.—it acquires a geographical significance.

In other words, the unity of geography is a certain unity of human action, a certain human interest. Unless, therefore, geographical data are presented in such a way as to appeal to this interest, the method of teaching geography is uncertain, vacillating, confusing; it throws the movement of the child's mind into lines of great, rather than of least, resistance, and leaves him with a mass of disconnected facts and a feeling of unreality in presence of which his interest dies out. All method means adaptation of means to a certain end; if the end is not grasped there is no rational principle for the selection of means; the method is haphazard and empirical—a chance selection from a bundle of expedients. But the elaboration of this interest, the discovery of the concrete ways in which the mind realizes it, is unquestionably the province of psychology. There are certain definite modes in which the mind images to itself the relation of environment and human activity in production and exchange; there is a certain order of growth in this imagery; to know this is psychology; and, once more, to know this is to be able to direct the teaching of geography rationally and fruitfully, and to secure the best results, both in culture and discipline, that can be had from the study of the subject.

Application to Arithmetic.—In the following pages an attempt has been made to present the psychology of number from this point of view. Number represents a certain interest, a certain psychical demand; it is not a bare property of facts, but is a certain way of interpreting and arranging them—a certain method of construing them. What is the interest, the demand, which gives rise to the psychical activity by which objects are taken as numbered or measured? And how does this activity develop? In so far as we can answer these questions we have a sure guide to methods of instruction in dealing with number. We have a positive basis for testing and criticising various proposed methods and devices; we have only to ask whether they are true to this specific activity, whether they build upon it and further it. In addition to this we have a standard at our disposal for setting forth correct methods; we have but to translate the theory of mental activity in this direction—the psychical nature of number and the problem of its origin—over into its practical meaning.

Knowing the nature and origin of number and numerical properties as psychological facts, the teacher knows how the mind works in the construction of number, and is prepared to help the child to think number: is prepared to use a method, helpful to the normal movement of the mind. In other words, rational method in arithmetic must be based on the psychology of number.

2

Education, Direct and Indirect (1904)

"Education, Direct and Indirect" moves us ahead almost a decade. It debuted as an address to the Francis Parker School in Chicago, a progressive "demonstration school" that later merged with the Deweys' Lab School (see the introduction for more about the school). The piece was later published in 1909 in the *Progressive Journal of Education*. Dewey begins by reflecting on the formalities of "direct education," things like lesson plans, tests, and the grading and sorting of students. He then contrasts them with what might be called "indirect education," the informal things children learn, both in and out of school, independently from (or perhaps in spite of) these formalities. Such informal learning experiences are often genuinely engaging and immediately relevant to students' lives, while free of the mundane formalities of "studenting." Dewey asks us to consider the value of this indirect education and reflect on why it often contrasts so markedly with its more formal and direct counterpart. Might it have anything to teach us about the artificialities of traditional schooling?

The other day a parent of a little boy who recently entered our elementary school, after having been in a public school, told me that her son came to her and said, "I think we learn almost as much at that school as we did at the John Smith school—I believe, maybe, we learn more, only we have such a good time that we do not stop to think that we are learning anything." This story I tell to help illustrate the meaning of the term "indirect education." We have our choice between two methods. We may shape the conditions and direct the influences of school work so that pupils are forever reminded that they are pupils—that they are there to study lessons and do tasks. We may make the child conscious at every point that he is going to school, and that he goes to school to do something quite different from what he does anywhere else—namely, to learn. This is "direct education." Put in this bald way, however, the idea may well arouse some mental searchings of heart. Are we really willing to admit that the child does not learn anything outside of school—that he is not getting his education all the time by what he is thinking and feeling and doing, and in spite of the fact that his consciousness is not upon the fact that he is learning? This, then, is the other alternative—the child may be given something fixed up for purposes of learning it, and we may trust to the learning, instruction and training which results out of and along with this doing and inquiring for its own sake. This is "indirect education."

Having got thus far, we are ready to ask the question as to whether and how this indirect education has a place inside the school walls. Shall we show the door of the school as that kind of development which comes with doing things that are worth doing for their own sake, the growth that comes with contact with the realities of the physical and social world, which is had for the sake of the fullness and reality of the contact? Shall we frame our school in such a way that the child is perpetually and insistently reminded that here is the place where he comes to learn things, to study, to get and recite lessons?

Before trying to answer this question, let us ask some of the ways in which we succeed in making so prominent, so overpowering in the consciousness of the child, the fact that in school he is undergoing education. I begin with one of the most obvious aspects of the matter, not because it is so very important in itself, but because it is such an admirable symbol and index of what lies back. I refer to all of the school machinery that hinges around the giving of marks—the eternal presence of the record book, the never-absent consciousness on the part of the child that he is to be marked for the poorness or goodness of his lesson, the sending home of graded reports upon purely conventional, mathematical or alphabetical schemes, the comparing by the children of their respective grades and all the scheming (sometimes cheating) thereby called forth.

That acute humorist who wrote under the name of John Phoenix tells a story of how he became disgusted with the inaccuracy of our descriptive language, having in mind such terms as little, remarkably, exceedingly, etc., etc., and evolved a scheme, which he thought would meet the whole difficulty, of substituting a decimal system of notation. The idea was that instead of saying that it was a moderately fine day, one would say that the weather was about 53 per cent good, while a particularly fine sunset might be described as a 95 per cent sunset. He goes on to say that, much elated with his project, he submitted it to his wife, who replied that she thought it was a fine scheme, and that she would put it in operation by telling him that he was a 99 per cent idiot.

I do not know whether this was intended as a caricature of the methods of our schools or not, but it may stand as a parody. Suppose we were to watch the child at his sports and games, and not having any confidence in an inherent development of power and knowledge through the very experience, thought it necessary to accentuate in his mind the fact that he had something to learn by giving him a mark of 60 per cent upon his game of marbles, and marking him "A" for his excellence in baseball. Suppose we tried to apply the same scheme to what the child gets from his daily conversation with older people; to the results accruing from the necessity he is under of adapting his modes of behavior to the demands of the social circle in which he lives and moves and has his being; suppose when our boy comes home fresh and elated from what he has seen in the park, or from a trip to the country, that after seeing his interest expressed by his telling, in his animated way, of his experiences, we were under obligation to decide that he was entitled to 82 per cent upon his accuracy of observation, while we should be compelled to give him not above 60 per cent upon his grammatical accuracy—all this so that he might be tested upon his growth or stimulated to further learning!

This is so clearly ridiculous that it may seem extremely unfair to the marking system in the schools. But what I want to point out is that the marking system implies as a fundamental and unquestionable axiom that the actual subject matter with which the child is engaged, and the responsive play of his own emotional and mental activities upon it, do not suffice to supply educative motive and material—that over and above them some further stimulus in the way of an externally imposed conventional scheme of rating is required to keep attention fixed upon the importance of learning.

Now this assumption that education is not natural and attractive—inherently so—reacts most disastrously upon the responsibility of both the teacher and the child. Human nature being what it is, any teacher who works under the conditions imposed by considering the school just as a place to learn lessons, comes to feel that he has done his whole duty by the individual (so far as judging and estimating the work and worth of that individual is concerned) when he has, after full and impartial investigation as possible, given that student his mark—i.e., determined his success in learning lessons. If some scheme had been intentionally devised in order to prevent the teacher from assuming the full responsibility he ought to feel for keeping constant watch and ward over the life of the child, for relating the child's work to his temperament, capacities, and to [the] totality of influences operating him—if the scheme, I say, had been intentionally devised for relieving the teacher of the necessity of the most intimate and unremitting acquaintance with the child, nothing better could have been found.

I should not have the slightest hesitation in making the statement that, given two schools of otherwise equal conditions, in one of which the marking system prevailed, and in the other did not, the latter would in time possess the teachers who had the most thorough and sympathetic knowledge of all the children, both as to their weak points and their strong points. All the influences at work, unconscious as well as conscious, compel the teachers to know the individuals with whom they are dealing, and to judge not merely their external work, to consider fairly how it should rank between the letters A and E, or zero and 100, but to judge the individual himself as a living, struggling, failing and succeeding individual. In one case, the individual has to be known and judged in terms of his own unique self, unrepeatable in any other self; and in the last analysis, incomparable with any other self just because he is his own self. The other scheme permits and encourages the teacher to escape with the feeling that he has done his whole duty when he has impartially graded the external and dead product of such a personality.

The same tendency to lack of full responsibility imposes itself upon the children and spreads among them. I have seen a powerful indictment against the marking and examination system, as ordinarily conducted, to the effect that it sets up a false and demoralizing standard by which the students come to judge their own work. Instead of each one considering himself responsible for the highest excellency to which he can possibly attain, the tendency is to suppose that one is doing well enough if he comes up to the average expectation; and that, indeed, everything above the required pass mark is so much to the student's credit—representing a sort of accumulation of merit, which in case of an emergency justifies a falling off. The point here is a far-reaching one. I have sometimes heard arguments which imply that there is something particularly strenuous in the disciplinary ideals of rigid tests and marks, and that their surrender means the substitution of a less severe and exacting standard—that it is a part of what is sometimes called "soft pedagogy." As I see it, the exact contrary holds. Where there is a system which fastens upon learning set lessons, the student cannot be reasonably held up to the best of which he himself is capable. All but the obvious failures can point in justification of themselves to the fact that they have come up to the standard which the school itself has officially set. If the student has done what the school proclaims it exacts of him, what further right to blame him? The "average" is a false and demoralizing standard.

Please do not think I am over-concerned about marks. They are indeed an evil, yet not in themselves of supreme importance. But they externally symbolize what I have said about the situation in the schools where the learning of lessons is made the measure of education. Any standard which can be stated, which can be put in external form, is by the necessity of the case a mechanical and quantitative thing. It points out to students certain particular things which are to be done and certain particular things which are to be avoided. And it not only permits but encourages them to believe that the whole duty of man is done when just these special things have been performed, and just these special things avoided. Neither the intellectual nor moral standard of life is capable of any such restriction. What the laws of life demand of everyone is that he always do absolutely the best that he can under all circumstances. The only reasonable, and, in the long run, the only effective standard by which students should learn to judge their own work is whether they have developed the subject that is given them to the utmost; whether they have seen all in the subject of study that it is possible for them to see; and whether by engaging it with their full attention may have got out of it all gain or power which is possible. To let the student substitute the standard of "passing," of coming up to a certain external limit, is to let him off altogether too easily; and the worst of it is that this easy-going standard tends to become habitual—it radiates to other spheres of life and makes itself at home in them.

The marking system in itself is a minor matter. It is an effect rather than a cause; a symptom rather than an underlying disease. The root of the evil lies much deeper. The artificial division of subject-matter, and the assignment of particular chopped-off sections of it as tasks to be accomplished in the form of lessons, lies much nearer the centre of the evils of this "direct education." Subjects are first rigidly marked off from each other, and then this arbitrarily selected subject-matter is arranged so as to provide the material which will make the student most conscious that he has before him just and only something which is to be learned by him. The reality of experience, the substance of truth or beauty that may be involved, becomes a wholly secondary matter. The main thing is that so many lines or pages have been assigned for the next lesson, and that the educational work is judged not by the refinement and growth of the organ of vision which it brings, not by the strengthening of the hunger and thirst after what is fine and true, but by exhibition of the mastery of specific tasks assigned.

It ought not to be necessary to point to the crippling and paralysis that result. There is, after all, a presumption that there are certain great currents of truth and rightness flowing through all subject-matter which has any right to occupy a place in the school curriculum. It is true, is it not, that the universe is really a wonderful place, and that history is a record of all the absorbing struggles, failures and successes of human aspiration and endeavor? If this be true, are we doing quite the fair thing by either the world of nature or of history, or the child, the newcomer into this wonderful world, when we manage to present all this to him as if it constituted just so many lessons which for no very obvious and vital reason have to be learned? If it were not pathetic, it would make one smile to hear the argument used sometimes against having eager and alert interest play a part in the school room. The argument rests on supposing that interest is something which simply attaches to the child's side of the educational problem—as if the things in themselves, the realities of nature and human life and art through which the child receives his education, were themselves quite uninteresting or even repulsive! The purpose of the newer movement in education is not to make things interesting to the child by environing him with a sort of vaudeville divertissement, with all sorts of spectacular accompaniments. The aim is to permit the intrinsic wonder and value which attach to all the realities which lie behind the school curriculum to come home to the child, and to take him up and carry him on in their own onward sweep. It is true that we adults get too easily blasé, overcome by the mere routine of living, and somehow constitutionally distrustful of the surprising values that reside in the bare facts of living. But it requires, I think, an unusually hardened pessimism to assume that the universe of nature and society, which, after all, is the only thing which can form the material of studies and lessons, is without inherent inspiration and appeal to the child, or that the child, of all beings, is so made as to be dull and slow in responding to this appeal. Yet this is the assumption which underlies the treatment of the material of education as if it were something only fit to be given out in lessons and tasks—the assumption which underlies the notion that education is a purely and direct conscious process—conscious to him who receives as well as to him who gives. The simile of a friend who was herself a teacher always occurs to my mind. Education, she said, reminded her of nothing so much as a corpse. It was all so silent, composed and laid out, and so dead.

Here also I should resent the interpretation that that idea of education which believes in educating by bringing boy and girl into proper relations of contact and responsiveness to the things in experience which are best worth seeing and doing, represents a lowering of standards, a decrease of severity intellectually or morally. It is the converse which is true. The standard which the truth and order of the universe set up when they are given a fair chance, an open and free field, when they secure adequate access to the individual, is infinitely more exacting than the conventions which textbook and school teacher can manage to agree upon and to set up. The responsibility of responding to what is right and worthy is a much more significant thing than the responsibility for reciting a given lesson. And the influence of the teacher becomes much more real and lively when it takes the form of cooperating with the influences that proceed from occupations and subject-matter than when it is felt purely as an independent and direct source.

More particularly, "direct education" involves a low standard because it fixes the attention of pupils upon the demands which teacher and textbook make, instead of the demands of the subject-matter, moving in the medium of individual thought and endeavor. It substitutes the standard, "Have I got this well enough to recite today? What are the chances of my being called upon to recite today, anyway, since I recited yesterday?" for the standard of "What is there in this that is so real as to make it imperative that I rise to it and move along with it?" There is one inevitable tendency of treating subject-matter simply as lessons or tasks: the desires, wishes or real expectations of the teacher, the teacher's own peculiar interests, tastes and standards become the controlling element. For moral purposes it makes comparatively little difference whether the pupils look at these expectations and demands from the standpoint of seeing in how many cases and by what ingenious methods they may evade them and still go through the show of conformity, or whether (because of greater skill of the teacher, or what is called tact) the children devote themselves to measuring up in the most amiable way possible—and children rightly approached are amiable to the level of the teacher's methods and ideals. In either case, the children are getting set in external habits of morality, and are learning to find their centre of intellectual gravity outside their own selves.

I know by experience that even after we come to believe in certain modes of educational practice, because we find that in spite of our theories they actually work well with our own children, we are yet somewhat "hard of heart and slow to believe" in their underlying theory and ideals. I am reminded of a gentleman who used periodically to insist that his children be taken out of the school where the method that I have called indirect education was in vogue, and be sent to a school where they would really have to learn lessons (to work, as he called it), but who, after he had won his wife's assent, always ended by stating that although the theory of the thing was absurd and demoralizing, at just that time it seemed to be working so well that he thought they had better leave the children where they were a little longer. Indeed, the point of view is so relatively recent in educational practice that I think that even the most ardent believers in it need to at times remind themselves of its fundamental reasonableness, and of the basic realities upon which it rests. We need to remind ourselves that the newer types of study, the various forms of social occupations, the cooking, the shop work, weaving, music, painting and clay modeling, are not merely devices for making old studies more pleasing, nor for disguising the inherent disagreeableness they have for boys and girls, that they are not simply effective methods for getting children to study more and learn their lessons easier and better than they used to, but that they stand for something which is fundamentally moral. They stand for the belief that the only final educative force in the world is participation in the realities of life, and that these realities are inherently moral in effect. It is because the various studies and occupations, which play so prominent a part in what is called the new education, are just modes of participating in the moving forces of truth and rightness that they insist upon being made central in everything that has a right to be termed a school. When this centre is the heart of school life, I have no fears as to the quality of education that is the outcome.

3

From *How We Think* (1933)

The final readings in this section come from Dewey's popular book *How We Think*. Written expressly for teachers, it was originally published in 1910 and later revised for greater clarity and coverage in 1933. In the portions entitled "What Is Thinking?" and "Analysis of Reflective Thinking," Dewey examines the constituents of reflective thinking and explores its role in inquiry and problem-solving. He also asks us to consider how we might teach and utilize it more effectively in the classroom. In Dewey's view, every instance of reflective thinking is experientially unique and cannot (and should not) be automatically reduced to the more abstract and finite processes of mathematical computation or formal logic. Indeed, Dewey argues that the holistic elements of reflective thinking—which include things like intuition, imagination, and directly "had" or felt meanings—are integral to effective problem-solving. This defies the popular notion that math and logic are the pinnacle of rationality, while the above are irrational and "merely subjective." (Dewey, in contrast, calls these holistic elements "suprarational.") Dewey also observes that reflective thinking is situation specific. Its stages or phases do not always occur in the same sequence; and the lengths of these stages can vary considerably. This encourages us to reflect on how teachers might help students attend to the different dimensions of reflective thinking in a more mindful and intentional way.

What Is Thinking?

I. Different Meanings of Thought

The Best Way of Thinking

No one can tell another person in any definite way how he *should* think, any more than how he ought to breathe or to have his blood circulate. But the various ways in which men *do* think can be told and can be described in their general features. Some of these ways are better than others; the reasons why they are better can be set forth. The person who understands what the better ways of thinking are and why they are better can, if he will, change his own personal ways until they become more effective; until, that is to say, they do better the work that thinking can do and that other mental operations cannot do so well. The better way of thinking that is to be considered in this book is called reflective thinking: the kind of thinking that consists in turning a subject over in the mind and giving it serious and consecutive consideration. Before we take up this main theme, we shall, however, first take note briefly of some other mental processes to which the name *thought* is sometimes given.

The "Stream of Consciousness"

All the time we are awake and sometimes when we are asleep, something is, as we say, going through our heads. When we are asleep we call that kind of sequence "dreaming." We also have daydreams, reveries, castles built in the air, and mental streams that are even more idle and chaotic. To this uncontrolled coursing of ideas through our heads the name of "thinking" is sometimes given. It is automatic and unregulated. Many a child has attempted to see whether he could not "stop thinking"—that is, stop this procession of mental states through his mind—and in vain. More of our waking life than most of us would care to admit is whiled away in this inconsequential trifling with mental pictures, random recollections, pleasant but unfounded hopes, flitting, half-developed impressions. Hence it is that he who offers "a penny for your thoughts" does not expect to drive any great bargain if his offer is taken; he will only find out what happens to be "going through the mind" and what "goes" in this fashion rarely leaves much that is worth while behind.

Reflective Thought Is a Chain

In this sense, silly folk and dullards *think*. The story is told of a man in slight repute for intelligence, who, desiring to be chosen selectman in his New England town, addressed a knot of neighbors in this wise: "I hear you don't believe I know enough to hold office. I wish you to understand that I am thinking about something or other most of the time." Now, reflective thought is like this random coursing of things through the mind in that it consists of a succession of things thought of, but it is unlike in that the mere chance occurrence of any chance "something or other" in an irregular sequence does not suffice. Reflection involves not simply a sequence of ideas, but a *con*-sequence—a consecutive ordering in such a way that each determines the next as its proper outcome, while each outcome in turn leans back on, or refers to, its predecessors. The successive portions of a reflective thought grow out of one another and support one another; they do not come and go in a medley. Each phase is a step from something to something—technically speaking, it is a *term* of thought. Each term leaves a deposit that is utilized in the next term. The stream or flow becomes a train or chain. There are in any reflective thought definite units that are linked together so that there is a sustained movement to a common end.

Thinking Usually Restricted to Things Not Directly Perceived

The second meaning of thinking limits it to things not sensed or directly perceived, to things *not* seen, heard, touched, smelt, or tasted. We ask the man telling a story if he saw a certain incident happen, and his reply may be, "No, I only thought of it." A note of invention, as distinct from faithful record of observation, is present. Most important in this class are successions of imaginative incidents and episodes that have a certain coherence, hang together on a continuous thread, and thus lie between kaleidoscopic flights of fancy and considerations deliberately employed to establish a conclusion. The imaginative stories poured forth by children possess all degrees of internal congruity; some are disjointed, some are articulated. When connected, they simulate reflective thought; indeed, they usually occur in minds of logical capacity. These imaginative enterprises often precede thinking of the close-knit type and prepare the way for it. In this sense, a thought or idea is a mental picture of something not actually present, and thinking is the succession of such pictures.

Reflective Thinking Aims at a Conclusion

In contrast, reflective thinking has a purpose beyond the entertainment afforded by the train of agreeable mental inventions and pictures. The train must lead somewhere; it must tend to a conclusion that can be substantiated outside the course of the images. A story of a giant may satisfy merely because of the story itself; a reflective conclusion that a giant lived at a certain date and place on the earth would have to have some justification outside of the chain of ideas in order to be a valid or sound conclusion. This contrasting element is probably best conveyed in the ordinary saying: "Think it *out*." The phrase suggests an entanglement to be straightened out, something obscure to be cleared up through the application of thought. There is a goal to be reached, and this end sets a task that controls the sequence of ideas.

Thinking as Practically Synonymous with Believing

A third meaning of thought is practically synonymous with *belief*. "I think it is going to be colder tomorrow," or "I think Hungary is larger than Jugo-Slavia" is equivalent to "I believe so-and-so." When we say, "Men used to think the world was flat," we obviously refer to a belief that was held by our ancestors. This meaning of thought is narrower than those previously mentioned. A belief refers to something beyond itself by which its value is tested; it makes an assertion about some matter of fact or some principle or law. It means that a specified state of fact or law is accepted or rejected, that it is something proper to be affirmed or at least acquiesced in. It is hardly necessary to lay stress upon the importance of belief. It covers all the matters of which we have no sure knowledge and yet which we are sufficiently confident of to act upon and also the matters that we now accept as certainly true, as knowledge, but which nevertheless may be questioned in the future—just as much that passed as knowledge in the past has now passed into the limbo of mere opinion or of error.

There is nothing in the mere fact of thought as identical with belief that reveals whether the belief is well founded or not. Two different men say, "I believe the world is spherical." One man, if challenged, could produce little or no evidence for thinking as he does. It is an idea that he has picked up from others and that he accepts because the idea is generally current, not because he has examined into the matter and not because his own mind has taken any active part in reaching and framing the belief.

Such "thoughts" grow up unconsciously. They are picked up—we know not how. From obscure sources and by unnoticed channels they insinuate themselves into the mind and become unconsciously a part of our mental furniture. Tradition, instruction, imitation—all of which depend upon authority in some form, or appeal to our own advantage, or fall in with a strong passion—are responsible for them. Such thoughts are prejudices; that is, prejudgments, not conclusions reached as the result of personal mental activity, such as observing, collecting, and examining evidence. Even when they happen to be correct, their correctness is a matter of accident as far as the person who entertains them is concerned.

Reflective Thinking Impels to Inquiry

Thus we are brought again, by way of contrast, to the particular kind of thinking that we are to study in this volume, *reflective thinking*. Thought, in the two first senses mentioned, may be harmful to the mind because it distracts attention from the real world, and because it may be a waste of time. On the other hand, if indulged in judiciously these thoughts may afford genuine enjoyment and also be a source of needed recreation. But in either case they can make no claim to truth; they cannot hold themselves up as something that the mind should accept, assert, and be willing to act upon. They may involve a kind of emotional commitment, but not intellectual and practical commitment. Beliefs, on the other hand, do involve precisely this commitment and consequently sooner or later they demand our investigation to find out upon what grounds they rest. To think of a cloud as a whale or a camel—in the sense of to "fancy"—does not commit one to the conclusion that the person having the idea would ride the camel or extract oil from the whale. But when Columbus "thought" the world was round, in the sense of "believed it to be so," he and his followers were thereby committed to a series of other beliefs and actions: to beliefs about routes to India, about what would happen if ships traveled far westward on the Atlantic, etc., precisely as thinking that the world was flat had committed those who held it to belief in the impossibility of circumnavigation, and in the limitation of the earth to regions in the small civilized part of it Europeans were already acquainted with, etc.

The earlier thought, belief in the flatness of the earth, had some foundation in evidence; it rested upon what men could see easily within the limits of their vision. But this evidence was not further looked into; it was not checked by considering other evidence; there was no search for new evidence. Ultimately the belief rested on laziness, inertia, custom, absence of courage and energy in investigation. The later belief rests upon careful and extensive study, upon purposeful widening of the area of observation, upon reasoning out the conclusions of alternative conceptions to see what would follow in case one or the other were adopted for belief. As distinct from the first kind of thinking there was an orderly chain of ideas; as distinct from the second, there was a controlling purpose and end; as distinct from the third, there was personal examination, scrutiny, inquiry.

Because Columbus did not accept unhesitatingly the current traditional theory, because he doubted and inquired, he arrived at his thought. Skeptical of what, from long habit, seemed most certain, and credulous of what seemed impossible, he went on thinking until he could produce evidence for both his confidence and his disbelief. Even if his conclusion had finally turned out wrong, it would have been a different sort of belief from those it antagonized, because it was reached by a different method. *Active, persistent, and careful consideration of any belief or supposed form of knowledge in the light of the grounds that support it and the further conclusions to which it tends* constitutes reflective thought. Any one of the first three kinds of thought may elicit this type; but once begun, it includes a conscious and voluntary effort to establish belief upon a firm basis of evidence and rationality.

II. The Central Factor in Thinking

The Suggestion of Something Not Observed

There are, however, no sharp lines of demarcation between the various operations just outlined. The problem of attaining correct habits of reflection would be much easier than it is, did not the different modes of thinking blend insensibly into one another. So far, we have considered rather extreme instances of each kind in order to get the field clearly before us. Let us now reverse this operation; let us consider a rudimentary case of thinking, lying between careful examination of evidence and a mere irresponsible stream of fancies. A man is walking on a warm day. The sky was clear the last time he observed it; but presently he notes, while occupied primarily with other things, that the air is cooler. It occurs to him that it is probably going to rain; looking up, he sees a dark cloud between him and the sun, and he then quickens his steps. What, if anything, in such a situation can be called thought? Neither the act of walking nor the noting of the cold is a thought. Walking is one direction of activity;

looking and noting are other modes of activity. The likelihood that it will rain is, however, something *suggested*. The pedestrian *feels* the cold; first he *thinks* of clouds, then he looks and perceives them, and then he thinks of something he does not see: a storm. This *suggested possibility* is the idea, the thought. If it is believed in as a genuine possibility which may occur, it is the kind of thought which falls within the scope of knowledge and which requires reflective consideration.

Up to a certain point there is the same sort of situation as when one who looks at a cloud is reminded of a human figure and face. Thinking in both of these cases (the cases of belief and of fancy) involves noting or perceiving a fact, followed by something else that is not observed but that is brought to mind, suggested by the thing seen. One thing reminds us, as we say, of the other. Side by side, however, with this factor of agreement in the two cases of suggestion is a factor of marked disagreement. We do not *believe* in the face suggested by the cloud; we do not consider at all the probability of its being a fact. There is no *reflective* thought. The danger of rain, on the contrary, presents itself to us as a genuine possibility—a fact of the same nature as the observed coolness. Put differently, we do not regard the cloud as meaning or indicating a face, but merely as suggesting it, while we do consider that the coolness may *mean* rain. In the first case, on seeing an object, we just happen, as we say, to think of something else; in the second, we consider the *possibility and nature of the connection between the object seen and the object suggested*. The seen thing is regarded as in some way *the ground or basis of belief* in the suggested thing; it possesses the quality of *evidence*.

The Function of Signifying

This function whereby one thing signifies or indicates another, thus leading us to consider how far the one may be regarded as warrant for belief in the other, is, then, the central factor in all reflective or distinctively intellectual thinking. By calling up various situations to which such terms as *signifies* and *indicates* apply, the student will realize for himself the actual facts denoted. Synonyms for these terms are: points to, tells of, betokens, prognosticates, represents, stands for, implies.[1] We also say one thing portends another, is ominous of another, or a symptom of it, or a key to it, or (if the connection is quite obscure) that it gives a hint, clue, or intimation. Reflection is not identical with the mere fact that one thing indicates, means, another thing. It commences when we begin to inquire into the reliability, the worth, of any particular indication; when we try to test its value and see what guarantee there is that the existing data *really* point to the idea that is suggested in such a way as to *justify* acceptance of the latter.

Reflection Implies Belief on Evidence

Reflection thus implies that something is believed in (or disbelieved in), not on its own direct account, but through something else which stands as witness, evidence, proof, voucher, warrant; that is, as *ground of belief.* At one time, rain is actually felt or directly experienced; at another time, we *infer* that it has rained from the appearance of the grass and trees, or that it is going to rain because of the condition of the air or the state of the barometer. At one time, we see a man (or suppose we do) without any intermediary fact; at another time, we are not quite sure what we see, and hunt for accompanying facts that will serve as signs, indications, tokens of what we are to believe.

Thinking, for the purposes of this inquiry, is accordingly defined as *that operation in which present facts suggest other facts (or truths) in such a way as to induce belief in what is suggested on the ground of real relation in the things themselves, a relation between what suggests and what is suggested.* A cloud *suggests* a weasel or a whale; it does not mean the latter, because there is no tie, or bond, in the things themselves between what is seen and what is suggested. Ashes not merely suggest a previous fire, but they signify there has been a fire, because ashes are produced by combustion and, if they are genuine ashes, only by combustion. It is an objective connection, the link in actual things, that makes one thing the ground, warrant, evidence, for believing in something else.

III. PHASES OF REFLECTIVE THINKING

We may carry our account further by noting that *reflective* thinking, in distinction from other operations to which we apply the name of thought, involves (1) a state of doubt, hesitation, perplexity, mental difficulty, in which thinking originates, and (2) an act of searching, hunting, inquiring, to find material that will resolve the doubt, settle and dispose of the perplexity.

The Importance of Uncertainty and of Inquiry

In our illustration, the shock of coolness generated confusion and suspended belief, at least momentarily. Because it was unexpected, it was a shock or an interruption needing to be accounted for, identified, or placed. To say that the abrupt occurrence of the change of temperature constitutes a problem may sound forced and artificial; but if we are willing to extend the meaning of the word *problem* to whatever—no matter how slight and commonplace in character—perplexes and challenges the mind so that it makes a belief at all uncertain, there is a genuine problem, or question, involved in an experience of sudden change.

The turning of the head, the lifting of the eyes, the scanning of the heavens, are activities adapted to bring to recognition facts that will answer the question presented by the sudden coolness. The facts as they first presented themselves were perplexing; they suggested, however, clouds. The act of looking was an act to discover whether this suggested explanation held good. It may again seem forced to speak of this looking, almost automatic, as an act of research, or inquiry. But once more, if we are willing to generalize our conceptions of our mental operations to include the trivial and ordinary as well as the technical and recondite, there is no good reason for refusing to give this title to the act of looking. For the result of the act is to bring facts before the mind that enable a person to reach a conclusion on the basis of evidence. In so far, then, as the act of looking was deliberate, was performed with the intention of getting an external basis on which to rest a belief, it exemplifies in an elementary way the operation of hunting, searching, inquiring, involved in any reflective operation.

Another instance, commonplace also, yet not quite so trivial, may enforce this lesson. A man traveling in an unfamiliar region comes to a branching of the road. Having no sure knowledge to fall back upon, he is brought to a standstill of hesitation and suspense. Which road is right? And how shall his perplexity be resolved? There are but two alternatives: he must either blindly and arbitrarily take his course, trusting to luck for the outcome, or he must discover grounds for the conclusion that a given road is right. Any attempt to decide the matter by thinking will involve inquiring into other facts, whether brought to mind by memory, or by further observation, or by both. The perplexed wayfarer must carefully scrutinize what is before him and he must cudgel his memory. He looks for evidence that will support belief in favor of either of the roads—for evidence that will weight down one suggestion. He may climb a tree; he may go first in this direction, then in that, looking, in either case, for signs, clues, indications. He wants something in the nature of a signboard or a map, and *his reflection is aimed at the discovery of facts that will serve this purpose.*

The foregoing illustration may be generalized. Thinking begins in what may fairly enough be called a *forked-road* situation, a situation that is ambiguous, that presents a dilemma, that proposes alternatives. As long as our activity glides smoothly along from one thing to another, or as long as we permit our imagination to entertain fancies at pleasure, there is no call for reflection. Difficulty or obstruction in the way of reaching a belief brings us, however, to a pause. In the suspense of uncertainty, we metaphorically climb a tree; we try to find some standpoint from which we may survey additional facts and, getting a more commanding view of the situation, decide how the facts stand related to one another.

The Regulation of Thinking by Its Purpose

Demand for the solution of a perplexity is the steadying and guiding factor in the entire process of reflection. Where there is no question of a problem to be solved or a difficulty to be surmounted, the course of suggestions flows on at random; we have the first type of thought described. If the stream of suggestions is controlled simply by their emotional congruity, their fitting agreeably into a single picture or story, we have the second type. But a question to be answered, an ambiguity to be resolved, sets up an end and holds the current of ideas to a definite channel. Every suggested conclusion is tested by its reference to this regulating end, by its pertinence to the problem in hand. This need of straightening out a perplexity also controls the kind of inquiry undertaken. A traveler whose end is the most beautiful path will look for other signs and will test suggestions on another basis than if he wishes to discover the way to a given city. *The nature of the problem fixes the end of thought,* and *the end controls the process of thinking.*

IV. Summary

We may recapitulate by saying that the origin of thinking is some perplexity, confusion, or doubt. Thinking is not a case of spontaneous combustion; it does not occur just on "general principles." There is something that occasions and evokes it. General appeals to a child (or to a grown-up) to think, irrespective of the existence in his own experience of some difficulty that troubles him and disturbs his equilibrium, are as futile as advice to lift himself by his boot-straps.

Given a difficulty, the next step is suggestion of some way out—the formation of some tentative plan or project, the entertaining of some theory that will account for the peculiarities in question, the consideration of some solution for the problem. The data at hand cannot supply the solution;

they can only suggest it. What, then, are the sources of the suggestion? Clearly, past experience and a fund of relevant knowledge at one's command. If the person has had some acquaintance with similar situations, if he has dealt with material of the same sort before, suggestions more or less apt and helpful will arise. But unless there has been some analogous experience, confusion remains mere confusion. Even when a child (or a grown-up) has a problem, it is wholly futile to urge him to think when he has no prior experiences that involve some of the same conditions.

There may, however, be a state of perplexity and also previous experience out of which suggestions emerge, and yet thinking need not be reflective. For the person may not be sufficiently *critical* about the ideas that occur to him. He may jump at a conclusion without weighing the grounds on which it rests; he may forego or unduly shorten the act of hunting, inquiring; he may take the first "answer," or solution, that comes to him because of mental sloth, torpor, impatience to get something settled. One can think reflectively only when one is willing to endure suspense and to undergo the trouble of searching. To many persons both suspense of judgment and intellectual search are disagreeable; they want to get them ended as soon as possible. They cultivate an over-positive and dogmatic habit of mind, or feel perhaps that a condition of doubt will be regarded as evidence of mental inferiority. It is at the point where examination and test enter into investigation that the difference between reflective thought and bad thinking comes in. To be genuinely thoughtful, we must be willing to sustain and protract that state of doubt which is the stimulus to thorough inquiry, so as not to accept an idea or make positive assertion of a belief until justifying reasons have been found.

Analysis of Reflective Thinking

I. Facts and Ideas

When a situation arises containing a difficulty or perplexity, the person who finds himself in it may take one of a number of courses. He may dodge it, dropping the activity that brought it about, turning to something else. He may indulge in a flight of fancy, imagining himself powerful or wealthy, or in some other way in possession of the means that would enable him to deal with the difficulty. Or, finally, he may face the situation. In this case, he begins to reflect.

Reflection Includes Observation

The moment he begins to reflect, he begins of necessity to observe in order to take stock of conditions. Some of these observations are made by direct use of the senses; others by recollecting observations previously made either by himself or by others. The person who had the engagement to keep, notes with his eyes his present location, recalls the place where he should arrive at one o'clock, and brings back to mind the means of transportation with which he is acquainted and their respective locations. In this way he gets as clear and distinct a recognition as possible of the nature of the situation with which he has to deal. Some of the conditions are obstacles and others are aids, resources. No matter whether these conditions come to him by direct perception or by memory, they form the "*facts* of the case." They are the things that are *there*, that have to be reckoned with. Like all facts, they are stubborn. They cannot be got out of the way by magic just because they are disagreeable. It is no use to *wish* they did not exist or were different. They must be taken for just what they are. Hence observation and recollection must be used to the full so as not to glide over or to mistake important features. Until the habit of thinking is well formed, facing the situation to discover the facts requires an effort. For the mind tends to dislike what is unpleasant and so to sheer off from an adequate notice of that which is especially annoying.

Reflection Includes Suggestions

Along with noting the conditions that constitute the facts to be dealt with, suggestions arise of possible courses of action. Thus the person of our illustration thinks of surface cars, elevated trains, and the subway. These alternative suggestions compete with one another. By comparison he judges which alternative is best, which one is the more likely to give a satisfactory solution. The comparison takes place indirectly. The moment one thinks of a possible solution and holds it in suspense, he turns back to the facts. He has now a point of view that leads him to new observations and recollections and to a reconsideration of observations already made in order to test the worth of the suggested way out. Unless he uses the suggestion so as to guide to new observations instead of exercising suspended judgment, he accepts it as soon as it presents itself. Then he falls short of truly reflective thought. The newly noted facts may (and in any complex situation surely will) cause new suggestions to spring up. These become clews to further investigation of conditions. The results of this survey test and correct the proposed inference or suggest a new one. This continuous interaction of the facts disclosed by observation and of the suggested proposals of solution and the suggested methods of dealing with conditions goes on till some suggested solution meets all the conditions of the case and does not run counter to any discoverable feature of it.

Data and Ideas Are Correlative and Indispensable Factors in Reflection

A technical term for the observed facts is *data*. The data form the material that has to be interpreted, accounted for, explained; or, in the case of deliberation as to what to do or how to do it, to be managed and utilized. The suggested solutions for the difficulties disclosed by observation form *ideas*. Data (facts) and ideas (suggestions, possible solutions) thus form the two indispensable and correlative factors of all reflective activity. The two factors are carried on by means respectively of *observation* (in which for convenience is included memory of prior observations of similar cases) and *inference*. The latter runs beyond what is actually noted, beyond what is found, upon careful examination, to be actually present. It relates, therefore, to what is *possible*, rather than to what is actual. It proceeds by anticipation, supposition, conjecture, imagination. All foresight, prediction, planning, as well as theorizing and speculation, are characterized by excursion from the actual into the possible. Hence (as we have already seen) what is inferred demands a double test: first, the process of forming the idea or supposed solution is checked by constant cross reference to the conditions observed to be actually present; secondly, the idea *after* it is formed is tested by *acting* upon it, overtly if possible, otherwise in imagination. The consequences of this action confirm, modify, or refute the idea.

We shall illustrate what has been said by a simple case. Suppose you are walking where there is no regular path. As long as everything goes smoothly, you do not have to think about your walking; your already formed habit takes care of it. Suddenly you find a ditch in your way. You think you will jump it (supposition, plan); but to make sure, you survey it with your eyes (observation), and you find that it is pretty wide and that the bank on the other side is slippery (facts, data). You then wonder if the ditch may not be narrower somewhere else (idea), and you look up and down the stream (observation) to see how matters stand (test of idea by observation). You do not find any good place and so are thrown back upon forming a new plan. As you are casting about, you discover a log (fact again). You ask yourself whether you could not haul that to the ditch and get it across the ditch to use as a bridge (idea again). You judge that idea is worth trying, and so you get the log and manage to put it in place and walk across (test and confirmation by overt action).

If the situation were more complicated, thinking would of course be more elaborate. You can imagine a case in which making a raft, constructing a pontoon bridge, or making a dugout would be the ideas that would finally come to mind and have to be checked by reference to conditions of action (facts). Simple or complicated, relating to what to do in a practical predicament or what to infer in a scientific or philosophic problem, there will always be the two sides: the conditions to be accounted for, dealt with, and the ideas that are plans for dealing with them or are suppositions for interpreting and explaining the phenomena.

In predicting an eclipse, for example, a multitude of observed facts regarding position and movements of earth, sun, and moon, comes in on one side, while on the other side the ideas employed to predict and explain involve extensive mathematical calculations. In a philosophic problem, the facts or data may be remote and not susceptible of direct observation by the senses. But still there will be data, perhaps of science, or of morals, art, or the conclusions of past thinkers, that supply the subject matter to be dealt with and by which theories are checked. On the other side, there are the speculations that come to mind and that lead to search for additional subject matter which will both develop the proposed theories as ideas and test their value. Mere facts or data are dead, as far as mind is concerned, unless they are used to suggest and test some idea, some way out of a difficulty. Ideas, on the other hand, are *mere* ideas, idle speculations, fantasies, dreams, unless they are used to guide new observations of, and reflections upon, actual situations, past, present, or future. Finally, they must be brought to some sort of check by actual given material or else remain ideas. Many ideas are of great value as material of poetry, fiction, or the drama, but not as the stuff of knowledge. However, ideas may be of intellectual use to a penetrating mind even when they do not find any immediate reference to actuality, provided they stay in the mind for use when new facts come to light.

II. The Essential Functions of Reflective Activity

We now have before us the material for the analysis of a complete act of reflective activity. In the preceding chapter we saw that the two limits of every unit of thinking are a perplexed, troubled, or confused situation at the beginning and a cleared-up, unified, resolved situation at the close. The first of these situations may be called pre-reflective. It sets the problem to be solved; out of it grows the question that reflection has to answer. In the final situation the doubt has been dispelled; the situation is post-reflective; there results a direct experience of mastery, satisfaction, enjoyment. Here, then, are the limits within which reflection falls.

Five Phases, or Aspects, of Reflective Thought

In between, as states of thinking, are (1) *suggestions*, in which the mind leaps forward to a possible solution; (2) an intellectualization of the difficulty or perplexity that has been *felt* (directly experienced) into a *problem* to be solved, a question for which the answer must be sought; (3) the use of one suggestion after another as a leading idea, or *hypothesis*, to initiate and guide observation and other operations in collection of factual material; (4) the mental elaboration of the idea or supposition as an idea or supposition *(reasoning*, in the sense in which reasoning is a part, not the whole, of inference); and (5) testing the hypothesis by overt or imaginative action.

We shall now take up the five phases, or functions, one by one.

THE FIRST PHASE, SUGGESTION

The most "natural" thing for anyone to do is to go ahead; that is to say, to *act* overtly. The disturbed and perplexed situation arrests such direct activity temporarily. The tendency to continue *acting* nevertheless persists. It is diverted and takes the form of an idea or a suggestion. The *idea* of what to do when we find ourselves "in a hole" is a substitute for direct action. It is a vicarious, anticipatory way of acting, a kind of dramatic rehearsal. Were there only one suggestion popping up, we should undoubtedly adopt it at once. But where there are two or more, they collide with one another, maintain the state of suspense, and produce further inquiry. The first suggestion in the instance recently cited was to jump the ditch, but the perception of conditions inhibited that suggestion and led to the occurrence of other ideas.

Some inhibition of *direct* action is necessary to the condition of hesitation and delay that is essential to thinking. Thought is, as it were, conduct turned in upon itself and examining its purpose and its conditions, its resources, aids, and difficulties and obstacles.

THE SECOND PHASE, INTELLECTUALIZATION

We have already noted that it is artificial, so far as thinking is concerned, to start with a ready-made problem, a problem made out of whole cloth or arising out of a vacuum. In reality such a "problem" is simply an assigned *task*. There is not at first a situation *and* a problem, much less just a problem and no situation. There is a troubled, perplexed, trying situation, where the difficulty is, as it were, spread throughout the entire situation, infecting it as a whole. If we knew just what the difficulty was and where it lay, the job of reflection would be much easier than it is. As the saying truly goes, a question well put is half answered. In fact, we know what the problem *exactly* is simultaneously with finding a way out and getting it resolved. Problem and solution stand out *completely* at the same time. Up to that point, our grasp of the problem has been more or less vague and tentative.

A blocked suggestion leads us to reinspect the conditions that confront us. Then our uneasiness, the shock of disturbed activity, gets stated in some degree on the basis of observed conditions, of objects. The width of the ditch, the slipperiness of the banks, not the mere presence of a ditch, is the trouble. The difficulty is getting located and defined; it is becoming a true problem, something intellectual, not just an annoyance at being held up in what we are doing. The person who is suddenly blocked and troubled in what he is doing by the thought of an engagement to keep at a time that is near and a place that is distant has the suggestion of getting there at once. But in order to carry this suggestion into effect, he has to find means of transportation. In order to find them he has to note his present position and its distance from the station, the present time, and the interval at his disposal. Thus the perplexity is more precisely located: just so much ground to cover, so much time to do it in.

The word "problem" often seems too elaborate and dignified to denote what happens in minor cases of reflection. But in every case where reflective activity ensues, there is a process of *intellectualizing* what at first is merely an *emotional* quality of the whole situation. This conversion is effected by noting more definitely the conditions that constitute the trouble and cause the stoppage of action.

THE THIRD PHASE, THE GUIDING IDEA, HYPOTHESIS

The first suggestion occurs spontaneously; it comes to mind automatically; it *springs* up; it "pops," as we have said, "into the mind"; it flashes upon us. There is no direct control of its occurrence; the idea just comes or it does not come; that is all that can be said. There is nothing *intellectual* about its occurrence. The intellectual element consists in *what we do with it,* how we use it, *after* its sudden occurrence as an idea. A controlled use of it is made possible by the state of affairs just described. In the degree in which we define the difficulty (which is effected by stating it in terms of objects), we get a better idea of the kind of solution that is needed. The facts or data set the problem before us, and insight into the problem corrects, modifies, expands the suggestion that originally occurred. In this fashion the suggestion becomes a definite supposition or, stated more technically, a *hypothesis.*

Take the case of a physician examining a patient or a mechanic inspecting a piece of complicated machinery that does not behave properly. There is something wrong, so much is sure. But how to remedy it cannot be told until it is known *what* is wrong. An untrained person is likely to make a wild guess—the suggestion—and then proceed to act upon it in a random way, hoping that by good luck the right thing will be hit upon. So some medicine that appears to have worked before or that a neighbor has recommended is tried. Or the person fusses, monkeys, with the machine, poking here and hammering there on the chance of making the right move. The trained person proceeds in a very different fashion. He *observes* with unusual care, using the methods, the techniques, that the experience of physicians and expert mechanics in general, those familiar with the structure of the organism or the machine, have shown to be helpful in detecting trouble.

The idea of the solution is thus controlled by the diagnosis that has been made. But if the case is at all complicated, the physician or mechanic does not foreclose further thought by assuming that the suggested method of remedy is certainly right. He proceeds to act upon it tentatively rather than decisively. That is, he treats it as a guiding idea, a working hypothesis, and is led by it to make more observations, to collect more facts, so as to see if the *new* material is what the hypothesis calls for. He reasons that *if* the disease is typhoid, *then* certain phenomena will be found; and he looks particularly to see if *just* these conditions are present. Thus both the first and second operations are brought under control; the sense of the problem becomes more adequate and refined and the suggestion ceases to be a *mere* possibility, becoming a *tested* and, if possible, a *measured* probability.

THE FOURTH PHASE, REASONING (IN THE NARROWER SENSE)

Observations pertain to what exists in nature. They constitute the facts, and these facts both regulate the formation of suggestions, ideas, hypotheses, and test their probable value as indications of solutions. The ideas, on the other hand, occur, as we say, in our heads, in our minds. They not only occur there, but are capable, as well, of great development there. Given a fertile suggestion occurring in an experienced, well-informed mind, that mind is capable of elaborating it until there results an idea that is quite different from the one with which the mind started.

For example, the idea of heat in the third instance in the earlier chapter was linked up with what the person already knew about heat—in his case, its expansive force—and this in turn with the contractive tendency of cold, so that the idea of expansion could be used as an explanatory idea, though the mere idea of heat would not have been of any avail. Heat was quite directly suggested by the observed conditions; water was felt to be hot. But only a mind with some prior information about heat would have reasoned that heat meant expansion, and then used the idea of expansion as a working hypothesis. In more complex cases, there are long trains of reasoning in which one idea leads up to another idea known by previous test to be related to it. The stretch of links brought to light by reasoning depends, of course, upon the store of knowledge that the mind is already in possession of. And this depends not only upon the prior experience and special education of the individual who is carrying on the inquiry, but also upon the state of culture and science of the age and place. Reasoning helps extend knowledge, while at the same time it depends upon what is already known and upon the facilities that exist for communicating knowledge and making it a public, open resource.

A physician to-day can develop, by reasoning from his knowledge, the implications of the disease that symptoms suggest to him as probable in a way that would have been impossible even a generation ago; just as, on the other hand, he can carry his observation of symptoms much farther because of improvement in clinical instruments and the technique of their use.

Reasoning has the same effect upon a suggested solution that more intimate and extensive observation has upon the original trouble. Acceptance of a suggestion in its first form is prevented by looking into it more thoroughly. Conjectures that seem plausible at first sight are often found unfit or even absurd when their full consequences are traced out. Even when reasoning out the bearings of a supposition does not lead to its rejection, it develops the idea into a form in which it is more apposite to the problem. Only when, for example, the conjecture that a pole was an index pole had been thought out in its implications could its particular applicability to the case in hand be judged. Suggestions at first seemingly remote and wild are frequently so transformed by being elaborated into what follows from them as to become apt and fruitful. The development of an idea through reasoning helps supply intervening or intermediate terms which link together into a consistent whole elements that at first seemingly conflict with each other, some leading the mind to one inference and others to an opposed one.

Mathematics as Typical Reasoning. Mathematics affords the typical example of how far can be carried the operation of relating ideas to one another, without having to depend upon the observations of the senses. In geometry we start with a few simple conceptions, line, angle, parallel, surfaces formed by lines meeting, etc., and a few principles defining equalities. Knowing something about the equality of angles made by parallel lines when they intersect a straight line, and knowing, by definition, that a perpendicular to a straight line forms two right angles, by means of a combination of these ideas we readily determine that the sum of the interior angles of a triangle is equal to two right angles. By continuing to trace the implications of theorems already demonstrated, the whole subject of plane figures is finally elaborated. The manipulation of algebraic symbols so as to establish a series of equations and other mathematical functions affords an even more striking example of what can be accomplished by developing the relation of ideas to one another.

When the hypothesis indicated by a series of scientific observations and experiments can be stated in mathematical form, that idea can be transformed to almost any extent, until it assumes a form in which a problem can be dealt with most expeditiously and effectively. Much of the accomplishment of physical science depends upon an intervening mathematical elaboration of ideas. It is not the mere presence of measurements in quantitative form that yields scientific knowledge, but that particular kind of mathematical statement which can be developed by reasoning into other and more fruitful forms—a consideration which is fatal to the claim to scientific standing of many educational measurements merely because they have a quantitative form.

THE FIFTH PHASE, TESTING THE HYPOTHESIS BY ACTION

The concluding phase is some kind of testing by overt action to give *experimental corroboration,* or *verification,* of the conjectural idea. Reasoning shows that *if* the *idea* be adopted, certain consequences follow. So far the conclusion is hypothetical or conditional. If when we look we find present all the conditions demanded by the theory, and if we find the characteristic traits called for by rival alternatives to be lacking, the tendency to believe, to accept, is almost irresistible. Sometimes direct observation furnishes corroboration, as in the case of the pole on the boat. In other cases, as in that of the bubbles, experiment is required; that is, *conditions are deliberately arranged in accord with the requirements of an idea or hypothesis to see whether the results theoretically indicated by the idea actually occur.* If it is found that the experimental results agree with the theoretical, or rationally deduced, results, and if there is reason to believe that *only* the conditions in question would yield such results, the confirmation is so strong as to induce a conclusion—at least until contrary facts shall indicate the advisability of its revision.

Of course, verification does not always follow. Sometimes consequences show failure to confirm instead of corroboration. The idea in question is refuted by the court of final appeal. But a great advantage of possession of the habit of reflective activity is that failure is not *mere* failure. It is instructive. The person who really thinks learns quite as much from his failures as from his successes. For a failure indicates to the person whose thinking has been involved in it, and who has not come to it by mere blind chance, what further observations should be made. It suggests to him what modifications should be introduced in the hypothesis upon which he has been operating. It either brings to light a new problem or helps to define and clarify the problem on which he has been engaged. Nothing shows the trained thinker better than the use he makes of his errors and mistakes. What merely annoys and discourages a person not accustomed to thinking, or what starts him out on a new course of aimless attack by mere cut-and-try methods, is a stimulus and a guide to the trained inquirer.

The Sequence of the Five Phases Is Not Fixed

The five phases, terminals, or functions of thought, that we have noted do not follow one another in a set order. On the contrary, each step in genuine thinking does something to perfect the formation of a suggestion and promote its change into a leading idea or directive hypothesis. It does something to promote the location and definition of the problem. Each improvement in the idea leads to new observations that yield new facts or data and help the mind judge more accurately the relevancy of facts already at hand. The elaboration of the hypothesis does not wait until the problem has been defined and adequate hypothesis has been arrived at; it may come in at any intermediate time. And as we have just seen, any particular overt test need not be final; it may be introductory to new observations and new suggestions, according to what happens in consequence of it.

There is, however, an important difference between test by overt action in practical deliberations and in scientific investigations. In the former the practical commitment involved in overt action is much more serious than in the latter. An astronomer or a chemist performs overt actions, but they are for the sake of knowledge; they serve to test and develop his conceptions and theories. In practical matters, the main result desired lies outside of knowledge. One of the great values of thinking, accordingly, is that it defers the commitment to action that is irretrievable, that, once made, cannot be revoked. Even in moral and other practical matters, therefore, a thoughtful person treats his overt deeds as experimental so far as possible; that is to say, while he cannot call them back and must stand their consequences, he gives alert attention to what they teach him about his conduct as well as to the non-intellectual consequences. He makes a problem out of consequences of conduct, looking into the causes from which they probably resulted, especially the causes that lie in his own habits and desires.

In conclusion, we point out that the five phases of reflection that have been described represent only in outline the indispensable traits of reflective thinking. In practice, two of them may telescope, some of them may be passed over hurriedly, and the burden of reaching a conclusion may fall mainly on a single phase, which will then require a seemingly disproportionate development. No set rules can be laid down on such matters. The way they are managed depends upon the intellectual tact and sensitiveness of the individual. When things have come out wrong, it is, however, a wise practice to review the methods by which the unwise decision was reached, and see where the misstep was made.

One Phase May Be Expanded

In complicated cases some of the five phases are so extensive that they include definite subphases within themselves. In this case it is arbitrary whether the minor functions are regarded as parts or are listed as distinct phases. There is nothing especially sacred about the number five. For example, in matters of practical deliberation where the object is to decide what to do, it may be well to undertake a scrutiny of the underlying desires and motives that are operating; that is, instead of asking what ends and means will best satisfy one's wish, one may turn back to the attitudes of which the wish is the expression. It is a matter of indifference whether this search be listed as an independent problem, having its own phases, or as an additional phase in the original problem.

Reference to the Future and to the Past

Again, it has been suggested that reflective thinking involves a look into the future, a forecast, an anticipation, or a prediction, and that this should be listed as a sixth aspect, or phase. As a matter of fact, every intellectual suggestion or idea is anticipatory of some possible future experience, while the final solution gives a definite set toward the future. It is both a record of something accomplished and an assignment of a future method of operation. It helps set up an enduring habit of procedure. When a physician, for example, has diagnosed a case, he usually makes also a *prognosis*, a forecast, of the probable future course of the disease. And not only is his treatment a verification—or the reverse—of the idea or hypothesis about the disease upon which he has proceeded, but the result also affects his treatment of future patients. In some cases, the future reference may be so important as to require special elaboration. In this case, it may be presented as an added, distinct phase. Some of the investigations of an astronomical expedition to watch an eclipse of the sun may be directly intended, for example, to get material bearing on Einstein's theory. But the theory, itself, is so important that its confirmation or refutation will give a decided turn to the future of physical science, and this consideration is likely to be uppermost in the minds of scientists.

Of equal importance is the reference to the *past* involved in reflection. Of course, suggestions are dependent in any case upon one's past experience; they do not arise out of nothing. But while sometimes we go ahead with the suggestion without stopping to go back to the original experience of which it is the fruit, at other times we go consciously over the past experience in considerable detail as part of the process of testing the value of the suggestion.

For example, it occurs to a man to invest in real estate. Then he recalls that a previous investment of this kind turned out unfortunately. He goes over the former case, comparing it bit by bit with the present, to see how far the two cases are alike or unlike. Examination of the past may be the chief and decisive factor in thought. The most valuable reference to the past is likely, however, to come at the time the conclusion is reached. We noted earlier the importance of a final survey to secure a net formulation of the exact result and of the premises upon which it logically depends. This is not only an important part of the process of *testing*, but, as was stated in the earlier discussion, is almost necessary if good habits are to be built up. Ability to *organize* knowledge consists very largely in the habit of reviewing previous facts and ideas and relating them to one another on a new basis; namely, that of the conclusion that has been reached. A certain amount of this operation is included in the testing phase that has been described. But its influence upon the attitude of students is so important that it may be well at times so to emphasize it that it becomes a definite function, or phase, on its own account.

Note

1. *Implies* is more often used when a principle or general truth brings about belief in some other truth; the other phrases are more frequently used to denote the cases in which a fact or event leads us to believe in some other fact or in a law.

II
THE NATURE OF METHOD

4

Method in Science Teaching (1916)

Written as an address to the Science Section of the National Education Association (NEA), "Method in Science Teaching" was subsequently published in the inaugural issue of *General Science Quarterly*. It is no secret that Dewey was a great admirer of the sciences, espousing the belief that they offer "knowledge at its best." Yet he also expressed concern at the time with their increasing specialization and exclusivity. The level of expertise this required led many teachers to suggest that work in science be confined to high school and college. Dewey worried, however, that this would detach advanced study in science from the more basic scientific spirit and habits of mind preferably developed in younger students. In short, treating high-school students as novice scientists, without this foundation, ultimately does a disservice both to the students and to science.

Method means a way to a result, a means to an end, a path to a goal. Method therefore varies with the end to be reached. Without a clear notion of the end, we cannot proceed intelligently upon the journey toward it. When we try to state the end of science teaching we are, however, likely to find ourselves involved in such vague generalities that all might use the same words and yet differ radically about the actual method of procedure. It is therefore only to make clear my own point of approach and not to foreclose discussion that I say that the end of science teaching is to make us aware what constitutes the most effective use of mind, of intelligence; to give us a working sense of the real nature of knowledge, of sound knowledge as distinct from mere guess work, opinion, dogmatic belief or whatever. Obviously science is not only knowledge, but it is knowledge at its best, knowledge in its tested and surest form. Educationally then what differentiates its value from that of other knowledge is precisely this superior quality. Unless it is so taught that students acquire a realizing sense of what gives it its superiority, something is lost. If we ask how this superior type of knowledge came into existence we find that men have been working their minds, more or less effectively for many thousand years, and that for a very long time it was less rather than more effectively. But the most efficient ways of using or working intelligence have gradually been selected and cultivated. And science as a personal power and resource is an equipment of those found most successful, most effective. A man may have a great deal of cultivation; a great deal of information, correct information at that, about things, but if he has never made a first-hand acquaintance at some point with scientific ways of dealing with a subject-matter, he has no sure way of telling the difference between all-wool knowledge and shoddy goods. He has no sure way of knowing how, or when, he is using his mental powers most capably and fruitfully. The ability to detect the genuine in our beliefs and ideas, the ability to control one's mind to its own best working is a very precious thing. Hence the rightful place of science in education is a fundamental one, and it is correspondingly important to see to it that methods of teaching are such as to fulfill its true purpose.

When we pass from this generality, it seems to me that the first need is to discriminate certain stages in the educational development of science. The first stage belongs of necessity to the elementary school, for I do not think that any amount of pains and ability in the high school can make up for a wrong start or even a failure to get the right start in the grades. This is contrary in appearance to a common assertion of secondary teachers that they prefer that their pupils come to them without any science instruction at all—which is paralleled by a similar statement on the part of college teachers. I think the inconsistency is only in appearance. The remark is really proof of the necessity of a right start. I do not believe that the problem of successful science will be met until teachers in college and high school exchange experience with those in the elementary school, and all take a mutual interest in one another's work.

At this stage, the purpose should be to give a first-hand acquaintance with a fair area of natural facts of such a kind as to arouse interest in the discovery of causes, dynamic processes, operating forces. I would emphasize the phrase "of such a kind." I think the chief defect, upon the whole, in our present elementary nature study is that while it may arouse a certain interest in observation and accumulate a certain store of information, it is too static, and hence too miscellaneous. By static I mean that observation is not directed to some active process. No amount of information of this sort can supply even a background for science. Space, however, forbids my dwelling upon this point, and its underlying point can perhaps be brought out by reference to something which lies within the high-school program, namely, so-called general science. Like the nature-study movement the tendency to general-science courses is animated by a praiseworthy desire to get away from the specialized technicalities of a highly matured science. I will not say that these reduce themselves for the average beginning student to mere acquisition of a vocabulary, though there is danger of this. But except with the few this science of the accomplished specialist remains, even when fairly well understood, just an isolated thing, a thing of a world superadded to the everyday world, when it ought to be an enlightening and an intellectual control of the everyday world.

As an attempt to get back nearer to the world in which the pupil lives, and away from a world which exists only for the scientist, the general-science tendency has, as I have just said, its justification. But I have an impression that in practice it may mean two quite different things. It may take its departure from sciences which are already differentiated, and simply pick out pieces from them, some from physics, some from chemistry, some from physiography, some from botany, etc., and out of this varied selection form something to serve as an introduction to sciences in a more specialized form. Now this method I believe to be of the static type after all. It gives scope for variety and adaptation, and will work with the right teacher. But urged as a general movement, I believe it retains the essential mistake of any method which begins with scientific knowledge in its already made form, while in addition it lends itself very easily to scrappy and superficial work, and even to a distaste for the continued and serious thinking necessary to a real mastery of science.

General science may, however, have another meaning. It may mean that a person who is himself an expert in scientific knowledge, forgets for the time being the conventional divisions of the sciences, and puts himself at the standpoint of pupils' experience of natural forces together with their ordinary useful applications. He does not however forget the scientific possibilities of these experiences, nor does he forget that there is an order of relative importance in scientific principles—that is to say, that some are more fundamental, some necessary in order to understand others, and thus more fruitful and ramifying.

While then he may take his subject-matter from any of the ordinary and more familiar materials of daily life, he does not allow that material in its obvious and superficial form to dictate to him the nature of the subsequent study. It may be varnish or cleansers, or bleachers, or a gasoline engine. But he never for a moment allows in his educational planning that thing to become the end of study; when he does, we have simply the wrong kind of elementary nature study over again. To him, as a teacher, the material is simply a means, a tool, a road. It is a way of getting at some process of nature's activity which is widely exemplified in other phenomena and which when grasped will render them more significant and more intelligible. While the student's attention may remain, so far as his conscious interest is concerned, upon the phenomena directly in front of him, it is the teacher's duty to see that he gets below the surface to the perception of whatever is scientifically in the experience. This need not be labelled a principle or law—in fact, if it is so labelled at first, the name principle or law will be merely a label. But if further material is selected so that what the pupil got hold of before serves as a means of intellectual approach and understanding, it becomes a principle or law for him: a law of his own thinking and inquiries, a standpoint from which he surveys facts and attempts to reduce them to order.

This same method of procedure means of course that choice is made in fixing the kind of familiar material with which one sets out. The interests and occupations of the environment will play a part. A farming environment would tend to provide one point of departure, a district in which electric apparatus was made another, a railway centre a third, and so on. But in each case, there will always be room for choice between material which tends to begin and end in itself and that from which something may be easily extracted which will give pupils a momentum to other things.

My point may perhaps be stated by saying that the right course lies between two erroneous courses. One method is the scrappy one of picking up isolated materials just because they happen to be familiar objects within the pupil's experience, and of merely extending and deepening the range of the pupil's familiarity, and then passing on to something else.

No amount of this process will make an introduction to science, to say nothing of science, for an introduction leads or draws into a subject, while the scrappy method never, save by accident, gets the pupil within range of the problems and explanatory methods of science. The other erroneous course is taken when the teacher's imagination is so limited that he cannot conceive of science existing except in the definitely segregated areas, concepts and terms which are found in books under the heads of physics, chemistry, etc., and who is thus restricted to moving within these boundaries. Such a person forgets that there is no material in existence which is physical or chemical or botanical, but that a certain ordinary subject-matter becomes physical or chemical or botanical when certain questions are raised, and when it is subjected to certain modes of inquiry. What is desired of the pupil is that starting from the ordinary unclassed material of experience he shall acquire command of the points of view, the ideas and methods, which make it physical or chemical or whatever.

I return to what I said at first about the dynamic point of view as the really scientific one, or the understanding of process as the heart of the scientific attitude. What are called physics and chemistry deal in effect with the lawful energies which bring about changes. To master their method means to be able to see any observed fact, no matter how seemingly fixed and stubborn, as a change, as a part of a larger process or on going. In this sense, they are central (along with mathematics which only deals with the fixed, the formal and structural side of the fact) in all scientific understanding. There is a sound instinct in the tendency to insist upon them as the heart of the secondary course in science and to look with jealousy upon whatever narrows their sphere of influence. But it does not follow that the material which is found in the texts which segregate certain considerations under the heads of physics or chemistry is the material to begin with. That is the fallacy against which I have been arguing. Plant and animal life, the operations of machines and the familiar appliances and processes of industrial life, are much more likely to furnish the actual starting material. What the principle calls for is that the pupil shall be led in his study of plant and animal life, of the machine and its operations, to the basic operations which enable him to understand what is before him to be led inevitably to physical and chemical principles. Nothing is more unfortunate for education than the usual separation between the sciences of life and the physical sciences. Living phenomena are natural and interesting material from which to set out, especially in all rural environments. But they are educationally significant in the degree in which they are used to procure an insight into just those principles which are not plants and animals, but which, when they are formulated by themselves, constitute physics and chemistry. It is the failure to carry nature study on to this insight which is responsible for its pedagogically unsatisfactory character, and the movement toward general science will repeat the failure unless it keeps the goal of physical and chemical principle steadily in view.

An extension of the method I have spoken of should in my judgment constitute the bulk of the secondary course in science, which ideally should be continuous throughout the four years—or the six. We must remember that although in school we are always treating pupils as embryonic scientists who somehow are interrupted and cut off before they get very far, the great mass of the pupils will never be scientific specialists. The value of science for them resides in the added meaning it gives to the usual occurrences of their everyday surroundings and occupations. None the less, we want a high school which will tend to attract those who have a distinct calling for specialized inquiry, and one which prepares them to enter upon it. I can only express my belief that there are many more such in the pupil population than we succeed at present in selecting and carrying on, and that I believe this is largely because we follow to so great an extent the method of feeding them all from the start as if they were full-fledged minute specialists. As a result large numbers who might otherwise be drawn later into the paths of scientific inquiry now become shunted off into the more concrete and appealing paths of engineering, industrial invention and application—simply because they have been repelled by a premature diet of abstract scientific propositions, lacking in meaning to them because abstracted from familiar facts of experience.

I believe there are scores, if not hundreds, of boys, for example, who now go from courses of abstract physics into automobile factories and the like, who, if they had begun with the automobile under a teacher who realized its scientific possibilities, might have gone on into abstract physics. I can sum up by saying that it seems to me that our present methods too largely put the cart before the horse; and that when we become aware of this mistake we are all too likely to cut the horse entirely loose from the cart, and let him browse around at random in the pastures without going anywhere. What we need is to hitch the horse of concrete experience with daily occupation and surroundings to a cart loaded with specialized scientific knowledge. It is not the duty of high-school science to pack the cart full—that will come later. It is its part to make such a good job of the hitching that every pupil who comes under its influence will always find in himself a tendency to turn his crude experiences over into a more scientific form, and to translate the bare science he reads and hears back into the terms of his daily life. When we do this, we shall find, I am confident, the crop of scientific specialists increased, not diminished, while we shall have a citizenship of men and women really intelligent in judging the affairs of life.

5

The Classroom Teacher (1923)

"The Classroom Teacher" originated as an address to the Massachusetts State Conference of Normal School Instructors. (Normal schools specialized in teacher preparation, with an emphasis on instructional methods.) It, too, was later published in *General Science Quarterly*. (*General Science Quarterly* became *Science Education* in 1929.) Here we find Dewey connecting the art of teaching with the need to be responsive to students' individuality. This opposed the growing tendency to view students en masse, like industrial workers at a machine—a future that unfortunately awaited many immigrant children, students of color, and the poor. Dewey voices a similar concern with the conditions faced by many classroom teachers: their invaluable firsthand knowledge of students was increasingly superseded by standardized tests and other bureaucratic devices that reduced quality to quantity, depersonalized relationships, and obstructed vital human interactions.[1] Is it not foolish, Dewey asks, to depend on forms of educational organization, administration, and standardization that substantially devalue teacher experience and the realities of school and classroom life? The former exist to support the latter, not the reverse.

What I have to say this afternoon is more in continuation of the talk of this morning than might seem from the title. I hope the reasons for making this connection between the two subjects will become apparent as I go on. As I suggested this morning, it is not so much in theory or philosophy of education that we need to provide greater recognition of individuality in the schools, but rather in certain practical considerations. It is easier, more convenient, and cheaper to handle persons in masses and classes than it is to deal with them individually. A very large number of people can learn to run a machine; a comparatively small number of people can be artists of a creative sort. The tendency toward treating students in masses and classes rather than individually results in the comparative ease and comfort there is in working with a smoothly-running machine. In learning the behavior of a machine, how to adjust it, much more is required.

When we come to dealing with living things, especially living characters that vary as human individuals do, and attempt to modify their individual dispositions, develop their individual powers, counteract their individual interests, we have to deal with them in an artistic way, a way which requires sympathy and interest to make all of the needed adjustments to the particular emergencies of the act. The more mechanical a thing is, the more we can manage it; the more vital it is, the more we have to use our observation and interest in order to adjust ourselves properly to it. It is not easy, in other words, to maintain a truly artistic standard, which is, of course, the real business of the teacher; hence the emphasis upon quantity rather than quality.

Our whole system of education, with the graded, classified system of inspection and examination, necessitates the handling of large numbers of students at a time, and moving them on according to some time schedule in large groups. These things, rather than philosophy or theory, are the great forces working against a more general recognition of the principle of individuality in education. The whole effect of organized administration sometimes seems to force a kind of standardization which is unfavorable to the development of the teacher's individuality and to the teacher's cooperating in the development of the pupil's individuality.

Wherever there is a mechanical element, wherever we are dealing with physical conditions—space, time, money conditions—there is room, and a necessity, for standardization or uniformity. The danger is, however, that those who become interested in this work of standardizing conditions—the external side of the school work—will forget the limits of standardized uniformity, and attempt to carry it over into the strictly human, spiritual element that cannot be standardized. At bottom, this is very largely a matter of money, like so many other things. But if we ask why it is that the best known and best tested educational ideas are not more widely practised than they actually are, we are quite apt to come up against the fact of professed inability of the community to supply the material means to do the best thing that is possible. I repeat this! Our whole system of examination, inspection, grading, classification, tends almost automatically to introduce a factitious factor that gets between the educator and the human individual that is being developed.

There was an English novel published a few years ago, wherein a young girl, whose parents having died, was brought up in an institution, an orphan asylum. Later on, when someone inquired about her education, she replied, "We never had any education; we were just brought up in batches." That tendency to treat children in batches instead of individually is enforced as a measure of economy.

I was very much interested in what Professor [Clifford] Kirkpatrick said this morning about the subject of intelligence tests. He put the emphasis in the right place, I think. There is some danger in putting the emphasis in the wrong place. I do not think the leaders in the movement put the emphasis on the wrong place, but I do think there is considerable danger in the mind of the public who have not had a share in the scientific use of the test. There is some danger that the impression should get abroad that when you have a student's intelligence quotient—his I.Q.—you have a certain insight and measurement of him as an individual. If you stop to think what these tests are and what they propose to do, you will see that an intelligence quotient is something quite different from an insight into the make-up of the individual as an individual. It is a method, as the word "quotient" shows, of getting a certain average, in order to show what class of person he belongs in, a wholly relative matter.

If you take the children of the country at large, you will find a certain number of an average of such and such ability. This particular class belongs in that group having this average intellectual ability. One might say you do not know any more about the individual than you did before. Suppose he has the mental age of 13 and 1/2, while his physiological age is so and so. He is above or below the average of his age. He is one of certain hundreds of thousands of children in the country who have been tested. We would know so many hundreds of thousands of children attain a mental age of so and so, and that this child belongs in that group. This finding is valuable for purposes of classification, which places the individual where he will work most effectively with others, and prevents useless retardation, of which Dr. Kirkpatrick spoke. It guards against the mistake of trying to make an individual go at a faster pace than he is capable of moving. However, when the teacher has determined this mental level, her work is really just beginning, so far as the psychological interest is concerned.

To turn now to the announced subject for the afternoon. It is the classroom teacher who is in contact with the individuals who are being educated. We might well say that all the rest of the system, organization and administration, is really so much superstructure for enabling the classroom teacher to do his or her work more effectively. It is true that actual education, whatever there is in the way of actual teaching and learning, is done in the classroom, through vital contact, intellectual and moral, between teacher and student. Like many other things self-evident, we give this basic fact a glance of passing recognition and then do not take it further into account. We emphasize the machinery of administration, the formation and laying out of the course of study, the functions of the school board, functions of the superintendent, principals and supervisors. All these stand in the public eye, at least very often, as the most important elements in the school system. To a certain extent, all these exist for the sake of the ultimate consumers, the teacher and the pupil as they come into direct personal relationship with each other in the school. If these factors of organization, administration and supervision of instruction do not stimulate, assist and reinforce the worker in the classroom, then they are useless, or even worse, since they become encumbrances in the way of the teacher. After all, the truest thing said in education is, "As is the teacher, so is the school." We all know that. The difference between one school and another, between one class in school and another, goes back to the personality of the principal or teacher. The problem is then: How are we going to concentrate all of these more external elements so that they really will emancipate, assist and safeguard the individual teacher in the classroom? Have we not, to some extent, been looking through the wrong end of the telescope? Do we not need to look more frequently through the end that magnifies the work of the classroom teacher and places that work in a better position?

Referring briefly to the course of study, I would have the best experts in the country studying the proper course of study. I would have experts in history, geography, arithmetic, and other subjects in the curriculum. Let them meet together and discuss what is the best subject matter out of the vast range of subject matter to be had. That may be, and should be, of great assistance to the classroom teacher, but it does not wholly determine what the actual subject matter is that comes home to the pupil. The course of study should be a *course*; it ought to be a flowing, moving thing, for its subject matter comes into continuous contact with the minds of the pupils.

There is no way by which subject matter, as laid out by experts, can get over to the pupils, except through the medium of the teacher. We can have a text-book written in accordance with the recommendation of experts. But after all, will not the last thing that counts be how the teacher uses that text-book; how it is handled; the questions that are asked? You can have very rich, full subject matter laid down on paper, and yet the personality and intelligence of the teacher may be such that the subject matter will shrink, dry up, and become a mere trickle of dull fact when it gets to the pupil. You can have an outline of a course of study, in the form of a bare skeleton on paper, and yet that course of study, as it gets over to the pupils in the classroom, may be very full, rich and alive, because of the spirit that the teacher puts into it; the methods the teacher uses; the assignment of outside study that the teacher gives, and new points of view in the student mind. What is true here of the course of study, as it comes to the pupils through the teacher's mind and personality, is true, in my judgment, of many other things in the educational system. It is the failure to concentrate all of the various school resources upon the power of the teacher that is a fundamental cause of some stereotyped mechanizing of our educational system. I repeat. Because the classroom teacher stands for this element of personal individual contact, while administration and organization are influences which are modified as they reach the pupil through the teacher, the central problem is how to use all of our existing resources in developing the classroom teacher.

We all know that there is a very great gap between our theories and our practices. Many of the wisest and truest things about education have been said for many hundreds of years—some of them by Plato, over 2,000 years ago; others, in the educational reforms of the last three or four hundred years. Many have come through discoveries in recent years and in our own day. But we all know that, even if these discoveries had not been made, there was enough known before as true and wise by educational experts immensely to improve our schools, indeed to have revolutionized them. I remember a few years ago a young woman who, for some reason, had escaped a secondary school education, for better or worse, and decided she wished to be a teacher. She went to Teachers College to study all of the improved theories of teaching. She later took a place in a school, and she had a surprise, not to say shock, which most of us who have come through an educational system would not have. Here were those things taught by the authorities, agreed to by the authorities as true, as well as modern and up-to-date, and she assumed she was going to find schools run on the basis of these advanced theories of which she had learned. It was the discrepancy between the teaching she had and the actual practice and teaching in the schools that gave her this shock. It brought home to me how wide this gap is, after all, and how the crucial problem of the improvement of education is to make those advances that we have in theory and administration, effective upon the work of the teacher, so that they will seriously affect the life of the pupil.

A teacher, a short time ago, at the suggestion of another teacher, made a study over a number of years of the volumes of reports of the N.E.A., with a view to seeing who was making the vital contributions to educational thought; contributions that were supposed to influence practice. As perhaps you will guess, a very small percentage of the papers read at the N.E.A., the addresses made, came from classroom teachers. If we eliminate the number coming from high school classroom teachers, the number coming from elementary classroom teachers was negligible. I doubt if it was one per cent, going over a series of years. That seems to me to be a deplorable fact. It indicates that, for some reason, classroom teachers are not being the active force in the improvement of educational practice that they should be. The people who are doing the actual work of instruction, that are in personal contact, are personal influences on the character and minds of the students, are not the ones who are actively carrying forward the theory. I realize how many explanations can be given for this condition,—such as lack of time, teachers overburdened with work, etc. The university or normal school teacher or principal may have more leisure to study these things, but, after all, since it is the teachers who make the final application, ought they not to play a large part in developing and making concrete and real the ideas which they are engaged in executing?

In industry and factory life we have a sharp separation between those who plan and those who execute. I wonder, however, from the standpoint of the welfare of the country, whether, even in a factory, it is advisable to have so sharp a line of division between those who plan and those who execute. But certainly, when we come to such a vital thing as education, it is still more dangerous to have this sharp distinction between those who plan and those who do the work of execution. The result is that the teacher, who does not have part in developing ideas, cannot have that sympathetic understanding of them that one has who has taken part in working them out. The principle of learning by experience, if it is a good principle for pupils, is a good principle for teachers. If our ideas and theories ought to be arrived at inductively, if they ought to grow up out of actual experience, why should not the concrete experience of the classroom teacher develop more in the way of educational ideas and principles than it does at present? I think one reason for the gap between our modern theories and what is known and accepted in school practice, is largely due to the fact that the intellectual responsibility of the classroom teacher has not been sufficiently recognized or magnified. You know, if you are engaged in carrying out plans and ideas of one person, you do not, and cannot, throw yourself into it with the same enthusiasm and wholeheartedness, or same desire to learn and improve, that you do when you are carrying out plans and ideas which you yourself have had some share in developing. The function of the supervisor is important and valuable. Obviously, it should be one of inspiration and of education, rather than that of simply writing prescriptions such as those the doctor writes, and which are then handed to a drug-store clerk to fill out. Teachers should not be clerks filling out recipes that are prescribed by others. They should not be like cooks in the kitchen, who take a cook-book and mix ingredients in the proportion called for by the recipe in the book, not knowing why they do this or that, or with any expectation that they are going to make any discoveries or improvement. The real cook is the one who originates all the improved dishes that we like to eat. And the permanent improvements in the course of study must be those which are either contributed to, tested by, worked out, experimented upon intelligently by the teacher in the classroom.

A good deal of supervision, so-called, especially when class supervision is the watchword of the day, seems to have a great deal of "super" in it and not much of "vision." It is the business of the supervisor to look over the field, to get a larger, wider, more thorough view of it than the conditions of the classroom teacher can permit. It is the privilege of the supervisor and directing officer to give the classroom teacher the benefit of this larger, more comprehensive vision of the field.

There are, of course, some valuable short cuts and mechanical devices. It is difficult always to be a creative artist. I think, however, that we should get on more rapidly if we realized that, if education is going to live up to its profession, it must be seen as a work of art which requires the same qualities of personal enthusiasm and imagination as are required by the musician, painter or artist. Each one of these artists needs a technique which is more or less mechanical, but in the degree to which he loses his personal vision to become subordinate to the more formal rules of the technique he falls below the level and grade of the artist. He becomes reduced again to the level of the artisan who follows the blue prints, drawings, and plans that are made by other people.

I think what first interested me in this problem of the greater freedom on the part of the teacher, was carried or transferred from an interest in more varied and creative, independent and original work on the part of the pupil. Finally, I saw how inconsistent it was to expect this greater amount of creative, independent work from the student when the teachers were still unemancipated; when the teachers were still shackled by too many rules and prescriptions and too much of a desire for uniformity of method and subject matter.

As Mr. [William] Baldwin said this morning, every course of study put in print is more or less out of date by the time it is in print. It can serve only as a suggestion for the teacher, and every classroom teacher ought to be regarded by others, and regard himself or herself, as responsible not only for the teaching of recognized subject matter, but for the making of new contributions to subject matter. Think of the variety of the universe we live in, the history of society and human life! There is no end to the riches of the material that it is possible to draw upon. We can only begin to attack the reservoir of subject matter in education. There is not a teacher fit for the work, who is really stimulated to do her best, who will not find in her own locality, suggested by the needs of the locality, or stimulated or aroused by the questions that pupils ask, some new field of subject matter which will satisfy the mental hunger of the pupils at the present time. We shall not make our theoretical improvements in education practically effective, we shall not realize upon them and get them over into concrete cash values, until we expect, as well as give, opportunity where every individual pupil can exercise freedom and discuss certain lines of subject matter in the school in contact with the teacher, quite irrespective of any formula or prescribed course of study.

The imagination of everybody today, their unconscious way of seeing things, is more influenced by industrial considerations than we realize. The way business is done influences unconsciously all our ideas. So we have from business practices carried over into education too much standardization, too much concentration of responsibility. There should be concentration of responsibility, but if, in a school system, you concentrate responsibility in a small number of people, what does that mean for the rest of the people? Is it not a division of irresponsibility, when you have concentrated your responsibility in a few? Responsibility needs to be concentrated, but in everybody. Every part of the school system needs to have responsibility for improvements in subject matter, in methods of instruction, in methods of discipline. When we try to place all responsibility on a few administrative officers, we are practically depriving the greater number of teachers of responsibility. That is why I say that concentration of responsibility is a division of irresponsibility. Too often the relation between pupils and teachers is reduplicated in the relation between teachers and supervisory officers. Pupils, many of them, strive to come up to the external standards that are set by the teacher, and the main question with them is whether they can get by; whether they can do enough at the proper time to satisfy the demands and expectation of the teacher. This situation is often reduplicated in the relation between teacher and the supervisory officer. The teacher is simply concerned with the things that will meet external standards that are set for her.

My attention was first called to this by one of the finest women I ever knew, Mrs. Ella Flagg Young of Chicago. Mrs. Young began as a classroom teacher, and became a supervisor, an associate superintendent, and finally, superintendent. From forty years' experience she knew from every angle the public schools of a large city. She saw the schools from the standpoint of the teacher and supervisory officer, and was acutely aware of the situation that could exist in a highly organized school system between two parts of the system.

The classroom teacher has this advantage. She is on the job all the time. There are not enough supervisory officers to go around and be on the job all the time. They can only visit now and then. But under a regime of class supervision, the teachers often develop a very great skill in doing what they like to do, and at the same time appearing to be carrying out the directions of supervisors. The advantage is on the side of the classroom teacher, because she is there all the time.

Let me repeat a story told by a teacher: "As a high school teacher in algebra I had what I thought was an unusually successful recitation, because the pupils were doing all the work. I was acting as umpire. The principal came in and did not see me doing anything. He reproved me afterwards, and said that I was lazy. I remedied that immediately. Every time he came into the room after that, I began to lecture to the pupils, and he thought I was a good teacher. Personally I do not think I was teaching so successfully."

I sometimes think the greatest human loss there is at the present time is in the loss of experience as to our human contacts with each other.

Parents too often start out having to take and train their own children as if nobody had ever done it before. There is some improvement now, but, after all, how much experience goes unrecorded and unutilized that might be rendered available for others. And so in the school, because the teacher is not given a responsible position, how much in the way of experience there is that goes unused, that does not become food for their further teaching, and, because of that, other people, perhaps professors like myself in universities, who are more or less at arm's length from the situation, have to provide ideas and theories that are more or less abstract. These ideas and theories do not get translated over into vital results because the teacher has not had share enough in building them up and contributing to them.

Note

1. Dewey's concerns were borne out in his Columbia colleague, E. L. Thorndike. A staunch behaviorist, Thorndike famously argued, "All that exists, exists in some amount and can be measured." Regrettably, the paltry empiricism of Thorndike's methodology rationalized his support for eugenics and other toxic forms of bigotry. See E. L. Thorndike, "The Nature, Purposes, and General Methods of Measurements of Educational Products," in *Seventeenth Yearbook of the National Society for the Study of Education*, vol. 2, ed. G. M. Whipple (Public School Publishing, 1918), 16.

6

From *Experience and Education* (1938)

Experience and Education derives from an invited lecture for the Kappa Delta Pi education honor society. It is also one of Dewey's most frequently read books. This is due largely to its brevity (it is highly condensed), as well as Dewey's efforts to (once again) divorce his theory of experience from the polarizing debate between the "old" or traditional education and the child-centered variety of the "new" or progressive education. Using a favorite rhetorical technique, Dewey presents the arguments of each side before declaring them both misguided, the victims of a false dichotomy between the active learner and the meaning-making possibilities of subject matter. To move beyond this either/or mentality, he says, we have "The Need of a Theory of Experience": one cannot simply reject the experiential paradigm of the "old" education and embrace its polar opposite as the only viable alternative. After summarizing his holistic theory of experience, Dewey proceeds in "Criteria of Experience" to explain the need for educators to address the connections or continuities in students' experiences both over time and across different situations: isolation and disconnect in experience, he stresses, result in a loss of purpose and meaning, not freedom or independence, and constitute "waste in education." In the end, the most relevant distinctions are between educative and mis-educative experience and democratic and undemocratic social arrangements. This is where individual human potential is either furthered or frustrated.

The Need of a Theory of Experience

Rejection of the philosophy and practice of traditional education sets a new type of difficult educational problem for those who believe in the new type of education. We shall operate blindly and in confusion until we recognize this fact; until we thoroughly appreciate that departure from the old solves no problems. What is said in the following pages is, accordingly, intended to indicate some of the main problems with which the newer education is confronted and to suggest the main lines along which their solution is to be sought. I assume that amid all uncertainties there is one permanent frame of reference: namely, the organic connection between education and personal experience; or, that the new philosophy of education is committed to some kind of empirical and experimental philosophy. But experience and experiment are not self-explanatory ideas. Rather, their meaning is part of the problem to be explored. To know the meaning of empiricism we need to understand what experience is.

The belief that all genuine education comes about through experience does not mean that all experiences are genuinely or equally educative. Experience and education cannot be directly equated to each other. For some experiences are mis-educative. Any experience is mis-educative that has the effect of arresting or distorting the growth of further experience. An experience may be such as to engender callousness; it may produce lack of sensitivity and of responsiveness. Then the possibilities of having richer experience in the future are restricted. Again, a given experience may increase a person's automatic skill in a particular direction and yet tend to land him in a groove or rut; the effect again is to narrow the field of further experience. An experience may be immediately enjoyable and yet promote the formation of a slack and careless attitude; this attitude then operates to modify the quality of subsequent experiences so as to prevent a person from getting out of them what they have to give. Again, experiences may be so disconnected from one another that, while each is agreeable or even exciting in itself, they are not linked cumulatively to one another. Energy is then dissipated and a person becomes scatter-brained. Each experience may be lively, vivid, and "interesting," and yet their disconnectedness may artificially generate dispersive, disintegrated, centrifugal habits. The consequence of formation of such habits is inability to control future experiences. They are then taken, either by way of enjoyment or of discontent and revolt, just as they come. Under such circumstances, it is idle to talk of self-control.

Traditional education offers a plethora of examples of experiences of the kinds just mentioned. It is a great mistake to suppose, even tacitly, that the traditional schoolroom was not a place in which pupils had experiences. Yet this is tacitly assumed when progressive education as a plan of learning by experience is placed in sharp opposition to the old. The proper line of attack is that the experiences which were had, by pupils and teachers alike, were largely of a wrong kind. How many students, for example, were rendered callous to ideas, and how many lost the impetus to learn because of the way in which learning was experienced by them? How many acquired special skills by means of automatic drill so that their power of judgment and capacity to act intelligently in new situations was limited? How many came to associate the learning process with ennui and boredom? How many found what they did learn so foreign to the situations of life outside the school as to give them no power of control over the latter? How many came to associate books with dull drudgery, so that they were "conditioned" to all but flashy reading matter?

If I ask these questions, it is not for the sake of wholesale condemnation of the old education. It is for quite another purpose. It is to emphasize the fact, first, that young people in traditional schools do have experiences; and, secondly, that the trouble is not the absence of experiences, but their defective and wrong character—wrong and defective from the standpoint of connection with further experience. The positive side of this point is even more important in connection with progressive education. It is not enough to insist upon the necessity of experience, nor even of activity in experience. Everything depends upon the *quality* of the experience which is had. The quality of any experience has two aspects. There is an immediate aspect of agreeableness or disagreeableness, and there is its influence upon later experiences. The first is obvious and easy to judge. The *effect* of an experience is not borne on its face. It sets a problem to the educator. It is his business to arrange for the kind of experiences which, while they do not repel the student, but rather engage his activities are, nevertheless, more than immediately enjoyable since they promote having desirable future experiences. Just as no man lives or dies to himself, so no experience lives and dies to itself. Wholly independent of desire or intent, every experience lives on in further experiences. Hence the central problem of an education based upon experience is to select the kind of present experiences that live fruitfully and creatively in subsequent experiences.

Later, I shall discuss in more detail the principle of the continuity of experience or what may be called the experiential continuum. Here I wish simply to emphasize the importance of this principle for the philosophy of educative experience. A philosophy of education, like any theory, has to be stated in words, in symbols. But so far as it is more than verbal it is a plan for conducting education. Like any plan, it must be framed with reference to what is to be done and how it is to be done. The more definitely and sincerely it is held that education is a development within, by, and for experience, the more important it is that there shall be clear conceptions of what experience is. Unless experience is so conceived that the result is a plan for deciding upon subject-matter, upon methods of instruction and discipline, and upon material equipment and social organization of the school, it is wholly in the air. It is reduced to a form of words which may be emotionally stirring but for which any other set of words might equally well be substituted unless they indicate operations to be initiated and executed. Just because traditional education was a matter of routine in which the plans and programs were handed down from the past, it does not follow that progressive education is a matter of planless improvisation.

The traditional school could get along without any consistently developed philosophy of education. About all it required in that line was a set of abstract words like culture, discipline, our great cultural heritage, etc., actual guidance being derived not from them but from custom and established routines. Just because progressive schools cannot rely upon established traditions and institutional habits, they must either proceed more or less haphazardly or be directed by ideas which, when they are made articulate and coherent, form a philosophy of education. Revolt against the kind of organization characteristic of the traditional school constitutes a demand for a kind of organization based upon ideas. I think that only slight acquaintance with the history of education is needed to prove that educational reformers and innovators alone have felt the need for a philosophy of education. Those who adhered to the established system needed merely a few fine-sounding words to justify existing practices. The real work was done by habits which were so fixed as to be institutional. The lesson for progressive education is that it requires in an urgent degree, a degree more pressing than was incumbent upon former innovators, a philosophy of education based upon a philosophy of experience.

I remarked incidentally that the philosophy in question is, to paraphrase the saying of Lincoln about democracy, one of education of, by, and for experience. No one of these words, *of*, *by*, or *for*, names anything which is self-evident. Each of them is a challenge to discover and put into operation a principle of order and organization which follows from understanding what educative experience signifies.

It is, accordingly, a much more difficult task to work out the kinds of materials, of methods, and of social relationships that are appropriate to the new education than is the case with traditional education. I think many of the difficulties experienced in the conduct of progressive schools and many of the criticisms leveled against them arise from this source. The difficulties are aggravated and the criticisms are increased when it is supposed that the new education is somehow easier than the old. This belief is, I imagine, more or less current. Perhaps it illustrates again the *Either-Or* philosophy, springing from the idea that about all which is required is *not* to do what is done in traditional schools.

I admit gladly that the new education is *simpler* in principle than the old. It is in harmony with principles of growth, while there is very much which is artificial in the old selection and arrangement of subjects and methods, and artificiality always leads to unnecessary complexity. But the easy and the simple are not identical. To discover what is really simple and to act upon the discovery is an exceedingly difficult task. After the artificial and complex is once institutionally established and ingrained in custom and routine, it is easier to walk in the paths that have been beaten than it is, after taking a new point of view, to work out what is practically involved in the new point of view. The old Ptolemaic astronomical system was more complicated with its cycles and epicycles than the Copernican system. But until organization of actual astronomical phenomena on the ground of the latter principle had been effected the easiest course was to follow the line of least resistance provided by the old intellectual habit. So we come back to the idea that a coherent *theory* of experience, affording positive direction to selection and organization of appropriate educational methods and materials, is required by the attempt to give new direction to the work of the schools. The process is a slow and arduous one. It is a matter of growth, and there are many obstacles which tend to obstruct growth and to deflect it into wrong lines.

I shall have something to say later about organization. All that is needed, perhaps, at this point is to say that we must escape from the tendency to think of organization in terms of the *kind* of organization, whether of content (or subject-matter), or of methods and social relations, that mark traditional education. I think that a good deal of the current opposition to the idea of organization is due to the fact that it is so hard to get away from the picture of the studies of the old school. The moment "organization" is mentioned imagination goes almost automatically to the kind of organization that is familiar, and in revolting against that we are led to shrink from the very idea of any organization. On the other hand, educational reactionaries, who are now gathering force, use the absence of adequate intellectual and moral organization in the newer type of school as proof not only of the need of organization, but to identify any and every kind of organization with that instituted before the rise of experimental science. Failure to develop a conception of organization upon the empirical and experimental basis gives reactionaries a too easy victory. But the fact that the empirical sciences now offer the best type of intellectual organization which can be found in any field shows that there is no reason why we, who call ourselves empiricists, should be "pushovers" in the matter of order and organization.

Criteria of Experience

If there is any truth in what has been said about the need of forming a theory of experience in order that education may be intelligently conducted upon the basis of experience, it is clear that the next thing in order in this discussion is to present the principles that are most significant in framing this theory. I shall not, therefore, apologize for engaging in a certain amount of philosophical analysis, which otherwise might be out of place. I may, however, reassure you to some degree by saying that this analysis is not an end in itself but is engaged in for the sake of obtaining criteria to be applied later in discussion of a number of concrete and, to most persons, more interesting issues.

I have already mentioned what I called the category of continuity, or the experiential continuum. This principle is involved, as I pointed out, in every attempt to discriminate between experiences that are worth while educationally and those that are not. It may seem superfluous to argue that this discrimination is necessary not only in criticizing the traditional type of education but also in initiating and conducting a different type. Nevertheless, it is advisable to pursue for a little while the idea that it is necessary. One may safely assume, I suppose, that one thing which has recommended the progressive movement is that it seems more in accord with the democratic ideal to which our people is committed than do the procedures of the traditional school, since the latter have so much of the autocratic about them. Another thing which has contributed to its favorable reception is that its methods are humane in comparison with the harshness so often attending the policies of the traditional school.

The question I would raise concerns why we prefer democratic and humane arrangements to those which are autocratic and harsh. And by "why," I mean the *reason* for preferring them, not just the *causes* which lead us to the preference. One *cause* may be that we have been taught not only in the schools but by the press, the pulpit, the platform, and our laws and law-making bodies that democracy is the best of all social institutions. We may have so assimilated this idea from our surroundings that it has become an habitual part of our mental and moral make-up. But similar causes have led other persons in different surroundings to widely varying conclusions—to prefer fascism, for example. The cause for our preference is not the same thing as the reason why we *should* prefer it.

It is not my purpose here to go in detail into the reason. But I would ask a single question: Can we find any reason that does not ultimately come down to the belief that democratic social arrangements promote a better quality of human experience, one which is more widely accessible and enjoyed, than do nondemocratic and anti-democratic forms of social life? Does not the principle of regard for individual freedom and for decency and kindliness of human relations come back in the end to the conviction that these things are tributary to a higher quality of experience on the part of a greater number than are methods of repression and coercion or force? Is it not the reason for our preference that we believe that mutual consultation and convictions reached through persuasion, make possible a better quality of experience than can otherwise be provided on any wide scale?

If the answer to these questions is in the affirmative (and personally I do not see how we can justify our preference for democracy and humanity on any other ground), the ultimate reason for hospitality to progressive education, because of its reliance upon and use of humane methods and its kinship to democracy, goes back to the fact that discrimination is made between the inherent values of different experiences. So I come back to the principle of continuity of experience as a criterion of discrimination.

At bottom, this principle rests upon the fact of habit, when *habit* is interpreted biologically. The basic characteristic of habit is that every experience enacted and undergone modifies the one who acts and undergoes, while this modification affects, whether we wish it or not, the quality of subsequent experiences. For it is a somewhat different person who enters into them. The principle of habit so understood obviously goes deeper than the ordinary conception of *a* habit as a more or less fixed way of doing things, although it includes the latter as one of its special cases. It covers the formation of attitudes, attitudes that are emotional and intellectual; it covers our basic sensitivities and ways of meeting and responding to all the conditions which we meet in living. From this point of view, the principle of continuity of experience means that every experience both takes up something from those which have gone before and modifies in some way the quality of those which come after. As the poet states it,

> . . . all experience is an arch wherethro'
> Gleams that untravell'd world, whose margin fades
> Forever and forever when I move.[1]

So far, however, we have no ground for discrimination among experiences. For the principle is of universal application. There is *some* kind of continuity in every case. It is when we note the different forms in which continuity of experience operates that we get the basis of discriminating among experiences. I may illustrate what is meant by an objection which has been brought against an idea which I once put forth—namely, that the educative process can be identified with growth when that is understood in terms of the active participle, *growing*.

Growth, or growing as developing, not only physically but intellectually and morally, is one exemplification of the principle of continuity. The objection made is that growth might take many different directions: a man, for example, who starts out on a career of burglary may grow in that direction, and by practice may grow into a highly expert burglar. Hence it is argued that "growth" is not enough; we must also specify the direction in which growth takes place, the end towards which it tends. Before, however, we decide that the objection is conclusive we must analyze the case a little further.

That a man may grow in efficiency as a burglar, as a gangster, or as a corrupt politician, cannot be doubted. But from the standpoint of growth as education and education as growth the question is whether growth in this direction promotes or retards growth in general. Does this form of growth create conditions for further growth, or does it set up conditions that shut off the person who has grown in this particular direction from the occasions, stimuli, and opportunities for continuing growth in new directions? What is the effect of growth in a special direction upon the attitudes and habits which alone open up avenues for development in other lines? I shall leave you to answer these questions, saying simply that when and *only* when development in a particular line conduces to continuing growth does it answer to the criterion of education as growing. For the conception is one that must find universal and not specialized limited application.

I return now to the question of continuity as a criterion by which to discriminate between experiences which are educative and those which are mis-educative. As we have seen, there is some kind of continuity in any case since every experience affects for better or worse the attitudes which help decide the quality of further experiences, by setting up certain preference and aversion, and making it easier or harder to act for this or that end. Moreover, every experience influences in some degree the objective conditions under which further experiences are had. For example, a child who learns to speak has a new facility and new desire. But he has also widened the external conditions of subsequent learning. When he learns to read, he similarly opens up a new environment. If a person decides to become a teacher, lawyer, physician, or stockbroker, when he executes his intention he thereby necessarily determines to some extent the environment in which he will act in the future. He has rendered himself more sensitive and responsive to certain conditions, and relatively immune to those things about him that would have been stimuli if he had made another choice.

But, while the principle of continuity applies in some way in every case, the quality of the present experience influences the *way* in which the principle applies. We speak of spoiling a child and of the spoilt child. The effect of overindulging a child is a continuing one. It sets up an attitude which operates as an automatic demand that persons and objects cater to his desires and caprices in the future. It makes him seek the kind of situation that will enable him to do what he feels like doing at the time. It renders him averse to and comparatively incompetent in situations which require effort and perseverance in overcoming obstacles. There is no paradox in the fact that the principle of the continuity of experience may operate so as to leave a person arrested on a low plane of development, in a way which limits later capacity for growth.

On the other hand, if an experience arouses curiosity, strengthens initiative, and sets up desires and purposes that are sufficiently intense to carry a person over dead places in the future, continuity works in a very different way. Every experience is a moving force. Its value can be judged only on the ground of what it moves toward and into. The greater maturity of experience which should belong to the adult as educator puts him in a position to evaluate each experience of the young in a way in which the one having the less mature experience cannot do. It is then the business of the educator to see in what direction an experience is heading. There is no point in his being more mature if, instead of using his greater insight to help organize the conditions of the experience of the immature, he throws away his insight. Failure to take the moving force of an experience into account so as to judge and direct it on the ground of what it is moving into means disloyalty to the principle of experience itself. The disloyalty operates in two directions. The educator is false to the understanding that he should have obtained from his own past experience. He is also unfaithful to the fact that all human experience is ultimately social: that it involves contact and communication. The mature person, to put it in moral terms, has no right to withhold from the young on given occasions whatever capacity for sympathetic understanding his own experience has given him.

No sooner, however, are such things said than there is a tendency to react to the other extreme and take what has been said as a plea for some sort of disguised imposition from outside. It is worth while, accordingly, to say something about the way in which the adult can exercise the wisdom his own wider experience gives him without imposing a merely external control. On one side, it is his business to be on the alert to see what attitudes and habitual tendencies are being created. In this direction he must, if he is an educator, be able to judge what attitudes are actually conducive to continued growth and what are detrimental. He must, in addition, have that sympathetic understanding of individuals as individuals which gives him an idea of what is actually going on in the minds of those who are learning. It is, among other things, the need for these abilities on the part of the parent and teacher which makes a system of education based upon living experience a more difficult affair to conduct successfully than it is to follow the patterns of traditional education.

But there is another aspect of the matter. Experience does not go on simply inside a person. It does go on there, for it influences the formation of attitudes of desire and purpose. But this is not the whole of the story. Every genuine experience has an active side which changes in some degree the objective conditions under which experiences are had. The difference between civilization and savagery, to take an example on a large scale, is found in the degree in which previous experiences have changed the objective conditions under which subsequent experiences take place. The existence of roads, of means of rapid movement and transportation, tools, implements, furniture, electric light and power, are illustrations. Destroy the external conditions of present civilized experience, and for a time our experience would relapse into that of barbaric peoples.

In a word, we live from birth to death in a world of persons and things which in large measure is what it is because of what has been done and transmitted from previous human activities. When this fact is ignored, experience is treated as if it were something which goes on exclusively inside an individual's body and mind. It ought not to be necessary to say that experience does not occur in a vacuum. There are sources outside an individual which give rise to experience. It is constantly fed from these springs. No one would question that a child in a slum tenement has a different experience from that of a child in a cultured home; that the country lad has a different kind of experience from the city boy, or a boy on the seashore one different from the lad who is brought up on inland prairies. Ordinarily we take such facts for granted as too commonplace to record. But when their educational import is recognized, they indicate the second way in which the educator can direct the experience of the young without engaging in imposition. A primary responsibility of educators is that they not only be aware of the general principle of the shaping of actual experience by environing conditions, but that they also recognize in the concrete what surroundings are conducive to having experiences that lead to growth. Above all, they should know how to utilize the surroundings, physical and social, that exist so as to extract from them all that they have to contribute to building up experiences that are worth while.

Traditional education did not have to face this problem; it could systematically dodge this responsibility. The school environment of desks, blackboards, a small school yard, was supposed to suffice. There was no demand that the teacher should become intimately acquainted with the conditions of the local community, physical, historical, economic, occupational, etc., in order to utilize them as educational resources. A system of education based upon the necessary connection of education with experience must, on the contrary, if faithful to its principle, take these things constantly into account. This tax upon the educator is another reason why progressive education is more difficult to carry on than was ever the traditional system.

It is possible to frame schemes of education that pretty systematically subordinate objective conditions to those which reside in the individuals being educated. This happens whenever the place and function of the teacher, of books, of apparatus and equipment, of everything which represents the products of the more mature experience of elders, is systematically subordinated to the immediate inclinations and feelings of the young. Every theory which assumes that importance can be attached to these objective factors only at the expense of imposing external control and of limiting the freedom of individuals rests finally upon the notion that experience is truly experience only when objective conditions are subordinated to what goes on within the individuals having the experience.

I do not mean that it is supposed that objective conditions can be shut out. It is recognized that they must enter in: so much concession is made to the inescapable fact that we live in a world of things and persons. But I think that observation of what goes on in some families and some schools would disclose that some parents and some teachers are acting upon the idea of *subordinating* objective conditions to internal ones. In that case, it is assumed not only that the latter are primary, which in one sense they are, but that just as they temporarily exist they fix the whole educational process.

Let me illustrate from the case of an infant. The needs of a baby for food, rest, and activity are certainly primary and decisive in one respect. Nourishment must be provided; provision must be made for comfortable sleep, and so on. But these facts do not mean that a parent shall feed the baby at any time when the baby is cross or irritable, that there shall not be a program of regular hours of feeding and sleeping, etc. The wise mother takes account of the needs of the infant but not in a way which dispenses with her own responsibility for regulating the objective conditions under which the needs are satisfied. And if she is a wise mother in this respect, she draws upon past experiences of experts as well as her own for the light that these shed upon what experiences are in general most conducive to the normal development of infants. Instead of these conditions being subordinated to the immediate internal condition of the baby, they are definitely ordered so that a particular kind of *interaction* with these immediate internal states may be brought about.

The word "interaction," which has just been used, expresses the second chief principle for interpreting an experience in its educational function and force. It assigns equal rights to both factors in experience—objective and internal conditions. Any normal experience is an interplay of these two sets of conditions. Taken together, or in their interaction, they form what we call a *situation*. The trouble with traditional education was not that it emphasized the external conditions that enter into the control of the experiences but that it paid so little attention to the internal factors which also decide what kind of experience is had. It violated the principle of interaction from one side. But this violation is no reason why the new education should violate the principle from the other side—except upon the basis of the extreme *Either-Or* educational philosophy which has been mentioned.

The illustration drawn from the need for regulation of the objective conditions of a baby's development indicates, first, that the parent has responsibility for arranging the conditions under which an infant's experience of food, sleep, etc., occurs, and, secondly, that the responsibility is fulfilled by utilizing the funded experience of the past, as this is represented, say, by the advice of competent physicians and others who have made a special study of normal physical growth. Does it limit the freedom of the mother when she uses the body of knowledge thus provided to regulate the objective conditions of nourishment and sleep? Or does the enlargement of her intelligence in fulfilling her parental function widen her freedom? Doubtless if a fetish were made of the advice and directions so that they came to be inflexible dictates to be followed under every possible condition then restriction of freedom of both parent and child would occur. But this restriction would also be a limitation of the intelligence that is exercised in personal judgment.

In what respect does regulation of objective conditions limit the freedom of the baby? Some limitation is certainly placed upon its immediate movements and inclinations when it is put in its crib, at a time when it wants to continue playing, or does not get food at the moment it would like it, or when it isn't picked up and dandled when it cries for attention. Restriction also occurs when mother or nurse snatches a child away from an open fire into which it is about to fall. I shall have more to say later about freedom. Here it is enough to ask whether freedom is to be thought of and adjudged on the basis of relatively momentary incidents or whether its meaning is found in the continuity of developing experience.

The statement that individuals live in a world means, in the concrete, that they live in a series of situations. And when it is said that they live *in* these situations, the meaning of the word "in" is different from its meaning when it is said that pennies are "in" a pocket or paint is "in" a can. It means, once more, that interaction is going on between an individual and objects and other persons. The conceptions of *situation* and of *interaction* are inseparable from each other. An experience is always what it is because of a transaction taking place between an individual and what, at the time, constitutes his environment, whether the latter consists of persons with whom he is talking about some topic or event, the subject talked about being also a part of the situation; or the toys with which he is playing; the book he is reading (in which his environing conditions at the time may be England or ancient Greece or an imaginary region); or the materials of an experiment he is performing. The environment, in other words, is whatever conditions interact with personal needs, desires, purposes, and capacities to create the experience which is had. Even when a person builds a castle in the air he is interacting with the objects which he constructs in fancy.

The two principles of continuity and interaction are not separate from each other. They intercept and unite. They are, so to speak, the longitudinal and lateral aspects of experience. Different situations succeed one another. But because of the principle of continuity something is carried over from the earlier to the later ones. As an individual passes from one situation to another, his world, his environment, expands or contracts. He does not find himself living in another world but in a different part or aspect of one and the same world. What he has learned in the way of knowledge and skill in one situation becomes an instrument of understanding and dealing effectively with the situations which follow. The process goes on as long as life and learning continue. Otherwise the course of experience is disorderly, since the individual factor that enters into making an experience is split. A divided world, a world whose parts and aspects do not hang together, is at once a sign and a cause of a divided personality. When the splitting-up reaches a certain point we call the person insane. A fully integrated personality, on the other hand, exists only when successive experiences are integrated with one another. It can be built up only as a world of related objects is constructed.

Continuity and interaction in their active union with each other provide the measure of the educative significance and value of an experience. The immediate and direct concern of an educator is then with the situations in which interaction takes place. The individual, who enters as a factor into it, is what he is at a given time. It is the other factor, that of objective conditions, which lies to some extent within the possibility of regulation by the educator. As has already been noted, the phrase "objective conditions" covers a wide range. It includes what is done by the educator and the way in which it is done, not only words spoken but the tone of voice in which they are spoken. It includes equipment, books, apparatus, toys, games played. It includes the materials with which an individual interacts, and, most important of all, the total *social* set-up of the situations in which a person is engaged.

When it is said that the objective conditions are those which are within the power of the educator to regulate, it is meant, of course, that his ability to influence directly the experience of others and thereby the education they obtain places upon him the duty of determining that environment which will interact with the existing capacities and needs of those taught to create a worth-while experience. The trouble with traditional education was not that educators took upon themselves the responsibility for providing an environment. The trouble was that they did not consider the other factor in creating an experience; namely, the powers and purposes of those taught. It was assumed that a certain set of conditions was intrinsically desirable, apart from its ability to evoke a certain quality of response in individuals. This lack of mutual adaptation made the process of teaching and learning accidental. Those to whom the provided conditions were suitable managed to learn. Others got on as best they could. Responsibility for selecting objective conditions carries with it, then, the responsibility for understanding the needs and capacities of the individuals who are learning at a given time. It is not enough that certain materials and methods have proved effective with other individuals at other times. There must be a reason for thinking that they will function in generating an experience that has educative quality with particular individuals at a particular time.

It is no reflection upon the nutritive quality of beefsteak that it is not fed to infants. It is not an invidious reflection upon trigonometry that we do not teach it in the first or fifth grade of school. It is not the subject *per se* that is educative or that is conducive to growth. There is no subject that is in and of itself, or without regard to the stage of growth attained by the learner, such that inherent educational value can be attributed to it. Failure to take into account adaptation to the needs and capacities of individuals was the source of the idea that certain subjects and certain methods are intrinsically cultural or intrinsically good for mental discipline. There is no such thing as educational value in the abstract. The notion that some subjects and methods and that acquaintance with certain facts and truths possess educational value in and of themselves is the reason why traditional education reduced the material of education so largely to a diet of predigested materials. According to this notion, it was enough to regulate the quantity and difficulty of the material provided, in a scheme of quantitative grading, from month to month and from year to year.

Otherwise a pupil was expected to take it in the doses that were prescribed from without. If the pupil left it instead of taking it, if he engaged in physical truancy, or in the mental truancy of mind-wandering and finally built up an emotional revulsion against the subject, he was held to be at fault. No question was raised as to whether the trouble might not lie in the subject-matter or in the way in which it was offered. The principle of interaction makes it clear that failure of adaptation of material to needs and capacities of individuals may cause an experience to be non-educative quite as much as failure of an individual to adapt himself to the material.

The principle of continuity in its educational application means, nevertheless, that the future has to be taken into account at every stage of the educational process. This idea is easily misunderstood and is badly distorted in traditional education. Its assumption is, that by acquiring certain skills and by learning certain subjects which would be needed later (perhaps in college or perhaps in adult life) pupils are as a matter of course made ready for the needs and circumstances of the future. Now "preparation" is a treacherous idea. In a certain sense every experience should do something to prepare a person for later experiences of a deeper and more expansive quality. That is the very meaning of growth, continuity, reconstruction of experience. But it is a mistake to suppose that the mere acquisition of a certain amount of arithmetic, geography, history, etc., which is taught and studied because it may be useful at some time in the future, has this effect, and it is a mistake to suppose that acquisition of skills in reading and figuring will automatically constitute preparation for their right and effective use under conditions very unlike those in which they were acquired.

Almost everyone has had occasion to look back upon his school days and wonder what has become of the knowledge he was supposed to have amassed during his years of schooling, and why it is that the technical skills he acquired have to be learned over again in changed form in order to stand him in good stead. Indeed, he is lucky who does not find that in order to make progress, in order to go ahead intellectually, he does not have to unlearn much of what he learned in school. These questions cannot be disposed of by saying that the subjects were not actually learned, for they were learned at least sufficiently to enable a pupil to pass examinations in them. One trouble is that the subject-matter in question was learned in isolation; it was put, as it were, in a water-tight compartment. When the question is asked, then, what has become of it, where has it gone to, the right answer is that it is still there in the special compartment in which it was originally stowed away. If exactly the same conditions recurred as those under which it was acquired, it would all recur and be available. But it was segregated when it was acquired and hence is so disconnected from the rest of experience that it is not available under the actual conditions of life. It is contrary to the laws of experience that learning of this kind, no matter how thoroughly engrained at the time, should give genuine preparation.

Nor does failure in preparation end at this point. Perhaps the greatest of all pedagogical fallacies is the notion that a person learns only the particular thing he is studying at the time. Collateral learning in the way of formation of enduring attitudes, of likes and dislikes, may be and often is much more important than the spelling lesson or lesson in geography or history that is learned. For these attitudes are fundamentally what count in the future. The most important attitude that can be formed is that of desire to go on learning. If impetus in this direction is weakened instead of being intensified, something much more than mere lack of preparation takes place. The pupil is actually robbed of native capacities which otherwise would enable him to cope with the circumstances that he meets in the course of his life. We often see persons who have had little schooling and in whose case the absence of set schooling proves to be a positive asset. They have at least retained their native common sense and power of judgment, and its exercise in the actual conditions of living has given them the precious gift of ability to learn from the experiences they have. What avail is it to win prescribed amounts of information about geography and history, to win ability to read and write, if in the process the individual loses his own soul: loses his appreciation of things worth while, of the values to which these things are relative; if he loses desire to apply what he has learned and, above all, loses the ability to extract meaning from his future experiences as they occur?

What, then, is the true meaning of preparation in the educational scheme? In the first place, it means that a person, young or old, gets out of his present experience all that there is in it for him at the time in which he has it. When preparation is made the controlling end, then the potentialities of the present are sacrificed to a supposititious future. When this happens, the actual preparation for the future is missed or distorted. The ideal of using the present simply to get ready for the future contradicts itself. It omits, and even shuts out, the very conditions by which a person can be prepared for his future. We always live at the time we live and not at some other time, and only by extracting at each present time the full meaning of each present experience are we prepared for doing the same thing in the future. This is the only preparation which in the long run amounts to anything. All this means that attentive care must be devoted to the conditions which give each present experience a worthwhile meaning. Instead of inferring that it doesn't make much difference what the present experience is as long as it is enjoyed, the conclusion is the exact opposite. Here is another matter where it is easy to react from one extreme to the other. Because traditional schools tended to sacrifice the present to a remote and more or less unknown future, therefore it comes to be believed that the educator has little responsibility for the kind of present experiences the young undergo. But the relation of the present and the future is not an *Either-Or* affair. The present affects the future anyway. The persons who should have some idea of the connection between the two are those who have achieved maturity. Accordingly, upon them devolves the responsibility for instituting the conditions for the kind of present experience which has a favorable effect upon the future. Education as growth or maturity should be an ever-present process.

Note

1. These brief lines come from Alfred Lord Tennyson's blank verse poem "Ulysses."

III
THE NATURE OF SUBJECT-MATTER AND CURRICULUM

7

The Child and the Curriculum (1902)

The Child and the Curriculum is one of Dewey's best-known early works on education. Its contents provide an overview of the organic approach to the relations between the child and the curriculum practiced at the Chicago Lab School. For example, curricular frameworks at the school were not preestablished but allowed to develop with time and experience in the actual process of teaching and learning. Similarly, lesson plans were general guidelines for conducting broader forms of inquiry informed by student interests. In this way neither the child nor the curriculum predominated: they functioned together as part of one evolving situation with a unified purpose and goal. And there was no rigid compartmentalization of subject matter. The curriculum, especially with the younger students, was highly interdisciplinary: It provided hands-on shared experience with engaging "real world" problems. (Learning "hands-on," for Dewey, means interacting directly or firsthand with subject matter.) These problems were not posed (or imposed) by teachers, but, as immediately felt difficulties, grew naturally out of student-driven inquiries and projects. The intention was not to prepare children for specific occupations, something Dewey strongly opposed, but to use everyday occupations as vehicles for bringing together different educational subject matter in a directly meaningful and imaginative way, "psychologizing" the curriculum. This, in a nutshell, is education *through* occupations, not *for* occupations.

∽

Profound differences in theory are never gratuitous or invented. They grow out of conflicting elements in a genuine problem—a problem which is genuine just because the elements, taken as they stand, are conflicting. Any significant problem involves conditions that for the moment contradict each other. Solution comes only by getting away from the meaning of terms that is already fixed upon and coming to see the conditions from another point of view, and hence in a fresh light. But this reconstruction means travail of thought. Easier than thinking with surrender of already formed ideas and detachment from facts already learned, is just to stick by what is already said, looking about for something with which to buttress it against attack.

Thus sects arise; schools of opinion. Each selects that set of conditions that appeal to it; and then erects them into a complete and independent truth, instead of treating them as a factor in a problem, needing adjustment.

The fundamental factors in the educative process are an immature, undeveloped being; and certain social aims, meanings, values incarnate in the matured experience of the adult. The educative process is the due interaction of these forces. Such a conception of each in relation to the other as facilitates completest and freest interaction is the essence of educational theory.

But here comes the effort of thought. It is easier to see the conditions in their separateness, to insist upon one at the expense of the other, to make antagonists of them, than to discover a reality to which each belongs. The easy thing is to seize upon something in the nature of the child, or upon something in the developed consciousness of the adult, and insist upon *that* as the key to the whole problem. When this happens a really serious practical problem—that of interaction—is transformed into an unreal, and hence insoluble, theoretic problem. Instead of seeing the educative steadily and as a whole, we see conflicting terms. We get the case of the child *vs.* the curriculum; of the individual nature *vs.* social culture. Below all other divisions in pedagogic opinion lies this opposition.

The child lives in a somewhat narrow world of personal contacts. Things hardly come within his experience unless they touch, intimately and obviously, his own well-being, or that of his family and friends. His world is a world of persons with their personal interests, rather than a realm of facts and laws. Not truth, in the sense of conformity to external fact, but affection and sympathy, is its keynote. As against this, the course of study met in the school presents material stretching back indefinitely in time, and extending outward indefinitely into space. The child is taken out of his familiar physical environment, hardly more than a square mile or so in area, into the wide world—yes, and even to the bounds of the solar system. His little span of personal memory and tradition is overlaid with the long centuries of the history of all peoples.

Again, the child's life is an integral, a total one. He passes quickly and readily from one topic to another, as from one spot to another, but is not conscious of transition or break. There is no conscious isolation, hardly conscious distinction. The things that occupy him are held together by the unity of the personal and social interests which his life carries along. Whatever is uppermost in his mind constitutes to him, for the time being, the whole universe. That universe is fluid and fluent; its contents dissolve and re-form with amazing rapidity. But, after all, it is the child's own world. It has the unity and completeness of his own life. He goes to school, and various studies divide and fractionize the world for him. Geography selects, it abstracts and analyzes one set of facts, and from one particular point of view. Arithmetic is another division, grammar another department, and so on indefinitely.

Again, in school each of these subjects is classified. Facts are torn away from their original place in experience and rearranged with reference to some general principle. Classification is not a matter of child experience; things do not come to the individual pigeon-holed. The vital ties of affection, the connecting bonds of activity, hold together the variety of his personal experiences. The adult mind is so familiar with the notion of logically ordered facts that it does not recognize—it cannot realize—the amount of separating and reformulating which the facts of direct experience have to undergo before they can appear as a "study," or branch of learning. A principle, for the intellect, has had to be distinguished and defined; facts have had to be interpreted in relation to this principle, not as they are in themselves. They have had to be regathered about a new centre which is wholly abstract and ideal. All this means a development of a special intellectual interest. It means ability to view facts impartially and objectively; that is, without reference to their place and meaning in one's own experience. It means capacity to analyze and to synthesize. It means highly matured intellectual habits and the command of a definite technique and apparatus of scientific inquiry. The studies as classified are the product, in a word, of the science of the ages, not of the experience of the child.

These apparent deviations and differences between child and curriculum might be almost indefinitely widened. But we have here sufficiently fundamental divergences: first, the narrow but personal world of the child against the impersonal but infinitely extended world of space and time;

second, the unity, the single whole-heartedness of the child's life, and the specializations and divisions of the curriculum; third, an abstract principle of logical classification and arrangement, and the practical and emotional bonds of child life.

From these elements of conflict grow up different educational sects. One school fixes its attention upon the importance of the subject-matter of the curriculum as compared with the contents of the child's own experience. It is as if they said: Is life petty, narrow, and crude? Then studies reveal the great, wide universe with all its fullness and complexity of meaning. Is the life of the child egoistic, self-centered, impulsive? Then in these studies is found an objective universe of truth, law, and order. Is his experience confused, vague, uncertain, at the mercy of the moment's caprice and circumstance? Then studies introduce a world arranged on the basis of eternal and general truth; a world where all is measured and defined. Hence the moral: ignore and minimize the child's individual peculiarities, whims, and experiences. They are what we need to get away from. They are to be obscured or eliminated. As educators our work is precisely to substitute for these superficial and casual affairs stable and well-ordered realities; and these are found in studies and lessons.

Subdivide each topic into studies; each study into lessons; each lesson into specific facts and formulae. Let the child proceed step by step to master each one of these separate parts, and at last he will have covered the entire ground. The road which looks so long when viewed in its entirety, is easily traveled, considered as a series of particular steps. Thus emphasis is put upon the logical subdivisions and consecutions of the subject-matter. Problems of instruction are problems of procuring texts giving logical parts and sequences, and of presenting these portions in class in a similar definite and graded way. Subject-matter furnishes the end, and it determines method. The child is simply the immature being who is to be matured; he is the superficial being who is to be deepened; his is narrow experience which is to be widened. It is his to receive, to accept. His part is fulfilled when he is ductile and docile.

Not so, says the other sect. The child is the starting-point, the centre, and the end. His development, his growth, is the ideal. It alone furnishes the standard. To the growth of the child all studies are subservient; they are instruments valued as they serve the needs of growth. Personality, character, is more than subject-matter. Not knowledge or information, but self-realization, is the goal. To possess all the world of knowledge and lose one's own self is as awful a fate in education as in religion. Moreover, subject-matter never can be got into the child from without. Learning is active. It involves reaching out of the mind. It involves organic assimilation starting from within. Literally, we must take our stand with the child and our departure from him. It is he and not the subject-matter which determines both quality and quantity of learning.

The only significant method is the method of the mind as it reaches out and assimilates. Subject-matter is but spiritual food, possible nutritive material. It cannot digest itself; it cannot of its own accord turn into bone and muscle and blood. The source of whatever is dead, mechanical, and formal in schools is found precisely in the subordination of the life and experience of the child to the curriculum. It is because of this that "study" has become a synonym for what is irksome, and a lesson identical with a task.

This fundamental opposition of child and curriculum set up by these two modes of doctrine can be duplicated in a series of other terms. "Discipline" is the watchword of those who magnify the course of study; "interest" that of those who blazon "The Child" upon their banner. The standpoint of the former is logical; that of the latter psychological. The first emphasizes the necessity of adequate training and scholarship on the part of the teacher; the latter that of need of sympathy with the child, and knowledge of his natural instincts. "Guidance and control" are the catchwords of one school; "freedom and initiative" of the other. Law is asserted here; spontaneity proclaimed there. The old, the conservation of what has been achieved in the pain and toil of the ages, is dear to the one; the new, change, progress, wins the affection of the other. Inertness and routine, chaos and anarchism, are accusations bandied back and forth. Neglect of the sacred authority of duty is charged by one side, only to be met by counter-charges of suppression of individuality through tyrannical despotism.

Such oppositions are rarely carried to their logical conclusion. Common sense recoils at the extreme character of these results. They are left to theorists, while common sense vibrates back and forward in a maze of inconsistent compromise. The need of getting theory and practical common sense into closer connection suggests a return to our original thesis: that we have here conditions which are necessarily related to each other in the educative process, since this is precisely one of interaction and adjustment.

What, then, is the problem? It is just to get rid of the prejudicial notion that there is some gap in kind (as distinct from degree) between the child's experience and the various forms of subject-matter that make up the course of study. From the side of the child, it is a question of seeing how his experience already contains within itself elements—facts and truths—of just the same sort as those entering into the formulated study; and, what is of more importance, of how it contains within itself the attitudes, the motives, and the interests which have operated in developing and organizing the subject-matter to the plane which it now occupies. From the side of the studies, it is a question of interpreting them as outgrowths of forces operating in the child's life, and of discovering the steps that intervene between the child's present experience and their richer maturity.

Abandon the notion of subject-matter as something fixed and ready-made in itself, outside the child's experience; cease thinking of the child's experience as also something hard and fast; see it as something fluent, embryonic, vital; and we realize that the child and the curriculum are simply two limits which define a single process. Just as two points define a straight line, so the present standpoint of the child and the facts and truths of studies define instruction. It is continuous reconstruction, moving from the child's present experience out into that represented by the organized bodies of truth that we call studies.

On the face of it, the various studies, arithmetic, geography, language, botany, etc., are themselves experience—they are that of the race. They embody the cumulative outcome of the efforts, the strivings, and successes of the human race generation after generation. They present this, not as a mere accumulation, not as a miscellaneous heap of separate bits of experience, but in some organized and systematized way—that is, as reflectively formulated.

Hence, the facts and truths that enter into the child's present experience, and those contained in the subject-matter of studies, are the initial and final terms of one reality. To oppose one to the other is to oppose the infancy and maturity of the same growing life; it is to set the moving tendency and the final result of the same process over against each other; it is to hold that the nature and the destiny of the child war with each other.

If such be the case, the problem of the relation of the child and the curriculum presents itself in this guise: Of what use, educationally speaking, is it to be able to see the end in the beginning? How does it assist us in dealing with the early stages of growth to be able to anticipate its later phases? The studies, as we have agreed, represent the possibilities of development inherent in the child's immediate crude experience. But, after all, they are not parts of that present and immediate life. Why, then, or how, make account of them?

Asking such a question suggests its own answer. To see the outcome is to know in what direction the present experience is moving, provided it move normally and soundly. The far-away point, which is of no significance to us simply as far away, becomes of huge importance the moment we take it as defining a present direction of movement. Taken in this way it is no remote and distant result to be achieved, but a guiding method in dealing with the present. The systematized and defined experience of the adult mind, in other words, is of value to us in interpreting the child's life as it immediately shows itself, and in passing on to guidance or direction.

Let us look for a moment at these two ideas: interpretation and guidance. The child's present experience is in no way self-explanatory. It is not final, but transitional. It is nothing complete in itself, but just a sign or index of certain growth-tendencies. As long as we confine our gaze to what the child here and now puts forth, we are confused and misled. We cannot read its meaning. Extreme depreciations of the child morally and intellectually, and sentimental idealizations of him, have their root in a common fallacy. Both spring from taking stages of a growth or movement as something cut off and fixed. The first fails to see the promise contained in feelings and deeds which, taken by themselves, are unpromising and repellant; the second fails to see that even the most pleasing and beautiful exhibitions are but signs, and that they begin to spoil and rot the moment they are treated as achievements.

What we need is something which will enable us to interpret, to appraise, the elements in the child's present puttings forth and fallings away, his exhibitions of power and weakness, in the light of some larger growth-process in which they have their place. Only in this way can we discriminate. If we isolate the child's present inclinations, purposes, and experiences from the place they occupy and the part they have to perform in a developing experience, all stand upon the same level; all alike are equally good and equally bad. But in the movement of life different elements stand upon different planes of value. Some of the child's deeds are symptoms of a waning tendency; they are survivals in functioning of an organ which has done its part and is passing out of vital use. To give positive attention to such qualities is to arrest development upon a lower level. It is systematically to maintain a rudimentary phase of growth. Other activities are signs of a culminating power and interest; to them applies the maxim of striking while the iron is hot. As regards them, it is perhaps a matter of now or never. Selected, utilized, emphasized, they may mark a turning-point for good in the child's whole career; neglected, an opportunity goes, never to be recalled. Other acts and feelings are prophetic; they represent the dawning of flickering light that will shine steadily only in the far future. As regards them there is little at present to do but give them fair and full chance, waiting for the future for definite direction.

Just as, upon the whole, it was the weakness of the "old education" that it made invidious comparisons between the immaturity of the child and the maturity of the adult, regarding the former as something to be got away from as soon as possible and as much as possible; so it is the danger of the "new education" that it regard the child's present powers and interests as something finally significant in themselves. In truth, his learnings and achievements are fluid and moving. They change from day to day and from hour to hour.

It will do harm if child-study leave in the popular mind the impression that a child of a given age has a positive equipment of purposes and interests to be cultivated just as they stand. Interests in reality are but attitudes toward possible experiences; they are not achievements; their worth is in the leverage they afford, not in the accomplishment they represent. To take the phenomena presented at a given age as in any way self-explanatory or self-contained is inevitably to result in indulgence and spoiling. Any power, whether of child or adult, is indulged when it is taken on its given and present level in consciousness. Its genuine meaning is in the propulsion it affords toward a higher level. It is just something to do with. Appealing to the interest upon the present plane means excitation; it means playing with a power so as continually to stir it up without directing it toward definite achievement. Continuous initiation, continuous starting of activities that do not arrive, is, for all practical purposes, as bad as the continual repression of initiative in conformity with supposed interests of some more perfect thought or will. It is as if the child were forever tasting and never eating; always having his palate tickled upon the emotional side, but never getting the organic satisfaction that comes only with digestion of food and transformation of it into working power.

As against such a view, the subject-matter of science and history and art serves to reveal the real child to us. We do not know the meaning either of his tendencies or of his performances excepting as we take them as germinating seed, or opening bud, of some fruit to be borne. The whole world of visual nature is all too small an answer to the problem of the meaning of the child's instinct for light and form. The entire science of physics is none too much to interpret adequately to us what is involved in some simple demand of the child for explanation of some casual change that has attracted his attention. The art of Rafael [Raphael]or of Corot is none too much to enable us to value the impulses stirring in the child when he draws and daubs.

So much for the use of the subject-matter in interpretation. Its further employment in direction or guidance is but an expansion of the same thought. To interpret the fact is to see it in its vital movement, to see it in its relation to growth. But to view it as a part of a normal growth is to secure the basis for guiding it. Guidance is not external imposition. *It is freeing the life-process for its own most adequate fulfillment.* What was said about disregard of the child's present experience because of its remoteness from mature experience; and of the sentimental idealization of the child's naive caprices and performances, may be repeated here with slightly altered phrase. There are those who see no alternative between forcing the child from without, or leaving him entirely alone. Seeing no alternative, some choose one mode, some another. Both fall into the same fundamental error. Both fail to see that development is a definite process, having its own law which can be fulfilled only when adequate and normal conditions are provided. Really to interpret the child's present crude impulses in counting, measuring, and arranging things in rhythmic series, involves mathematical scholarship—a knowledge of the mathematical formulae and relations which have, in the history of the race, grown out of just such crude beginnings. To see the whole history of development which intervenes between these two terms is simply to see what step the child needs to take just here and now; to what use he needs to put his blind impulse in order that it may get clarity and gain force.

If, once more, the "old education" tended to ignore the dynamic quality, the developing force inherent in the child's present experience, and therefore to assume that direction and control were just matters of arbitrarily putting the child in a given path and compelling him to walk there, the "new education" is in danger of taking the idea of development in altogether too formal and empty a way. The child is expected to "develop" this or that fact or truth out of his own mind. He is told to think things out, or work things out for himself, without being supplied any of the environing conditions which are requisite to start and guide thought. Nothing can be developed from nothing; nothing but the crude can be developed out of the crude—and this is what surely happens when we throw the child back upon his achieved self as a finality, and invite him to spin new truths of nature or of conduct out of that. It is certainly as futile to expect a child to evolve a universe out of his own mere mind as it is for a philosopher to attempt that task. Development does not mean just getting something out of the mind. It is a development of experience and into experience that is really wanted. And this is impossible save as just that educative medium is provided which will enable the powers and interests that have been selected as valuable to function. They must operate, and how they operate will depend almost entirely upon the stimuli which surround them, and the material upon which they exercise themselves. The problem of direction is thus the problem of selecting appropriate stimuli for instincts and impulses which it is desired to employ in the gaining of new experience. What new experiences are desirable, and thus what stimuli are needed, it is impossible to tell except as there is some comprehension of the development which is aimed at; except, in a word, as the adult knowledge is drawn upon as revealing the possible career open to the child.

It may be of use to distinguish and to relate to each other the logical and the psychological aspects of experience—the former standing for subject-matter in itself, the latter for it in relation to the child. A psychological statement of experience follows its actual growth; it is historic; it notes steps actually taken, the uncertain and tortuous, as well as the efficient and successful. The logical point of view, on the other hand, assumes that the development has reached a certain positive stage of fulfillment. It neglects the process and considers the outcome. It summarizes and arranges, and thus separates the achieved results from the actual steps by which they were forthcoming in the first instance. We may compare the difference between the logical and the psychological to the difference between the notes which an explorer makes in a new country, blazing a trail and finding his way along as best he may, and the finished map that is constructed after the country has been thoroughly explored. The two are mutually dependent. Without the more or less accidental and devious paths traced by the explorer there would be no facts which could be utilized in the making of the complete and related chart. But no one would get the benefit of the explorer's trip if it was not compared and checked up with similar wanderings undertaken by others; unless the new geographical facts learned, the streams crossed, the mountains climbed, etc., were viewed, not as mere incidents in the journey of the particular traveler, but (quite apart from the individual explorer's life) in relation to other similar facts already known. The map orders individual experiences, connecting them with one another irrespective of the local and temporal circumstances and accidents of their original discovery.

Of what use is this formulated statement of experience? Of what use is the map?

Well, we may first tell what the map is not. The map is not a substitute for a personal experience. The map does not take the place of an actual journey. The logically formulated material of a science or branch of learning, of a study, is no substitute for the having of individual experiences. The mathematical formula for a falling body does not take the place of personal contact and immediate individual experience with the falling thing. But the map, a summary, an arranged and orderly view of previous experiences, serves as a guide to future experience; it gives direction; it facilitates control; it economizes effort, preventing useless wandering, and pointing out the paths which lead most quickly and most certainly to a desired result. Through the map every new traveler may get for his own journey the benefits of the results of others' explorations without the waste of energy and loss of time involved in their wanderings—wanderings which he himself would be obliged to repeat were it not for just the assistance of the objective and generalized record of their performances. That which we call a science or study puts the net product of past experience in the form which makes it most available for the future. It represents a capitalization which may at once be turned to interest. It economizes the workings of the mind in every way. Memory is less taxed because the facts are grouped together about some common principle, instead of being connected solely with the varying incidents of their original discovery. Observation is assisted; we know what to look for and where to look. It is the difference between looking for a needle in a haystack, and searching for a given paper in a well-arranged cabinet. Reasoning is directed, because there is a certain general path or line laid out along which ideas naturally march, instead of moving from one chance association to another.

There is, then, nothing final about a logical rendering of experience. Its value is not contained in itself; its significance is that of standpoint, outlook, method. It intervenes between the more casual, tentative, and round-about experiences of the past, and more controlled and orderly experiences of the future. It gives past experience in that net form which renders it most available and most significant, most fecund for future experience. The abstractions, generalizations, and classifications which it introduces all have prospective meaning.

The formulated result is then not to be opposed to the process of growth. The logical is not set over against the psychological. The surveyed and arranged result occupies a critical position in the process of growth. It marks a turning-point. It shows how we may get the benefit of past effort in controlling future endeavor. In the largest sense the logical standpoint is itself psychological; it has its meaning as a point in the development of experience, and its justification is in its functioning in the future growth which it insures.

Hence the need of reinstating into experience the subject-matter of the studies, or branches of learning. It must be restored to the experience from which it has been abstracted. It needs to be *psychologized*; turned over, translated into the immediate and individual experiencing within which it has its origin and significance.

Every study or subject thus has two aspects: one for the scientist as a scientist; the other for the teacher as a teacher. These two aspects are in no sense opposed or conflicting. But neither are they immediately identical. For the scientist, the subject-matter represents simply a given body of truth to be employed in locating new problems, instituting new researches, and carrying them through to a verified outcome. To him the subject-matter of the science is self-contained. He refers various portions of it to each other; he connects new facts with it. He is not, as a scientist, called upon to travel outside its particular bounds; if he does, it is only to get more facts of the same general sort. The problem of the teacher is a different one. As a teacher he is not concerned with adding new facts to the science he teaches; in propounding new hypotheses or in verifying them. He is concerned with the subject-matter of the science as *representing a given stage and phase of the development of experience*. His problem is that of inducing a vital and personal experiencing. Hence, what concerns him, as teacher, is the ways in which that subject may become a part of experience; what there is in the child's present that is usable with reference to it; how such elements are to be used; how his own knowledge of the subject-matter may assist in interpreting the child's needs and doings, and determine the medium in which the child should be placed in order that his growth may be properly directed. He is concerned, not with the subject-matter as such, but with the subject-matter as a related factor in a total and growing experience. Thus to see it is to psychologize it.

It is the failure to keep in mind the double aspect of subject-matter which causes the curriculum and child to be set over against each other as described in our early pages. The subject-matter, just as it is for the scientist, has no direct relationship to the child's present experience. It stands outside of it. The danger here is not a merely theoretical one. We are practically threatened on all sides. Text-book and teacher vie with each other in presenting to the child the subject-matter as it stands to the specialist. Such modification and revision as it undergoes are a mere elimination of certain scientific difficulties, and the general reduction to a lower intellectual level. The material is not translated into life-terms, but is directly offered as a substitute for, or an external annex to, the child's present life.

Three typical evils result: In the first place, the lack of any organic connection with what the child has already seen and felt and loved makes the material purely formal and symbolic. There is a sense in which it is impossible to value too highly the formal and the symbolic. The genuine form, the real symbol, serve as methods in the holding and discovery of truth. They are tools by which the individual pushes out most surely and widely into unexplored areas. They are means by which he brings to bear whatever of reality he has succeeded in gaining in past searchings. But this happens only when the symbol really symbolizes—when it stands for and sums up in shorthand actual experiences which the individual has already gone through. A symbol which is induced from without, which has not been led up to in preliminary activities, is, as we say, a *bare* or *mere* symbol; it is dead and barren. Now, any fact, whether of arithmetic, or geography, or grammar, which is not led up to and into out of something which has previously occupied a significant position in the child's life for its own sake, is forced into this position. It is not a reality, but just the sign of a reality which *might* be experienced if certain conditions were fulfilled. But the abrupt presentation of the fact as something known by others, and requiring only to be studied and learned by the child, rules out such conditions of fulfillment. It condemns the fact to be a hieroglyph: it would mean something if one only had the key. The clue being lacking, it remains an idle curiosity, to fret and obstruct the mind, a dead weight to burden it.

The second evil in this external presentation is lack of motivation. There are not only no facts or truths which have been previously felt as such with which to appropriate and assimilate the new, but there is no craving, no need, no demand. When the subject-matter has been psychologized, that is, viewed as an outgrowth of present tendencies and activities, it is easy to locate in the present some obstacle, intellectual, practical, or ethical, which can be handled more adequately if the truth in question be mastered. This need supplies motive for the learning. An end which is the child's own carries him on to possess the means of its accomplishment. But when material is directly supplied in the form of a lesson to be learned as a lesson, the connecting links of need and aim are conspicuous for their absence. What we mean by the mechanical and dead in instruction is a result of this lack of motivation. The organic and vital mean interaction—they mean play of mental demand and material supply.

The third evil is that even the most scientific matter, arranged in most logical fashion, loses this quality, when presented in external, ready-made fashion, by the time it gets to the child. It has to undergo some modification in order to shut out some phases too hard to grasp, and to reduce some of the attendant difficulties. What happens? Those things which are most significant to the scientific man, and most valuable in the logic of actual inquiry and classification, drop out. The really thought-provoking character is obscured, and the organizing function disappears. Or, as we commonly say, the child's reasoning powers, the faculty of abstraction and generalization, are not adequately developed. So the subject-matter is evacuated of its logical value, and, though it is what it is only from the logical standpoint, is presented as stuff only for "memory." This is the contradiction: the child gets the advantage neither of the adult logical formulation, nor of his own native competencies of apprehension and response. Hence the logic of the child is hampered and mortified, and we are almost fortunate if he does not get actual non-science, flat and commonplace residual of what was gaining scientific vitality a generation or two ago—degenerate reminiscence of what someone else once formulated on the basis of the experience that some further person had, once upon a time, experienced.

The train of evils does not cease. It is all too common for opposed erroneous theories to play straight into each other's hands. Psychological considerations may be slurred or shoved one side; they cannot be crowded out. Put out of the door, they come back through the window. Somehow and somewhere motive must be appealed to, connection must be established between the mind and its material. There is no question of getting along without this bond of connection; the only question is whether it be such as grows out of the material itself in relation to the mind, or be imported and hitched on from some outside source. If the subject-matter of the lessons be such as to have an appropriate place within the expanding consciousness of the child, if it grows out of his own past doings, thinkings, and sufferings, and grows into application in further achievements and receptivities, then no device or trick of method has to be resorted to in order to enlist "interest." The psychologized *is* of interest—that is, it is placed in the whole of conscious life so that it shares the worth of that life. But the externally presented material, that, conceived and generated in standpoints and attitudes remote from the child, and developed in motives alien to him, has no such place of its own. Hence the recourse to adventitious leverage to push it in, to factitious drill to drive it in, to artificial bribe to lure it in.

Three aspects of this recourse to outside ways for giving the subject-matter some psychological meaning may be worth mentioning. Familiarity breeds contempt, but it also breeds something like affection. We get used to the chains we wear, and we miss them when removed. 'Tis an old story that through custom we finally embrace what at first wore a hideous mien. Unpleasant, because meaningless, activities may get agreeable if long enough persisted in. *It is possible for the mind to develop interest in a routine or mechanical procedure, if conditions are continually supplied which demand that mode* of *operation and preclude any other sort.* I frequently hear dulling devices and empty exercises defended and extolled because "the children take such an 'interest' in them." Yes, that is the worst of it; the mind, shut out from worthy employ and missing the taste of adequate performance, comes down to the level of that which is left to it to know and do, and perforce takes an interest in a cabined and cramped experience. To find satisfaction in its own exercise is the normal law of mind, and if large and meaningful business for the mind be denied, it tries to content itself with the formal movements that remain to it—and too often succeeds, save in those cases of more intense activity which cannot accommodate themselves, and that make up the unruly and *declassé* of our school product. An interest in the formal apprehension of symbols and in their memorized reproduction becomes in many pupils a substitute for the original and vital interest in reality; and all because, the subject-matter of the course of study being out of relation to the concrete mind of the individual, some substitute bond to hold it in some kind of working relation to the mind must be discovered and elaborated.

The second substitute for living motivation in the subject-matter is that of contrast-effects; the material of the lesson is rendered interesting, if not in itself, at least in contrast with some alternative experience. To learn the lesson is more interesting than to take a scolding, be held up to general ridicule, stay after school, receive degradingly low marks, or fail to be promoted. And very much of what goes by the name of "discipline," and prides itself upon opposing the doctrines of a soft pedagogy and upon upholding the banner of effort and duty, is nothing more or less than just this appeal to "interest" in its obverse aspect—to fear, to dislike of various kinds of physical, social, and personal pain. The subject-matter does not appeal; it cannot appeal; it lacks origin and bearing in a growing experience. So the appeal is to the thousand and one outside and irrelevant agencies which may serve to throw, by sheer rebuff and rebound, the mind back upon the material from which it is constantly wandering.

Human nature being what it is, however, it tends to seek its motivation in the agreeable rather than in the disagreeable, in direct pleasure rather than in alternative pain. And so has come up the modern theory and practice of the "interesting," in the false sense of that term. The material is still left; so far as its own characteristics are concerned, just material externally selected and formulated. It is still just so much geography and arithmetic and grammar study; not so much potentiality of child-experience with regard to language, earth, and numbered and measured reality. Hence the difficulty of bringing the mind to bear upon it; hence its repulsiveness; the tendency for attention to wander; for other acts and images to crowd in and expel the lesson. The legitimate way out is to transform the material; to psychologize it—that is, once more, to take it and to develop it within the range and scope of the child's life. But it is easier and simpler to leave it as it is, and then by trick of method to *arouse* interest, to *make* it *interesting*; to cover it with sugar-coating; to conceal its barrenness by intermediate and unrelated material; and finally, as it were, to get the child to swallow and digest the unpalatable morsel while he is enjoying tasting something quite different. But alas for the analogy! Mental assimilation is a matter of consciousness; and if the attention has not been playing upon the actual material, that has not been apprehended, nor worked into faculty.

How, then, stands the case of Child *vs.* Curriculum? What shall the verdict be? The radical fallacy in the original pleadings with which we set out is the supposition that we have no choice save either to leave the child to his own unguided spontaneity or to inspire direction upon him from without. Action is response; it is adaptation, adjustment. There is no such thing as sheer self-activity possible—because all activity takes place in a medium, in a situation, and with reference to its conditions. But, again, no such thing as imposition of truth from without, as insertion of truth from without, is possible. All depends upon the activity which the mind itself undergoes in responding to what is presented from without. Now, the value of the formulated wealth of knowledge that makes up the course of study is that it may enable the educator *to determine the environment of the child,* and thus by indirection to direct. Its primary value, its primary indication, is for the teacher, not for the child. It says to the teacher: Such and such are the capacities, the fulfillments, in truth and beauty and behavior, open to these children. Now see to it that day by day the conditions are such that *their own activities* move inevitably in this direction, toward such culmination of themselves. Let the child's nature fulfill its own destiny, revealed to you in whatever of science and art and industry the world now holds as its own.

The case is of Child. It is his present powers which are to assert themselves; his present capacities which are to be exercised; his present attitudes which are to be realized. But save as the teacher knows, knows wisely and thoroughly, the race-experience which is embodied in that thing we call the Curriculum, the teacher knows neither what the present power, capacity, or attitude is, nor yet how it is to be asserted, exercised, and realized.

8

From *Democracy and Education* (1916)

When *Democracy and Education* was first published, Dewey declared that it was not only his most complete statement on education, but also the best demonstration of his "entire philosophical position." In the chapter titled "The Nature of Subject Matter," Dewey expands on several fundamental themes first introduced in *The School and Society* and *The Child and the Curriculum*. He reminds us that successful learning necessitates a healthy and dynamic social environment. This promotes the development of democratic habits and attitudes, as students engage meaningfully together with subject matter. (Shared experience, for Dewey, is "the greatest of human goods.") This subject matter is a "working resource" for the purposeful construction of meaning and knowledge, not a uniform collection of facts or ready-made units of study. For students to participate effectively in this meaning-construction process, the subject matter must be encountered in a way that is both intellectually accessible and relevant experientially. Over time, students' knowledge of curricular material is increasingly refined. It typically begins with the ability to do or make things without fully grasping the underlying structures and processes. This later culminates in understanding curricular material in a logically organized, intellectual way that allows for new and creative applications and more complex problem-solving. Importantly, the development of student knowledge of subject matter does not occur on any fixed timetable or in a lockstep process. Nor, then, can assessment of student learning. Why would we expect this to be the case, Dewey asks, if the subject matter itself did not evolve in a predetermined and uniform way?

The Nature of Subject Matter

1. *Subject Matter of Educator and of Learner.*—So far as the nature of subject matter in principle is concerned, there is nothing to add to what has been said. It consists of the facts observed, recalled, read, and talked about, and the ideas suggested, in course of a development of a situation having a purpose. This statement needs to be rendered more specific by connecting it with the materials of school instruction, the studies which make up the curriculum. What is the significance of our definition in application to reading, writing, mathematics, history, nature study, drawing, singing, physics, chemistry, modern and foreign languages, and so on? Let us recur to two of the points made earlier in our discussion. The educator's part in the enterprise of education is to furnish the environment which stimulates responses and directs the learner's course. In last analysis, *all* that the educator can do is modify stimuli so that response will as surely as is possible result in the formation of desirable intellectual and emotional dispositions. Obviously studies or the subject matter of the curriculum have intimately to do with this business of supplying an environment. The other point is the necessity of a social environment to give meaning to habits formed. In what we have termed informal education, subject matter is carried directly in the matrix of social intercourse. It is what the persons with whom an individual associates do and say. This fact gives a clue to the understanding of the subject matter of formal or deliberate instruction. A connecting link is found in the stories, traditions, songs, and liturgies which accompany the doings and rites of a primitive social group. They represent the stock of meanings which have been precipitated out of previous experience, which are so prized by the group as to be identified with their conception of their own collective life. Not being obviously a part of the skill exhibited in the daily occupations of eating, hunting, making war and peace, constructing rugs, pottery, and baskets, etc., they are consciously impressed upon the young; often, as in the initiation ceremonies, with intense emotional fervor. Even more pains are consciously taken to perpetuate the myths, legends, and sacred verbal formulae of the group than to transmit the directly useful customs of the group just because they cannot be picked up, as the latter can be in the ordinary processes of association.

As the social group grows more complex, involving a greater number of acquired skills which are dependent, either in fact or in the belief of the group, upon standard ideas deposited from past experience, the content of social life gets more definitely formulated for purposes of instruction.

As we have previously noted, probably the chief motive for consciously dwelling upon the group life, extracting the meanings which are regarded as most important and systematizing them in a coherent arrangement, is just the need of instructing the young so as to perpetuate group life. Once started on this road of selection, formulation, and organization, no definite limit exists. The invention of writing and of printing gives the operation an immense impetus. Finally, the bonds which connect the subject matter of school study with the habits and ideals of the social group are disguised and covered up. The ties are so loosened that it often appears as if there were none; as if subject matter existed simply as knowledge on its own independent behoof, and as if study were the mere act of mastering it for its own sake, irrespective of any social values. Since it is highly important for practical reasons to counteract this tendency, the chief purposes of our theoretical discussion are to make clear the connection which is so readily lost from sight, and to show in some detail the social content and function of the chief constituents of the course of study.

The points need to be considered from the standpoint of instructor and of student. To the former, the significance of a knowledge of subject matter, going far beyond the present knowledge of pupils, is to supply definite standards and to reveal to him the possibilities of the crude activities of the immature. *(i)* The material of school studies translates into concrete and detailed terms the meanings of current social life which it is desirable to transmit. It puts clearly before the instructor the essential ingredients of the culture to be perpetuated, in such an organized form as to protect him from the haphazard efforts he would be likely to indulge in if the meanings had not been standardized. *(ii)* A knowledge of the ideas which have been achieved in the past as the outcome of activity places the educator in a position to perceive the meaning of the seeming impulsive and aimless reactions of the young, and to provide the stimuli needed to direct them so that they will amount to something. The more the educator knows of music the more he can perceive the possibilities of the inchoate musical impulses of a child. Organized subject matter represents the ripe fruitage of experiences like theirs, experiences involving the same world, and powers and needs similar to theirs. It does not represent perfection or infallible wisdom; but it is the best at command to further new experiences which may, in some respects at least, surpass the achievements embodied in existing knowledge and works of art.

From the standpoint of the educator, in other words, the various studies represent working resources, available capital. Their remoteness from the experience of the young is not, however, seeming; it is real. The subject matter of the learner is not, therefore, and cannot be, identical with the formulated, the crystallized, and systematized subject matter of the adult; the material as found in books and in works of art, etc. The latter represents the *possibilities* of the former; not its existing state. It enters directly into the activities of the expert and the educator, not into that of the beginner, the learner. Failure to bear in mind the difference in subject matter from the respective standpoints of teacher and student is responsible for most of the mistakes made in the use of texts and other expressions of preexistent knowledge.

The need for a knowledge of the constitution and functions, in the concrete, of human nature is great just because the teacher's attitude to subject matter is so different from that of the pupil. The teacher presents in actuality what the pupil represents only in *posse*. That is, the teacher already knows the things which the student is only learning. Hence the problem of the two is radically unlike. When engaged in the direct act of teaching, the instructor needs to have subject matter at his fingers' ends; his attention should be upon the attitude and response of the pupil. To understand the latter in its interplay with subject matter is his task, while the pupil's mind, naturally, should be not on itself but on the topic in hand. Or to state the same point in a somewhat different manner: the teacher should be occupied not with subject matter in itself but in its interaction with the pupil's present needs and capacities. Hence simple scholarship is not enough. In fact, there are certain features of scholarship or mastered subject matter—taken by itself—which get in the way of effective teaching *unless* the instructor's habitual attitude is one of concern with its interplay in the pupil's own experience. In the first place, his knowledge extends indefinitely beyond the range of the pupil's acquaintance. It involves principles which are beyond the immature pupil's understanding and interest. In and of itself, it may no more represent the living world of the pupil's experience than the astronomer's knowledge of Mars represents a baby's acquaintance with the room in which he stays. In the second place, the method of organization of the material of achieved scholarship differs from that of the beginner. It is not true that the experience of the young is unorganized—that it consists of isolated scraps. But it is organized in connection with direct practical centres of interest. The child's home is, for example, the organizing centre of his geographical knowledge. His own movements about the locality, his journeys abroad, the tales of his friends, give the ties which hold his items of information together. But the geography of the geographer, of the one who has already developed the implications of these smaller experiences, is organized on the basis of the relationship which the various facts bear to one another—not the relations which they bear to his house, bodily movements, and friends. To the one who is learned, subject matter is extensive, accurately defined, and logically interrelated. To the one who is learning, it is fluid, partial, and connected through his personal occupations.[1] The problem of teaching is to keep the experience of the student moving in the direction of what the expert already knows. Hence the need that the teacher know both subject matter and the characteristic needs and capacities of the student.

2. *The Development of Subject Matter in the Learner.*—It is possible, without doing violence to the facts, to mark off three fairly typical stages in the growth of subject matter in the experience of the learner. In its first estate, knowledge exists as the content of intelligent ability—power to do. This kind of subject matter, or known material, is expressed in familiarity or acquaintance with things. Then this material gradually is surcharged and deepened through communicated knowledge or information. Finally, it is enlarged and worked over into rationally or logically organized material—that of the one who, relatively speaking, is expert in the subject.

I. The knowledge which comes first to persons, and that remains most deeply engrained, is knowledge of *how to do*; how to walk, talk, read, write, skate, ride a bicycle, manage a machine, calculate, drive a horse, sell goods, manage people, and so on indefinitely. The popular tendency to regard instinctive acts which are adapted to an end as a sort of miraculous knowledge, while unjustifiable, is evidence of the strong tendency to identify intelligent control of the means of action with knowledge. When education, under the influence of a scholastic conception of knowledge which ignores everything but scientifically formulated facts and truths, fails to recognize that primary or initial subject matter always exists as matter of an active doing, involving the use of the body and the handling of material, the subject matter of instruction is isolated from the needs and purposes of the learner, and so becomes just a something to be memorized and reproduced upon demand. Recognition of the natural course of development, on the contrary, always sets out with situations which involve learning by doing. Arts and occupations form the initial stage of the curriculum, corresponding as they do to knowing how to go about the accomplishment of ends.

Popular terms denoting knowledge have always retained the connection with ability in action lost by academic philosophies. Ken and can are allied words. Attention means caring for a thing, in the sense of both affection and of looking out for its welfare. Mind means carrying out instructions in action—as a child minds his mother—and taking care of something—as a nurse minds the baby. To be thoughtful, considerate, means to heed the claims of others. Apprehension means dread of undesirable consequences, as well as intellectual grasp. To have good sense or judgment is to know the conduct a situation calls for; discernment is not making distinctions for the sake of making them, an exercise reprobated as hair splitting, but is insight into an affair with reference to acting. Wisdom has never lost its association with the proper direction of life. Only in education, never in the life of farmer, sailor, merchant, physician, or laboratory experimenter, does knowledge mean primarily a store of information aloof from doing.

Having to do with things in an intelligent way issues in acquaintance or familiarity. The things we are best acquainted with are the things we put to frequent use—such things as chairs, tables, pen, paper, clothes, food, knives and forks on the commonplace level, differentiating into more special objects according to a person's occupations in life. Knowledge of things in that intimate and emotional sense suggested by the word acquaintance is a precipitate from our employing them with a purpose. We have acted with or upon the thing so frequently that we can anticipate how it will act and react—such is the meaning of familiar acquaintance. We are ready for a familiar thing; it does not catch us napping, or play unexpected tricks with us. This attitude carries with it a sense of congeniality or friendliness, of ease and illumination; while the things with which we are not accustomed to deal are strange, foreign, cold, remote, "abstract."

II. But it is likely that elaborate statements regarding this primary stage of knowledge will darken understanding. It includes practically all of our knowledge which is not the result of deliberate technical study. Modes of purposeful doing includes dealings with persons as well as things. Impulses of communication and habits of intercourse have to be adapted to maintaining successful connections with others; a large fund of social knowledge accrues. As a part of this intercommunication one learns much from others. They tell of their experiences and of the experiences which, in turn, have been told them. In so far as one is interested or concerned in these communications, their matter becomes a part of one's own experience. Active connections with others are such an intimate and vital part of our own concerns that it is impossible to draw sharp lines, such as would enable us to say, "Here my experience ends; there yours begins." In so far as we are partners in common undertakings, the things which others communicate to us as the consequences of their particular share in the enterprise blend at once into the experience resulting from our own special doings. The ear is as much an organ of experience as the eye or hand; the eye is available for reading reports of what happens beyond its horizon. Things remote in space and time affect the issue of our actions quite as much as things which we can smell and handle. They really concern us, and, consequently, any account of them which assists us in dealing with things at hand falls within personal experience.

Information is the name usually given to this kind of subject matter. The place of communication in personal doing supplies us with a criterion for estimating the value of informational material in school. Does it grow naturally out of some question with which the student is concerned? Does it fit into his more direct acquaintance so as to increase its efficacy and deepen its meaning? If it meets these two requirements, it is educative. The amount heard or read is of no importance—the more the better, *provided* the student has a need for it and can apply it in some situation of his own. But it is not so easy to fulfill these requirements in actual practice as it is to lay them down in theory. The extension in modern times of the area of intercommunication; the invention of appliances for securing acquaintance with remote parts of the heavens and bygone events of history; the cheapening of devices, like printing, for recording and distributing information—genuine and alleged—have created an immense bulk of communicated subject matter. It is much easier to swamp a pupil with this than to work it into his direct experiences. All too frequently it forms another strange world which just overlies the world of personal acquaintance. The sole problem of the student is to learn, for school purposes, for purposes of recitations and promotions, the constituent parts of this strange world. Probably the most conspicuous connotation of the word knowledge for most persons to-day is just the body of facts and truths ascertained by others; the material found in the rows and rows of atlases, cyclopedias, histories, biographies, books of travel, scientific treatises, on the shelves of libraries.

The imposing stupendous bulk of this material has unconsciously influenced men's notions of the nature of knowledge itself. The statements, the propositions, in which knowledge, the issue of active concern with problems, is deposited, are taken to be themselves knowledge. The record of knowledge, independent of its place as an outcome of inquiry and a resource in further inquiry, is taken to *be* knowledge. The mind of man is taken captive by the spoils of its prior victories; the spoils, not the weapons and the acts of waging the battle against the unknown, are used to fix the meaning of knowledge, of fact, and truth.

If this identification of knowledge with propositions stating information has fastened itself upon logicians and philosophers, it is not surprising that the same ideal has almost dominated instruction. The "course of study" consists largely of information distributed into various branches of study, each study being subdivided into lessons presenting in serial cut-off portions of the total store. In the seventeenth century, the store was still small enough so that men set up the ideal of a complete encyclopedic mastery of it. It is now so bulky that the impossibility of any one man's coming into possession of it all is obvious. But the educational ideal has not been much affected. Acquisition of a modicum of information in each branch of learning, or at least in a selected group, remains the principle by which the curriculum, from elementary school through college, is formed; the easier portions being assigned to the earlier years, the more difficult to the later.

The complaints of educators that learning does not enter into character and affect conduct; the protests against memoriter work, against cramming, against gradgrind preoccupation with "facts," against devotion to wire-drawn distinctions and ill-understood rules and principles, all follow from this state of affairs. Knowledge which is mainly second-hand, other men's knowledge, tends to become merely verbal. It is no objection to information that it is clothed in words; communication necessarily takes place through words. But in the degree in which what is communicated cannot be organized into the existing experience of the learner, it becomes *mere* words: that is, pure sense-stimuli, lacking in meaning. Then it operates to call out mechanical reactions, ability to use the vocal organs to repeat statements, or the hand to write or to do "sums."

To be informed is to be posted; it is to have at command the subject matter needed for an effective dealing with a problem, and for giving added significance to the search for solution and to the solution itself. Informational knowledge is the material which can be fallen back upon as given, settled, established, assured in a doubtful situation. It is a kind of bridge for mind in its passage from doubt to discovery. It has the office of an intellectual middleman. It condenses and records in available form the net results of the prior experiences of mankind, as an agency of enhancing the meaning of new experiences. When one is told that Brutus assassinated Caesar, or that the length of the year is three hundred sixty-five and one fourth days, or that the ratio of the diameter of the circle to its circumference is 3.1415 . . . one receives what is indeed knowledge for others, but for him it is a stimulus to knowing. His acquisition of *knowledge* depends upon his response to what is communicated.

3. *Science or Rationalized Knowledge.*—Science is a name for knowledge in its most characteristic form. It represents in its degree, the perfected outcome of learning,—its consummation. What is known, in a given case, is what is sure, certain, settled, disposed of; that which we think *with* rather than that which we think about. In its honorable sense, knowledge is distinguished from opinion, guesswork, speculation, and mere tradition. In knowledge, things are *ascertained* they are *so* and not dubiously otherwise. But experience makes us aware that there is difference between intellectual certainty of *subject matter* and *our* certainty. We are made, so to speak, for belief; credulity is natural. The undisciplined mind is averse to suspense and intellectual hesitation; it is prone to assertion. It likes things undisturbed, settled, and treats them as such without due warrant. Familiarity, common repute, and congeniality to desire are readily made measuring rods of truth. Ignorance gives way to opinionated and current error,—a greater foe to learning than ignorance itself. A Socrates is thus led to declare that consciousness of ignorance is the beginning of effective love of wisdom, and a Descartes to say that science is born of doubting.

We have already dwelt upon the fact that subject matter, or data, and ideas have to have their worth tested experimentally: that in themselves they are tentative and provisional. Our predilection for premature acceptance and assertion, our aversion to suspended judgment, are signs that we tend naturally to cut short the process of testing. We are satisfied with superficial and immediate short-visioned applications. If these work out with moderate satisfactoriness, we are content to suppose that our assumptions have been confirmed. Even in the case of failure, we are inclined to put the blame not on the inadequacy and incorrectness of our data and thoughts, but upon our hard luck and the hostility of circumstance. We charge the evil consequence not to the error of our schemes and our incomplete inquiry into conditions (thereby getting material for revising the former and stimulus for extending the latter) but to untoward fate. We even plume ourselves upon our firmness in clinging to our conceptions in spite of the way in which they work out.

Science represents the safeguard of the race against these natural propensities and the evils which flow from them. It consists of the special appliances and methods which the race has slowly worked out in order to conduct reflection under conditions whereby its procedures and results are tested. It is artificial (an acquired art), not spontaneous; learned, not native. To this fact is due the unique, the invaluable place of science in education, and also the dangers which threaten its right use. Without initiation into the scientific spirit one is not in possession of the best tools which humanity has so far devised for effectively directed reflection. One in that case not merely conducts inquiry and learning without the use of the best instruments, but fails to understand the full meaning of knowledge. For he does not become acquainted with the traits that mark off opinion and assent from authorized conviction. On the other hand, the fact that science marks the perfecting of knowing in highly specialized conditions of technique renders its results, taken by themselves, remote from ordinary experience—a quality of aloofness that is popularly designated by the term abstract. When this isolation appears in instruction, scientific information is even more exposed to the dangers attendant upon presenting ready-made subject matter than are other forms of information.

Science has been defined in terms of method of inquiry and testing. At first sight, this definition may seem opposed to the current conception that science is organized or systematized knowledge. The opposition, however, is only seeming, and disappears when the ordinary definition is completed. Not organization but the *kind* of organization effected by adequate methods of tested discovery marks off science. The knowledge of a farmer is systematized in the degree in which he is competent. It is organized on the basis of relation of means to ends—practically organized. Its organization *as* knowledge (that is, in the eulogistic sense of adequately tested and confirmed) is incidental to its organization with reference to securing crops, live-stock, etc. But scientific subject matter is organized with specific reference to the successful conduct of the enterprise of discovery, to knowing as a specialized undertaking.

Reference to the kind of assurance attending science will shed light upon this statement. It is *rational* assurance,—logical warranty. The ideal of scientific organization is, therefore, that every conception and statement shall be of such a kind as to follow from others and to lead to others. Concepts and propositions mutually imply and support one another. This double relation of "leading to and confirming" is what is meant by the terms logical and rational. The everyday conception of water is more available for ordinary uses of drinking, washing, irrigation, etc., than the chemist's notion of it. The latter's description of it as H_2O is superior from the standpoint of place and use in inquiry. It states the nature of water in a way which connects it with knowledge of other things, indicating to one who understands it how the knowledge is arrived at and its bearings upon other portions of knowledge of the structure of things. Strictly speaking, it does not indicate the objective relations of water any more than does a statement that water is transparent, fluid, without taste or odor, satisfying to thirst, etc. It is just as true that water has these relations as that it is constituted by two molecules of hydrogen in combination with one of oxygen. But for the *particular purpose* of conducting discovery with a view to ascertainment of fact, the latter relations are fundamental. The more one emphasizes organization as a mark of science, then, the more he is committed to a recognition of the primacy of method in the definition of science. For method defines the kind of organization in virtue of which science is science.

4. *Subject Matter as Social.*—Our next chapters will take up various school activities and studies and discuss them as successive stages in that evolution of knowledge which we have just been discussing. It remains to say a few words upon subject matter as social, since our prior remarks have been mainly concerned with its intellectual aspect. A difference in breadth and depth exists even in vital knowledge; even in the data and ideas which are relevant to real problems and which are motivated by purposes. For there is a difference in the social scope of purposes and the social importance of problems. With the wide range of possible material to select from, it is important that education (especially in all its phases short of the most specialized) should use a criterion of social worth.

All information and systematized scientific subject matter have been worked out under the conditions of social life and have been transmitted by social means. But this does not prove that all is of equal value for the purposes of forming the disposition and supplying the equipment of members of present society. The scheme of a curriculum must take account of the adaptation of studies to the needs of the existing community life; it must select with the intention of improving the life we live in common so that the future shall be better than the past. Moreover, the curriculum must be planned with reference to placing essentials first, and refinements second. The things which are socially most fundamental, that is, which have to do with the experiences in which the widest groups share, are the essentials. The things which represent the needs of specialized groups and technical pursuits are secondary. There is truth in the saying that education must first be human and only after that professional. But those who utter the saying frequently have in mind in the term human only a highly specialized class: the class of learned men who preserve the classic traditions of the past. They forget that material is humanized in the degree in which it connects with the common interests of men as men.

Democratic society is peculiarly dependent for its maintenance upon the use in forming a course of study of criteria which are broadly human. Democracy cannot flourish where the chief influences in selecting subject matter of instruction are utilitarian ends narrowly conceived for the masses, and, for the higher education of the few, the traditions of a specialized cultivated class. The notion that the "essentials" of elementary education are the three R's mechanically treated, is based upon ignorance of the essentials needed for realization of democratic ideals. Unconsciously it assumes that these ideals are unrealizable; it assumes that in the future, as in the past, getting a livelihood, "making a living," must signify for most men and women doing things which are not significant, freely chosen, and ennobling to those who do them; doing things which serve ends unrecognized by those engaged in them, carried on under the direction of others for the sake of pecuniary reward. For preparation of large numbers for a life of this sort, and only for this purpose, are mechanical efficiency in reading, writing, spelling and figuring, together with attainment of a certain amount of muscular dexterity, "essentials." Such conditions also infect the education called liberal, with illiberality. They imply a somewhat parasitic cultivation bought at the expense of not having the enlightenment and discipline which come from concern with the deepest problems of common humanity. A curriculum which acknowledges the social responsibilities of education must present situations where problems are relevant to the problems of living together, and where observation and information are calculated to develop social insight and interest.

Summary.—The subject matter of education consists primarily of the meanings which supply content to existing social life. The continuity of social life means that many of these meanings are contributed to present activity by past collective experience. As social life grows more complex, these factors increase in number and import. There is need of special selection, formulation, and organization in order that they may be adequately transmitted to the new generation. But this very process tends to set up subject matter as something of value just by itself, apart from its function in promoting the realization of the meanings implied in the present experience of the immature. Especially is the educator exposed to the temptation to conceive his task in terms of the pupil's ability to appropriate and reproduce the subject matter in set statements, irrespective of its organization into his activities as a developing social member.

The positive principle is maintained when the young begin with active occupations having a social origin and use, and proceed to a scientific insight in the materials and laws involved, through assimilating into their more direct experience the ideas and facts communicated by others who have had a larger experience.

Note

1. Since the learned man should also still be a learner, it will be understood that these contrasts are relative, not absolute. But in the earlier stages of learning at least they are practically all-important.

9

From *The Way Out of Educational Confusion* (1931)

The Way Out of Educational Confusion debuted as a lecture on secondary education at Harvard University. The confusion Dewey references stemmed from growing uncertainty at the time over a wide range of issues in education, including questions regarding curricular standards, instructional goals, and teaching methods. Inevitably, this uncertainty fostered conflict among educators of opposing viewpoints and beliefs. In his remarks, Dewey proposes to use this conflict as a means of clearing up some of the educational confusion. He begins by pointing out the intellectual consequences of the increasing separation and specialization of the traditional academic disciplines. Most notable is conceptual confusion regarding the scope and substance of the subjects that make up the secondary school and college curriculums. How, for instance, do we determine in what subject area a particular topic belongs? What about topics that subsume multiple subject areas? What do subject area titles like history, political science, art, and physics really signify? Dewey argues that the "project method" provides one (not the only) way out of this confusion. He credits it with three main attributes: (1) It pulls together material from multiple subjects as needed for the situation at hand, not as established certainties with identifying labels preattached. (2) It requires actively doing something purposeful with this material utilizing intelligence and the exercise of judgment. (3) It puts the results of this (sometimes lengthy) process to the test through the aims or goals of the particular project. The "project method," then, as conceived by Dewey, is first and foremost a means of subject matter integration and only secondarily of curricular integration: curriculum, in most cases, entails prior organization of subject matter.

∾

It is fair for an objector to ask what is the substitute, the alternative, to organization of courses on the basis of adherence to traditional divisions and classifications of knowledge. The reply which goes furthest to the left is found in reference to the so-called "project," "problem," or "situation" method, now adopted for trial in many elementary schools. I shall indicate later that I do not believe that this is the only alternative. But the method has certain characteristics which are significant for any plan for change that may be adopted, and accordingly I shall call attention to these features. The method mentioned is called a method; it might be taken, therefore, to be *only* a method. In fact, like anything that *is* a method other than in name, it has definite implications for subject-matter. There cannot be a problem that is not a problem of *something*, nor a project that does not involve doing something in a way which demands inquiry into fresh fields of subject-matter. Many so-called projects are of such a short time-span and are entered upon for such casual reasons, that extension of acquaintance with facts and principles is at a minimum. In short, they are too trivial to be educative. But the defect is not inherent. It only indicates the need that educators should assume their educational responsibility. It is possible to find problems and projects that come within the scope and capacities of the experience of the learner and which have a sufficiently long span so that they raise new questions, introduce new and related undertakings, and create a demand for fresh knowledge. The difference between this procedure and the traditional one is not that the latter involves acquisition of new knowledge and the former does not. It is that in one a relatively fixed and isolated body of knowledge is assumed in advance; while in the other, material is drawn from any field as it is needed to carry on an intellectual enterprise.

Nor is the difference that in one procedure organization exists and in the other it does not. It is a difference in the type of organization effected. Material may be drawn from a variety of fields, number and measure from mathematics when they are needed, from historical, geographical, biological facts when they carry forward the undertaking, and so on. But the central question acts as a magnet to draw them together. Organization in one case consists in formal relations within a particular field as they present themselves to an expert who has mastered the subject. In the other case, it consists in noting the bearing and function of things acquired. The latter course has at least the advantage of being of the kind followed in study and learning outside of school walls, where data and principles do not offer themselves in isolated segments with labels already affixed.

Another feature of the problem method is that activity is exacted. I suppose that if there is one principle which is not a monopoly of any school of educational thought, it is the need of intellectual activity on the part of teacher and student, the condemnation of passive receptivity. But in practice there persist methods in which the pupil is a recording phonograph, or one who stands at the end of a pipe line receiving material conducted from a distant reservoir of learning. How is this split between theory and practice to be explained? Does not the presentation in doses and chunks of a ready-made subject-matter inevitably conduce to passivity? The mentally active scholar will acknowledge, I think, that his mind roams far and wide. All is grist that comes to his mill, and he does not limit his supply of grain to any one fenced-off field. Yet the mind does not merely roam abroad. It returns with what is found, and there is constant exercise of judgment to detect relations, relevancies, bearings upon the central theme. The outcome is a continuously growing intellectual integration. There is absorption; but it is eager and willing, not reluctant and forced. There is digestion, assimilation, not merely the carrying of a load by memory, a load to be cast off as soon as the day comes when it is safe to throw it off. Within the limits set by capacity and experience this kind of seeking and using, of amassing and organizing, is the process of learning everywhere and at any age.

In the third place, while the student with a proper "project" is intellectually active, he is also overtly active; he applies, he constructs, he expresses himself in new ways. He puts his knowledge to the test of operation. Naturally, he does something with what he learns. Because of this feature the separation between the practical and the liberal does not even arise. It does not have to be done away with, because it is not there. In practical subjects, this doing exists in laboratories and shops. But too often it is of a merely technical sort, not a genuine carrying forward of theoretical knowledge. It aims at mere manual facility, at an immediate external product, or a driving home into memory of something already learned as a matter of mere information.

I have referred, as already indicated, to the "project" method because of these traits, which seem to me proper and indispensable aims in all study by whatever name it be called, not because this method seems to be the only alternative to that usually followed. I do not urge it as the sole way out of educational confusion, not even in the elementary school, though I think experimentation with it is desirable in college and secondary school. But it is possible to retain traditional titles and still reorganize the subject-matter under them, so as to take account of interdependencies of knowledge and connection of knowledge with use and application. As the time grows to a close let me mention one illustration, Julian Huxley's and H. G. Wells' recent volumes on Life. They cut across all conventional divisions in the field: yet not at the expense of scientific accuracy but in a way which increases both intellectual curiosity and understanding, while disclosing the world about us as a perennial source of esthetic delight.

I have referred to intellectual interest. It is only too common to hear students (in name) say in reference to some subject that they "have *had* it." The use of the past tense is only too significant. The subject is over and done with; it is very much in the past. Every intelligent observer of the subsequent career of those who come from our schools deplores the fact that they do not carry away from school into later life abiding intellectual interests in what they have studied. After all, the period from, say, fourteen to twenty-two is a comparatively short portion of a normal life time. The best that education can do during these years is to arouse intellectual interests which carry over and onwards. The worst condemnation that can be passed is that these years are an interlude, a passing interval. If a student does not take into subsequent life an enduring concern for some field of knowledge and art, lying outside his immediate profession preoccupations, schooling for him has been a failure, no matter how good a "student" he was.

The failure is again due, I believe, to segregation of subjects. A pupil can say he has "had" a subject, because the subject has been treated as if it were complete in itself, beginning and terminating within limits fixed in advance. A reorganization of subject-matter which takes account of out-leadings into the wide world of nature and man, of knowledge and of social interests and uses, cannot fail save in the most callous and intellectually obdurate to awaken some permanent interest and curiosity. Theoretical subjects will become more practical, because more related to the scope of life; practical subjects will become more charged with theory and intelligent insight. Both will be vitally and not just formally unified.

I see no other way out of our educational confusion. The obvious objection is that this way takes too abrupt a turn. But what alternative is there save a further cluttering up of the curriculum and a steeper dividing wall between the cultural and liberal? The change is in many respects revolutionary. Yet the intelligence needed to bring it about is not lacking, but rather a long-time patience and a will to cooperation and coordination. I can see schools of education leading in the movement. They will hardly do much to reduce the existing confusion if they merely move in the direction of refining existing practices, striving to bring them under the protective shield of "scientific method." That course is more likely to increase confusion. But they can undertake consecutive study of the interrelation of subjects with one another and with social bearing and application; they can contribute a reorganization that will give direction to an aimless and divided situation.

For confusion is due ultimately to aimlessness, as much of the conflict is due to the attempt to follow tradition and yet introduce radically new material and interests into it—the attempt to superimpose the new on the old. The simile of new wines in old bottles is trite. Yet no other is so apt. We use leathern bottles in an age of steel and glass. The bottles leak and sag. The new wine spills and sours. No prohibitory holds against the attempt to make a new wine of culture and to provide new containers. Only new aims can inspire educational effort for clarity and unity. They alone can reduce confusion; if they do not terminate conflict they will at least render it intelligent and profitable.

IV
THEORY AND PRACTICE IN EDUCATION

10

The Relation of Theory to Practice in Education (1904)

This excerpt from "The Relation of Theory to Practice in Education" was initially published (in full) in the *Thirteenth Yearbook of the National Society for the Study of Education*. Throughout the piece, Dewey demonstrates his belief in the practical value of intelligently developed theory. Without a knowledge of theory, he explains, teachers are forced to fall back on antiquated or guesswork approaches to instruction, especially when present methods seem, for whatever reason, to be ineffectual. Moreover, even if teachers hit upon something that appears effective, there can be significant negative outcomes, short term and long term, that go unrecognized. Focusing only on what "works" is consequently a red flag for Dewey. Frequently, the more important issues are how and why something works or doesn't work. Dewey touches specifically on the student-teaching experience. During this time, "practice-teachers" have the opportunity to experience and reflect on the functioning and value of theory firsthand, in the context of actual teaching. It can then become a seamless dimension of practice, leading to deeper understanding and enhanced professional judgement. If this is the case, why do we regularly treat theory and practice as unrelated, even contrary, things?

༄

The difficulties which face a beginning teacher, who is set down for the first time before a class of from thirty to sixty children, in the responsibilities not only of instruction, but of maintaining the required order in the room as a whole, are most trying. It is almost impossible for an old teacher who has acquired the requisite skill of doing two or three distinct things simultaneously—skill to see the room as a whole while hearing one individual in one class recite, of keeping the program of the day and, yes, of the week and of the month in the fringe of consciousness while the work of the hour is in its centre—it is almost impossible for such a teacher to realize all the difficulties that confront the average beginner.

There is a technique of teaching, just as there is a technique of piano-playing. The technique, if it is to be educationally effective, is dependent upon principles. But it is possible for a student to acquire outward form of method without capacity to put it to genuinely educative use. As every teacher knows, children have an inner and an outer attention. The inner attention is the giving of the mind without reserve or qualification to the subject in hand. It is the first-hand and personal play of mental powers. As such, it is a fundamental condition of mental growth. To be able to keep track of this mental play, to recognize the signs of its presence or absence, to know how it is initiated and maintained, how to test it by results attained, and to test *apparent* results by it, is the supreme mark and criterion of a teacher. It means insight into soul-action, ability to discriminate the genuine from the sham, and capacity to further one and discourage the other.

External attention, on the other hand, is that given to the book or teacher as an independent object. It is manifested in certain conventional postures and physical attitudes rather than in the movement of thought. Children acquire great dexterity in exhibiting in conventional and expected ways the *form* of attention to school work, while reserving the inner play of their own thoughts, images, and emotions for subjects that are more important to them, but quite irrelevant.

Now, the teacher who is plunged prematurely into the pressing and practical problem of keeping order in the schoolroom has almost of necessity to make supreme the matter of external attention. The teacher has not yet had the training which affords psychological insight—which enables him to judge promptly (and therefore almost automatically) the kind and mode of subject-matter which the pupil needs at a given moment to keep his attention moving forward effectively and healthfully. He does know, however, that he must maintain order; that he must keep the attention of the pupils fixed upon his own questions, suggestions, instructions, and remarks, and upon their "lessons." The inherent tendency of the situation therefore is for him to acquire his technique in relation to the outward rather than the inner mode of attention.

III. Along with this fixation of attention upon the secondary at the expense of the primary problem, *there goes the foundation of habits of work which have an empirical, rather than a scientific, sanction.* The student adjusts his actual methods of teaching, not to the principles which he is acquiring, but to what he sees succeed and fail in an empirical way from moment to moment: to what he sees other teachers doing who are more experienced and successful in keeping order than he is; and to the injunctions and directions given him by others. In this way the controlling habits of the teacher finally get fixed with comparatively little reference to principles in the psychology, logic, and history of education. In theory, these latter are dominant; in practice, the moving forces are the devices and methods which are picked up through blind experimentation; through examples which are not rationalized; through precepts which are more or less arbitrary and mechanical; through advice based upon the experience of others. Here we have the explanation, in considerable part at least, of the dualism, the unconscious duplicity, which is one of the chief evils of the teaching profession. There is an enthusiastic devotion to certain principles of lofty theory in the abstract—principles of self-activity, self-control, intellectual and moral—and there is a school practice taking little heed of the official pedagogic creed. Theory and practice do not grow together out of and into the teacher's personal experience.

Ultimately there are two bases upon which the habits of a teacher as a teacher may be built up. They may be formed under the inspiration and constant criticism of intelligence, applying the best that is available. This is possible only where the would-be teacher has become fairly saturated with his subject-matter, and with his psychological and ethical philosophy of education. Only when such things have become incorporated in mental habit, have become part of the working tendencies of observation, insight, and reflection, will these principles work automatically, unconsciously, and hence promptly and effectively. And this means that practical work should be pursued primarily with reference to its reaction upon the professional pupil in making him a thoughtful and alert student of education, rather than to help him get immediate proficiency.

For immediate skill may be got at the cost of power to go on growing. The teacher who leaves the professional school with power in managing a class of children may appear to superior advantage the first day, the first week, the first month, or even the first year, as compared with some other teacher who has a much more vital command of the psychology, logic, and ethics of development. But later "progress" may with such consist only in perfecting and refining skill already possessed. Such persons seem to know how to teach, but they are not students of teaching. Even though they go on studying books of pedagogy, reading teachers' journals, attending teachers' institutes, etc., yet the root of the matter is not in them, unless they continue to be students of subject-matter, and students of mind-activity. Unless a teacher is such a student, he may continue to improve in the mechanics of school management, but he can not grow as a teacher, an inspirer and director of soul-life. How often do candid instructors in training schools for teachers acknowledge disappointment in the later career of even their more promising candidates! They seem to strike twelve at the start. There is an unexpected and seemingly unaccountable failure to maintain steady growth. Is this in some part due to the undue premature stress laid in early practice work upon securing immediate capability in teaching?

I might go on to mention other evils which seem to me to be more or less the effect of this same cause. Among them are the lack of intellectual independence among teachers, their tendency to intellectual subserviency. The "model lesson" of the teachers' institute and of the educational journal is a monument, on the one hand, of the eagerness of those in authority to secure immediate practical results at any cost; and, upon the other, of the willingness of our teaching corps to accept without inquiry or criticism any method or device which seems to promise good results. Teachers, actual and intending, flock to those persons who give them clear-cut and definite instructions as to just how to teach this or that.

The tendency of educational development to proceed by reaction from one thing to another, to adopt for one year, or for a term of seven years, this or that new study or method of teaching, and then as abruptly to swing over to some new educational gospel, is a result which would be impossible if teachers were adequately moved by their own independent intelligence. The willingness of teachers, especially of those occupying administrative positions, to become submerged in the routine detail of their callings, to expend the bulk of their energy upon forms and rules and regulations, and reports and percentages, is another evidence of the absence of intellectual vitality. If teachers were possessed by the spirit of an abiding student of education, this spirit would find some way of breaking through the mesh and coil of circumstance and would find expression for itself.

B. Let us turn from the practical side to the theoretical. What must be the aim and spirit of theory in order that practice work may really serve the purpose of an educational laboratory? We are met here with the belief that instruction in theory is merely theoretical, abstruse, remote, and therefore relatively useless to the teacher as a teacher, unless the student is at once set upon the work of teaching; that only "practice" can give a motive to a professional learning, and supply material for educational courses. It is not infrequently claimed (or at least unconsciously assumed) that students will not have a professional stimulus for their work in subject-matter and in educational psychology and history, will not have any outlook upon their relation to education, unless these things are immediately and simultaneously reinforced by setting the student upon the work of teaching. But is this the case? Or are there practical elements and bearings already contained in theoretical instruction of the proper sort?

I. Since it is impossible to cover in this paper all phases of the philosophy and science of education, I shall speak from the standpoint of psychology, believing that this may be taken as typical of the whole range of instruction in educational theory as such.

In the first place, beginning students have without any reference to immediate teaching a very large capital of an exceedingly practical sort in their own experience. The argument that theoretical instruction is merely abstract and in the air unless students are set at once to test and illustrate it by practice teaching of their own, *overlooks the continuity of the classroom mental activity with that of other normal experience.* It ignores the tremendous importance for educational purposes of this continuity. Those who employ this argument seem to isolate the psychology of learning that goes on in the schoolroom from the psychology of learning found elsewhere.

This isolation is both unnecessary and harmful. It is unnecessary, tending to futility, because it throws away or makes light of the greatest asset in the student's possession—the greatest, moreover, that ever will be in his possession—his own direct and personal experience. There is every presumption (since the student is not an imbecile) that he has been learning all the days of his life, and that he is still learning from day to day. He must accordingly have in his own experience plenty of practical material by which to illustrate and vitalize theoretical principles and laws of mental growth in the process of learning. Moreover, since none of us is brought up under ideal conditions, each beginning student has plenty of practical experience by which to illustrate cases of arrested development—instances of failure and maladaptation and retrogression, or even degeneration. The material at hand is pathological as well as healthy. It serves to embody and illustrate both achievement and failure, in the problem of learning.

But it is more than a serious mistake (violating the principle of proceeding from the known to the unknown) to fail to take account of this body of practical experience. Such ignoring tends also to perpetuate some of the greatest evils of current school methods. Just because the student's attention is not brought to the point of recognizing that *his own* past and present growth is proceeding in accordance with the very laws that control growth in the school, and that there is no psychology of the schoolroom different from that of the nursery, the playground, the street, and the parlor, he comes unconsciously to assume that education in the class-room is a sort of unique thing, having its own laws.[1] Unconsciously, but none the less surely, the student comes to believe in certain "methods" of learning, and hence of teaching which are somehow especially appropriate to the school—which somehow have their particular residence and application there. Hence he comes to believe in the potency for schoolroom purposes of materials, methods, and devices which it never occurs to him to trust to in his experience outside of school.

I know a teacher of teachers who is accustomed to say that when she fails to make clear to a class of teachers some point relative to children, she asks these teachers to stop thinking of their own pupils and to think of some nephew, niece, cousin, some child of whom they have acquaintance in the unformalities of home life. I do not suppose any great argument is needed to prove that breach of continuity between learning within and without the school is the great cause in education of wasted power and misdirected effort. I wish rather to take advantage of this assumption (which I think will be generally accepted) to emphasize the danger of bringing the would-be teacher into an abrupt and dislocated contact with the psychology of the schoolroom—abrupt and dislocated because not prepared for by prior practice in selecting and organizing the relevant principles and data contained within the experience best known to him, his own.[2]

From this basis, a transition to educational psychology may be made in observation of the teaching of others—visiting classes. I should wish to note here, however, the same principle that I have mentioned as regards practice work, specifically so termed. The first observation of instruction given by model- or critic-teachers should not be too definitely practical in aim. The student should not be observing to find out how the good teacher does it, in order to accumulate a store of methods by which he also may teach successfully. He should rather observe with reference to seeing the interaction of mind, to see how teacher and pupils react upon each other—how mind answers to mind. Observation should at first be conducted from the psychological rather than from the "practical" standpoint. If the latter is emphasized before the student has an independent command of the former, the principle of imitation is almost sure to play an exaggerated part in the observer's future teaching, and hence at the expense of personal insight and initiative. What the student needs most at this stage of growth is ability to see what is going on in the minds of a group of persons who are in intellectual contact with one another. He needs to learn to observe psychologically—a very different thing from simply observing how a teacher gets "good results" in presenting any particular subject.

It should go without saying that the student who has acquired power in psychological observation and interpretation may finally go on to observe more technical aspects of instruction, namely, the various methods and instrumentalities used by a good teacher in giving instruction in any subject. If properly prepared for, this need not tend to produce copiers, followers of tradition and example. Such students will be able to translate the practical devices which are such an important part of the equipment of a good teacher over into their psychological equivalents; to know not merely as a matter of brute fact that they do work, but to know how and why they work. Thus he will be an independent judge and critic of their proper use and adaptation.

In the foregoing I have assumed that educational psychology is marked off from general psychology simply by the emphasis which it puts upon two factors. The first is the stress laid upon a certain end, namely, growth or development—with its counterparts, arrest and adaptation. The second is the importance attached to the social factor—to the mutual interaction of different minds with each other. It is, I think, strictly true that no educational procedure nor pedagogical maxim can be derived directly from pure psychological data. The psychological data taken without qualification (which is what I mean by their being pure) cover everything and anything that may take place in a mind. Mental arrest and decay occur according to psychological laws, just as surely as do development and progress.

We do not make practical maxims out of physics by telling persons to move according to laws of gravitation. If people move at all, they *must* move in accordance with the conditions stated by this law. Similarly, if mental operations take place at all, they *must* take place in accordance with the principles stated in correct psychological generalizations. It is superfluous and meaningless to attempt to turn these psychological principles directly into rules of teaching. But the person who knows the laws of mechanics knows the conditions of which he must take account when he wishes to reach a certain end. He knows that *if* he aims to build a bridge, he must build it in a certain way and of certain materials, or else he will not have a bridge, but a heap of rubbish. So in psychology. Given an end, say promotion of healthy growth, psychological observations and reflection put us in control of the conditions concerned in that growth. We know that if we are to get that *end,* we must do it in a certain way. It is the subordination of the psychological material to the problem of effecting growth and avoiding arrest and waste which constitutes a distinguishing mark of educational psychology.

I have spoken of the importance of the social factor as the other mark. I do not mean, of course, that general theoretical psychology ignores the existence and significance of the reaction of mind to mind—though it would be within bounds to say that till recently the social side was an unwritten chapter of psychology. I mean that considerations of the ways in which one mind responds to the stimuli which another mind is consciously or unconsciously furnishing possess a relative importance for the educator which they have not for the psychologist as such. From the teacher's standpoint, it is not too much to say that every habit which a pupil exhibits is to be regarded as a reaction to stimuli which some persons or group of persons have presented to the child. It is not too much to say that the most important thing for the teacher to consider, as regards his present relations to his pupils, is the attitudes and habits which his own modes of being, saying, and doing are fostering or discouraging in them.

Now, if these two assumptions regarding educational psychology be granted, I think it will follow as a matter of course, that only by beginning with the values and laws contained in the student's own experience of his own mental growth, and by proceeding gradually to facts connected with other persons of whom he can know little; and by proceeding still more gradually to the attempt actually to influence the mental operations of others, can educational theory be made most effective. Only in this way can the most essential trait of the mental habit of the teacher be secured—that habit which looks upon the internal, not upon the external; which sees that the important function of the teacher is direction of the mental movement of the student, and that the mental element must be known before it can be directed.

II. I turn now to the side of subject-matter, or scholarship, with the hope of showing that here too the material, when properly presented, is not so *merely* theoretical, remote from the practical problems of teaching, as is sometimes supposed. I recall that once a graduate student in a university made inquiries among all the leading teachers in the institution with which he was connected as to whether they had received any professional training, whether they had taken courses in pedagogy. The inquirer threw the results, which were mostly negative, into the camp of the local pedagogical club. Some may say that this proves nothing, because college teaching is proverbially poor, considered simply as teaching. Yet no one can deny that there is *some* good teaching, and some teaching of the very first order, done in colleges, and done by persons who have never had any instruction in either the theory or the practice of teaching.

This fact cannot be ignored any more than can the fact that there were good teachers before there was any such thing as pedagogy. Now, I am not arguing for not having pedagogical training—that is the last thing I want. But I claim the facts mentioned prove that scholarship *per se* may itself be a most effective tool for training and turning out good teachers. If it has accomplished so much when working unconsciously and without set intention, have we not good reason to believe that, when acquired in a training school for teachers—with the end of making teachers held definitely in view and with conscious reference to its relation to mental activity—it may prove a much more valuable pedagogical asset than we commonly consider it?

Scholastic knowledge is sometimes regarded as if it were something quite irrelevant to method. When this attitude is even unconsciously assumed, method becomes an external attachment to knowledge of subject-matter. It has to be elaborated and acquired in relative independence from subject-matter, and *then* applied.

Now the body of knowledge which constitutes the subject-matter of the student-teacher must, by the nature of the case, be organized subject-matter. It is not a miscellaneous heap of separate scraps. Even if (as in the case of history and literature), it be not technically termed "science," it is none the less material which has been subjected to method—has been selected and arranged with reference to controlling intellectual principles. There is, therefore, method in subject-matter itself—method indeed of the highest order which the human mind has yet evolved, scientific method.

It cannot be too strongly emphasized that this scientific method is the method of mind itself.[3] The classifications, interpretations, explanations, and generalizations which make subject-matter a branch of study do not lie externally in facts apart from mind. They reflect the attitudes and workings of mind in its endeavor to bring raw material of experience to a point where it at once satisfies and stimulates the needs of active thought. Such being the case, there is something wrong in the "academic" side of professional training, if by means of it the student does not constantly get object-lessons of the finest type in the kind of mental activity which characterizes mental growth and, hence, the educative process.

It is necessary to recognize the importance for the teacher's equipment of his own habituation to superior types of method of mental operation. The more a teacher in the future is likely to have to do with elementary teaching, the more, rather than the less, necessary is such exercise. Otherwise, the current traditions of elementary work with their tendency to talk and write down to the supposed intellectual level of children, will be likely to continue. Only a teacher thoroughly trained in the higher levels of intellectual method and who thus has constantly in his own mind a sense of what adequate and genuine intellectual activity means, will be likely, in deed, not in mere word, to respect the mental integrity and force of children.

Of course, this conception will be met by the argument that the scientific organization of subject-matter, which constitutes the academic studies of the student-teacher is upon such a radically different basis from that adapted to less mature students that too much preoccupation with scholarship of an advanced order is likely actually to get in the way of the teacher of children and youth. I do not suppose anybody would contend that teachers really can know more than is good for them, but it may reasonably be argued that continuous study of a specialized sort forms mental habits likely to throw the older student out of sympathy with the type of mental impulses and habits which are found in younger persons.

Right here, however, I think normal schools and teachers' colleges have one of their greatest opportunities—an opportunity not merely as to teachers in training, but also for reforming methods of education in colleges and higher schools having nothing to do with the training of teachers. It is the business of normal schools and collegiate schools of education to present subject-matter in science, in language, in literature and the arts, in such a way that the student both sees and feels that these studies *are* significant embodiments of mental operations. He should be led to realize that they are not products of technical methods, which have been developed for the sake of the specialized branches of knowledge in which they are used, but represent fundamental mental attitudes and operations—that, indeed, particular scientific methods and classifications simply express and illustrate in their most concrete form that of which simple and common modes of thought-activity are capable when they work under satisfactory conditions.

In a word, it is the business of the "academic" instruction of future teachers to carry back subject-matter to its common psychical roots.[4] In so far as this is accomplished, the gap between the higher and the lower treatment of subject-matter, upon which the argument of the supposed objector depends, ceases to have the force which that argument assigns to it. This does not mean, of course, that exactly the same subject-matter, in the same mode of presentation, is suitable to a student in the elementary or high schools that is appropriate to the normal student. But it does mean that a mind which is habituated to viewing subject-matter from the standpoint of the function of that subject-matter in connection with *mental* responses, attitudes, and methods will be sensitive to *signs of intellectual activity* when exhibited in the child of four, or the youth of sixteen, and will be trained to a spontaneous and unconscious appreciation of the subject-matter which is fit to call out and direct mental activity. We have here, I think, the explanation of the success of some teachers who violate every law known to and laid down by pedagogical science. They are themselves so full of the spirit of inquiry, so sensitive to every sign of its presence and absence, that no matter what they do, nor how they do it, they succeed in awakening and inspiring like alert and intense mental activity in those with whom they come in contact.

This is not a plea for the prevalence of these irregular, inchoate methods. But I feel that I may recur to my former remark: if some teachers, by sheer plentitude of knowledge, keep by instinct in touch with the mental activity of their pupils, and accomplish so much without, and even in spite of, principles which are theoretically sound, then there must be in this same scholarship a tremendous resource when it is more consciously used—that is, employed in clear connection with psychological principles.

When I said above that schools for training teachers have here an opportunity to react favorably upon general education, I meant that no instruction in subject-matter (wherever it is given) is adequate if it leaves the student with just acquisition of certain information about external facts and laws, or even a certain facility in the intellectual manipulation of this material. It is the business of our higher schools in all lines, and not simply of our normal schools, to furnish the student with the realization that, after all, it is the human mind, trained to effective control of its natural attitudes, impulses, and responses, that is the significant thing in all science and history and art so far as these are formulated for purposes of study.

The present divorce between scholarship and method is as harmful on one side as upon the other—as detrimental to the best interests of higher academic instruction as it is to the training of teachers. But the only way in which this divorce can be broken down is by so presenting all subject-matter, for whatever ultimate, practical, or professional purpose, that it shall be apprehended as an objective embodiment of methods of mind in its search for, and transactions with, the truth of things.

Upon the more practical side, this principle requires that, so far as students appropriate new subject-matter (thereby improving their own scholarship and realizing more consciously the nature of method), they should finally proceed to organize this same subject-matter with reference to its use in teaching others. The curriculum of the elementary and the high school constituting the "practice" or "model" school ought to stand in the closest and most organic relation to the instruction in subject-matter which is given by the teachers of the professional school. If in any given school this is not the case, it is either because in the *training class* subject-matter is presented in an isolated way, instead of as a concrete expression of methods of mind, or else because the *practice school* is dominated by certain conventions and traditions regarding material and the methods of teaching it, and hence is not engaged in work of an adequate educational type.

As a matter of fact, as everybody knows, both of these causes contribute to the present state of things. On the one hand, inherited conditions impel the elementary school to a certain triviality and poverty of subject-matter, calling for mechanical drill, rather than for thought-activity, and the high school to a certain technical mastery of certain conventional culture subjects, taught as independent branches of the same tree of knowledge! On the other hand traditions of the different branches of science (the academic side of subject-matter) tend to subordinate the teaching in the normal school to the attainment of certain facilities, and the acquirement of certain information, both in greater or less isolation from their value as exciting and directing mental power.

The great need is convergence, concentration. Every step taken in the elementary and the high school toward intelligent introduction of more worthy and significant subject-matter, one requiring consequently for its assimilation thinking rather than "drill," must be met by a like advance step in which the mere isolated specialization of collegiate subject-matter is surrendered, and in which there is brought to conscious and interested attention its significance in expression of fundamental modes of mental activity—so fundamental as to be common to both the play of the mind upon the ordinary material of everyday experience and to the systematized material of the sciences.

III. As already suggested, this point requires that training students be exercised in making the connections between the course of study of the practice or model school, and the wider horizons of learning coming within their ken. But it is consecutive and systematic exercise in the consideration of the subject-matter of the elementary and high schools that is needed. The habit of making isolated and independent lesson plans for a few days' or weeks' instruction in a separate grade here or there not only does not answer this purpose, but is likely to be distinctly detrimental. Everything should be discouraged which tends to put the student in the attitude of snatching at the subject-matter which he is acquiring in order to see if by some hook or crook it may be made immediately available for a lesson in this or that grade. What is needed is the habit of viewing the entire curriculum as a continuous growth, reflecting the growth of mind itself. This in turn demands, so far as I can see, consecutive and longitudinal consideration of the curriculum of the elementary and high school rather than a cross-sectional view of it. The student should be led to see that the same subject-matter in geography, nature-study, or art develops not merely day to day in a given grade, but from year to year throughout the entire movement of the school; and he should realize this before he gets much encouragement in trying to adapt subject-matter in lesson plans for this or that isolated grade.

C. If we attempt to gather together the points which have been brought out, we should have a view of practice work something like the following—though I am afraid even this formulates a scheme with more appearance of rigidity than is desirable:

At first, the practice school would be used mainly for purposes of observation. This observation, moreover, would not be for the sake of seeing how good teachers teach, or for getting "points" which may be employed in one's own teaching, but to get material for psychological observation and reflection, and some conception of the educational movement of the school as a whole.

Secondly, there would then be more intimate introduction to the lives of the children and the work of the school through the use as assistants of such students as had already got psychological insight and a good working acquaintance with educational problems. Students at this stage would not undertake much direct teaching, but would make themselves useful in helping the regular class instructor. There are multitudes of ways in which such help can be given and be of real help—that is, of use to the school, to the children, and not merely of putative value to the training student.[5] Special attention to backward children, to children who have been out of school, assisting in the care of material, in forms of hand-work, suggest some of the avenues of approach.

This kind of practical experience enables, in the third place, the future teacher to make the transition from his more psychological and theoretical insight to the observation of the more technical points of class teaching and management. The informality, gradualness, and familiarity of the earlier contact tend to store the mind with material which is unconsciously assimilated and organized, and thus supplies a background for work involving greater responsibility.

As a counterpart of this work in assisting, such students might well at the same time be employed in the selection and arrangement of subject-matter, as indicated in the previous discussion. Such organization would at the outset have reference to at least a group of grades, emphasizing continuous and consecutive growth. Later it might, without danger of undue narrowness, concern itself with finding supplementary materials and problems bearing upon the work in which the student is giving assistance; might elaborate material which could be used to carry the work still farther, if it were desirable; or, in case of the more advanced students, to build up a scheme of possible alternative subjects for lessons and studies.

Fourthly, as fast as students are prepared through their work of assisting for more responsible work, they could be given actual teaching to do. Upon the basis that the previous preparation has been adequate in subject-matter, in educational theory, and in the kind of observation and practice already discussed, such practice-teachers should be given the maximum amount of liberty possible. They should not be too closely supervised, nor too minutely and immediately criticised upon either the matter or the method of their teaching. Students should be given to understand that they not only are *permitted* to act upon their own intellectual initiative, but that they are *expected* to do so, and that their ability to take hold of situations for themselves would be a more important factor in judging them than their following any particular set method or scheme.

Of course, there should be critical discussion with persons more expert of the work done, and of the educational results obtained. But sufficient time should be permitted to allow the practice-teacher to recover from the shocks incident to the newness of the situation, and also to get enough experience to make him capable of seeing the *fundamental* bearings of criticism upon work done. Moreover, the work of the expert or supervisor should be directed to getting the student to judge his own work critically, to find out for himself in what respects he has succeeded and in what failed, and to find the probable reasons for both failure and success, rather than to criticising him too definitely and specifically upon special features of his work.

It ought to go without saying (unfortunately, it does not in all cases) that criticism should be directed to making the professional student thoughtful about his work in the light of principles, rather than to induce in him a recognition that certain special methods are good, and certain other special methods bad. At all events, no greater travesty of real intellectual criticism can be given than to set a student to teaching a brief number of lessons, have him under inspection in practically all the time of every lesson, and then criticise him almost, if not quite, at the very end of each lesson, upon the particular way in which that particular lesson has been taught, pointing out elements of failure and of success. Such methods of criticism may be adapted to giving a training-teacher command of some of the knacks and tools of the trade, but are not calculated to develop a thoughtful and independent teacher.

Moreover, while such teaching (as already indicated) should be extensive or continuous enough to give the student time to become at home and to get a body of funded experience, it ought to be intensive in purpose rather than spread out miscellaneously. It is much more important for the teacher to assume responsibility for the consecutive development of some one topic, to get a feeling for the movement of that subject, than it is to teach a certain number (necessarily smaller in range) of lessons in a larger number of subjects. What we want, in other words, is not so much technical skill, as a realizing sense in the teacher of what the educational development of a subject means, and, in some typical case, command of a method of control, which will then serve as a standard for self-judgment in other cases.

Fifthly, if the practical conditions permit—if, that is to say, the time of the training course is sufficiently long, if the practice schools are sufficiently large to furnish the required number of children, and to afford actual demand for the work to be done—students who have gone through the stages already referred to should be ready for work of the distinctly apprenticeship type.

Nothing that I have said heretofore is to be understood as ruling out practice teaching which is designed to give an individual mastery of the actual technique of teaching and management, provided school conditions permit it in reality and not merely in external form—provided, that is, the student has gone through a training in educational theory and history, in subject-matter, in observation, and in practice work of the laboratory type, before entering upon the latter. The teacher must acquire his technique some time or other; and if conditions are favorable, there are some advantages in having this acquisition take place in cadetting or in something of that kind. By means of this probation, persons who are unfit for teaching may be detected and eliminated more quickly than might otherwise be the case and before their cases have become institutionalized.

Even in this distinctly apprenticeship stage, however, it is still important that the student should be given as much responsibility and initiative as he is capable of taking, and hence that supervision should not be too unremitting and intimate, and criticism not at too short range or too detailed. The advantage of this intermediate probationary period does not reside in the fact that thereby supervisory officers may turn out teachers who will perpetuate their own notions and methods, but in the inspiration and enlightenment that come through prolonged contact with mature and sympathetic persons. If the conditions in the public schools were just what they ought to be, if all superintendents and principals had the knowledge and the wisdom which they should have, and if they had time and opportunity to utilize their knowledge and their wisdom in connection with the development of the younger teachers who come to them, the value of this apprenticeship period would be reduced, I think, very largely to its serving to catch in time and to exclude persons unfitted for teaching.

In conclusion, I may say that I do not believe that the principles presented in this paper call for anything utopian. The present movement in normal schools for improvement of range and quality of subject-matter is steady and irresistible. All the better classes of normal schools are already, in effect, what are termed "junior colleges." That is, they give two years' work which is almost, and in many cases quite, of regular college grade. More and more, their instructors are persons who have had the same kind of scholarly training that is expected of teachers in colleges. Many of these institutions are already of higher grade than this; and the next decade will certainly see a marked tendency on the part of many normal schools to claim the right to give regular collegiate bachelor degrees.

The type of scholarship contemplated in this paper is thus practically assured for the near future. If two other factors cooperate with this, there is no reason why the conception of relation of theory and practice here presented should not be carried out. The second necessary factor is that the elementary and high schools, which serve as schools of observation and practice, should represent an advanced type of education properly corresponding to the instruction in academic subject-matter and in educational theory given to the training classes. The third necessity is that work in psychology and educational theory make concrete and vital the connection between the normal instruction in subject-matter and the work of the elementary and high schools. If it should prove impracticable to realize the conception herein set forth, it will not be, I think, because of any impossibility resident in the outward conditions, but because those in authority, both within and without the schools, believe that the true function of training schools is just to meet the needs of which people are already conscious. In this case, of course, training schools will be conducted simply with reference to perpetuating current types of educational practice, with simply incidental improvement in details.

The underlying assumption of this paper is, accordingly, that training schools for teachers do not perform their full duty in accepting and conforming to present educational standards, but that educational leadership is an indispensable part of their office. The thing needful is improvement of education, not simply by turning out teachers who can do better the things that are now necessary to do, but rather by changing the conception of what constitutes education.

Notes

1. There is where the plea for "adult" psychology has force. The person who does not know himself is not likely to know others. The adult psychology ought, however, to be just as genetic as that of childhood.

2. It may avoid misapprehension if I repeat the word *experience*. It is not a *metaphysical* introspection that I have in mind but the process of turning back upon one's own experiences, and turning them over to see how they were developed, what helped and hindered, the stimuli and the inhibitions both within and without the organism.

3. Professor Ella F. Young's *Scientific Method in Education* (University of Chicago Decennial Publications) is a noteworthy development of this conception, to which I am much indebted. [Another of Dewey's important mentors, Young was superintendent of Chicago Public Schools.]

4. It is hardly necessary to refer to Dr. [William Torrey] Harris's continued contention that normal training should give a higher view or synthesis of even the most elementary subjects.

5. This question of some real need in the practice school itself for the work done is very important in its moral influence and in assimilating the conditions of "practice work" to those of real teaching.

11

From *The Sources of a Science of Education*, Part 1 (1929)

In *The Sources of a Science of Education*, part I, Dewey considers the question whether or not there can be a science of education. If so, he asks, what would it look like and how would it function? Importantly, Dewey uses the word "science" very broadly to include a range of "systematic methods of inquiry." Such methods address the genuine processes and practices of teaching and learning, not isolated fragments of teacher and student behaviors. These multifaceted activities can be viewed from the perspectives of many subject areas, including sociology, psychology, ethics, and biology, among others. (Dewey also affirms that teaching is an art, but we must remember that he sees art and science as complementary, not oppositional.) All of these subject areas potentially have something to contribute to our understanding of teaching and learning. None, though, Dewey argues, is sufficient by itself or capable of providing a "one best approach," especially given the complexity and diversity of human learners and learning environments. Thoughtfully utilized, however, these subject areas can help us be more knowledgeable, more artful, and more democratic as educators.

∼

Part I: Education as a Science

The title may suggest to some minds that it begs a prior question: Is there a science of education? And still more fundamentally, Can there be a science of education? Are the procedures and aims of education such that it is possible to reduce them to anything properly called a science? Similar questions exist in other fields. The issue is not unknown in history; it is raised in medicine and law. As far as education is concerned, I may confess at once that I have put the question in its apparently question-begging form in order to avoid discussion of questions that are important but that are also full of thorns and attended with controversial divisions.

It is enough for our purposes to note that the word "science" has a wide range.

There are those who would restrict the term to mathematics or to disciplines in which exact results can be determined by rigorous methods of demonstration. Such a conception limits even the claims of physics and chemistry to be sciences, for according to it the only scientific portion of these subjects is the strictly mathematical. The position of what are ordinarily termed the biological sciences is even more dubious, while social subjects and psychology would hardly rank as sciences at all, when measured by this definition. Clearly we must take the idea of science with some latitude. We must take it with sufficient looseness to include all the subjects that are usually regarded as sciences. The important thing is to discover those traits in virtue of which various fields are called scientific. When we raise the question in this way, we are led to put emphasis upon *methods* of dealing with subject-matter rather than to look for uniform objective traits in subject-matter. From this point of view, science signifies, I take it, the existence of systematic methods of inquiry, which, when they are brought to bear on a range of facts, enable us to understand them better and to control them more intelligently, less haphazardly and with less routine.

No one would doubt that our practices in hygiene and medicine are less casual, less results of a mixture of guess work and tradition, than they used to be, nor that this difference has been made by development of methods of investigating and testing. There is an intellectual technique by which discovery and organization of material go on cumulatively, and by means of which one inquirer can repeat the researches of another, confirm or discredit them, and add still more to the capital stock of knowledge. Moreover, the methods when they are used tend to perfect themselves, to suggest new problems, new investigations, which refine old procedures and create new and better ones.

The question as to the sources of a science of education is, then, to be taken in this sense. What are the ways by means of which the function of education in all its branches and phases—selection of material for the curriculum, methods of instruction and discipline, organization and administration of schools—can be conducted with systematic increase of intelligent control and understanding? What are the materials upon which we may—and should—draw in order that educational activities may become in a less degree products of routine, tradition, accident and transitory accidental influences? From what sources shall we draw so that there shall be steady and cumulative growth of intelligent, communicable insight and power of direction?

Here is the answer to those who decry pedagogical study on the ground that success in teaching and in moral direction of pupils is often not in any direct ratio to knowledge of educational principles. Here is "A" who is much more successful than "B" in teaching, awakening the enthusiasm of his students for learning, inspiring them morally by personal example and contact, and yet relatively ignorant of educational history, psychology, approved methods, etc., which "B" possesses in abundant measure. The facts are admitted. But what is overlooked by the objector is that the successes of such individuals tend to be born and to die with them: beneficial consequences extend only to those pupils who have personal contact with such gifted teachers. No one can measure the waste and loss that have come from the fact that the contributions of such men and women in the past have been thus confined, and the only way by which we can prevent such waste in the future is by methods which enable us to make an *analysis* of what the gifted teacher does intuitively, so that something accruing from his work can be communicated to others. Even in the things conventionally recognized as sciences, the insights of unusual persons remain important and there is no levelling down to a uniform procedure. But the existence of science gives common efficacy to the experiences of the genius; it makes it possible for the results of special power to become part of the working equipment of other inquirers, instead of perishing as they arose.

The individual capacities of the Newtons, Boyles, Joules, Darwins, Lyells, Helmholtzes, are not destroyed because of the existence of science; their differences from others and the impossibility of predicting on the basis of past science what discoveries they would make—that is, the impossibility of regulating their activities by antecedent sciences—persist. But science makes it possible for others to benefit systematically by what they achieved.

The existence of scientific method protects us also from a danger that attends the operations of men of unusual power; dangers of slavish imitation partisanship, and such jealous devotion to them and their work as to get in the way of further progress. Anybody can notice to-day that the effect of an original and powerful teacher is not all to the good. Those influenced by him often show a one-sided interest; they tend to form schools, and to become impervious to other problems and truths; they incline to swear by the words of their master and to go on repeating his thoughts after him, and often without the spirit and insight that originally made them significant. Observation also shows that these results happen oftenest in those subjects in which scientific method is least developed. Where these methods are of longer standing, students adopt methods rather than merely results, and employ them with flexibility rather than in literal reproduction.

This digression seems to be justified not merely because those who object to the idea of a science put personality and its unique gifts in opposition to science, but also because those who recommend science sometimes urge that uniformity of procedure will be its consequence. So it seems worth while to dwell on the fact that in the subjects best developed from the scientific point of view, the opposite is the case. Command of scientific methods and systematized subject-matter liberates individuals; it enables them to see new problems, devise new procedures, and, in general, makes for diversification rather than for set uniformity. But at the same time these diversifications have a cumulative effect in an advance shared by all workers in the field.

Education as an Art

This theme is, I think, closely connected with another point which is often urged, namely, that education is an art rather than a science. That, in concrete operation, education is an art, either a mechanical art or a fine art, is unquestionable. If there were an opposition between science and art, I should be compelled to side with those who assert that education is an art. But there is no opposition, although there is a distinction. We must not be misled by words. Engineering is, in actual practice, an art. But it is an art that progressively incorporates more and more of science into itself, more of mathematics, physics and chemistry. It is the kind of art it is precisely because of a content of scientific subject-matter which guides it as a practical operation. There is room for the original and daring projects of exceptional individuals. But their distinction lies not in the fact that they turn their backs upon science, but in the fact that they make new integrations of scientific material and turn it to new and previously unfamiliar and unforeseen uses. When, in education, the psychologist or observer and experimentalist in any field reduces his findings to a rule which is to be uniformly adopted, then, only, is there a result which is objectionable and destructive of the free play of education as an art.

But this happens not because of scientific method but because of departure from it. It is not the capable engineer who treats scientific findings as imposing upon him a certain course which is to be rigidly adhered to: it is the third- or fourth-rate man who adopts this course. Even more, it is the unskilled day laborer who follows it. For even if the practice adopted is one that follows from science and could not have been discovered or employed except for science, when it is converted into a uniform rule of procedure it becomes an empirical rule-of-thumb procedure—just as a person may use a table of logarithms mechanically without knowing anything about mathematics.

The danger is great in the degree in which the attempt to develop scientific method is recent. Nobody would deny that education is still in a condition of transition from an empirical to a scientific status. In its empirical form the chief factors determining education are tradition, imitative reproduction, response to various external pressures wherein the strongest force wins out, and the gifts, native and acquired, of individual teachers. In this situation there is a strong tendency to identify teaching ability with the use of procedures that yield immediately successful results, success being measured by such things as order in the classroom, correct recitations by pupils in assigned lessons, passing of examinations, promotion of pupils to a higher grade, etc.

For the most part, these are the standards by which a community judges the worth of a teacher. Prospective teachers come to training schools, whether in normal schools or colleges, with such ideas implicit in their minds. They want very largely to find out *how to do* things with the maximum prospect of success. Put baldly, they want recipes. Now, to such persons science is of value because it puts a stamp of final approval upon this and that specific procedure. It is very easy for science to be regarded as a guarantee that goes with the sale of goods rather than as a light to the eyes and a lamp to the feet. It is prized for its prestige value rather than as an organ of personal illumination and liberation. It is prized because it is thought to give unquestionable authenticity and authority to a specific procedure to be carried out in the school room. So conceived, science *is* antagonistic to education as an art.

～

Experience and Abstraction

The history of the more mature sciences shows two characteristics. Their original problems were set by difficulties that offered themselves in the ordinary region of practical affairs. Men obtained fire by rubbing sticks together and noted how things grew warm when they pressed on each other, long before they had any theory of heat. Such everyday experiences in their seeming inconsistency with the phenomena of flame and fire finally led to the conception of heat as a mode of molecular motion. But it led to this conception only when the ordinary phenomena were reflected upon in detachment from the conditions and uses under which they exhibit themselves in practices. There is no science without abstraction, and abstraction means fundamentally that certain occurrences are removed from the dimension of familiar practical experience into that of reflective or theoretical inquiry.

To be able to get away for the time being from entanglement in the urgencies and needs of immediate practical concerns is a condition of the origin of scientific treatment in any field. Preoccupation with attaining some direct end or practical utility, always limits scientific inquiry. For it restricts the field of attention and thought, since we note only those things that are immediately connected with what we want to do or get at the moment. Science signifies that we carry our observations and thinking further afield and become interested in what happens on its own account. Theory is in the end, as has been well said, the most practical of all things, because this widening of the range of attention beyond nearby purpose and desire eventually results in the creation of wider and farther-reaching purposes and enables us to use a much wider and deeper range of conditions and means than were expressed in the observation of primitive practical purposes. For the time being, however, the formation of theories demands a resolute turning aside from the needs of practical operations previously performed.

This detachment is peculiarly hard to secure in the case of those persons who are concerned with building up the scientific content of educational practices and arts. There is a pressure for immediate results, for demonstration of a quick, short-time span of usefulness in school. There is a tendency to convert the results of statistical inquiries and laboratory experiments into directions and rules for the conduct of school administration and instruction. Results tend to be directly grabbed, as it were, and put into operation by teachers. Then there is not the leisure for that slow and gradual independent growth of theories that is a necessary condition of the formation of a true science. This danger is peculiarly imminent in a science of education because its very recentness and novelty arouse skepticism as to its possibility and its value. The human desire to prove that the scientific mode of attack is really of value brings pressure to convert scientific conclusions into rules and standards of schoolroom practice.

It would perhaps be invidious to select examples too near to current situations. Some illustration, however, is needed to give definiteness to what has been said. I select an instance which is remote in time and crude in itself. An investigator found that girls between the ages of eleven and fourteen mature more rapidly than boys of the same age. From this fact, or presumed fact, he drew the inference that during these years boys and girls should be separated for purposes of instruction. He converted an intellectual finding into an immediate rule of school practice.

That the conversion was rash, few would deny. The reason is obvious. School administration and instruction is a much more complex operation than was the one factor contained in the scientific result. The significance of one factor for educational practice can be determined only as it is balanced with many other factors. Taken by itself, this illustration is so crude that to generalize from it might seem to furnish only a caricature. But the principle involved is of universal application. No conclusion of scientific research can be converted into an immediate rule of educational art. For there is no educational practice whatever which is not highly complex; that is to say, which does not contain many other conditions and factors than are included in the scientific finding.

Nevertheless, scientific findings are of practical utility, and the situation is wrongly interpreted when it is used to disparage the value of science in the art of education. What it militates against is the transformation of scientific findings into *rules* of action. Suppose for the moment that the finding about the different rates of maturing in boys and girls of a certain age is confirmed by continued investigation, and is to be accepted as fact. While it does not translate into a specific rule of fixed procedure, it is of some worth. The teacher who really knows this fact will have his personal attitude changed. He will be on the alert to make certain observations which would otherwise escape him; he will be enabled to interpret some facts which would otherwise be confused and misunderstood. This knowledge and understanding render his practice more intelligent, more flexible and better adapted to deal effectively with concrete phenomena of practice.

Nor does this tell the whole story. Continued investigation reveals other relevant facts. Each investigation and conclusion is special, but the tendency of an increasing number and variety of specialized results is to create new points of view and a wider field of observation. Various special findings have a cumulative effect; they reenforce and extend one another, and in time lead to the detection of principles that bind together a number of facts that are diverse and even isolated in their *prima facie* occurrence. These connecting principles which link different phenomena together we call laws.

Facts which are so interrelated form a system, a science. The practitioner who knows the system and its laws is evidently in possession of a powerful instrument for observing and interpreting what goes on before him. This intellectual tool affects his attitudes and modes of response in what he does. Because the range of understanding is deepened and widened he can take into account remote consequences which were originally hidden from view and hence were ignored in his actions. Greater continuity is introduced; he does not isolate situations and deal with them in separation as he was compelled to do when ignorant of connecting principles. At the same time, his practical dealings become more flexible. Seeing more relations he sees more possibilities, more opportunities. He is emancipated from the need of following tradition and special precedents. His ability to judge being enriched, he has a wider range of alternatives to select from in dealing with individual situations.

What Science Means

If we gather up these conclusions in a summary we reach the following results. In the first place, no genuine science is formed by isolated conclusions, no matter how scientifically correct the technique by which these isolated results are reached, and no matter how exact they are. Science does not emerge until these various findings are linked up together to form a relatively coherent system—that is, until they reciprocally confirm and illuminate one another, or until each gives the others added meaning. Now this development requires time, and it requires more time in the degree in which the transition from an empirical condition to a scientific one is recent and hence imperfect.

Illustrations from the Physical Sciences

The physical sciences have a much longer past behind them than psychological and social inquiries. In addition, they deal with subjects that are intrinsically less complex, involving fewer variables. This difference in the degree of maturity is at the bottom of what was said regarding the danger of premature transfer of special scientific findings into educational practice. It explains why scientific investigations regarding educational problems must go on, for a considerable time, in comparative remoteness and detachment from direct application, and why the pressure to demonstrate *immediate* utility in school administration and instruction is dangerous.

The way in which physical science was put upon its present foundations proves the scientific necessity of knowledge of relationships forming a system; it proves also the dependence of this knowledge upon a scheme of *general thought*, if experiments and measurements are to have scientific value. The history of physics proves conclusively that measurements and correlations, no matter how quantitatively exact, cannot yield a science except in connection with general principles which indicate *what* measurements to conduct and *how* they are to be interpreted. Galileo's experiments and measurements form the basis of modern science; they were made in connection with rolling of balls on an inclined plane, movements of pendulums and the dropping of balls from the Leaning Tower of Pisa.

Galileo had, however, first performed an experiment in thought, leading him to the hypothesis that the time of falling bodies is proportional to the square of the space traversed. It was this general idea, arrived at by thinking, that gave point to his experiment in Pisa, and that gave meaning to his measurement of the elapsed time of falling of bodies of various textures and volumes. His conception of what was measured, namely a generalization about relations of space, time and motion as the true objects of physical measurement, gave his measurements scientific status. Without these ideas he would not have known what to measure; he would have measured at random. Nor would he have known the meaning of his measurements after they were made; they would have remained mere intellectual curiosities.

It was also his preliminary hypotheses framed by thought which gave revolutionary import to his measurements of rolling balls. His experiments here and with pendulums went to confirm his theory that bodies in motion continue to move with the same velocity and direction unless externally acted upon. The result in connection with that at Pisa enabled acceleration to be measured and a general formula to be framed. In consequence, there was opened to subsequent experimenters the road of indirect measurement. Indirect measurements through calculation are much more important in science than are direct measurements, the latter merely supplying data and checks. The experimenters knew at the same time *what* they were measuring, namely, relations of mass, space, time, and motion. These general conceptions bound together their specific observations into a system.

12

The Need for a Philosophy of Education (1934)

The final piece in this section, "The Need for a Philosophy of Education," has rather unique origins. It was written for a South African education conference sponsored by a group called the New Education Fellowship. The paper then appeared in the Fellowship's journal *The New Era*. (Both the organization and the journal still exist, though under slightly different names: the World Education Fellowship and *New Era in Education*. The journal's mission, in a nutshell, is to support and promote a holistic education for students infused with themes of peace.) Dewey states at the outset that the need for a philosophy of education coincides with determining "what education actually is." Otherwise, educational philosophy too easily devolves into flights of fancy or uncritically accepts the status quo. As in other places, Dewey equates education with growth—not in the direction of any fixed or ultimate goal, but toward something at once tangible and open-ended across a range of possibilities. The idea is to open doors to new opportunities and experiences, rather than closing them by stifling natural impulses or forcing students down predetermined paths. For this growth to promote self-realization and genuine freedom, it also entails acquiring a democratic spirit of cooperation with others. Competition for the purpose of inflating egos or obtaining extrinsic rewards (e.g., extra credit or special privileges) results inevitably in detachment and divided attention by both teachers and students.

"Progressive education" is a phrase at least of contrast with an education predominantly static in subject-matter, authoritarian in methods, and mainly passive and receptive from the side of the young. But the philosophy of education must go beyond any method of education that is formed by way of contrast, reaction, and protest, as an attempt to discover what education *is* and how it takes place. Only as identified with schooling does a definition of actual education seem simple, though such definition gives the only criterion for judging and directing the work of schools.

Some suppose that the philosophy of education should tell what education *should* be and set up ideals and norms for it. In a sense this proposition is true, but not in the sense usually implied. For the only way of deciding what education should be, and which does not take us too far away from actual conditions and from tangible processes, is discovery of what actually takes place when education really occurs. Any ideal that is a genuine help in carrying on activity must rest upon a prior knowledge of concrete actual occurrences. A metallurgist's ideal of the best possible steel must rest upon knowledge of actual ores and of natural processes. Otherwise his ideal is not a directive idea but a fantasy.

So too with the ideal of education as affecting the philosophy of education we have to know how human nature is constituted in the concrete just as the steel-worker has to know about his raw material, to know about the working of actual social forces and about the operations through which basic raw materials are modified into things of greater value. The need for a philosophy of education is thus fundamentally the need for finding out what education really *is*. We have to take those cases in which we find there is a real development of desirable powers, find out how this development took place, and then project what has taken place as a guide for directing our other efforts. The need for this discovery and this projection is the need for a philosophy of education.

What then is education when we find actual satisfactory specimens of it in existence? Firstly, it is a process of development—of growth, and the *process*, not merely the end result, is important. A truly healthy person is not something fixed and completed. He is one who through his processes and activities will continue to be healthy. He cannot say "I am healthy" and stop at that as if health were bound to continue automatically, otherwise he would soon find himself ill. Similarly, an educated person has the power to go on and get more education, to grow and to expand his development. Hence sometimes learned, erudite persons, as having parted with the capacity to grow, are not educated.

What is growth? What is development? Early philosophers, like Rousseau and his followers, made much use of the analogy of the development of a seed into the full-grown plant, deducing the conclusion that in human beings there are latent capacities which, left to themselves, will ultimately flower and bear fruit. So they framed the notion of a *natural* development, as far as possible left alone, as opposed to a directed growth, direction here being an interference resulting in distortion and corruption of natural powers.

This idea has two fallacies. In the first place seed-growth is limited as compared with human growth; its future is much more prescribed by its antecedent nature; its line of growth is comparatively fixed; it has not the capacities for growth in different directions toward different outcomes characteristic of the human young, which is also, if you please, a seed embodying germinal powers but may develop any of many forms.

This fact suggests the second fallacy. Even the seed of a plant does not grow simply of itself without atmospheric aids. Its development is controlled by external conditions and forces. Native inherent forces must interact with external if there is to be life and development. In brief, development, even with a plant, depends on the *kind of interaction* between itself and its environment. A stunted oak, or a stalk of maize with few ears of scattered grains, exhibits natural development as truly as the noblest tree or the prize-winning ear of maize. The difference in result is due not only to native stock but also to environment; the finest native stock would come to an untimely end, or give a miserable product, if its own energies could not interact with favourable atmospheric conditions.

There being two factors involved in any interaction (and hence in every kind of growth) the idea and ideal of education must take account of both. Native capacities of growth and inherent traits provide the raw material. What is lacking cannot interact with even the very best of conditions; there is then no leverage, nothing with which to cooperate. Traditional school methods and subject-matter fail in three ways to take this factor into account. In the first place, they ignore the *diversity* of capacities and needs of different human beings which constitute *individuality*. They virtually assume that, for purposes of education, all human beings are as much alike as peas in a pod, hence their provision of a uniform curriculum, the same lessons assigned for all, and the same conduct of the recitation.

In the second place, they fail to recognize that the *initiative* in growth comes from the needs and powers of the pupil. The *first* step in the interaction for growth comes from the reaching out of the tentacles of the individual, from an effort, at first blind, to procure the materials that his potentialities demand if they are to come into action and find satisfaction. With the body, hunger and power of taking and assimilating food are the first necessities. Without the inner demand and impetus the most nutritious food is offered in vain; repulsion and indigestion result. No proper system of education could tolerate the common assumption, that the mind of the individual is naturally averse to learning, and has to be either browbeaten or coaxed into action. Every mind, even of the youngest, is naturally seeking for those modes of active operation within the limits of its capacities. The problem is to discover what tendencies are especially seeking expression at a particular time and just what materials and methods will serve to evoke and direct a truly educative development. The practical counterpart of this failure to see the source of initiative lies in the method of imposition by the teacher and of reception by the pupil. The idea of drill is only too suggestive of drilling a hole into a hard and resistant rock by means of repeated monotonous blows. Unwillingness to learn naturally follows failure to take into account tendencies urgent in the existing make-up of an individual. All sorts of external devices then are needed to achieve absorption and retention of imposed subject-matter and skills. This method of teaching may be compared to inscribing records upon a passive phonograph disc to secure their return when the proper button is pressed. Or again the pupil's mind is treated as an empty cistern passively waiting to be filled, while teacher and text-book form the reservoir from which pipelines lead.

The third failure is the result of the two already mentioned. Every teacher must observe that there *are* real differences among pupils. But, because these are not carried back to concrete differences of individuality in needs, in desires, in direction of native interest, they are too often generalized under two main heads. Some pupils are bright, others dull and stupid! Some are docile and obedient, others unruly and troublesome! Inability to fit into a cast-iron scheme of subject-matter or to meet the requirements of the set discipline is taken as a sign of either radical intrinsic incapacity or deliberate willfulness. Conformity then becomes the criterion of judgment in spite of the value of initiative, originality and independence in life.

While the raw material and the starting-point of growth are found in native capacities, the environing conditions to be furnished by the educator are the indispensable means of their development. They are not, and do not of themselves decide, the end. A gardener, a worker of metals, must observe and pay attention to the properties of his material. If he permits these properties in their original form to dictate his treatment, he will not get *anywhere*. If they decide his end, he will fixate raw materials in their primitive state. Development will be arrested, not promoted. He must bring to his consideration of his material an idea, an ideal, of possibilities not realized, which must be in line with the constitution of his plant or ore; it must not do violence to them; it must be *their* possibilities. Yet it cannot be extracted from any study of their present form but from seeing them imaginatively, reflectively, and hence from another source.

Similarly with the educator, save that the demand on him for imaginative insight into possibilities is greater. The gardener and worker in metals may take as their measures results already achieved with plants and ores, although originality and invention will introduce some variation. But the true educator while using results already accomplished cannot make them his final and complete standard. Like the artist he has the problem of creating something that is not the exact duplicate of some previous creation.

In any case, development and growth involve change and modification in definite directions. A teacher, under the supposed sanction of the idea of cultivating individuality, may fixate a pupil more or less at his existing level, confusing respect for individual traits with a catering for their present estate. Respect for individuality is primarily the *intellectual* study of the individual to discover material. With this sympathetic understanding the *practical* work then begins of modification, of changing, of reconstruction continued without end. The change must at least be toward more effective techniques, greater self-reliance, a more thoughtful and inquiring disposition more capable of persistent effort in meeting obstacles.

Some would-be progressive schools and teachers in their reaction from the method of external imposition stop short with the recognition of the importance of giving free scope to native capacities and interests. They do not examine closely or long enough what these may actually be; they judge too much from superficial and transitory reactions to accidental circumstances. In the second place, they are inclined to take the evident individual traits as finalities instead of as possibilities for suitable direction into something of greater significance. Under the alleged sanction of not violating freedom and individuality the responsibility for providing development conditions is overlooked. The idea persists that evolution and development are simply matters of automatic unfolding from within.

This is a natural reaction from the manifest evils of external imposition. But there is a radically different alternative between thinking of the young as clay to be moulded into traditional patterns and thinking of existing capacities and present interests and desires as laying down the whole law of development. Existing likes and powers are to be treated as possibilities necessary for any healthy development. But development involves a point of direction as well as a starting-point with constant movement in that direction, and the direction-point, as the temporary goal, is reached only as the starting-point of further reconstruction. The great problem of the educator is to see intellectually, and to feel deeply, the forces moving in the young as possibilities, as signs and promises, and to interpret them in the light of what they may become. Nor does the exacting task end there: it is bound up with the judging and devising of the conditions, the materials, the tools—physical, moral, and social—which will, once more by *interaction* with existing powers and preferences, bring about the desired transformation.

The old education emphasised the necessity for provision of definite subject-matter and activities, which *are* necessities for right education. The weakness was that its imagination did not go beyond provision of a rigid environment of subject-matter drawn from sources remote from any concrete experiences of the taught. Its conception of techniques was derived from the conventions of the past. The New Education needs more attention, not less, to subject-matter and to progress in technique for getting satisfactory results. More does not, however, mean more in quantity of the same old kind but an imaginative vision, which sees that no prescribed and ready-made scheme can determine the exact subject-matter for the educative growth of each individual, since each sets a new problem and calls for at least a somewhat different emphasis in either subject-matter or angle of presentation. Only blindly obtuse convention supposes that the actual contents of text-books will further the educational development of all children, or of any one child, if they be regarded as the prescription of a doctor to be taken just as they are. As [Robert] Louis Stevenson remarked, "the world is full of a number of things," and no teacher can know too much or have too ingenious an imagination in selecting and adapting this and that aspect of some of the many things in the world to meet the requirements that make for growth in this and that individual.

In short, departure from the rigidity of the old curriculum is only the negative side. If we do not go on and go far in the positive direction of providing, through persistent intelligent study and experiment, a body of subject-matter much richer, more varied and flexible, and also more definite in terms of the experience of those being educated, we shall tend to leave an educational vacuum in which anything may happen. The old saying that "nature abhors a vacuum" embodies a definite truth. Complete isolation is impossible in nature. The young live in some environment constantly interacting with what the young bring to it, and the result is the shaping of their interests, minds and characters—either educatively or mis-educatively. If the professed educator abdicates his responsibility for judging and selecting the kind of environment conducive, in his best understanding, to growth, then the young are left at the mercy of all the unorganized and casual forces that inevitably play upon them throughout life. In the educative environment the knowledge, judgment, or experience of the teacher becomes a greater, not a smaller factor. He now operates not as a magistrate set on high and possessed of arbitrary authority but as a friendly co-partner and guide in a common enterprise.

There is a further truism about education as development, difficult to carry out in practice and easily violated. Development is a *continuous* process and continually signifies consecutiveness of action—the strong point of the traditional education at its best. The subject-matter of the classics and mathematics involved a consecutive and orderly development along definite lines. In the newer education it is comparatively easy to improvise, to try a little of this to-day and something else tomorrow, on the basis of some immediate stimulus but without sufficient regard to its objective or whether or not something more difficult is led up to naturally, raising new questions and calling for acquisition of more adequate technique and for new modes of skill. There is genuine need for taking account of spontaneous interest and activity but, without care and thought, it readily results in a detached multiplicity of isolated brief-lived activities or projects, not in continuity of growth. Indeed, the new educational processes require much more planning ahead by the teachers, for whom the old planning was all effected in advance by the fixed curriculum, etc.

But a sound philosophy of education also requires that the general term environment be specified as dominantly human with its values social. Through its influence each person becomes saturated with the customs, the beliefs, the purposes, skills, hopes and fears, of his own cultural group. The features of even his physical surroundings come to him through the eyes and ears of his community. His geographical, climatical, and atmospherical experiences are clothed with the memories and traditions, the characteristic associations, of his particular society. In the early stages, then, it is particularly important that subject-matter be presented in its human context and setting. Here the school often fails when, in proceeding from the concrete to the abstract, it forgets that to the child only that which has human value and function is concrete. In his nature study and geography, physical things are presented to him from the standpoint of the adult specialist as if independent and complete in themselves. But to the child these things have a meaning only as they enter into human life. Even those distinctively human products, reading and writing, whose purpose is the furthering of human communication and association, are treated as if they were subjects of and in themselves, not used as is friendly everyday speech, and so for the child they become abstract, a mystery belonging to the school but not to daily life.

The same separation of school studies from social or human setting and function deadens the traditional recitation which, instead of being a scene of friendly intercourse as are the conversations of home and of ordinary life, clarified and organised by definite purpose, becomes an artificial exercise in repeating uniformly the identical material of some one text-book and a mere test of the faithfulness of the preparation. It thus becomes a first cause of the isolation of school from out-of-school life and experience.

As the material of genuine development is that of human contacts and associations, so the end, the value that is the criterion and directing guide of educational work, is social. The acquisition however perfectly of skills is not an end in itself. They are things to be put to use as a contribution to a common and shared life. They are intended, indeed, to make an individual more capable of self-support and of self-respecting independence. But unless this end is placed in the context of services rendered to others, services which they need to the fulfilment also of their lives, skills gained will be put to an egoistic and selfish use as means of a trained shrewdness for personal advantage at the cost of others' claims and opportunities for the good life. Too often, indeed, the schools, through reliance upon the spur of competition and the bestowal of special honours and prizes as for those who excel in a competitive race or even battle, only build up and strengthen the disposition that in after-school life employs special talents and superior skill to outwit others and "get on" personally without respect for their welfare.

And as with skills acquired in school so also with knowledge gained in school. The educational end and the ultimate test of the value of what is learned is its use and application in carrying on and improving the common life of all. The background of the traditional educational system is a class society, and opportunity for instruction in certain subjects, especially literary ones, and in mathematics beyond the rudiments of simple arithmetical subjects, was reserved for the well-born and the well-to-do, and thus knowledge of these subjects became a badge of cultural superiority and social status, which marked off those who had it from the vulgar herd and for many persons was a means of self-display. Useful knowledge, on the other hand, was necessary only for those compelled by their class status to work for a living. A class stigma attached to it, and the uselessness of knowledge, save for purely personal culture, was proof of its higher quality.

Even after education in many countries was made universal for all, these standards of value persisted. There is no greater egotism than that of learning when treated simply as a mark of personal distinction to be cherished for its own sake. Yet to eliminate this quality of exclusiveness all conditions of the school environment must tend in actual practice to develop in individuals the realization that knowledge is a trust for the furthering of the well-being of all.

Perhaps the greatest need of and for a philosophy of education to-day is the urgent need that exists for making clear in idea and effective in practice the social character of its end and that the criterion of value of school practices is social.

The aim of education is development of individuals to the utmost of their potentialities. But this statement as such leaves unanswered the question of the measure of the development to be desired and worked for. A society of free individuals in which all, in doing each his own work, contribute to the liberation and enrichment of the lives of others is the only environment for the normal growth to full stature. An environment in which some are limited will always in reaction create conditions that prevent the full development even of those who fancy they enjoy complete freedom for unhindered growth.

There are two outstanding reasons why in existing world conditions a philosophy of education must make the social aim of education the central article in its creed. The world is being rapidly industrialized. Individual groups, tribes and races, once living completely untouched by the economic regime of modern capitalistic industry, now find almost every phase of their lives affected by its expansion. The principle of a report of the Geneva Commission based on a study of conditions of life of mine-Natives in South Africa holds good of peoples all over the world, "The investment of Western capital in African industries has made the Native dependent upon the demand of the world markets for the products of his labour and the resources of his continent." In a world that has so largely engaged in a mad, often brutal, race for material gain by means of ruthless competition the school must make ceaseless and intelligently organized effort to develop above all else the will for cooperation and the spirit which sees in every other individual an equal right to share in the cultural and material fruits of collective human invention, industry, skill and knowledge. The supremacy of this aim in mind and character is necessary, not merely as an offset to the spirit of inhumanity bred by economic competition and exploitation but to prepare the coming generation for an inevitable new and more just and humane society which, unless hearts and minds are prepared by education, is likely to come attended with all the evils of social changes by violence.

The other especially urgent need is connected with the present unprecedented wave of nationalistic sentiment, of racial and national prejudice, of readiness to resort to force of arms. For this spirit to have arisen on such a scale the schools must have somehow failed grievously. Their best excuse is maybe that schools and educators were caught unawares. But that excuse is no longer available. We now know the enemy; it is out in the open. Unless the schools of the world can unite in effort to rebuild the spirit of common understanding, of mutual sympathy and goodwill among all peoples and races, to exorcise the demon of prejudice, isolation and hatred, they themselves are likely to be submerged by the general return to barbarism, the sure outcome of present tendencies if unchecked by the forces which education alone can evoke and fortify.

It is to this great work that any ideal worthy of the name of education summons the educational forces of all countries.

V

THE INDIVIDUAL AND SOCIETY IN DEMOCRATIC EDUCATION

13

Individuality in Education (1922)

Section V opens with "Individuality in Education." Like "The Classroom Teacher," it was prepared for the Massachusetts State Conference of Normal School Instructors. Dewey's remarks begin with an intentionally broad definition of individuality. Along with readily perceptible differences between people, individuality, he tells us, comprises each person's "irreplaceable uniqueness in value." That is to say, individuals contribute most fruitfully to democratic life and relationships through unique ways of "doing things, thinking things, and feeling things." This uniqueness goes beyond mere surface features and conduct to deeper personal qualities. As such it is an achievement, requiring a supportive and nurturing environment, and not a given. Unfortunately, Dewey observes, this uniqueness is easily endangered by school and classroom policies and procedures that sacrifice uniqueness and plurality for greater uniformity. (Some of this uniformity reflects social norms often referred to as the "hidden curriculum.") The physical culture of schools (e.g., self-contained classrooms with individual desks in rows) is an obvious means of promoting increased uniformity. Dewey, however, focuses on the harm to individuality caused by intellectual restraints that hinder the development of students' "unique and distinctive minds." He also reminds us that the creation of genuine forms of individuality cannot be realized, and uniqueness cultivated, without the habits necessary for active participation in social life.

∽

There are, I think, two important elements in individuality. First, is the distinctive difference, something that marks off one person from another. A noted philosopher, in emphasizing the principles of individuality, said that if one were to take all the leaves on all of the trees in the world, it would be impossible to find two leaves exactly alike. Two oaks or two maples might resemble each other, but there would be no duplicate. Certainly, as we go up the scale in existence, this element of diversity of distinction becomes more important. In the lower forms of life, for example, there is little difference of parts; the cells are all very much like each other. All jellyfish resemble each other. When we get to the height of the scale of life, to human beings, we find differences of parts, differences of form of structure, instead of similarity or close resemblance. One person is marked off from another; it is easy to tell them apart. However, this distinctiveness or difference, by itself would not give all that is really valuable in individuality. We may have two pennies and two nickels of different years and of different design, but we do not care about this difference,—one is just as good as the other. We do not care as long as one will buy as much as the other.

This additional principle of individuality means this: there is not merely difference or distinction, but something unique or irreplaceable in value, an unique difference of value. Human beings are not like the nickel or mechanical products which are as much like each other as peas in the pod. As long as we get peas enough we do not care which individual pea. They become substitutes for each other. When we get human individuals, we get the principle that each individual has something that is unique or irreplaceable. No one else will quite take his place in the world or do quite the same thing that he will do. I think that is what we mean by the idea of equality. We do not mean that people are physiologically or psychologically equal, but we do mean that every human being who is normal has something so distinctive that no other individual can be substituted for him.

The principle of individuality, then, is having a place and work in the world that no one else can quite do. This gives us a measure. The more mechanical, the more things are similar to each other; but as we rise to what is vital, rise in the sphere of life to what is spiritual, moral and intellectual, the principle of individuality counts for more and more. That is why the principle of individuality has such claims in education. It is the measure of whatever is elevating in the rank of life in spiritual, moral and intellectual beings.

The difficulties are practical rather than theoretical, when we come to the individual in education. On the theoretical side I think they come largely from a misapprehension of the meaning of individuality. The first misapprehension is that we often confuse individuality with "bumptiousness," or conceit, or self-assertion, or some kind of aggressiveness, instead of having something of distinctive worth or value to contribute to life. Real individuality is unconscious rather than conscious or self-conscious. Individuality is a particular way of feeling things, thinking things, and doing things, something which goes into, colors and dyes everything which a person has to do with.

Take, for example, two persons. Each uses the words, "I think." One emphasizes the "I." What he thinks may be very commonplace and may be what everyone else thinks is so; but because he emphasizes "*I* think,"—"I am the oracle; when I open my mouth let no dog bark." Another person says, "I *think* so and so." He may refer to something that is familiar and commonplace, but we will be struck by something distinctive, some peculiar form, something original in the particular expression about that very common thing. That illustrates what is meant by my saying that individuality is a certain way of doing things, thinking things, and feeling things, which runs through everything and gives it its peculiar color, something which irradiates unconsciously whatever the person has to deal with.

The opposition to the theory and practice of the principles of individuality in education seems to me to be based in a large measure upon the supposition that the recognition means something of the nature of conscious assertion of individuality, conceit, a kind of "bumptiousness." It is quite possible that some teachers, under the guise of individuality, are really simply engaged in cultivating this "bumptiousness," that is, giving the pupil an exaggerated idea of his own importance as compared with that of other people. What we need, then, is to view this matter right; to get rid of the notion that connects individuality with the conscious idea of importance and associate it rather with the more subtle characteristics of individuality, which make the person distinctive and stamp his personality in a more or less unconscious way upon everything that the person has to do with.

The personality to be recognized means that each one of us has his own bias, his own preferences, his own instinctive tendency to prefer, not only things, but also ways of doing things. Our respect for individuality does not mean that the teacher shall single out the pupil and make him think his ideas are more important than others, but rather give opportunity to the pupils to give expression to their own special interests and their own special ways of approach, instead of trying to impose purely artificial beliefs and standards.

Take an instance which may be somewhat exaggerated, but which still is found in many schools. Children are given problems in arithmetic. The teacher believes there is one scientific and proper method of approaching these problems. One child does the problem in a way which diverges from the orthodox conventional method laid down by the text-book, the teacher, or the particular course of study. Instead of recognizing something valuable, something precious, something to be encouraged, the teacher frowns upon the pupil and insists on the adoption of a certain uniform method of arranging the result.

In less extreme cases than that, teachers are emphasizing the value of uniformity, tending to suppress this distinctive angle of approach on the part of the pupil. This emphasis on the uniformity of approach tends to get the better of the natural individual way of dealing with the subject on the part of the pupil.

The grammar of old-fashioned teaching, the analysis of arithmetical problems, comes, from the standpoint of the children, to mean certain forms of words with changing figures. For example, a child in the third grade told his parents that they had in the third grade a new kind of multiplication from that of the second grade. The child said: "Last year we always said 'two times two is four cents,' and this year we say, 'two times two are four cents.'" Now this is extreme; but it illustrates the tendency to exaggerate or encourage uniformity, certain common forms of doing, instead of rightly assisting every individual to go at the matter in his own way.

I think that this is responsible for the disregard or even contempt in which many people outside of the teaching profession hold the whole matter of teaching or pedagogy. They have somehow come to associate every idea of pedagogy and every idea of method with a formulated, uniform way of doing things, while in actual life we realize that the individual should have his own way of doing things, throwing individuality into whatever he does.

Individuality really means a certain originality of method. Originality is not to be measured by newness or originality of product. Very few people can produce things really original in any important measure, but anyone can contribute something of originality to the way he goes at things.

Mr. [Samuel McChord] Crothers tells of a gentleman of an exploring turn of mind who climbed a tree to view the landscape, and as he climbed he saw a body of water. Coming down, he proclaimed he had discovered the Pacific Ocean. It turned out to be nothing but a local and circumscribed pond. He had the disposition, and if the Pacific Ocean had only been there he *would* have discovered it, for his heart was in the right place. We are not going to discover Pacific Oceans; we are only going to discover ponds; but nevertheless, there is possible an element of originality on the part of teachers and pupils in the way of discovering ponds and even puddles.

Why is it that children are such a constant source of delight to most grown people? Certainly the parents and fond relatives feel there is and never was anything like this baby. They somehow appreciate the uncommonness or originality of the small child, and feel that he has a certain element of original genius in him. Where does this all go to? Later on children become so much alike. Perhaps in earlier years it is because we recognize that the child is engaged in discovering a new world. He has to do it himself,—this discovering his own world,—and he cannot do it through anyone else's thoughts or feelings.

It is not a false belief that makes fond parents and relatives attribute originality to small children. There must be something wrong with the school and the home and the neighborhood if we allow this quality of originality to die out, and expect the individuals later on to be more or less copies of each other. It is a question if the school is not somehow or other responsible for the elimination of this individuality, because of the undue emphasis put on foreign matter, on strictly uniform methods of demonstration and instruction, on uniformity of subject matter, ground to be covered, and so on.

In the second place individuality is something that is internal and intellectual, rather than something which is external and physical. I have noticed, in the criticisms on ideas of freedom in the school, that it is generally assumed that individuality means a large amount of physical unrestraint: children "doing as they please;" something external and physical rather than internal and mental. There may be a great deal of "doing as a pupil pleases," absence of restraint, a great deal of physical activity, with very little display of individuality, with very little opportunity for individuality.

If you will notice a group of children under unusual circumstances, perhaps under some constraint, you will find that if one boy begins to "rough-house," others imitate him, and you get a scene of disorderliness. They are not displaying their individuality, but, on the contrary, they are imitating each other, for disorderliness is very largely imitation among children. The mere absence of physical restraint, or its presence, has practically nothing to do with the matter of individuality. Individuality is rather a distinctive way in which a person in his feelings and desires approaches any subject matter or any piece of work he has to do; that is, the way he puts himself into it. This does not mean that the presence or absence of physical restraint has nothing to do with the matter. It does,—but it is not an end in itself.

Respect for individuality certainly means that the teacher should respect his or her own individuality. Sometimes teachers carry respect of pupils' individuality to a point where they lack respect for their own individuality.

There is need for more outward freedom than is permitted in many schools; much more than was permitted in the traditional school, with the emphasis upon quiet, upon silence, upon physical immobility. The question of the amount and degree of activity has something to do with this matter of real individuality, but it is a question of *means* and conditions, rather than ends. We need enough physical freedom and mobility so the students can express their mental individuality, but we do not need any more.

I think the laboratory gives a good example of what I mean. The individual has to be using his hands, doing things, but his experimenting in the laboratory is not simply running wild and at random. He has to have enough physical activity to see that his ideas are made definite and precise; that he is getting principles rather than taking information on faith at the word of the teacher or textbook.

We need, on the whole, more elbow-room for activity of the outer sort, more freedom and spontaneity of action in the school room and on the playground than we usually get, not because that is the act of self-expression or end in itself, but because, with a certain degree of elbow-room we can get opportunity for the students to think for themselves, to work out their own plans, to formulate their own problems, to carry their ideas into execution, and to test their plans and ideas to determine how they work out.

That is one thing I meant, then, when I said that the difficulties are practical rather than theoretical. Real individuality is intellectual, inner, rather than physical. We talk about thinking for one's self. After all, the words "for one's self" are superfluous or redundant. It is not thought unless it is for one's self. To develop thinking we must have respect for the individual element, the distinctive element, which is unreplaceable in the workings of the mind. Respect for individuality is in its essence respect for the mind and the workings of the mind; and the teacher who has respect and reverence for individuality has reverence for the human spirit and for whatever is characteristic in the work of the human spirit. He recognizes that that which marks off humanity from the physical is that in the physical sphere we can have uniformity, a unit can be standardized. We find here the difference between the factory and the school. The factory deals with dead things, inanimate things, where one piece can replace another. This condition makes for economy and efficiency. The spirit, or soul, or mind is the element that cannot be standardized in this mechanical way without doing damage to the mind and reducing it to a lower level.

There is a third misapprehension. It is that individuality means a sort of isolation; that it is unsocial rather than social. Now exactly the contrary is the case. Only in social groups does a person have a chance to develop individuality. On the other hand, the more you get identical similarity and repetition in a number of persons, the more you are eliminating both individuality and the social element. We would not think of holding up a prison as a model of community life, but it is there that individuals are reduced to units like others, known by numbers not by name, with the chain-gang and the lock-step, attempting to have everyone do the same thing at the same time. In the community life of the ideal sort, the family marked by the spirit of unity, the town, or the nation, the more you have of real social unity the more diversity, the more division of labor, and the more differentiation of operations there is.

I think we owe a great deal to Madame [Maria] Montessori, but she has misled herself and others in assuring that there must be isolation or separation in order to get individuality; that each child must be doing something by himself rather than working with others; that it is impossible to combine the two principles of school work with the development of individuality. I think quite the opposite is the case. Children, of course, need a certain amount of isolation. They must get off by themselves and have time to think. This is true; but in the main, the best stimulus to the inventiveness and the ingenuity of the child, the calling out of his own individuality, is found when the individual is working with others, where there is a common project, something of interest to them all, but where each has his own part. There may be classes where there is no unity. There may be classes where there is no social group. Here again our emphasis on the class as a unit has not only had a tendency to depress, if not eliminate respect for individuality in education, but has also tended to eliminate the social element in education.

There is a good deal of talk about socializing the recitation. The word recitation to most minds suggests a uniform rehearsal. All the pupils are asked questions on the same subject matter, and if all of them have learned their lesson they are able to say the same thing in about the same way. Now what is there social about that? As all have the same book, the only child who would learn anything is the one who has not done his duty. The others sit there more or less bored. The result is, of course, that the motive instead of being social is purely competitive. One child is measured against another. If we are going to socialize the recitation, pupils must have an opportunity for the assignment of different matter, and each be required to make his own contribution. A large part of the value of the library is that it affords an opportunity to socialize the recitation by diversifying assignments, providing for different phases of the subject matter, so that the recitation period, instead of being a uniform recital, gives different responsibilities, so that the recitation becomes a clearing-house, a place of exchange, an intellectual give and take, where each person has something to give and also something to receive from the special studies which others have made. Thus you socialize and also individualize the recitation, and eliminate mechanical uniformity from the recitation.

Suppose you meet someone from Mexico. He tells you what he has seen there, of his own experiences. You are interested. He communicates to you something of his personal interest in the place. Now you meet him again, one, two, three, four, five, six, seven times. Each time he tells you of the same experiences, and then asks you questions about what he has told you of Mexico. Wouldn't you lose interest in Mexico? Wouldn't you dodge around the corner whenever you saw your friend coming?

How much of the children's aversion is thus caused? Is the mind really averse to learning? Isn't there an intellectual appetite for new books, new horizons, new outlooks? Haven't we imposed mechanical uniformity upon the minds of pupils, preventing them from displaying their own interests and preferences? Isn't that largely responsible for this acquired aversion to books and to study?

A mother was deploring the lack of interest of her boy in reading what she considered good classical literature. She said, "We never have suggested anything, but that he would reply, in an abrupt way, 'Oh, I have had that.'" His work in the university had not stimulated him to further reading, or to read literature of a different type. It was something he had been compelled to do, and had left him with an aversion to reading.

I think it would be possible to destroy a boy's interest in playing marbles and baseball by reducing it to prescribed exercises to be gone through in a regular way according to set instructions and at a certain time. The real reason why children are interested in play is not because of innate depravity, but because we have permitted the elements of individuality to remain in play, while we have unnecessarily eliminated them from what we call studies.

To go back to the point,—the problem of developing the individual is not a problem of isolating the child, is not giving something different to each, but rather in finding some community project in which each can take his own part, and in the carrying out of which each can make his own contribution.

It is like the life of the home, where the child is happier when he can do something with and for the parents than he is when shut off by himself and has no sense of participating in any undertaking in which others are engaged. The kind of individuality developed is that which is developed in some sort of social give and take, participating with one another. It is something where the different parts fit together, and the child knows that he, as an individual, contributes to what others are doing.

Now, my remarks, especially about the common apprehensions and confusions, if I may inject a personal element here, are largely a result of a somewhat prolonged experience. Trying to stand for freedom in dealing with teaching, I have found that I have been considered by many as upholding the doctrine "that children should do exactly as they please." Therefore, I was led to analyze more carefully what I really did believe, and I had to admit that I had set out without knowing what the real meaning of individuality was. I have tried to give you the net results of my thinking on this matter, to put the place and importance of individuality in a way which would inevitably avoid harmful apprehensions,—equally harmful whether accepted or rejected.

To sum up the points I have made: first, there is undue emphasis on the conscious acts. We are training the pupil to argue rather than to think. Second, there is undue emphasis on the external or more physical element of freedom of action. This latter is certainly important, but is a means and condition for developing the intellectual and moral element, rather than the end in itself. Third, there is an idea that to develop individuality means a sort of isolation or separation of one person from another, something opposed to the community spirit. Robinson Crusoe did not cease to be a social individual just because he was by himself on an island. He had his memories, his expectations, his experiences, which had come from his former association with other people.

You cannot define individuality physically or externally. It is a matter of spirit, of soul, of mind, and the way in which one enters into cooperative relations with others.

14

Education and Social Change (1937)

With the US struggling to recover from the Great Depression, Dewey contributed an article called "Education and Social Change" to the Progressive Era journal *Social Frontier*. Given the time, many reform-minded educators were questioning whether or not schools could be used to leverage significant social change. Moreover, they asked, *should* schools be used in this way? And if so, how? (Some of this discussion was fueled by George S. Counts's 1932 speech, and subsequent book, *Dare the Schools Build a New Social Order?*, which appeared to promote indoctrination in schools to bring about social change.) Other educators believed schools should promote social efficiency, economic stability, and employable skills by equipping new immigrants, students of color, and the poor for work in the industrial economy. (This was ostensibly justified by intelligence tests and "ability grouping.") Dewey insists, however, that schools be conceived as agencies of democratic life and not uncritically affirm and reproduce existing inequalities. Nor can they accomplish utopian reforms. Rather, schools should contribute to society through ongoing, incremental change by fostering democratic habits and "courageous intelligence and responsibility." Dewey clearly recognizes that this is no simple task, especially in a society where "social confusion and conflict" often prevail in public life, including the governance of public schools. Still, he refuses the kind of skepticism that leads inevitably to inaction and defeatism. Our commitment to democracy, Dewey counsels, must be our point of reference for nurturing in students the attitudes and habits necessary for meaningful social change.

Upon certain aspects of my theme there is nothing new to be said. Attention has been continually called of late to the fact that society is in process of change, and that the schools tend to lag behind. We are all familiar with the pleas that are urged to bring education in the schools into closer relation with the forces that are producing social change and with the needs that arise from these changes. Probably no question has received so much attention in educational discussion during the last few years as the problem of integration of the schools with social life. Upon these general matters, I could hardly do more than reiterate what has often been said.

Nevertheless, there is as yet little consensus of opinion as to what the schools can do in relation to the forces of social change and how they should do it. There are those who assert in effect that the schools must simply reflect social changes that have already occurred, as best they may. Some would go so far as to make the work of schools virtually parasitic. Others hold that the schools should take an active part in *directing* social change, and share in the construction of a new social order. Even among the latter there is, however, marked difference of attitude. Some think the schools should assume this directive role by means of indoctrination; others oppose this method. Even if there were more unity of thought than exists, there would still be the practical problem of overcoming institutional inertia so as to realize in fact an agreed-upon program.

There is, accordingly, no need to justify further discussion of the problem of the relation of education to social change. I shall do what I can, then, to indicate the factors that seem to me to enter into the problem, together with some of the reasons that prove that the schools do have a role—and an important one—in *production* of social change.

One factor inherent in the situation is that schools *do* follow and reflect the social "order" that exists. I do not make this statement as a grudging admission, nor yet in order to argue that they should *not* do so. I make it rather as a statement of a *conditioning* factor which supports the conclusion that the schools thereby do take part in the determination of a future social order; and that, accordingly, the problem is not whether the schools *should* participate in the production of a future society (since they do so anyway) but whether they should do it blindly and irresponsibly or with the maximum possible of courageous intelligence and responsibility.

The grounds that lead me to make this statement are as follows: The existing state of society, which the schools reflect, is not something fixed and uniform. The idea that such is the case is a self-imposed hallucination.

Social conditions are not only in process of change, but the changes going on are in different directions, so different as to produce social confusion and conflict. There is no single and clear-cut pattern that pervades and holds together in a unified way the social conditions and forces that operate. It would be easy to cite highly respectable authorities who have stated, as matter of historic fact and not on account of some doctrinal conclusion to be drawn, that social conditions in all that affects the relations of human beings to one another have changed more in the last one hundred and fifty years than in all previous time, and that the process of change is still going on. It requires a good deal of either ignorance or intellectual naiveté to suppose that these changes have all been tending to one coherent social outcome. The plaint of the conservative about the imperiling of old and time-tried values and truths, and the efforts of reactionaries to stem the tide of changes that occur, are sufficient evidence, if evidence be needed to the contrary.

Of course the schools have mirrored the social changes that take place. The efforts of Horace Mann and others a century ago to establish a public, free, common school system were a reflection primarily of the social conditions that followed the war by the colonies for political independence and the establishment of republican institutions. The evidential force of this outstanding instance would be confirmed in detail if we went through the list of changes that have taken place in (1) the kind of schools that have been established, (2) the new courses that have been introduced, (3) the shifts in subject-matter that have occurred, and (4) the changes in methods of instruction and discipline that have occurred in intervening years. The notion that the educational system has been static is too absurd for notice; it has been and still is in a state of flux.

The fact that it is possible to argue about the desirability of many of the changes that have occurred, and to give valid reasons for deploring aspects of the flux, is not relevant to the main point. For the stronger the arguments brought forth on these points, and the greater the amount of evidence produced to show that the educational system is in a state of disorder and confusion, the greater is the proof that the schools have responded to, and have reflected, social conditions which are themselves in a state of confusion and conflict.

Do those who hold the idea that the schools should not attempt to give direction to social change accept complacently the confusion that exists, because the schools *have* followed in the track of one social change after another? They certainly do not, although the logic of their position demands it. For the most part they are severe critics of the existing state of education. They are as a rule opposed to the studies called modern and the methods called progressive. They tend to favor return to older types of studies and to strenuous "disciplinary" methods. What does this attitude mean? Does it not show that its advocates in reality adopt the position that the schools can do something to affect positively and constructively social conditions? For they hold in effect that the school should discriminate with respect to the social forces that play upon it; that instead of accepting the latter *in toto,* education should select and organize in a given direction. The adherents of this view can hardly believe that the effect of selection and organization will stop at the doors of school rooms. They must expect some ordering and healing influence to be exerted sooner or later upon the structure and movement of life outside. What they are really doing when they deny directive social effect to education is to express their opposition to some of the directions social change is actually taking, and their choice of other social forces as those with which education should throw in its lot so as to promote as far as may be their victory in the strife of forces. They are conservatives in education because they are socially conservative and vice-versa.

This is as it should be in the interest of clearness and consistency of thought and action. If these conservatives in education were more aware of what is involved in their position, and franker in stating its implications, they would help bring out the real issue. It is not whether the schools shall or shall not influence the course of future social life, but in what direction they shall do so and how. In some fashion or other, the schools will influence social life anyway. But they can exercise such influence in different ways and to different ends, and the important thing is to become conscious of these different ways and ends, so that an intelligent choice may be made, and so that if opposed choices are made, the further conflict may at least be carried on with understanding of what is at stake, and not in the dark.

There are three possible directions of choice. Educators may act so as to perpetuate the present confusion and possibly increase it. That will be the result of drift, and under present conditions to drift is in the end to make a choice. Or they may select the newer scientific, technological, and cultural forces that are producing change in the old order; may estimate the direction in which they are moving and their outcome if they are given freer play, and see what can be done to make the schools their ally. Or, educators may become intelligently conservative and strive to make the schools a force in maintaining the old order intact against the impact of new forces.

If the second course is chosen—as of course I believe it should be—the problem will be other than merely that of accelerating the rate of the change that is going on. The problem will be to develop the insight and understanding that will enable the youth who go forth from the schools to take part in the great work of construction and organization that will have to be done, and to equip them with the attitudes and habits of action that will make their understanding and insight practically effective.

There is much that can be said for an intelligent conservatism. I do not know anything that can be said for perpetuation of a wavering, uncertain, confused condition of social life and education. Nevertheless, the easiest thing is to refrain from fundamental thinking and let things go on drifting. Upon the basis of any other policy than drift—which after all is a policy, though a blind one—every special issue and problem, whether that of selection and organization of subject-matter of study, of methods of teaching, of school buildings and equipment, of school administration, is a special phase of the inclusive and fundamental problem: What movement of social forces, economic, political, religious, cultural, shall the school take to be controlling in its aims and methods, and with which forces shall the school align itself?

Failure to discuss educational problems from this point of view but intensifies the existing confusion. Apart from this background, and outside of this perspective, educational questions have to be settled *ad hoc* and are speedily unsettled. What is suggested does not mean that the schools shall throw themselves into the political and economic arena and take sides with some party there. I am not talking about parties; I am talking about social forces and their movement. In spite of absolute claims that are made for this party or that, it is altogether probable that existing parties and sects themselves suffer from existing confusions and conflicts, so that the understanding, the ideas, and attitudes that control their policies, need re-education and re-orientation. I know that there are some who think that the implications of what I have said point to abstinence and futility; that they negate the stand first taken. But I am surprised when educators adopt this position, for it shows a profound lack of faith in their own calling. It assumes that education as education has nothing or next to nothing to contribute; that formation of understanding and disposition counts for nothing; that only immediate overt action counts and that it can count equally whether or not it has been modified by education.

Before leaving this aspect of the subject, I wish to recur to the utopian nature of the idea that the schools can be completely neutral. This idea sets up an end incapable of accomplishment. So far as it is acted upon, it has a definite social effect, but that effect is, as I have said, perpetuation of disorder and increase of blind because unintelligent conflict. Practically, moreover, the weight of such action falls upon the reactionary side. Perhaps the most effective way of re-inforcing reaction under the name of neutrality, consists in keeping the oncoming generation ignorant of the conditions in which they live and the issues they have to face. This effect is the more pronounced because it is subtle and indirect; because neither teachers nor those taught are aware of what they are doing and what is being done to them. Clarity can develop only in the extent to which there is frank acknowledgment of the basic issue: Where shall the social emphasis of school life and work fall, and what are the educational policies which correspond to this emphasis?

So far I have spoken of those who assert, in terms of the views of a conservative group, the doctrine of complete impotence of education. But it is an old story that politics makes strange bed fellows. There is another group which holds the schools are completely impotent; that they so necessarily reflect the dominant economic and political regime, that they are committed, root and branch, to its support. This conclusion is based upon the belief that the organization of a given society is fixed by the control exercised by a particular economic class, so that the school, like every other social institution, is of necessity the subservient tool of a dominant class. This viewpoint takes literally the doctrine that the school can only reflect the existing social order. Hence the conclusion in effect that it is a waste of energy and time to bother with the schools. The only way, according to advocates of this theory, to change education in any important respect is first to overthrow the existing class-order of society and transfer power to another class. Then the needed change in education will follow automatically and will be genuine and thorough-going.

This point of view serves to call attention to another factor in the general issue being discussed. I shall not here take up in detail the basic premise of this school of social thought, namely the doctrine of domination of social organization by a single rather solidly-unified class; a domination so complete and pervasive that it can be thrown off only by the violent revolutionary action of another distinct unified class. It will be gathered, however, from what has been said that I believe the existing situation is so composite and so marked by conflicting criss-cross tendencies that this premise represents an exaggeration of actual conditions so extreme as to be a caricature. Yet I do recognize that so far as any general characterization of the situation can be made, it is on the basis of a conflict of older and newer forces—forces cultural, religious, scientific, philosophic, economic, and political.

But suppose it is admitted for the sake of argument that a social revolution is going on, and that it will culminate in a transfer of power effected by violent action. The notion that schools are completely impotent under existing conditions then has disastrous consequences. The schools, according to the theory, are engaged in shaping as far as in them lies a mentality, a type of belief, desire, and purpose that is consonant with the present class-capitalist system. It is evident that if such be the case, any revolution that is brought about is going to be badly compromised and even undermined. It will carry with it the seeds, the vital seeds, of counter-revolutions. There is no basis whatever, save doctrinaire absolutism, for the belief that a complete economic change will produce of itself the mental, moral, and cultural changes that are necessary for its enduring success. The fact is practically recognized by the school of thought under discussion in that part of their doctrine which asserts that no genuine revolution can occur until the old system has passed away in everything but external political power, while within its shell a new economic system has grown to maturity. What is ignored is that the new system cannot grow to maturity without an accompanying widespread change of habits of belief, desire, and purpose.

It is unrealistic, in my opinion, to suppose that the schools can be a *main* agency in producing the intellectual and moral changes, the changes in attitudes and disposition of thought and purpose, which are necessary for the creation of a new social order. Any such view ignores the constant operation of powerful forces outside the school which shape mind and character. It ignores the fact that school education is but one educational agency out of many, and at the best is in some respects a minor educational force. Nevertheless, while the school is not a sufficient condition, it is a necessary condition of forming the understanding and the dispositions that are required to maintain a genuinely changed social order. No social change is more than external unless it is attended by and rooted in the attitudes of those who bring it about and of those who are affected by it. In a genuine sense, social change is accidental unless it has also a psychological and oral foundation. For it is then at the mercy of currents that veer and shift. The utmost that can be meant by those who hold that schools are impotent is that education in the form of *systematic indoctrination* can only come about when some government is sufficiently established to make schools undertake the task of single-minded inculcation in a single direction.

The discussion has thus reached the point in which it is advisable to say a few words about indoctrination. The word is not free from ambiguity. One definition of the dictionary makes it a synonym for teaching. In order that there may be a definite point to consider, I shall take indoctrination to mean the systematic use of every possible means to impress upon the minds of pupils a particular set of political and economic views to the exclusion of every other. This meaning is suggested by the word "inculcation," whose original signification was "to stamp in with the heel." This signification is too physical to be carried over literally. But the idea of stamping in is involved, and upon occasion does include physical measures. I shall discuss this view only as far as to state, in the first place, that indoctrination so conceived is something very different from education, for the latter involves, as I understand it, the active participation of students in reaching conclusions and forming attitudes. Even in the case of something as settled and agreed upon as the multiplication table, I should say if it is taught educatively, and not as a form of animal training, the active participation, the interest, reflection, and understanding of those taught are necessary.

The upholders of indoctrination rest their adherence to the theory in part upon the fact that there is a great deal of indoctrination now going on in the schools, especially with reference to narrow nationalism under the name of patriotism, and with reference to the dominant economic regime. These facts unfortunately *are* facts. But they do not prove that the right course is to seize upon the method of indoctrination and reverse its objective. A much stronger argument is that unless education has some frame of reference it is bound to be aimless, lacking a unified objective. The necessity for a frame of reference must be admitted. There exists in this country such a unified frame. It is called democracy. I do not claim for a moment that the significance of democracy as a mode of life is so settled that there can be no disagreement as to its significance. The moment we leave glittering generalities and come to concrete details, there is great divergence. I certainly do not mean either that our political institutions as they have come to be, our parties, legislatures, laws, and courts constitute a model upon which a clear idea of democracy can be based. But there is a tradition and an idea which we can put in opposition to the very much that is undemocratic in our institutions. The idea and ideal involve at least the necessity of personal and voluntary participation in reaching decisions and executing them—in so far it is the contrary of the idea of indoctrination. And I, for one, am profoundly sceptical of the notion that because we now have a rather poor embodiment of democracy we can ultimately produce a genuine democracy by sweeping away what we have left of one.

The positive point, however, is that the democratic ideal, in its human significance, provides us with a frame of reference. The frame is not filled in, either in society at large or in its significance for education. I am not implying that it is so clear and definite that we can look at it as a traveler can look at a map and tell where to go from hour to hour. Rather the point I would make is that the *problem* of education in its relation to direction of social change is all one with the *problem* of finding out what democracy means in its total range of concrete applications; economic, domestic, international, religious, cultural, *and* political.

I cannot wish for anything better to happen for, and in, our schools than that this problem should become the chief theme for consideration until we have attained clarity concerning the concrete significance of democracy—which like everything concrete means its application in living action, individual and collective. The trouble, at least one great trouble, is that we have taken democracy for granted; we have thought and acted as if our forefathers had founded it once for all. We have forgotten that it has to be enacted anew in every generation, in every year and day, in the living relations of person to person in all social forms and institutions. Forgetting this, we have allowed our economic and hence our political institutions to drift away from democracy; we have been negligent even in creating a school that should be the constant nurse of democracy.

I conclude by saying that there is at least one thing in which the idea of democracy is not dim, however far short we have come from striving to make it reality. Our public school system was founded in the name of equality of opportunity for all, independent of birth, economic status, race, creed, or color. The school cannot by itself alone create or embody this idea. But the least it can do is to create individuals who understand the concrete meaning of the idea with their minds, who cherish it warmly in their hearts, and who are equipped to battle in its behalf in their actions.

Democracy also means voluntary choice, based on an intelligence that is the outcome of free association and communication with others. It means a way of living together in which mutual and free consultation rule instead of force, and in which cooperation instead of brutal competition is the law of life; a social order in which all the forces that make for friendship, beauty, and knowledge are cherished in order that each individual may become what he, and he alone, is capable of becoming. These things at least give a point of departure for the filling in of the democratic idea and aim as a frame of reference. If a sufficient number of educators devote themselves to striving courageously and with full sincerity to find the answers to the concrete questions which the idea and the aim put to us, I believe that the question of the relation of the schools to direction of social change will cease to be a question, and will become a moving answer in action.

15

Democracy and Education in the World of Today (1938)

With fascism rapidly advancing in Europe, Dewey wrote a piece entitled "Democracy and Education in the World of Today" for a pamphlet by the New York Society for Ethical Culture (founded in 1876). Using a time-honored motif, Dewey opens by asserting that "democracy is itself an educational principle." In other words, democratic life is (or should be) its own form of education. This education requires that everyone have the opportunity to achieve their unique potential in pursuing a meaningful life while contributing to and sharing in the well-being of others. That means, for Dewey, that the citizens of a democracy should value a rich and full school experience not only for their own children, but for all children: the work of establishing a pluralistic democracy is necessarily a shared endeavor. As Dewey puts it, "every generation has to accomplish democracy over again for itself." Conditions change, after all, even if inequities like racism and gender discrimination stubbornly remain. Consequently, schools must recognize that the meaning of democracy, as more than a mere abstraction, itself changes whenever new social and economic conditions emerge. Is democracy really being instilled in students, Dewey asks, when they honor the flag while reciting the Pledge of Allegiance every morning? Or "are we permitting a symbol to become a substitute for that reality?"

Addendum: Dewey wrote little about what we now call disability. However, his criticisms of high-stakes psychometric testing, and insistence that democratic equality requires providing everyone opportunities to develop their unique potential, are directly relevant to issues concerning disability and schooling. Dewey's views are especially germane to the pathological ideology of the medical remedial model of disability. Within this model, students are diagnosed and identified in terms of their deficiencies and then assigned to, and de facto defined by, preconceived categories of illness or abnormality. From a Deweyan perspective, we therefore fail to *perceive* the whole person and their best possibilities as a unique human being. Instead, we merely *recognize* them as members of a certain category of disability requiring prescribed treatments (or "cures") based on conventions of normality. This failure of moral perception is something John and Alice Dewey experienced firsthand in attempting to secure equal education for their adopted son Sabino. For more on Dewey and disability, see Scot Danforth, "John Dewey's Contributions to an Educational Philosophy of Intellectual Disability," *Educational Theory* 58, no. 1 (2008): 45–62, and "Disability in the Family: John and Alice Dewey Raising Their Son, Sabino," *Teachers College Record* 120, no. 2 (February 2008): 1–30. In addition, groundbreaking scholar Thomas Skrtic draws on Dewey in calling for special educators to "reconstruct their practices and discourses using interpretations that promote the values of democracy, community, participation, and inclusion." See Thomas M. Skrtic, "A Political Economy of Learning Disabilities," *Learning Disability Quarterly* 28 (Spring 2005): 149–55.

∽

It is obvious that the relation between democracy and education is a reciprocal one, a mutual one, and vitally so. Democracy is itself an educational principle, an educational measure and policy. There is nothing novel in saying that even an election campaign has a greater value in educating the citizens of the country who take any part in it than it has in its immediate external results. Our campaigns are certainly not always as educational as they might be, but by and large they certainly do serve the purpose of making the citizens of the country aware of what is going on in society, what the problems are and the various measures and policies that are proposed to deal with the issues of the day.

Mussolini remarked that democracy was passé, done with, because people are tired of liberty. There is a certain truth in that remark, not about the democracy being done with, at least we hope not, but in the fact that human beings do get tired of liberty, of political liberty and of the responsibilities, the duties, the burden that the acceptance of political liberty involves. There is an educational principle and policy in a deeper sense than that which I have just mentioned in that it proposes in effect, if not in words, to every member of society just that question: do you want to be a free human being standing on your own feet, accepting the responsibilities, the duties that go with that position as an effective member of society?

The meaning of democracy, especially of political democracy which, of course, is far from covering the whole scope of democracy, as over against every aristocratic form of social control and political authority, was expressed by Abraham Lincoln when he said that no man was good enough or wise enough to govern others without their consent; that is, without some expression on their part of their own needs, their own desires and their own conception of how social affairs should go on and social problems be handled.

A woman told me once that she asked a very well known American statesman what he would do for the people of this country if he were God. He said, "Well, that is quite a question. I should look people over and decide what it was that they needed and then try and give it to them."

She said, "Well, you know, I expected that to be the answer that you would give. There are people that would *ask* other people what they wanted before they tried to give it to them."

That asking other people what they would like, what they need, what their ideas are, is an essential part of the democratic idea. We are so familiar with it as a matter of democratic political practice that perhaps we don't always think about it even when we exercise the privilege of giving an answer. That practice is an educational matter because it puts upon us as individual members of a democracy the responsibility of considering what it is that we as individuals want, what our needs and troubles are.

Dr. Felix Adler expressed very much the same idea. I am not quoting his words, but this was what he said, that "no matter how ignorant any person is there is one thing that he knows better than anybody else and that is where the shoes pinch on his own feet"; and because it is the individual that knows his own troubles, even if he is not literate or sophisticated in other respects, the idea of democracy as opposed to any conception of aristocracy is that every individual must be consulted in such a way, actively not passively, that he himself becomes a part of the process of authority, of the process of social control; that his needs and wants have a chance to be registered in a way where they count in determining social policy. Along with that goes, of course, the other feature which is necessary for the realization of democracy—mutual conference and mutual consultation and arriving ultimately at social control by pooling, by putting together all of these individual expressions of ideas and wants.

The ballot box and majority rule are external and very largely mechanical symbols and expressions of this. They are expedients, the best devices that at a certain time have been found, but beneath them there are the two ideas: first, the opportunity, the right and the duty of every individual to form some conviction and to express some conviction regarding his own place in the social order, and the relations of that social order to his own welfare; second, the fact that each individual counts as one and one only on an equality with others, so that the final social will comes about as the cooperative expression of the ideas of many people. And I think it is perhaps only recently that we are realizing that that idea is the essence of all sound education.

Even in the classroom we are beginning to learn that learning which develops intelligence and character does not come about when only the textbook and the teacher have a say; that every individual becomes educated only as he has an opportunity to contribute something from his own experience, no matter how meagre or slender that background of experience may be at a given time; and finally that enlightenment comes from the give and take, from the exchange of experiences and ideas.

The realization of that principle in the schoolroom, it seems to me, is an expression of the significance of democracy as the educational process without which individuals cannot come into the full possession of themselves nor make a contribution, if they have it in them to make, to the social well-being of others.

I said that democracy and education bear a reciprocal relation, for it is not merely that democracy is itself an educational principle, but that democracy cannot endure, much less develop, without education in that narrower sense in which we ordinarily think of it, the education that is given in the family, and especially as we think of it in the school. The school is the essential distributing agency for whatever values and purposes any social group cherishes. It is not the only means, but it is the first means, the primary means and the most deliberate means by which the values that any social group cherishes, the purposes that it wishes to realize, are distributed and brought home to the thought, the observation, judgment and choice of the individual.

What would a powerful dynamo in a big power-house amount to if there were no line of distribution leading into shops and factories to give power, leading into the home to give light? No matter what fine ideals or fine resources, the products of past experience, past human culture, exist somewhere at the centre, they become significant only as they are carried out, or are distributed. That is true of any society, not simply of a democratic society; but what is true of a democratic society is, of course, that its special values and its special purposes and aims must receive such distribution that they become part of the mind and the will of the members of society. So that the school in a democracy is contributing, if it is true to itself as an educational agency, to the democratic idea of making knowledge and understanding, in short the power of action, a part of the intrinsic intelligence and character of the individual.

I think we have one thing to learn from the anti-democratic states of Europe, and that is that we should take as seriously the preparation of the members of our society for the duties and responsibilities of democracy, as they take seriously the formation of the thoughts and minds and characters of their population for their aims and ideals.

This does not mean that we should imitate their universal propaganda, that we should prostitute the schools, the radio and the press to the inculcation of one single point of view and the suppression of everything else; it means that we should take seriously, energetically and vigorously the use of democratic schools and democratic methods in the schools; that we should educate the young and the youth of the country in freedom for participation in a free society. It may be that with the advantage of great distance from these troubled scenes in Europe we may learn something from the terrible tragedies that are occurring there, so as to take the idea of democracy more seriously, asking ourselves what it means, and taking steps to make our schools more completely the agents for preparation of free individuals for intelligent participation in a free society.

I don't need to tell these readers that our free public school system was founded, promoted, just about 100 years ago, because of the realization of men like Horace Mann and Henry Barnard that citizens need to participate in what they called a republican form of government; that they need enlightenment which could come about only through a system of free education.

If you have read the writings of men of those times, you know how few schools existed, how poor they were, how short their terms were, how poorly most of the teachers were prepared, and, judging from what Horace Mann said, how general was the indifference of the average well-to-do citizen to the education of anybody except his own children.

You may recall the terrible indictment that he drew of the well-to-do classes because of their indifference to the education of the masses, and the vigor with which he pointed out that they were pursuing a dangerous course; that, no matter how much they educated their own children, if they left the masses ignorant they would be corrupted and that they themselves and their children would be the sufferers in the end. As he said, "We did not mean to exchange a single tyrant across the sea for a hydra-headed tyrant here at home"; yet that is what we will get unless we educate our citizens.

I refer to him particularly because to such a very large extent the ideas, the ideals which Horace Mann and the others held have been so largely realized. I think even Horace Mann could hardly have anticipated a finer, more magnificent school plan, school building and school equipment than we have in some parts of our country. On the side of the mechanical and the external, the things that these educational statesmen 100 years ago strove for have been to a considerable extent realized. I should have to qualify that. We know how poor many of the rural schools are, especially in backward states of the country, how poorly they are equipped, how short their school years are; but, in a certain sense, taking what has been done at the best, the immediate ideals of Horace Mann and the others have been realized. Yet the problem we have today of the relation of education and democracy is as acute and as serious a problem as the problem of providing school buildings, school equipment, school teachers and school monies was a hundred years ago.

If, as we all know, democracy is in a more or less precarious position throughout the world, and has even in our own country enemies of growing strength, we cannot take it for granted as something that is sure to endure. If this is the actual case, one reason for it is that we have been so complacent about the idea of democracy that we have more or less unconsciously assumed that the work of establishing a democracy was completed by the founding fathers or when the Civil War abolished slavery. We tend to think of it as something that has been established and that it remains for us simply to enjoy.

We have had, without formulating it, a conception of democracy as something static, as something that is like an inheritance that can be bequeathed, a kind of lump sum that we could live off and upon. The crisis that we are undergoing will turn out, I think, to be worthwhile if we learn through it that every generation has to accomplish democracy over again for itself; that its very nature, its essence, is something that cannot be handed on from one person or one generation to another, but has to be worked out in terms of needs, problems and conditions of the social life of which, as the years go by, we are a part, a social life that is changing with extreme rapidity from year to year.

I find myself resentful and really feeling sad when, in relation to present social, economic and political problems, people point simply backward as if somewhere in the past there were a model for what we should do today. I hope I yield to none in appreciation of the great American tradition, for tradition is something that is capable of being transmitted as an emotion and as an idea from generation to generation. We have a great and precious heritage from the past, but to be realized, to be translated from an idea and an emotion, this tradition has to be embodied by active effort in the social relations which we as human beings bear to each other under present conditions. It is because the conditions of life change, that the problem of maintaining a democracy becomes new, and the burden that is put upon the school, upon the educational system is not that of stating merely the ideas of the men who made this country, their hopes and their intentions, but of teaching what a democratic society means under existing conditions.

The other day I read a statement to the effect that more than half of the working people in shops and factories in this country today are working in industries that didn't even exist forty years ago. It would seem to mean that, as far as the working population is concerned, half of the old industries have gone into obsolescence and been replaced by new ones. The man who made that statement, a working scientist, pointed out that every worker in every industry today is doing what he is doing either directly or indirectly because of the progress that has been made in the last half century in the physical sciences. In other words, in the material world, in the world of production, of material commodities and material entities, the progress of knowledge, of science, has revolutionized activity (revolutionized is not too strong a word) in the last fifty years.

How can we under these circumstances think that we can live from an inheritance, noble and fine as it is, that was formed in earlier days—one might as well say pre-scientific and pre-industrial days—except as we deliberately translate that tradition and that inheritance into the terms of the realities of present society which means simply our relations to one another.

Horace Mann and other educators 100 years ago worked when the United States was essentially agricultural. The things with which we are most familiar that enter into the formation of a material part of our life didn't exist. Railways were just beginning, but all the other great inventions that we take for granted were hidden in the darkness of future time. Even then in those earlier days, Thomas Jefferson predicted evils that might come to man with the too-rapid development of manufacturing industries, because, as he saw it, the backbone of any democratic society was the [yeoman] farmer who owned and cultivated his own land. He saw the farmer as a man who could control his own economic destiny, a man who, therefore, could stand on his own feet and be really a free citizen of a free country. What he feared was what might happen when men lost the security of economic independence and became dependent upon others.

Even Alexander Hamilton, who belonged to the other school of thought, when speaking of judges, maintained that those who controlled a man's subsistence controlled his will. If that is true of judges on the bench it is certainly true to a considerable extent of all people; and now we have economic conditions, because of the rapid change in industry and in finance, where there are thousands and millions of people who have the minimum of control over the conditions of their own subsistence. That is a problem, of course, that will need public and private consideration, but it is a deeper problem than that; it is a problem of the future of democracy, of how political democracy can be made secure if there is economic insecurity and economic dependence of great sections of the population if not upon the direct will of others, at least upon the conditions under which the employing sections of society operate.

I mention this simply as one of the respects in which the relation of education and democracy assumes a very different form than it did in the time when these men supposed that "If we can only have schools enough, only have school buildings and good school equipment and prepared teachers, the necessary enlightenment to take care of republican institutions will follow almost as a matter of course."

The educational problem today is deeper, it is more acute, it is infinitely more difficult because it has to face all of the problems of the modern world. Recently we have been reading in some quarters about the necessity of coalition, whether in arms or not, at least some kind of a coalition of democratic nations, formed to oppose and resist the advance of Fascist, totalitarian, authoritarian states. I am not going to discuss that issue, but I do want to ask a few questions. What do we mean when we assume that we, in common with certain other nations, are really democratic, that we have already so accomplished the ends and purposes of democracy that all we have to do is to stand up and resist the encroachments of non-democratic states?

We are unfortunately familiar with the tragic racial intolerance of Germany and now of Italy. Are we entirely free from that racial intolerance, so that we can pride ourselves upon having achieved a complete democracy? Our treatment of the Negroes, anti-Semitism, the growing (at least I fear it is growing) serious opposition to the alien immigrant within our gates, is, I think, a sufficient answer to that question. Here, in relation to education, we have a problem; what are our schools doing to cultivate not merely passive toleration that will put up with people of different racial birth or different colored skin, but what are our schools doing positively and aggressively and constructively to cultivate understanding and goodwill which are essential to democratic society?

We object, and object very properly, to the constant stream of false propaganda that is put forth in the states for the suppression of all free inquiry and freedom, but again how do we stand in those respects? I know we have in many schools a wonderful school pledge where the children six years old and up probably arise and pledge allegiance to a flag and to what that stands for—one indivisible nation, justice and liberty. How far are we permitting a symbol to become a substitute for the reality? How far are our citizens, legislators and educators salving their conscience with the idea that genuine patriotism is being instilled in these children because they recite the words of that pledge? Do they know what allegiance and loyalty mean? What do they mean by an indivisible nation when we have a nation that is still more or less torn by factional strife and class division? Is that an indivisible nation and is the reciting of a verbal pledge any educational guarantee of the existence of an indivisible nation?

And so I might go on about liberty and justice. What are we doing to translate those great ideas of liberty and justice out of a formal ceremonial ritual into the realities of the understanding, the insight and the genuine loyalty of the boys and girls in our schools?

We say we object, and rightly so, to this exaggerated, one-sided nationalism inculcated under the name of devotion to country, but until our schools have themselves become clear upon what public spirit and good citizenship mean in all the relations of life, youth cannot meet the great responsibilities that rest upon them.

We deplore, also, and deplore rightly, the dependence of these authoritarian states in Europe upon the use of force. What are we doing to cultivate the idea of the supremacy of the method of intelligence, of understanding, the method of goodwill and of mutual sympathy over and above force? I know that in many respects our public schools have and deserve a good reputation for what they have done in breaking down class division, creating a feeling of greater humanity and of membership in a single family, but I do not believe that we have as yet done what can be done and what needs to be done in breaking down even the ordinary snobbishness and prejudices that divide people from each other, and that our schools have done what they can and should do in this respect.

And when it comes to this matter of force as a method of settling social issues, we have unfortunately only to look at our own scene, both domestic and international. In the present state of the world apparently a great and increasing number of people feel that the only way we can make ourselves secure is by increasing our army and navy and making our factories ready to manufacture munitions. In other words, somehow we too have a belief that force, physical and brute force, after all is the best final reliance.

With our fortunate position in the world I think that if we used our resources, including our financial resources, to build up among ourselves a genuine, true and effective democratic society, we would find that we have a surer, a more enduring and a more powerful defense of democratic institutions both within ourselves and with relation to the rest of the world than the surrender to the belief in force, violence and war can ever give. I know that our schools are doing a great deal to inculcate ideas of peace, but I sometimes wonder how far this goes beyond a certain sentimental attachment to a realization of what peace would actually mean in the world in the way of cooperation, goodwill and mutual understanding.

I have endeavored to call your attention first to the inherent, the vital and organic relation that there is between democracy and education from both sides, from the side of education, the schools, and from the side of the very meaning of democracy. I have simply tried to give a certain number of more or less random illustrations of what the problems of the schools are today with reference to preparing the youth of the country for active, intelligent participation in the building and the rebuilding and the eternal rebuilding—because, as I have said, it never can be done once for all—of a genuinely democratic society, and, I wish to close (as I began) with saying, that after all the cause of democracy is the moral cause of the dignity and the worth of the individual. Through mutual respect, mutual toleration, give and take, the pooling of experiences, it is ultimately the only method by which human beings can succeed in carrying on this experiment in which we are all engaged, whether we want to be or not, the greatest experiment of humanity—that of living together in ways in which the life of each of us is at once profitable in the deepest sense of the word, profitable to himself and helpful in the building up of the individuality of others.

VI

MORALS, ETHICS, AND THE EDUCATION OF HABIT

16

From *Moral Principles in Education* (1909)

The following excerpts from *Moral Principles in Education* outline Dewey's holistic views on moral education and the ethical responsibilities of schools. They do so through three interrelated perspectives. These include the moral education provided by (a) the school community, (b) the methods of instruction, and (c) the educational subject matter. Here, for Dewey, is the "moral trinity of the school." Ideally, it equips young people with social intelligence: the ability to observe and understand social situations; social power: effective habits for participation in social life; and social interests: the willingness and capacity to work for the greater good. As Aristotle observed long ago, acquiring the appropriate habits requires more than a mere intellectual grasp of the moral: it necessitates participation in activities that foster and nourish the moral dimensions of habit. A school that fails to fulfill this responsibility, Dewey argues, is "derelict and a defaulter." Dewey then uses subject matter from geography, history, and mathematics to exemplify the purpose of school studies as a "means of bringing the child to realize the social scene of action"—that is, the child's unique contribution to social life, including the ability to participate in a variety of situations and assume diverse roles. (It should be noted here that Dewey does not begrudge individuals the right, in remaining true to their convictions, to withdraw from situations where participation would entail betraying those convictions. As he explains, "Only the voluntary initiative and voluntary cooperation of individuals can produce social institutions that will protect the liberties necessary for achieving development of genuine individuality" [see Dewey's "I Believe," 1939, *LW* 14, 91–92.])

The Moral Training Given by the School Community

There cannot be two sets of ethical principles, one for life in the school, and the other for life outside of the school. As conduct is one, so also the principles of conduct are one. The tendency to discuss the morals of the school as if the school were an institution by itself is highly unfortunate. The moral responsibility of the school, and of those who conduct it, is to society. The school is fundamentally an institution erected by society to do a certain specific work,—to exercise a certain specific function in maintaining the life and advancing the welfare of society. The educational system which does not recognize that this fact entails upon it an ethical responsibility is derelict and a defaulter. It is not doing what it was called into existence to do, and what it pretends to do. Hence the entire structure of the school in general and its concrete workings in particular need to be considered from time to time with reference to the social position and function of the school.

The idea that the moral work and worth of the public-school system as a whole are to be measured by its social value is, indeed, a familiar notion. However, it is frequently taken in too limited and rigid a way. The social work of the school is often limited to training for citizenship, and citizenship is then interpreted in a narrow sense as meaning capacity to vote intelligently, disposition to obey laws, etc. But it is futile to contract and cramp the ethical responsibility of the school in this way. The child is one, and he must either live his social life as an integral unified being, or suffer loss and create friction. To pick out one of the many social relations which the child bears, and to define the work of the school by that alone, is like instituting a vast and complicated system of physical exercise which would have for its object simply the development of the lungs and the power of breathing, independent of other organs and functions. The child is an organic whole, intellectually, socially, and morally, as well as physically. We must take the child as a member of society in the broadest sense, and demand for and from the schools whatever is necessary to enable the child intelligently to recognize all his social relations and take his part in sustaining them.

To isolate the formal relationship of citizenship from the whole system of relations with which it is actually interwoven; to suppose that there is some one particular study or mode of treatment which can make the child a good citizen; to suppose, in other words, that a good citizen is anything more than a thoroughly efficient and serviceable member of society, one with all his powers of body and mind under control, is a hampering superstition which it is hoped may soon disappear from educational discussion.

The child is to be not only a voter and a subject of law; he is also to be a member of a family, himself in turn responsible, in all probability, for rearing and training of future children, thereby maintaining the continuity of society. He is to be a worker, engaged in some occupation which will be of use to society, and which will maintain his own independence and self-respect. He is to be a member of some particular neighborhood and community, and must contribute to the values of life, add to the decencies and graces of civilization wherever he is. These are bare and formal statements, but if we let our imagination translate them into their concrete details, we have a wide and varied scene. For the child properly to take his place in reference to these various functions means training in science, in art, in history; means command of the fundamental methods of inquiry and the fundamental tools of intercourse and communication; means a trained and sound body, skillful eye and hand; means habits of industry, perseverance; in short, habits of serviceableness.

Moreover, the society of which the child is to be a member is, in the United States, a democratic and progressive society. The child must be educated for leadership as well as for obedience. He must have power, of self-direction and power of directing others, power of administration, ability to assume positions of responsibility. This necessity of educating for leadership is as great on the industrial as on the political side.

New inventions, new machines, new methods of transportation and intercourse are making over the whole scene of action year by year. It is an absolute impossibility to educate the child for any fixed station in life. So far as education is conducted unconsciously or consciously on this basis, it results in fitting the future citizen for no station in life, but makes him a drone, a hanger-on, or an actual retarding influence in the onward movement. Instead of caring for himself and for others, he becomes one who has himself to be cared for. Here, too, the ethical responsibility of the school on the social side must be interpreted in the broadest and freest spirit; it is equivalent to that training of the child which will give him such possession of himself that he may take charge of himself; may not only adapt himself to the changes that are going on, but have power to shape and direct them.

Apart from participation in social life, the school has no moral end nor aim. As long as we confine ourselves to the school as an isolated institution, we have no directing principles, because we have no object. For example, the end of education is said to be the harmonious development of all the powers of the individual. Here no reference to social life or membership is apparent, and yet many think we have in it an adequate and thoroughgoing definition of the goal of education. But if this definition be taken independently of social relationship we have no way of telling what is meant by any one of the terms employed. We do not know what a power is; we do not know what development is; we do not know what harmony is. A power is a power only with reference to the use to which it is put, the function it has to serve. If we leave out the uses supplied by social life we have nothing but the old "faculty psychology" to tell what is meant by power and what the specific powers are. The principle reduces itself to enumerating a lot of faculties like perception, memory, reasoning, etc., and then stating that each one of these powers needs to be developed.

Education then becomes a gymnastic exercise. Acute powers of observation and memory might be developed by studying Chinese characters; acuteness in reasoning might be got by discussing the scholastic subtleties of the Middle Ages. The simple fact is that there is no isolated faculty of observation, or memory, or reasoning any more than there is an original faculty of black-smithing, carpentering, or steam engineering. Faculties mean simply that particular impulses and habits have been coordinated or framed with reference to accomplishing certain definite kinds of work. We need to know the social situations in which the individual will have to use ability to observe, recollect, imagine, and reason, in order to have any way of telling what a training of mental powers actually means.

What holds in the illustration of this particular definition of education holds good from whatever point of view we approach the matter. Only as we interpret school activities with reference to the larger circle of social activities to which they relate do we find any standard for judging their moral significance.

The school itself must be a vital social institution to a much greater extent than obtains at present. I am told that there is a swimming school in a certain city where youth are taught to swim without going into the water, being repeatedly drilled in the various movements which are necessary for swimming. When one of the young men so trained was asked what he did when he got into the water, he laconically replied, "Sunk." The story happens to be true; were it not, it would seem to be a fable made expressly for the purpose of typifying the ethical relationship of school to society. The school cannot be a preparation for social life excepting as it reproduces, within itself, typical conditions of social life. At present it is largely engaged in the futile task of Sisyphus. It is endeavoring to form habits in children for use in a social life which, it would almost seem, is carefully and purposely kept away from vital contact with the child undergoing training. The only way to prepare for social life is to engage in social life. To form habits of social usefulness and serviceableness apart from any direct social need and motive, apart from any existing social situation, is, to the letter, teaching the child to swim by going through motions outside of the water. The most indispensable condition is left out of account, and the results are correspondingly partial.

The much lamented separation in the schools of intellectual and moral training, of acquiring information and growing in character, is simply one expression of the failure to conceive and construct the school as a social institution, having social life and value within itself. Except so far as the school is an embryonic typical community life, moral training must be partly pathological and partly formal. Training is pathological when stress is laid upon correcting wrong-doing instead of upon forming habits of positive service. Too often the teacher's concern with the moral life of pupils takes the form of alertness for failures to conform to school rules and routine. These regulations, judged from the standpoint of the development of the child at the time, are more or less conventional and arbitrary. They are rules which have to be made in order that the existing modes of school work may go on; but the lack of inherent necessity in these school modes reflects itself in a feeling, on the part of the child, that the moral discipline of the school is arbitrary. Any conditions that compel the teacher to take note of failures rather than of healthy growth give false standards and result in distortion and perversion. Attending to wrong-doing ought to be an incident rather than a principle. The child ought to have a positive consciousness of what he is about, so as to judge his acts from the standpoint of reference to the work which he has to do. Only in this way does he have a vital standard, one that enables him to turn failures to account for the future.

By saying that the moral training of the school is formal, I mean that the moral habits currently emphasized by the school are habits which are created, as it were, *ad hoc*. Even the habits of promptness, regularity, industry, noninterference with the work of others, faithfulness to tasks imposed, which are specially inculcated in the school, are habits that are necessary simply because the school system is what it is, and must be preserved intact. If we grant the inviolability of the school system as it is, these habits represent permanent and necessary moral ideas; but just in so far as the school system is itself isolated and mechanical, insistence upon these moral habits is more or less unreal, because the ideal to which they relate is not itself necessary. The duties, in other words, are distinctly school duties, not life duties. If we compare this condition with that of the well-ordered home, we find that the duties and responsibilities that the child has there to recognize do not belong to the family as a specialized and isolated institution, but flow from the very nature of the social life in which the family participates and to which it contributes. The child ought to have the same motives for right doing and to be judged by the same standards in the school, as the adult in the wider social life to which he belongs. Interest in community welfare, an interest that is intellectual and practical, as well as emotional—an interest, that is to say, in perceiving whatever makes for social order and progress, and in carrying these principles into execution—is the moral habit to which all the special school habits must be related if they are to be animated by the breath of life.

The Moral Training from Methods of Instruction

The principle of the social character of the school as the basic factor in the moral education given may be also applied to the question of methods of instruction,—not in their details, but their general spirit. The emphasis then falls upon construction and giving out, rather than upon absorption and mere learning. We fail to recognize how essentially individualistic the latter methods are, and how unconsciously, yet certainly and effectively, they react into the child's ways of judging and of acting. Imagine forty children all engaged in reading the same books, and in preparing and reciting the same lessons day after day. Suppose this process constitutes by far the larger part of their work, and that they are continually judged from the standpoint of what they are able to take in in a study hour and reproduce in a recitation hour. There is next to no opportunity for any social division of labor. There is no opportunity for each child to work out something specifically his own, which he may contribute to the common stock, while he, in turn, participates in the productions of others. All are set to do exactly the same work and turn out the same products. The social spirit is not cultivated,—in fact, in so far as the purely individualistic method gets in its work, it atrophies for lack of use. One reason why reading aloud in school is poor is that the real motive for the use of language—the desire to communicate and to learn—is not utilized. The child knows perfectly well that the teacher and all his fellow pupils have exactly the same facts and ideas before them that he has; he is not *giving* them anything at all. And it may be questioned whether the moral lack is not as great as the intellectual. The child is born with a natural desire to give out, to do, to serve. When this tendency is not used, when conditions are such that other motives are substituted, the accumulation of an influence working against the social spirit is much larger than we have any idea of,—especially when the burden of work, week after week, and year after year, falls upon this side.

But lack of cultivation of the social spirit is not all. Positively individualistic motives and standards are inculcated. Some stimulus must be found to keep the child at his studies. At the best this will be his affection for his teacher, together with a feeling that he is not violating school rules, and thus negatively, if not positively, is contributing to the good of the school. I have nothing to say against these motives so far as they go, but they are inadequate. The relation between the piece of work to be done and affection for a third person is external, not intrinsic. It is therefore liable to break down whenever the external conditions are changed. Moreover, this attachment to a particular person, while in a way social, may become so isolated and exclusive as to be selfish in quality. In any case, the child should gradually grow out of this relatively external motive into an appreciation, for its own sake, of the social value of what he has to do, because of its larger relations to life, not pinned down to two or three persons.

But, unfortunately, the motive is not always at this relative best, but mixed with lower motives which are distinctly egoistic. Fear is a motive which is almost sure to enter in,—not necessarily physical fear, or fear of punishment, but fear of losing the approbation of others; or fear of failure, so extreme as to be morbid and paralyzing. On the other side, emulation and rivalry enter in. Just because all are doing the same work, and are judged (either in recitation or examination with reference to grading and to promotion) not from the standpoint of their personal contribution, but from that of *comparative* success, the feeling of superiority over others is unduly appealed to, while timid children are depressed. Children are judged with reference to their capacity to realize the same external standard. The weaker gradually lose their sense of power, and accept a position of continuous and persistent inferiority. The effect upon both self-respect and respect for work need not be dwelt upon. The strong learn to glory, not in their strength, but in the fact that they are stronger. The child is prematurely launched into the region of individualistic competition, and this in a direction where competition is least applicable, namely, in intellectual and artistic matters, whose law is cooperation and participation.

Next, perhaps, to the evils of passive absorption and of competition for external standing come, perhaps, those which result from the eternal emphasis upon preparation for a remote future. I do not refer here to the waste of energy and vitality that accrues when children, who live so largely in the immediate present, are appealed to in the name of a dim and uncertain future which means little or nothing to them. I have in mind rather the habitual procrastination that develops when the motive for work is future, not present; and the false standards of judgment that are created when work is estimated, not on the basis of present need and present responsibility, but by reference to an external result, like passing an examination, getting promoted, entering high school, getting into college, etc. Who can reckon up the loss of moral power that arises from the constant impression that nothing is worth doing in itself, but only as a preparation for something else, which in turn is only a getting ready for some genuinely serious end beyond? Moreover, as a rule, it will be found that remote success is an end which appeals most to those in whom egoistic desire to get ahead—to get ahead of others—is already only too strong a motive. Those in whom personal ambition is already so strong that it paints glowing pictures of future victories may be touched; others of a more generous nature do not respond.

I cannot stop to paint the other side. I can only say that the introduction of every method that appeals to the child's active powers, to his capacities in construction, production, and creation, marks an opportunity to shift the centre of ethical gravity from an absorption which is selfish to a service which is social. Manual training is more than manual; it is more than intellectual; in the hands of any good teacher it lends itself easily, and almost as a matter of course, to development of social habits. Ever since the philosophy of Kant, it has been a commonplace of aesthetic theory, that art is universal; that it is not the product of purely personal desire or appetite, or capable of merely individual appropriation, but has a value participated in by all who perceive it. Even in the schools where most conscious attention is paid to moral considerations, the methods of study and recitation may be such as to emphasize appreciation rather than power, an emotional readiness to assimilate the experiences of others, rather than enlightened and trained capacity to carry forward those values which in other conditions and past times made those experiences worth having. At all events, separation between instruction and character continues in our schools (in spite of the efforts of individual teachers) as a result of divorce between learning and doing. The attempt to attach genuine moral effectiveness to the mere processes of learning, and to the habits which go along with learning, can result only in a training infected with formality, arbitrariness, and an undue emphasis upon failure to conform. That there is as much accomplished as there is shows the possibilities involved in methods of school activity which afford opportunity for reciprocity, cooperation, and positive personal achievement.

The Social Nature of the Course of Study

In many respects, it is the subject-matter used in school life which decides both the general atmosphere of the school and the methods of instruction and discipline which rule. A barren "course of study," that is to say, a meagre and narrow field of school activities, cannot possibly lend itself to the development of a vital social spirit or to methods that appeal to sympathy and cooperation instead of to absorption, exclusiveness, and competition. Hence it becomes an all-important matter to know how we shall apply our social standard of moral value to the subject-matter of school work, to what we call, traditionally, the "studies" that occupy pupils.

A study is to be considered as a means of bringing the child to realize the social scene of action. Thus considered it gives a criterion for selection of material and for judgment of values. We have at present three independent values set up: one of culture, another of information, and another of discipline. In reality, these refer only to three phases of social interpretation. Information is genuine or educative only in so far as it presents definite images and conceptions of materials placed in a context of social life. Discipline is genuinely educative only as it represents a reaction of information into the individual's own powers so that he brings them under control for social ends. Culture, if it is to be genuinely educative and not an external polish or factitious varnish, represents the vital union of information and discipline. It marks the socialization of the individual in his outlook upon life.

This point may be illustrated by brief reference to a few of the school studies. In the first place, there is a line of demarcation within facts themselves which classifies them belonging to science, history, or geography, respectively. The pigeon-hole classification which is so prevalent at present (fostered by introducing the pupil at the outset into a number of different studies contained in different text-books) gives an utterly erroneous idea of the relations of studies to one another and to the intellectual whole to which all belong. In fact, these subjects have to do with the same ultimate reality, namely, the conscious experience of man. It is only because we have different interests, or different ends, that we sort out the material and label part of it science, part of it history, part geography, and so on. Each "sorting" represents materials arranged with reference to some one dominant typical aim or process of the social life.

This social criterion is necessary, not only to mark off studies from one another, but also to grasp the reasons for each study,—the motives in connection with which it shall be presented. How, for example, should we define geography? What is the unity in the different so-called divisions of geography,—mathematical geography, physical geography, political geography, commercial geography? Are they purely empirical classifications dependent upon the brute fact that we run across a lot of different facts? Or is there some intrinsic principle through which the material is distributed under these various heads,—something in the interest and attitude of the human mind towards them? I should say that geography has to do with all those aspects of social life which are concerned with the interaction of the life of man and nature; or, that it has to do with the world considered as the scene of social interaction. Any fact, then, will be geographical in so far as it has to do with the dependence of man upon his natural environment, or with changes introduced in this environment through the life of man.

The four forms of geography referred to above represent, then, four increasing stages of abstraction in discussing the mutual relation of human life and nature. The beginning must be social geography, the frank recognition of the earth as the home of men acting in relations to one another. I mean by this that the essence of any geographical fact is the consciousness of two persons, or two groups of persons, who are at once separated and connected by their physical environment, and that the interest is in seeing how these people are at once kept apart and brought together in their actions by the instrumentality of the physical environment. The ultimate significance of lake, river, mountain, and plain is not physical but social; it is the part which it plays in modifying and directing human relationships. This evidently involves an extension of the term commercial. It has to do not simply with business, in the narrow sense, but with whatever relates to human intercourse and intercommunication as affected by natural forms and properties. Political geography represents this same social interaction taken in a static instead of in a dynamic way; taken, that is, as temporarily crystallized and fixed in certain forms. Physical geography (including under this not simply physiography, but also the study of flora and fauna) represents a further analysis or abstraction. It studies the conditions which determine human action, leaving out of account, temporarily, the ways in which they concretely do this. Mathematical geography carries the analysis back to more ultimate and remote conditions, showing that the physical conditions of the earth are not ultimate, but depend upon the place which the world occupies in a larger system. Here, in other words, are traced, step by step, the links which connect the immediate social occupations and groupings of men with the whole natural system which ultimately conditions them. Step by step the scene is enlarged and the image of what enters into the make-up of social action is widened and broadened; at no time is the chain of connection to be broken.

It is out of the question to take up the studies one by one and show that their meaning is similarly controlled by social considerations. But I cannot forbear saying a word or two upon history. History is vital or dead to the child according as it is, or is not, presented from the sociological standpoint. When treated simply as a record of what has passed and gone, it must be mechanical, because the past, as the past, is remote. Simply as the past there is no motive for attending to it. The ethical value of history teaching will be measured by the extent to which past events are made the means of understanding the present,—affording insight into what makes up the structure and working of society to-day. Existing social structure is exceedingly complex. It is practically impossible for the child to attack it *en masse* and get any definite mental image of it. But type phases of historical development may be selected which will exhibit, as through a telescope, the essential constituents of the existing order. Greece, for example, represents what art and growing power of individual expression stand for; Rome exhibits the elements and forces of political life on a tremendous scale. Or, as these civilizations are themselves relatively complex, a study of still simpler forms of hunting, nomadic, and agricultural life in the beginnings of civilization, a study of the effects of the introduction of iron, and iron tools, reduces the complexity to simpler elements.

One reason historical teaching is usually not more effective is that the student is set to acquire information in such a way that no epochs or factors stand out in his mind as typical; everything is reduced to the same dead level. The way to secure the necessary perspective is to treat the past as if it were a projected present with some of its elements enlarged.

The principle of contrast is as important as that of similarity. Because the present life is so close to us, touching us at every point, we cannot get away from it to see it as it really is. Nothing stands out clearly or sharply as characteristic. In the study of past periods, attention necessarily attaches itself to striking differences. Thus the child gets a locus of imagination, through which he can remove himself from the pressure of present surrounding circumstances and define them.

History is equally available in teaching the *methods* of social progress. It is commonly stated that history must be studied from the standpoint of cause and effect. The truth of this statement depends upon its interpretation. Social life is so complex and the various parts of it are so organically related to one another and to the natural environment, that it is impossible to say that this or that thing is the cause of some other particular thing. But the study of history can reveal the main instruments in the discoveries, inventions, new modes of life, etc., which have initiated the great epochs of social advance; and it can present to the child types of the main lines of social progress, and can set before him what have been the chief difficulties and obstructions in the way of progress. Once more this can be done only in so far as it is recognized that social forces in themselves are always the same,—that the same kind of influences were at work one hundred and one thousand years ago that are now working,—and that particular historical epochs afford illustration of the way in which the fundamental forces work.

Everything depends, then, upon history being treated from a social standpoint; as manifesting the agencies which have influenced social development and as presenting the typical institutions in which social life has expressed itself. The culture-epoch theory, while working in the right direction, has failed to recognize the importance of treating past periods with relation to the present,—as affording insight into the representative factors of its structure; it has treated these periods too much as if they had some meaning or value in themselves. The way in which the biographical method is handled illustrates the same point. It is often treated in such a way as to exclude from the child's consciousness (or at least not sufficiently to emphasize) the social forces and principles involved in the association of the masses of men. It is quite true that the child is easily interested in history from the biographical standpoint; but unless "the hero" is treated in relation to the community life behind him that he sums up and directs, there is danger that history will reduce itself to a mere exciting story. Then moral instruction reduces itself to drawing certain lessons from the life of the particular personalities concerned, instead of widening and deepening the child's imagination of social relations, ideals, and means.

It will be remembered that I am not making these points for their own sake, but with reference to the general principle that when a study is taught as a mode of understanding social life it has positive ethical import. What the normal child continuously needs is not so much isolated moral lessons upon the importance of truthfulness and honesty, or the beneficent results that follow from a particular act of patriotism, as the formation of habits of social imagination and conception.

I take one more illustration, namely, mathematics. This does, or does not, accomplish its full purpose according as it is, or is not, presented as a social tool. The prevailing divorce between information and character, between knowledge and social action, stalks upon the scene here. The moment mathematical study is severed from the place which it occupies with reference to use in social life, it becomes unduly abstract, even upon the purely intellectual side. It is presented as a matter of technical relations and formulae apart from any end or use. What the study of number suffers from in elementary education is lack of motivation. Back of this and that and the other particular bad method is the radical mistake of treating number as if it were an end in itself, instead of the means of accomplishing some end. Let the child get a consciousness of what is the use of number, of what it really is for, and half the battle is won. Now this consciousness of the use of reason implies some end which is implicitly social.

One of the absurd things in the more advanced study of arithmetic is the extent to which the child is introduced to numerical operations which have no distinctive mathematical principles characterizing them, but which represent certain general principles found in business relationships. To train the child in these operations, while paying no attention to the business realities in which they are of use, or to the conditions of social life which make these business activities necessary, is neither arithmetic nor common sense. The child is called upon to do examples in interest, partnership, banking, brokerage, and so on through a long string, and no pains are taken to see that, in connection with the arithmetic, he has any sense of the social realities involved. This part of arithmetic is essentially sociological in its nature. It ought either to be omitted entirely, or else be taught in connection with a study of the relevant social realities. As we now manage the study, it is the old case of learning to swim apart from the water over again, with correspondingly bad results on the practical side.

In concluding this portion of the discussion, we may say that our conceptions of moral education have been too narrow, too formal, and too pathological. We have associated the term ethical with certain special acts which are labeled virtues and are set off from the mass of other acts, and are still more divorced from the habitual images and motives of the children performing them. Moral instruction is thus associated with teaching about these particular virtues, or with instilling certain sentiments in regard to them. The moral has been conceived in too goody-goody a way. Ultimate moral motives and forces are nothing more or less than social intelligence—the power of observing and comprehending social situations,—and social power—trained capacities of control—at work in the service of social interest and aims. There is no fact which throws light upon the constitution of society, there is no power whose training adds to social resourcefulness that is not moral.

I sum up, then, this part of the discussion by asking your attention to the moral trinity of the school. The demand is for social intelligence, social power, and social interests. Our resources are (1) the life of the school as a social institution in itself; (2) methods of learning and of doing work; and (3) the school studies or curriculum. In so far as the school represents, in its own spirit, a genuine community life; in so far as what are called school discipline, government, order, etc., are the expressions of this inherent social spirit; in so far as the methods used are those that appeal to the active and constructive powers, permitting the child to give out and thus to serve; in so far as the curriculum is so selected and organized as to provide the material for affording the child a consciousness of the world in which he has to play a part, and the demands he has to meet; so far as these ends are met, the school is organized on an ethical basis. So far as general principles are concerned, all the basic ethical requirements are met. The rest remains between the individual teacher and the individual child.

17

From *Human Nature and Conduct* (1922)

Human Nature and Conduct is Dewey's extensive demonstration that human beings are fundamentally "creatures of habit." The book grew out of a series of Stanford University lectures delivered by Dewey in 1918 and, like other texts in this reader, it is part philosophy and part psychology. Dewey opens by arguing for the need to ground morality and ethics in an understanding of human nature. This, importantly, includes aspects of the everyday world of which human beings are necessarily a part. Accordingly, habits and customs should be viewed as the products of both persons and their social and material surroundings. In shaping these surroundings to fit our needs, we are at the same time being shaped by them through a transactional give-and-take relationship. While natural impulses assist us in reconstructing our habits, these impulses are meaningless apart from the familiar contexts of social life. At birth, for example, the cries of a hungry baby mean nothing to the infant: they are simply a physical discharge having meaning only to the baby's caregiver. In time, however, Dewey notes, the baby acquires habits (most notably language) to focus and direct this discharge of energy. More importantly, if developed effectively, these habits represent meaning and growth: As the baby's "organized habits are definitely deployed and focused, the confused situation takes on form, it is 'cleared up'—the essential function of intelligence." Rebuffing the idea that habits are limiting forces in human experience, Dewey places them at the center of human learning.

Introduction

"Give a dog a bad name and hang him." Human nature has been the dog of professional moralists, and consequences accord with the proverb. Man's nature has been regarded with suspicion, with fear, with sour looks, sometimes with enthusiasm for its possibilities but only when these were placed in contrast with its actualities. It has appeared to be so evilly disposed that the business of morality was to prune and curb it; it was thought better of if it could be replaced by something else. It has been supposed that morality would be quite superfluous were it not for the inherent weakness, bordering on depravity, of human nature. Some writers with a more genial conception have attributed the current blackening to theologians who have thought to honor the divine by disparaging the human. Theologians have doubtless taken a gloomier view of man than have pagans and secularists. But this explanation doesn't take us far. For after all these theologians are themselves human, and they would have been without influence if the human audience had not somehow responded to them.

Morality is largely concerned with controlling human nature. When we are attempting to control anything we are acutely aware of what resists us. So moralists were led, perhaps, to think of human nature as evil because of its reluctance to yield to control, its rebelliousness under the yoke. But this explanation only raises another question. Why did morality set up rules so foreign to human nature? The ends it insisted upon, the regulations it imposed, were after all outgrowths of human nature. Why then was human nature so adverse to them? Moreover rules can be obeyed and ideals realized only as they appeal to something in human nature and awaken in it an active response. Moral principles that exalt themselves by degrading human nature are in effect committing suicide. Or else they involve human nature in unending civil war, and treat it as a hopeless mess of contradictory forces.

We are forced therefore to consider the nature and origin of that control of human nature with which morals has been occupied. And the fact which is forced upon us when we raise this question is the existence of classes. Control has been vested in an oligarchy. Indifference to regulation has grown in the gap which separates the ruled from the rulers. Parents, priests, chiefs, social censors have supplied aims, aims which were foreign to those upon whom they were imposed, to the young, laymen, ordinary folk; a few have given and administered rule, and the mass have in a passable fashion and with reluctance obeyed. Everybody knows that good children are those who make as little trouble as possible for their elders, and since most of them cause a good deal of annoyance they must be naughty by nature. Generally speaking, good people have been those who did what they were told to do, and lack of eager compliance is a sign of something wrong in their nature.

But no matter how much men in authority have turned moral rules into an agency of class supremacy, any theory which attributes the origin of rule to deliberate design is false. To take advantage of conditions after they have come into existence is one thing; to create them for the sake of an advantage to accrue is quite another thing. We must go back of the bare fact of social division into superior and inferior. To say that accident produced social conditions is to perceive they were not produced by intelligence. Lack of understanding of human nature is the primary cause of disregard for it. Lack of insight always ends in despising or else unreasoned admiration. When men had no scientific knowledge of physical nature they either passively submitted to it or sought to control it magically. What cannot be understood cannot be managed intelligently. It has to be forced into subjection from without. The opaqueness of human nature to reason is equivalent to a belief in its intrinsic irregularity. Hence a decline in the authority of social oligarchy was accompanied by a rise of scientific interest in human nature. This means that the make-up and working of human forces afford a basis for moral ideas and ideals. Our science of human nature in comparison with physical sciences is rudimentary, and morals which are concerned with the health, efficiency and happiness of a development of human nature are correspondingly elementary. These pages are a discussion of some phases of the ethical change involved in positive respect for human nature when the latter is associated with scientific knowledge. We may anticipate the general nature of this change through considering the evils which have resulted from severing morals from the actualities of human physiology and psychology. There is a pathology of goodness as well as of evil; that is, of that sort of goodness which is nurtured by this separation. The badness of good people, for the most part recorded only in fiction, is the revenge taken by human nature for the injuries heaped upon it in the name of morality. In the first place, morals cut off from positive roots in man's nature is bound to be mainly negative. Practical emphasis falls upon avoidance, escape of evil, upon not doing things, observing prohibitions. Negative morals assume as many forms as there are types of temperament subject to it. Its commonest form is the protective coloration of a neutral respectability, an insipidity of character. For one man who thanks God that he is not as other men there are a thousand to offer thanks that they are as other men, sufficiently as others are to escape attention. Absence of social blame is the usual mark of goodness for it shows that evil has been avoided. Blame is most readily averted by being so much like everybody else that one passes unnoticed. Conventional morality is a drab morality in which the only fatal thing is to be conspicuous. If there be flavor left in it, then some natural traits have somehow escaped being subdued. To be so good as to attract notice is to be priggish, too good for this world. The same psychology that brands the convicted criminal as forever a social outcast makes it the part of a gentleman not to obtrude virtues noticeably upon others.

The Puritan is never popular, not even in a society of Puritans. In case of a pinch, the mass prefer to be good fellows rather than to be good men. Polite vice is preferable to eccentricity and ceases to be vice. Morals that professedly neglect human nature end by emphasizing those qualities of human nature that are most commonplace and average; they exaggerate the herd instinct to conformity. Professional guardians of morality who have been exacting with respect to themselves have accepted avoidance of conspicuous evil as enough for the masses. One of the most instructive things in all human history is the system of concessions, tolerances, mitigations and reprieves which the Catholic Church with its official supernatural morality has devised for the multitude. Elevation of the spirit above everything natural is tempered by organized leniency for the frailties of flesh. To uphold an aloof realm of strictly ideal realities is admitted to be possible only for a few. Protestantism, except in its most zealous forms, has accomplished the same result by a sharp separation between religion and morality in which a higher justification by faith disposes at one stroke of daily lapses into the gregarious morals of average conduct.

There are always ruder forceful natures who cannot tame themselves to the required level of colorless conformity. To them conventional morality appears as an organized futility; though they are usually unconscious of their own attitude since they are heartily in favor of morality for the mass as making it easier to manage them. Their only standard is success, putting things over, getting things done. Being good is to them practically synonymous with ineffectuality; and accomplishment, achievement is its own justification. They know by experience that much is forgiven to those who succeed, and they leave goodness to the stupid, to those whom they qualify as boobs. Their gregarious nature finds sufficient outlet in the conspicuous tribute they pay to all established institutions as guardians of ideal interests, and in their denunciations of all who openly defy conventionalized ideals. Or they discover that they are the chosen agents of a higher morality and walk subject to specially ordained laws. Hypocrisy in the sense of a deliberate covering up of a will to evil by loud-voiced protestations of virtue is one of the rarest of occurrences. But the combination in the same person of an intensely executive nature with a love of popular approval is bound, in the face of conventional morality, to produce what the critical term hypocrisy.

Another reaction to the separation of morals from human nature is a romantic glorification of natural impulse as something superior to all moral claims. There are those who lack the persistent force of the executive will to break through conventions and to use them for their own purposes, but who unite sensitiveness with intensity of desire. Fastening upon the conventional element in morality, they hold that all morality is a conventionality hampering to the development of individuality. Although appetites are the commonest things in human nature, the least distinctive or individualized, they identify unrestraint in satisfaction of appetite with free realization of individuality. They treat subjection to passion as a manifestation of freedom in the degree in which it shocks the bourgeois. The urgent need for a transvaluation of morals is caricatured by the notion that an avoidance of the avoidances of conventional morals constitutes positive achievement. While the executive type keeps its eyes on actual conditions so as to manipulate them, this school abrogates objective intelligence in behalf of sentiment, and withdraws into little coteries of emancipated souls.

There are others who take seriously the idea of morals separated from the ordinary actualities of humanity and who attempt to live up to it. Some become engrossed in spiritual egotism. They are preoccupied with the state of their character, concerned for the purity of their motives and the goodness of their souls. The exaltation of conceit which sometimes accompanies this absorption can produce a corrosive inhumanity which exceeds the possibilities of any other known form of selfishness. In other cases, persistent preoccupation with the thought of an ideal realm breeds morbid discontent with surroundings, or induces a futile withdrawal into an inner world where all facts are fair to the eye. The needs of actual conditions are neglected, or dealt with in a half-hearted way, because in the light of the ideal they are so mean and sordid. To speak of evils, to strive seriously for change, shows a low mind. Or, again, the ideal becomes a refuge, an asylum, a way of escape from tiresome responsibilities. In varied ways men come to live in two worlds, one the actual, the other the ideal. Some are tortured by the sense of their irreconcilability. Others alternate between the two, compensating for the strains of renunciation involved in membership in the ideal realm by pleasureable excursions into the delights of the actual.

If we turn from concrete effects upon character to theoretical issues, we single out the discussion regarding freedom of will as typical of the consequences that come from separating morals from human nature. Men are wearied with bootless discussion, and anxious to dismiss it as a metaphysical subtlety. But nevertheless it contains within itself the most practical of all moral questions, the nature of freedom and the means of its achieving. The separation of morals from human nature leads to a separation of human nature in its moral aspects from the rest of nature, and from ordinary social habits and endeavors which are found in business, civic life, the run of companionships and recreations. These things are thought of at most as places where moral notions need to be applied, not as places where moral ideas are to be studied and moral energies generated. In short, the severance of morals from human nature ends by driving morals inwards from the public open out-of-doors air and light of day into the obscurities and privacies of an inner life. The significance of the traditional discussion of free will is that it reflects precisely a separation of moral activity from nature and the public life of men.

One has to turn from moral theories to the general human struggle for political, economic and religious liberty, for freedom of thought, speech, assemblage and creed, to find significant reality in the conception of freedom of will. Then one finds himself out of the stiflingly close atmosphere of an inner consciousness and in the open-air world. The cost of confining moral freedom to an inner region is the almost complete severance of ethics from politics and economics. The former is regarded as summed up in edifying exhortations, and the latter as connected with arts of expediency separated from larger issues of good.

In short, there are two schools of social reform. One bases itself upon the notion of a morality which springs from an inner freedom, something mysteriously cooped up within personality. It asserts that the only way to change institutions is for men to purify their own hearts, and that when this has been accomplished, change of institutions will follow of itself. The other school denies the existence of any such inner power, and in so doing conceives that it has denied all moral freedom. It says that men are made what they are by the forces of the environment, that human nature is purely malleable, and that till institutions are changed, nothing can be done. Clearly this leaves the outcome as hopeless as does an appeal to an inner rectitude and benevolence. For it provides no leverage for change of environment. It throws us back upon accident, usually disguised as a necessary law of history or evolution, and trusts to some violent change, symbolized by civil war, to usher in an abrupt millennium. There is an alternative to being penned in between these two theories. We can recognize that all conduct is *interaction* between elements of human nature and the environment, natural and social. Then we shall see that progress proceeds in two ways, and that freedom is found in that kind of interaction which maintains an environment in which human desire and choice count for something. There are in truth forces in man as well as without him. While they are infinitely frail in comparison with exterior forces, yet they may have the support of a foreseeing and contriving intelligence. When we look at the problem as one of an adjustment to be intelligently attained, the issue shifts from within personality to an engineering issue, the establishment of arts of education and social guidance.

The idea persists that there is something materialistic about natural science and that morals are degraded by having anything seriously to do with material things. If a sect should arise proclaiming that men ought to purify their lungs completely before they ever drew a breath it ought to win many adherents from professed moralists. For the neglect of sciences that deal specifically with facts of the natural and social environment leads to a side-tracking of moral forces into an unreal privacy of an unreal self. It is impossible to say how much of the remediable suffering of the world is due to the fact that physical science is looked upon as merely physical. It is impossible to say how much of the unnecessary slavery of the world is due to the conception that moral issues can be settled within conscience or human sentiment apart from consistent study of facts and application of specific knowledge in industry, law and politics. Outside of manufacturing and transportation, science gets its chance in war. These facts perpetuate war and the hardest, most brutal side of modern industry. Each sign of disregard for the moral potentialities of physical science drafts the conscience of mankind away from concern with the interactions of man and nature which must be mastered if freedom is to be a reality. It diverts intelligence to anxious preoccupation with the unrealities of a purely inner life, or strengthens reliance upon outbursts of sentimental affection. The masses swarm to the occult for assistance. The cultivated smile contemptuously. They might smile, as the saying goes, out of the other side of their mouths if they realized how recourse to the occult exhibits the practical logic of their own beliefs. For both rest upon a separation of moral ideas and feelings from knowable facts of life, man and the world.

It is not pretended that a moral theory based upon realities of human nature and a study of the specific connections to these realities with those of physical science would do away with moral struggle and defeat. It would not make the moral life as simple a matter as wending one's way along a well-lighted boulevard. All action is an invasion of the future, of the unknown. Conflict and uncertainty are ultimate traits. But morals based upon concern with facts and deriving guidance from knowledge of them would at least locate the points of effective endeavor and would focus available resources upon them. It would put an end to the impossible attempt to live in two unrelated worlds. It would destroy fixed distinction between the human and the physical, as well as that between the moral and the industrial and political. Morals based on study of human nature instead of upon disregard for it would find the facts of man continuous with those of the rest of nature and would thereby ally ethics with physics and biology. It would find the nature and activities of one person coterminous with those of other human beings, and therefore link ethics with the study of history, sociology, law and economics.

Such a morals would not automatically solve moral problems, nor resolve perplexities. But it would enable us to state problems in such forms that action could be courageously and intelligently directed to their solution. It would not assure us against failure, but it would render failure a source of instruction. It would not protect us against the future emergence of equally serious moral difficulties, but it would enable us to approach the always recurring troubles with a fund of growing knowledge which would add significant values to our conduct even when we overtly failed—as we should continue to do. Until the integrity of morals with human nature and of both with the environment is recognized, we shall be deprived of the aid of past experience to cope with the most acute and deep problems of life. Accurate and extensive knowledge will continue to operate only in dealing with purely technical problems. The intelligent acknowledgment of the continuity of nature, man and society will alone secure a growth of morals which will be serious without being fanatical, aspiring without sentimentality, adapted to reality without conventionality, sensible without taking the form of calculation of profits, idealistic without being romantic.

Part One: The Place of Habit in Conduct

Habits as Social Functions

Habits may be profitably compared to physiological functions, like breathing, digesting. The latter are, to be sure, involuntary, while habits are acquired. But important as is this difference for many purposes it should not conceal the fact that habits are like functions in many respects, and especially in requiring the cooperation of organism and environment. Breathing is an affair of the air as truly as of the lungs; digesting an affair of food as truly as of tissues of stomach. Seeing involves light just as certainly as it does the eye and optic nerve. Walking implicates the ground as well as the legs; speech demands physical air and human companionship and audience as well as vocal organs. We may shift from the biological to the mathematical use of the word function, and say that natural operations like breathing and digesting, acquired ones like speech and honesty, are functions of the surroundings as truly as of a person. They are things done *by* the environment by means of organic structures or acquired dispositions. The same air that under certain conditions ruffles the pool or wrecks buildings, under other conditions purifies the blood and conveys thought. The outcome depends upon what air acts upon. The social environment acts through native impulses and speech and moral habitudes manifest themselves. There are specific good reasons for the usual attribution of acts to the person from whom they immediately proceed. But to convert this special reference into a belief of exclusive ownership is as misleading as to suppose that breathing and digesting are complete within the human body. To get a rational basis for moral discussion we must begin with recognizing that functions and habits are ways of using and incorporating the environment in which the latter has its say as surely as the former.

We may borrow words from a context less technical than that of biology, and convey the same idea by saying that habits are arts. They involve skill of sensory and motor organs, cunning or craft, and objective materials. They assimilate objective energies, and eventuate in command of environment. They require order, discipline, and manifest technique. They have a beginning, middle and end. Each stage marks progress in dealing with materials and tools, advance in converting material to active use. We should laugh at any one who said that he was master of stone working, but that the art was cooped up within himself and in no wise dependent upon support from objects and assistance from tools.

In morals we are however quite accustomed to such a fatuity. Moral dispositions are thought of as belonging exclusively to a self. The self is thereby isolated from natural and social surroundings. A whole school of morals flourishes upon capital drawn from restricting morals to character and then segregating character from conduct, motives from actual deeds. Recognition of the analogy of moral action with functions and arts uproots the causes which have made morals subjective and "individualistic." It brings morals to earth, and if they still aspire to heaven it is to the heavens *of* the earth, and not to another world. Honesty, chastity, malice, peevishness, courage, triviality, industry, irresponsibility are not private possessions of a person. They are working adaptations of personal capacities with environing forces. All virtues and vices are habits which incorporate objective forces. They are interactions of elements contributed by the make-up of an individual with elements supplied by the out-door world. They can be studied as objectively as physiological functions, and they can be modified by change of either personal or social elements.

If an individual were alone in the world, he would form his habits (assuming the impossible, namely, that he would be able to form them) in a moral vacuum. They would belong to him alone, or to him only in reference to physical forces. Responsibility and virtue would be his alone. But since habits involve the support of environing conditions, a society or some specific group of fellow-men, is always accessory before and after the fact. Some activity proceeds from a man; then it sets up reactions in the surroundings. Others approve, disapprove, protest, encourage, share and resist. Even letting a man alone is a definite response. Envy, admiration and imitation are complicities. Neutrality is non-existent. Conduct is always shared; this is the difference between it and a physiological process. It is not an ethical "ought" that conduct *should* be social. It *is* social, whether bad or good.

Washing one's hands of the guilt of others is a way of sharing guilt so far as it encourages in others a vicious way of action. Non-resistance to evil which takes the form of paying no attention to it is a way of promoting it. The desire of an individual to keep his own conscience stainless by standing aloof from badness may be a sure means of causing evil and thus of creating personal responsibility for it. Yet there are circumstances in which passive resistance may be the most effective form of nullification of wrong action, or in which heaping coals of fire on the evil-doer may be the most effective way of transforming conduct. To sentimentalize over a criminal—to "forgive" because of a glow of feeling—is to incur liability for production of criminals. But to suppose that infliction of retributive suffering suffices, without reference to concrete consequences, is to leave untouched old causes of criminality and to create new ones by fostering revenge and brutality. The abstract theory of justice which demands the "vindication" of law irrespective of instruction and reform of the wrong-doer is as much a refusal to recognize responsibility as is the sentimental gush which makes a suffering victim out of a criminal.

Courses of action which put the blame exclusively on a person as if his evil will were the sole cause of wrong-doing and those which condone offense on account of the share of social conditions in producing bad disposition, are equally ways of making an unreal separation of man from his surroundings, mind from the world. Causes for an act always exist, but causes are not excuses. Questions of causation are physical, not moral except when they concern future consequences. It is as causes of future actions that excuses and accusations alike must be considered. At present we give way to resentful passion, and then "rationalize" our surrender by calling it a vindication of justice. Our entire tradition regarding punitive justice tends to prevent recognition of social partnership in producing crime; it falls in with a belief in metaphysical freewill. By killing an evil-doer or by shutting him up behind stone walls, we are enabled to forget both him and our part in creating him. Society excuses itself by laying the blame on the criminal; he retorts by putting the blame on bad early surroundings, the temptations of others, lack of opportunities, and the persecutions of officers of the law. Both are right, except in the wholesale character of their recriminations. But the effect on both sides is to throw the whole matter back into antecedent causation, a method which refuses to bring the matter to truly moral judgment. For morals has to do with acts still within our control, acts still to be performed. No amount of guilt on the part of the evil-doer absolves us from responsibility for the consequences upon him and others of our way of treating him, or from our continuing responsibility for the conditions under which persons develop perverse habits.

We need to discriminate between the physical and the moral question. The former concerns what *has* happened, and how it happened. To consider this question is indispensable to morals. Without an answer to it we cannot tell what forces are at work nor how to direct our actions so as to improve conditions. Until we know the conditions which have helped form the characters we approve and disapprove, our efforts to create the one and do away with the other will be blind and halting. But the moral issue concerns the future. It is prospective. To content ourselves with pronouncing judgments of merit and demerit without reference to the fact that our judgments are themselves facts which have consequences and that their value depends upon *their* consequences, is complacently to dodge the moral issue, perhaps even to indulge ourselves in pleasurable passion just as the person we condemn once indulged himself. The moral problem is that of modifying the factors which now influence future results. To change the working character or will of another we have to alter objective conditions which enter into his habits. Our own schemes of judgment, of assigning blame and praise, of awarding punishment and honor, are part of these conditions.

In practical life, there are many recognitions of the part played by social factors in generating personal traits. One of them is our habit of making social classifications. We attribute distinctive characteristics to rich and poor, slum-dweller and captain of industry, rustic and suburbanite, officials, politicians, professors, to members of races, sets and parties. These judgments are usually too coarse to be of much use. But they show our practical awareness that personal traits are functions of social situations. When we generalize this perception and act upon it intelligently we are committed by it to recognize that we change character from worse to better only by changing conditions—among which, once more, are our own ways of dealing with the one we judge. We cannot change habit directly: that notion is magic. But we can change it indirectly by modifying conditions, by an intelligent selecting and weighting of the objects which engage attention and which influence the fulfilment of desires.

A savage can travel after a fashion in a jungle. Civilized activity is too complex to be carried on without smoothed roads. It requires signals and junction points; traffic authorities and means of easy and rapid transportation. It demands a congenial, antecedently prepared environment. Without it, civilization would relapse into barbarism in spite of the best of subjective intention and internal good disposition. The eternal dignity of labor and art lies in their effecting that permanent reshaping of environment which is the substantial foundation of future security and progress. Individuals flourish and wither away like the grass of the fields. But the fruits of their work endure and make possible the development of further activities having fuller significance. It is of grace not of ourselves that we lead civilized lives. There is sound sense in the old pagan notion that gratitude is the root of all virtue. Loyalty to whatever in the established environment makes a life of excellence possible is the beginning of all progress. The best we can accomplish for posterity is to transmit unimpaired and with some increment of meaning the environment that makes it possible to maintain the habits of decent and refined life. Our individual habits are links in forming the endless chain of humanity. Their significance depends upon the environment inherited from our forerunners, and it is enhanced as we foresee the fruits of our labors in the world in which our successors live.

For however much has been done, there always remains more to do. We can retain and transmit our own heritage only by constant remaking of our own environment. Piety to the past is not for its own sake nor for the sake of the past, but for the sake of a present so secure and enriched that it will create a better future. Individuals with their exhortations, their preachings and scoldings, their inner aspirations and sentiments have disappeared, but their habits endure, because these habits incorporate objective conditions in themselves. So will it be with *our* activities. We may desire abolition of war, industrial justice, greater equality of opportunity for all. But no amount of preaching good will or the golden rule or cultivation of sentiments of love and equity will accomplish the results. There must be change in objective arrangements and institutions. We must work on the environment not merely on the hearts of men. To think otherwise is to suppose that flowers can be raised in a desert or motor cars run in a jungle. Both things can happen and without a miracle. But only by first changing the jungle and desert.

Yet the distinctively personal or subjective factors in habit count. Taste for flowers may be the initial step in building reservoirs and irrigation canals. The stimulation of desire and effort is one preliminary in the change of surroundings. While personal exhortation, advice and instruction is a feeble stimulus compared with that which steadily proceeds from the impersonal forces and depersonalized habitudes of the environment, yet they may start the latter going. Taste, appreciation and effort always spring from some accomplished objective situation. They have objective support; they represent the liberation of something formerly accomplished so that it is useful in further operation. A genuine appreciation of the beauty of flowers is not generated within a self-enclosed consciousness. It reflects a world in which beautiful flowers have already grown and been enjoyed. Taste and desire represent a prior objective fact recurring in action to secure perpetuation and extension. Desire for flowers comes after actual enjoyment of flowers. But it comes before the work that makes the desert blossom, it comes before *cultivation* of plants. Every ideal is preceded by an actuality; but the ideal is more than a repetition in inner image of the actual. It projects in securer and wider and fuller form some good which has been previously experienced in a precarious, accidental, fleeting way.

Part Two: The Place of Impulse in Conduct

Impulses and Change of Habits

Habits as organized activities are secondary and acquired, not native and original. They are outgrowths of unlearned activities which are part of man's endowment at birth. The order of topics followed in our discussion may accordingly be questioned. Why should what is derived and therefore in some sense artificial in conduct be discussed before what is primitive, natural and inevitable? Why did we not set out with an examination of those instinctive activities upon which the acquisition of habits is conditioned?

The query is a natural one, yet it tempts to flinging forth a paradox. In conduct the acquired is the primitive. Impulses although first in time are never primary in fact; they are secondary and dependent. The seeming paradox in statement covers a familiar fact. In the life of the individual, instinctive activity comes first. But an individual begins life as a baby, and babies are dependent beings. Their activities could continue at most for only a few hours were it not for the presence and aid of adults with their formed habits. And babies owe to adults more than procreation, more than the continued food and protection which preserve life. They owe to adults the opportunity to express their native activities in ways which have meaning. Even if by some miracle original activity could continue without assistance from the organized skill and art of adults, it would not amount to anything. It would be mere sound and fury.

In short, the *meaning* of native activities is not native; it is acquired. It depends upon interaction with a matured social medium. In the case of a tiger or eagle, anger may be identified with a serviceable life-activity, with attack and defense. With a human being it is as meaningless as a gust of wind on a mudpuddle apart from a direction given it by the presence of other persons, apart from the responses they make to it. It is a physical spasm, a blind dispersive burst of wasteful energy. It gets quality, significance, when it becomes smouldering sullenness, an annoying interruption, a peevish irritation, a murderous revenge, a blazing indignation. And although these phenomena which have a meaning spring from original native reactions to stimuli, yet they depend also upon the responsive behavior of others. They and all similar human displays of anger are not pure impulses; they are habits formed under the influence of association with others who have habits already and who show their habits in the treatment which converts a blind physical discharge into a significant anger.

After ignoring impulses for a long time in behalf of sensations, modem psychology now tends to start out with an inventory and description of instinctive activities. This is an undoubted improvement. But when it tries to explain complicated events in personal and social life by direct reference to these native powers, the explanation becomes hazy and forced. It is like saying the flea and the elephant, the lichen and the redwood, the timid hare and the ravening wolf, the plant with the most inconspicuous blossom and the plant with the most glaring color are alike products of natural selection. There may be a sense in which the statement is true; but till we know the specific environing conditions under which selection took place we really know nothing. And so we need to know about the social conditions which have educated original activities into conditions and significant dispositions before we can discuss the psychological element in society. This is the true meaning of social psychology.

At some place on the globe, at some time, every kind of practice seems to have been tolerated or even praised. How is the tremendous diversity of institutions (including moral codes) to be accounted for? The native stock of instincts is practically the same everywhere. Exaggerate as much as we like the native differences of Patagonians and Greeks, Sioux Indians and Hindoos, Bushmen and Chinese, their original differences will bear no comparison to the amount of difference found in custom and culture. Since such a diversity can be attributed to an original identity, the development of native impulse must be stated in terms of acquired habits, not the growth of customs in terms of instincts.

The wholesale human sacrifices of Peru and the tenderness of St. Francis, the cruelties of pirates and the philanthropies of [John] Howard, the practice of Suttee and the cult of the Virgin, the war and peace dances of the Comanches and the parliamentary institutions of the British, the communism of the south-sea islander and the proprietary thrift of the Yankee, the magic of the medicine man and the experiments of the chemist in his laboratory, the non-resistance of Chinese and the aggressive militarism of an imperial Prussia, monarchy by divine right and government by the people; the countless diversity of habits suggested by such a random list springs from practically the same capital-stock of native instincts.

It would be pleasant if we could pick and choose those institutions which we like and impute them to human nature, and the rest to some devil; or those we like to our kind of human nature, and those we dislike to the nature of despised foreigners on the ground they are not really "native" at all. It would appear to be simpler if we could point to certain customs, saying that they are the unalloyed products of certain instincts, while those other social arrangements are to be attributed wholly to other impulses. But such methods are not feasible. The same original fears, angers, loves and hates are hopelessly entangled in the most opposite institutions. The thing we need to know is how native stock has been modified by interaction with different environments.

Yet it goes without saying that original, unlearned activity has its distinctive place and that an important one in conduct. Impulses are the pivots upon which re-organization of activities turn, they are agencies of deviation, for giving new directions to old habits and changing their quality. Consequently whenever we are concerned with understanding social transition and flux or with projects for reform, personal and collective, our study must go to analysis of native tendencies. Interest in progress and reform is, indeed, the reason for the present great development of scientific interest in primitive human nature. If we inquire why men were so long blind to the existence of powerful and varied instincts in human beings, the answer seems to be found in the lack of a conception of orderly progress. It is fast becoming incredible that psychologists disputed as to whether they should choose between innate ideas and an empty, passive, wax-like mind. For it seems as if a glance at a child would have revealed that the truth lay in neither doctrine, so obvious is the surging of specific native activities. But this obtuseness to facts was evidence of lack of interest in what could be done with impulses, due, in turn, to lack of interest in modifying existing institutions. It is no accident that men became interested in the psychology of savages and babies when they became interested in doing away with old institutions.

A combination of traditional individualism with the recent interest in progress explains why the discovery of the scope and force of instincts has led many psychologists to think of them as the fountain head of all conduct, as occupying a place before instead of after that of habits. The orthodox tradition in psychology is built upon isolation of individuals from their surroundings. The soul or mind or consciousness was thought of as self-contained and self-enclosed. Now in the career of an individual if it is regarded as complete in itself instincts clearly come before habits. Generalize this individualistic view, and we have an assumption that all customs, all significant episodes in the life of individuals can be carried directly back to the operation of instincts.

But, as we have already noted, if an individual be isolated in this fashion, along with the fact of primacy of instinct we find also the fact of death. The inchoate and scattered impulses of an infant do not coordinate into serviceable powers except through social dependencies and companionships. His impulses are merely starting points for assimilation of the knowledge and skill of the more matured beings upon whom he depends. They are tentacles sent out to gather that nutrition from customs which will in time render the infant capable of independent action. They are agencies for transfer of existing social power into personal ability; they are means of reconstructive growth. Abandon an impossible individualistic psychology, and we arrive at the fact that native activities are organs of re-organization and re-adjustment. The hen precedes the egg. But nevertheless this particular egg may be so treated as to modify the future type of hen.

Part Three: The Place of Intelligence in Conduct

Habit and Intelligence

In discussing habit and impulse we have repeatedly met topics where reference to the work of thought was imperative. Explicit consideration of the place and office of intelligence in conduct can hardly begin otherwise than by gathering together these incidental references and reaffirming their significance. The stimulation of reflective imagination by impulse, its dependence upon established habits, and its effect in transforming habit and regulating impulse forms, accordingly, our first theme.

Habits are conditions of intellectual efficiency. They operate in two ways upon intellect. Obviously, they restrict its reach, they fix its boundaries. They are blinders that confine the eyes of mind to the road ahead. They prevent thought from straying away from its imminent occupation to a landscape more varied and picturesque but irrelevant to practice. Outside the scope of habits, thought works gropingly, fumbling in confused uncertainty; and yet habit made complete in routine shuts in thought so effectually that it is no longer needed or possible. The routineer's road is a ditch out of which he cannot get, whose sides enclose him, directing his course so thoroughly that he no longer thinks of his path or his destination. All habit-forming involves the beginning of an intellectual specialization which if unchecked ends in thoughtless action.

Significantly enough this fullblown result is called absentmindedness. Stimulus and response are mechanically linked together in an unbroken chain. Each successive act facilely evoked by its predecessor pushes us automatically into the next act of a predetermined series. Only a signal flag of distress recalls consciousness to the task of carrying on. Fortunately nature which beckons us to this path of least resistance also puts obstacles in the way of our complete acceptance of its invitation. Success in achieving a ruthless and dull efficiency of action is thwarted by untoward circumstance. The most skillful aptitude bumps at times into the unexpected, and so gets into trouble from which only observation and invention extricate it. Efficiency in following a beaten path has then to be converted into breaking a new road through strange lands.

Nevertheless what in effect is love of ease has masqueraded morally as love of perfection. A goal of finished accomplishment has been set up which if it were attained would mean only mindless action. It has been complete and free activity when in truth it is only a treadmill activity or marching in one place. The practical impossibility of reaching, in an all around way and all at once such a "perfection" has been recognized. But such a goal has nevertheless been conceived as the ideal, and progress has been defined as approximation to it. Under diverse intellectual skies the ideal has assumed diverse forms and colors. But all of them have involved the conception of a completed activity, a static perfection. Desire and need have been treated as signs of deficiency, and endeavor as proof not of power but of incompletion.

In Aristotle this conception of an end which exhausts all realization and excludes all potentiality appears as a definition of the highest excellence. It of necessity excludes all want and struggle and all dependencies. It is neither practical nor social. Nothing is left but a self-revolving, self-sufficing thought engaged in contemplating its own sufficiency. Some forms of Oriental morals have united this logic with a profounder psychology, and have seen that the final terminus on this road is Nirvana, an obliteration of all thought and desire. In medieval science, the ideal reappeared as a definition of heavenly bliss accessible only to a redeemed immortal soul.

Herbert Spencer is far enough away from Aristotle, medieval Christianity and Buddhism; but the idea re-emerges in his conception of a goal of evolution in which adaptation of organism to environment is complete and final. In popular thought, the conception lives in the vague thought of a remote state of attainment in which we shall be beyond "temptation," and in which virtue by its own inertia will persist as a triumphant consummation. Even Kant who begins with a complete scorn for happiness ends with an "ideal" of the eternal and undisturbed union of virtue and joy, though in his case nothing but a symbolic approximation is admitted to be feasible.

The fallacy in these versions of the same idea is perhaps the most pervasive of all fallacies in philosophy. So common is it that one questions whether it might not be called *the* philosophical fallacy. It consists in the supposition that whatever is found true under certain conditions may forthwith be asserted universally or without limits and conditions. Because a thirsty man gets satisfaction in drinking water, bliss consists in being drowned. Because the success of any particular struggle is measured by reaching a point of frictionless action, therefore there is such a thing as an all-inclusive end of effortless smooth activity endlessly maintained. It is forgotten that success is success *of* a specific effort, and satisfaction the fulfilment *of* a specific demand, so that success and satisfaction become meaningless when severed from the wants and struggles whose consummations they are, or when taken universally. The philosophy of Nirvana comes the closest to admission of this fact, but even it holds Nirvana to be desirable.

Habit is however more than a restriction of thought. Habits become negative limits because they are first positive agencies. The more numerous our habits the wider the field of possible observation and foretelling. The more flexible they are, the more refined is perception in its discrimination and the more delicate the presentation evoked by imagination. The sailor is intellectually at home on the sea, the hunter in the forest, the painter in his studio, the man of science in his laboratory. These commonplaces are universally recognized in the concrete; but their significance is obscured and their truth denied in the current general theory of mind. For they mean nothing more or less than that habits formed in process of exercising biological aptitudes are the sole agents of observation, recollection, foresight and judgment: a mind or consciousness or soul in general which performs these operations is a myth.

The doctrine of a single, simple and indissoluble soul was the cause and the effect of failure to recognize that concrete habits are the means of knowledge and thought. Many who think themselves scientifically emancipated and who freely advertise the soul for a superstition, perpetuate a false notion of what knows, that is, of a separate knower. Nowadays they usually fix upon consciousness in general, as a stream or process or entity; or else, more specifically upon sensations and images as the tools of intellect. Or sometimes they think they have scaled the last heights of realism by adverting grandiosely to a formal knower in general who serves as one term in the knowing relation; by dismissing psychology as irrelevant to knowledge and logic, they think to conceal the psychological monster they have conjured up.

Now it is dogmatically stated that no such conceptions of the seat, agent or vehicle will go psychologically at the present time. Concrete habits do all the perceiving, recognizing, imagining, recalling, judging, conceiving and reasoning that is done. "Consciousness," whether as a stream or as special sensations and images, expresses functions of habits, phenomena of their formation, operation, their interruption and reorganization.

Yet habit does not, of itself, know, for it does not of itself stop to think, observe or remember. Neither does impulse of itself engage in reflection or contemplation. It just lets go. Habits by themselves are too organized, too insistent and determinate to need to indulge in inquiry or imagination. And impulses are too chaotic, tumultuous and confused to be able to know even if they wanted to. Habit as such is too definitely adapted to an environment to survey or analyze it, and impulse is too indeterminately related to the environment to be capable of reporting anything about it. Habit incorporates, enacts or overrides objects, but it doesn't know them. Impulse scatters and obliterates them with its restless stir. A certain delicate combination of habit and impulse is requisite for observation, memory and judgment. Knowledge which is not projected against the black unknown lives in the muscles, not in consciousness.

We may, indeed, be said to *know how* by means of our habits. And a sensible intimation of the practical function of knowledge has led men to identify all acquired practical skill, or even the instinct of animals, with knowledge. We walk and read aloud, we get off and on street cars, we dress and undress, and do a thousand useful acts without thinking of them. We know something, namely, how to do them. [Henri] Bergson's philosophy of intuition is hardly more than an elaborately documented commentary on the popular conception that by instinct a bird knows how to build a nest and a spider to weave a web. But after all, this practical work done by habit and instinct in securing prompt and exact adjustment to the environment is not knowledge, except by courtesy. Or, if we choose to call it knowledge—and no one has the right to issue an ukase to the contrary—then other things also called knowledge, knowledge *of* and *about* things, knowledge *that* things are thus and so, knowledge that involves reflection and conscious appreciation, remains of a different sort, unaccounted for and undescribed.

For it is a commonplace that the more suavely efficient a habit the more unconsciously it operates. Only a hitch in its workings occasions emotion and provokes thought. [Thomas] Carlyle and Rousseau, hostile in temperament and outlook, yet agree in looking at consciousness as a kind of disease, since we have no consciousness of bodily or mental organs as long as they work at ease in perfect health. The idea of disease is, however, aside from the point, unless we are pessimistic enough to regard every slip in total adjustment of a person to its surroundings as something abnormal—a point of view which once more would identify well-being with perfect automatism. The truth is that in every waking moment, the complete balance of the organism and its environment is constantly interfered with and as constantly restored. Hence the "stream of consciousness" in general, and in particular that phase of it celebrated by William James as alternation of flights and perchings. Life is interruptions and recoveries. Continuous interruption is not possible in the activities of an individual. Absence of perfect equilibrium is not equivalent to a complete crushing of organized activity. When the disturbance amounts to such a pitch as that, the self goes to pieces. It is like shell-shock. Normally, the environment remains sufficiently in harmony with the body of organized activities to sustain most of them in active function. But a novel factor in the surroundings releases some impulse which tends to initiate a different and incompatible activity, to bring about a redistribution of the elements of organized activity between those have been respectively central and subsidiary. Thus the hand guided by the eye moves toward a surface. Visual quality is the dominant element. The hand comes in contact with an object. The eye does not cease to operate but some unexpected quality of touch, a voluptuous smoothness or annoying heat, compels a readjustment in which the touching, handling activity strives to dominate the action. Now at these moments of a shifting in activity conscious feeling and thought arise and are accentuated. The disturbed adjustment of organism and environment is reflected in a temporary strife which concludes in a coming to terms of the old habit and the new impulse.

In this period of redistribution impulse determines the direction of movement. It furnishes the focus about which reorganization swirls. Our attention in short is always directed forward to bring to notice something which is imminent but which as yet escapes us. Impulse defines the peering, the search, the inquiry. It is, in logical language, the movement into the unknown, not into the immense inane of the unknown at large, but into that special unknown which when it is hit upon restores an ordered, unified action. During this search, old habit supplies content, filling, definite, recognizable, subject-matter. It begins as vague presentiment of what we are going towards. As organized habits are definitely deployed and focused, the confused situation takes on form, it is "cleared up"—the essential function of intelligence. Processes become objects. Without habit there is only irritation and confused hesitation. With habit alone there is a machine-like repetition, a duplicating recurrence of old acts. With conflict of habits and release of impulse there is conscious search.

VII
THE ARTS AND AESTHETIC EDUCATION

18

Individuality and Experience (1926)

In the 1920s, Dewey befriended Philadelphia philanthropist and art collector Albert C. Barnes. Barnes taught Dewey how to look at paintings, gave him access to his extraordinary art collection, and named him director of education at the Barnes Foundation. (The Barnes Foundation, which offers a variety of art education programs, is located in Philadelphia, Pennsylvania, next to the Philadelphia Museum of Art.) Dewey subsequently contributed several articles to the *Journal of the Barnes Foundation*, among them "Individuality and Experience." In this short piece, Dewey identifies another version of the artificial dualism between "child-centered" and "curriculum-centered" education. Here, it takes the form of "free-expression" in art education versus "direct instruction" in particular art methods and traditions. Again Dewey refuses to seek a compromise between the two approaches, rejecting the idea that they naturally constitute conflicting forms of education. He claims instead that methods and traditions in the arts embody practices that can help release and direct the individual creative and expressive abilities of students. These traditions, however, should not simply be told, copied, and rigidly adhered to. Rather, Dewey writes, each student must "*see* on [their] own behalf and in [their] own way the relations between means and methods employed and results achieved. Nobody else can see for [them]." In this way, methods and traditions can be liberating and facilitative, enhancing students' imaginative and expressive potentials, rather than limiting and restrictive.

The methods of picture-making employed in the classes of Professor [Franz] Cizek in Vienna raise a question that has to be dealt with in every branch of instruction. The question develops in two directions, one suggested by his statement that it is impossible to exclude outside influences, and the other by his report that upon the whole the more original constructions are those of younger pupils, that older students seem gradually to lose interest, so that no prominent artist has been produced. The problem thus defined consists in the relation of individuality and its adequate development to the work and responsibilities of the teacher, representing accumulated experience of the past.

Unfortunately, the history of schools not only in art but in all lines shows a swing of the pendulum between extremes, though it must be admitted that the simile of the pendulum is not a good one, for the schools remain, most of them, most of the time, near one extreme, instead of swinging periodically and evenly between the two. Anyway, the two extremes are external imposition and dictation and "free-expression." Revolt from the costly, nerve-taxing and inadequate results of mechanical control from without creates an enthusiasm for spontaneity and "development from within," as it is often phrased. It is found that children at first are then much happier in their work—anyone who has seen Cizek's class will testify to the wholesome air of cheerfulness, even of joy, which pervades the room—but gradually tend to become listless and finally bored, while there is an absence of cumulative, progressive development of power and of actual achievement in results. Then the pendulum swings back to regulation by the ideas, rules and orders of someone else, who being maturer, better informed and more experienced is supposed to know what should be done and how to do it.

The metaphor of the pendulum is faulty in another respect. It seems to suggest that the solution lies in finding a midpoint between the two extremes which would be at rest. But what is really wanted is a change in the direction of movement. As a general proposition no one would deny that personal mental growth is furthered in any branch of human undertaking by contact with the accumulated and sifted experience of others in that line. No one would seriously propose that all future carpenters should be trained by actually starting with a clean sheet, wiping out everything that the past has discovered about mechanics, about tools and their uses, and so on. It would not be thought likely that this knowledge would "cramp their style," limit their individuality, etc. But neither, on the other hand, have carpenters been formed by the methods often used in manual training shops where dinky tasks of a minute and technical nature are set, wholly independent of really making anything, having only specialized skill as their aim. As a rule carpenters are educated in their calling by working with others who have experience and skill, sharing in the simpler portions of the real undertakings, assisting in ways which enable them to observe methods and to see what results they are adapted to accomplish.

Such learning is controlled by two great principles: one is participation in something inherently worthwhile, or undertaken on its own account; the other, is perception of the relation of means to consequences. When these two conditions are met, a third consideration usually follows as a matter of course. Having had an experience of the meaning of certain technical processes and forms of skill there develops an interest in skill and "technique": the meaning of the result is "transferred" to the means of its attainment. Boys interested in base-ball as a game thus submit themselves voluntarily to continued practice in throwing, catching, batting, the separate elements of the game. Or boys who get interested in the game of marbles will practice to increase their skill in shooting and hitting. Just imagine, however, what would happen if they set these exercises as tasks in school, with no prior activity in the games and with no sense of what they were about or for, and without any such appeal to the social, or participating impulses, as takes place in games!

If we generalize from such a commonplace case as the education of artisans through their work, we may say that the customs, methods and *working* standards of the calling constitute a "tradition," and that initiation into the tradition is the means by which the powers of learners are released and directed. But we should also have to say that the urge or need of an individual to join in an undertaking is a necessary prerequisite of the tradition's being a factor in his personal growth in power and freedom; and also that he has to *see* on his own behalf and in his own way the relations between means and methods employed and results achieved. Nobody else can see for him, and he can't see just by being "told," although the right kind of telling may guide his seeing and thus help him see what he needs to see. And if he has no impelling desire of his own to become a carpenter, if his interest in being one is perfunctory, if it is not an interest in *being* a carpenter at all, but only in getting a pecuniary reward by doing jobs, the tradition will never of course really enter into and integrate with his own powers. It will remain, then, a mere set of mechanical and more or less meaningless rules that he is obliged to follow if he is to hold his job and draw his pay.

Supposing, again, that our imaginary pupil works for and with a master carpenter who believes in only one kind of house with a fixed design, and his aim is not only to teach his apprentice to make just that one kind of house, but to accept it with all his soul, heart and mind as the only kind of house that should ever be built, the very type and standard model of all houses. Then it is easy to see that limitation of personal powers will surely result, not merely, moreover, limitation of technical skill but, what is more important, of his powers of observation, imagination, judgment, and even his emotions, since his appreciations will be warped to conform to the one preferred style. The imaginary case illustrates what often happens when we pass from the education of artisans to that of artists. As a rule a carpenter has to keep more or less open; he is exposed to many demands and must be flexible enough to meet them. He is in no position to set up a final authority about ends and models and standards, no matter how expert he may be in methods and means. But an architect in distinction from a builder is likely to be an "authority"; he can dictate and lay down what is right and wrong, and thus prescribe certain ends and proscribe others. Here is a case where tradition is not enhancing and liberating, but is restrictive and enslaving. If he has pupils, he is a "master" and not an advanced fellow worker; his students are disciples rather than learners. Tradition is no longer tradition but a fixed and absolute convention.

In short, the practical difficulty does not reside in any antagonism of methods and rules and results worked out in past experience to individual desire, capacity and freedom. It lies rather in the hard and narrow and, we may truly say, uneducated habits and attitudes of teachers who set up as authorities, as rulers and judges in Israel. As a matter of course they know that as bare individuals they are not "authorities" and will not be accepted by others as such. So they clothe themselves with some tradition as a mantle, and henceforth it is not just "I" who speaks, but some Lord speaks through me. The teacher then offers himself as the organ of the voice of a whole school, of a *finished* classic tradition, and arrogates to himself the prestige that comes from what he is the spokesman for. Suppression of the emotional and intellectual integrity of pupils is the result; their freedom is repressed and the growth of their own personalities stunted. But it is not because of any opposition between the wisdom and skill of the past and the individual capacities of learners; the trouble lies in the habits, standards and ideas of the teacher. It is analogous to another case. There is no inherent opposition between theory and practice; the former enlarges, releases and gives significance to the latter; while practice supplies theory with its materials and with the test and check which keep it sincere and vital. But there is a whole lot of opposition between human beings who set themselves up as practical and those who set themselves up as theorists, an irresolvable conflict because both have put themselves into a wrong position.

This suggests that the proponents of freedom are in a false position as well as the would-be masters and dictators. There is a present tendency in so-called advanced schools of educational thought (by no means confined to art classes like those of Cizek) to say, in effect, let us surround pupils with certain materials, tools, appliances, etc., and then let pupils respond to these things according to their own desires. Above all let us not suggest any end or plan to the students; let us not suggest to them what they shall do, for that is an unwarranted trespass upon their sacred intellectual individuality since the essence of such individuality is to set up ends and aims.

Now such a method is really stupid. For it attempts the impossible, which is always stupid; and it misconceives the conditions of independent thinking. There are a multitude of ways of reacting to surrounding conditions, and without some guidance from experience these reactions are almost sure to be casual, sporadic and ultimately fatiguing, accompanied by nervous strain. Since the teacher has presumably a greater background of experience, there is the same presumption of the right of a teacher to make suggestions as to what to do, as there is on the part of the head carpenter to suggest to apprentices something of what they are to do. Moreover, the theory literally carried out would be obliged to banish all artificial materials, tools and appliances. Being the product of the skill, thought and matured experience of others, they would also, by the theory, "interfere" with personal freedom.

Moreover, when the child proposes or suggests what to do, some consequence to be attained, whence is the suggestion supposed to spring? There is no spontaneous germination in the mental life. If he does not get the suggestion from the teacher, he gets it from somebody or something in the home or the street or from what some more vigorous fellow pupil is doing. Hence the chances are great of its being a passing and superficial suggestion, without much depth and range—in other words, not specially conducive to the developing of freedom. If the teacher is really a teacher, and not just a master or "authority," he should know enough about his pupils, their needs, experiences, degrees of skill and knowledge, etc., to be able (not to dictate aims and plans) to share in a discussion regarding what is to be done and be as free to make suggestions as anyone else. (The implication that the teacher is the one and only person who has no "individuality" or "freedom" to "express" would be funny if it were not often so sad in its outworkings.) And his contribution, given the conditions stated, will presumably do more to getting something started which will really secure and increase the development of strictly individual capacities than will suggestions springing from uncontrolled haphazard sources.

The point is also worth dwelling upon, that the method of leaving the response entirely to pupils, the teacher supplying, in the language of the day, only the "stimuli," misconceives the nature of thinking. Any so-called "end" or "aim" or "project" which the average immature person can suggest in advance is likely to be highly vague and unformed, a mere outline sketch, not a suggestion of a definite result or consequence but rather a gesture which roughly indicates a field within which activities might be carried on. It hardly represents thought at all: it is a suggestion. The real intellectual shaping of the "end" or purpose comes during and because of the operations subsequently performed. This is as true of the suggestion which proceeds from the teacher as of those which "spontaneously" spring from the pupils, so that the former does not restrict thought. The advantage on the side of the teacher—if he or she has any business to be in that position—is the greater probability that it will be a suggestion which will permit and require thought in the subsequent activity which builds up a clear and organized conception of an end. There is no more fatal flaw in psychology than that which takes the original vague fore-feeling of some consequence to be realized as the equivalent of a *thought* of an end, a true purpose and directive plan. The thought of an end is strictly correlative to perception of means and methods. Only when, and as the latter becomes clear during the serial process of execution does the project and guiding aim and plan become evident and articulated. In the full sense of the word, a person becomes aware of what he wants to do and what he is about only when the work is actually complete.

The adjective "serial" is important in connection with the process of performance or execution. Each step forward, each "means" used, is a partial attainment of an "end." It makes clearer the character of that end, and hence suggests to an observing mind the next step to be taken, or the means and methods to be next employed. Originality and independence of thinking are therefore connected with the intervening process of execution rather than with the source of the initial suggestion. Indeed, genuinely fruitful and original suggestions are themselves usually the results of experience in the carrying out of undertakings. The "end" is not, in other words, an end or finality in the literal sense, but is in turn the starting point of new desires, aims and plans. By means of the process the mind gets power to make suggestions which are significant. There is now a past experience from which they can spring with an increased probability of their being worthwhile and articulate.

It goes without saying that a teacher may interfere and impose alien standards and methods during the operation. But as we have previously seen, this is not because of bringing to bear the results of previous experience, but because the habits of the teacher are so narrow and fixed, his imagination and sympathies so limited, his own intellectual horizon so bounded, that he brings them to bear in a wrong way. The fuller and richer the experience of the teacher, the more adequate his own knowledge of "traditions" the more likely is he, given the attitude of participator instead of that of master, to use them in a liberating way.

Freedom or individuality, in short, is not an original possession or gift. It is something to be achieved, to be wrought out. Suggestions as to things which may advantageously be taken, as to skill, as to methods of operation, are indispensable conditions of its achievement. These by the nature of the case must come from a sympathetic and discriminating knowledge of what has been done in the past and how it has been done.

19

Experience, Nature, and Art (1925)

Dewey's more philosophical piece "Experience, Nature, and Art" examines a related set of issues. It also appeared in the Barnes Foundation journal, but was published previously in extended form as chapter 9 of Dewey's magnum opus *Experience and Nature*, 1925 (*LW 1*). Dewey introduces his subject by recounting the age-old tradition in Western culture of separating mind and body, while deeming the former a superior form of being. This means valuing activities associated with mental life (e.g., contemplation) over those involving "hands-on" activity (e.g., creativity or making things). This dualism paved the way for the more modern distinction between fine art (or "art for art's sake") and the decorative or practical arts (e.g., crafts and the work of artisans). Dewey argues, however, that there is no fundamental difference between artist and artisan or the potential artistic and aesthetic qualities of their work. Each, at its best, can be immediately enjoyable *and* have instrumental or practical value. Indeed, writes Dewey, "It is the fact that art, so far as it is truly art, is a union of the serviceable and the immediately enjoyable, of the instrumental and the [aesthetic], that makes it impossible to institute a difference in kind between useful and fine art." So conceived, both forms of art can be infused with meaning, provide a feeling of completeness or consummation, stimulate the senses, and enhance perception, making them much more than a mere "frill" and expendable part of school curriculum.

∾

Contemporary theories of art generally suffer from inconsistency. They are only in part interpretations of art and of experience as these are to be observed today; in part, they represent a survival of opinions and assumptions inherited from the Greeks. According to Greek theory, art is a form of practice, and so incurs the reproach of being concerned with a merely subjective, changing and imperfect world. This was true of all arts, of those now classified as "fine" as well as of the useful crafts practiced by the artisan. In contrast with both, science was regarded as a revelation—in fact, the only true revelation—of reality. It was thought to be through science alone that access is provided to the world as it is in itself, not colored or distorted by human wants or preferences. Art corresponded to production, science to "contemplation," and the productive was branded as inferior, an activity proper only to mechanics and slaves.

This view was a reflection in theory of the Greek social system, in which a menial class performed all necessary labor, and freeman and citizens alone enjoyed the fruits of that labor. Since the leisure class held the position of power and honor, its part in life was regarded as intrinsically superior, and the artist, who by the labor of his hands shaped the objects which were the food of contemplation, belonged to the lower realm of nature and experience.

Contemporary opinion accepts, in the main, the Greek view that knowledge is contemplation, and that it alone reveals nature as nature is. The Greek disparagement of art, it partly accepts and partly rejects; accepts it as regards the useful arts, which are clearly modes of practice, but rejects it as regards the fine arts. In fine art it makes a distinction between the experience of the artist, which is considered to be creative, and the experience of the beholder or connoisseur, which is regarded as passive. Of these, it ranks the artist above the connoisseur, the producer above the consumer. At the same time, although it regards knowledge as contemplation, it recognizes that science, the systematic pursuit of knowledge, is active, an affair of making experiments, and so belongs to the realm of practice.

These notions are consistent neither with each other nor, as a whole, with experience. The Greek view was sound in recognizing the continuity of "useful" with "fine" art; it erred in neglecting the connection of knowledge with experiment, and so in isolating knowledge from practice. If knowledge is truly contemplation, and is on that account superior to mere practice, then all arts, that of the painter no less than that of the carpenter, are inferior to science, and the painter stands in rank below the dilettante who looks at paintings. If, however, not knowledge but art is the final flowering of experience, the crown and consummation of nature, and knowledge is only the means by which art, which includes all practice, is enabled to attain its richest development, then it is the artist who represents nature and life at their best.

Current discussion of aesthetics and art falls into inconsistency about the active and passive roles of art largely because it confuses art as a process of execution, of creation of a type of material things, and art as the enjoyable appreciation of things so created. To avoid this inconsistency it is advantageous to use the word "artistic" to designate the activities by which works of art are brought into being, and to reserve the term "aesthetic" for the appreciation of them when created, the enhanced or heightened perceptions in which they result.

Although the view here defended asserts that there is no ultimate difference between the artist and the artisan, there is an obvious empirical difference between the activities and experience of the artist, as we actually find him, and those of the artisan. That the artist's life is the more humanly desirable, that it is the richer, more self-rewarding, more humane, none would deny. The difference, however, is not one between aesthetic contemplation and mere labor, but between those activities which are charged with intrinsic significance—which are both instrumental, means to more remote ends, and consummatory, immediately enjoyable—and those forms which are *merely* instrumental, and in themselves nothing but drudgery. This fact is due to nothing in the nature of experience or practice, but only to defects in the present economic and social order. To call the greater part of the productive activities now carried on "useful arts" is mere euphemism, by which the essential irrationality of the existing régime is concealed. Innumerable commodities which are manufactured by the "useful arts" are only apparently and superficially useful; their employment results not in satisfaction of intelligent desire, but in confusion and extravagance, bought at the price of a narrowed and embittered experience. There can be no true understanding of either practice or aesthetic appreciation while practice is in large measure slavery, and while "esthetic appreciation" is merely one of the forms of distraction by which intervals of respite from slavery are whiled away.

The degradation of labor is paralleled by a degradation of art. Most of what passes for art at present falls under three captions:

First, there is mere indulgence in emotional outpouring, without reference to the conditions of intelligibility. Such "expression of emotion" is largely futile—futile partly because of its arbitrary and willfully eccentric character, but partly also because the channels of expression currently accepted as permissible are so rigidly laid down that novelty can find acceptance only with the aid of violence.

In addition to this type—and frequently mingled with it—there is experimentation in new modes of craftsmanship, cases where the seemingly bizarre and over-individualistic character of the products is due to discontent with existing technique, and is associated with an attempt to find new modes of expression. It is aside from the point to treat these manifestations as if they constituted art for the first time in human history, or to condemn them as not art because of their violent departure from received canons and methods. Some movement in this direction has always been a condition of growth of new forms, a condition of salvation from that mortal arrest and decay called academic art.

Then there is that which in quantity bulks most largely as fine art: the production of buildings in the name of the art of architecture; of pictures in the name of painting; of novels, dramas, etc., in the name of literary art; a production which in reality is largely a form of commercialized industry in production of a class of commodities that find their sale among well-to-do persons desirous of maintaining a conventionally approved status. As the first two modes carry to disproportionate excess that factor of difference, particularity and contingency, which is indispensable in all art, deliberately flaunting avoidance of the repetitions and order of nature, so this mode celebrates the regular and finished. It is reminiscent rather than commemorative of the meanings of things. Its products remind their owner of things pleasant in memory though hard in direct undergoing, and remind others that their owner has achieved an economic standard which makes possible cultivation and decoration of leisure.

Obviously no one of these classes of activity and products, or all of them put together, mark off anything that can be called distinctively fine art. They share their qualities and defects with many other activities and objects. But, fortunately, there may be mixed with any of them, and, still more fortunately, there may occur without mixture, process and product which are characteristically excellent. *This occurs when activity is productive of an object which affords continuously renewed delight.* This condition requires that the object be, with its successive consequences, indefinitely instrumental to *new* satisfying events. For otherwise the object is quickly exhausted and satiety sets in. Anyone who reflects upon the commonplace that a measure of artistic products is their capacity to attract and retain observation with satisfaction under whatever conditions they are approached, has a sure demonstration that a genuinely aesthetic object is not exclusively consummatory, but is causally productive as well. A consummatory object that is not also instrumental turns in time to the dust and ashes of boredom. The "eternal" quality of great art is its renewed instrumentality for further consummatory experiences.

When this fact is noted it is also seen that limitation of fineness of art to paintings, statues, poems, songs and symphonies is conventional, or even verbal. Any activity that is productive of objects whose perception is an immediate good, and whose operation is a continual source of enjoyable perception of other events, exhibits fineness of art. There are acts of all kinds that directly refresh and enlarge the spirit and that are instrumental to the production of new objects and dispositions which are in turn productive of further refinements and replenishments. Frequently moralists make the acts *they* find excellent or virtuous wholly final, and treat art and affection as mere means. Aestheticians reverse the performance, and see in good *acts* means to an ulterior external happiness, while aesthetic appreciation is called a good in itself, or that strange thing, an end in itself. But on both sides it is true that in being predominantly fructifying, the things designated means are immediately satisfying. They are their own excuses for being just because they are charged with an office in quickening apprehension, enlarging the horizon of vision, refining discrimination, creating standards of appreciation which are confirmed and deepened by further experiences. It would almost seem that when their non-instrumental character is insisted on, what is meant were an indefinitely expansive and radiating instrumental efficacy.

It is the fact that art, so far as it is truly art, is a union of the serviceable and the immediately enjoyable, of the instrumental and the consummatory, that makes it impossible to institute a difference in kind between useful and fine art. Many things are termed useful for reasons of social status, implying depreciation and contempt. Things are sometimes said to belong to the menial arts merely because they are cheap and used familiarly by common people. These things of daily use for ordinary ends may survive in later periods, or be transported to another culture, as from Japan and China to America, and being rare and sought by connoisseurs, rank forthwith as works of fine art. Other things may be called fine because their manner of use is decorative or socially ostentatious. It is tempting to make a distinction of degree and say that a thing belongs to the sphere of use when perception of its meaning is instrumental to something else; and that a thing belongs to fine art when its other uses are subordinate to its use in perception. The distinction has a rough practical value, but cannot be pressed too far. For in production of a painting or poem, as well as in making a vase or temple, a perception is also employed as a means for something beyond itself. Moreover, the perception of urns, pots and pans as commodities may be intrinsically enjoyable, although these things are primarily perceived with reference to some use to which they are put. The only *basic* distinction is that between bad art and good art, and this distinction between things that meet the requirements of art and those that do not applies equally to things of use and of beauty. Capacity to offer to perception meaning in which fruition and efficacy interpenetrate is met by different products in various degrees of fulness; it may be missed altogether by pans and poems alike. The difference between the ugliness of a meretriciously conceived and executed utensil and a meretricious and pretentious painting is one only of content or material; in form, both are articles, and bad articles.

The relation of the aesthetic and the artistic, as above defined, may now be stated more precisely. Both are incidental to practice, to performance, but in the aesthetic the attained vision with which the artist presents us releases energies which remain diffuse and inchoate, which raise the whole level of our existence, but do not find issue in any single or specific form. In the artistic the existing consummation is utilized to bring into existence further analogous perceptions. A painter, for example, uses a picture not only to guide his perception of the world, but as a source of suggestions for painting additional pictures. Art in being, the active productive process, may thus be defined as an aesthetic perception, together with an *operative* perception of the efficiencies of the aesthetic object. A parallel contrast is to be found in scientific experience. The layman may by his knowledge of science understand the world about him much more clearly, and regulate his actions more effectively, than he could without it, but he is not called a scientist until he is able to utilize his knowledge to make fresh scientific discoveries. As to the scientist, knowledge is a means to more knowledge, so to the artist aesthetic insight is a means to further aesthetic insight, and not merely to enhancement of life in general. The distinction between the aesthetic and the artistic, important as it is, is thus, in the last analysis, a matter of degree.

The meaning of the view accepted here may be made clearer if it is contrasted with the theory of art prevalent today in one school of critics, that aesthetic qualities in works of fine art are unique, separate not only from everything that is existential in nature but from all other forms of good. In proclaiming that such arts as music, poetry, painting, have characteristics unshared by any natural things whatever, such critics carry to its conclusion the isolation of fine art from the useful, of the final from the efficacious.

As an example, we may consider that theory of art which makes the distinguishing quality of the aesthetic object its possession of what is called "significant form." Unless the meaning of the term is so isolated as to be wholly occult, it denotes a selection, for the sake of emphasis, purity, subtlety, of those forms which give consummatory significance to everyday subject-matters of experience. "Forms" are not the peculiar property or creation of the aesthetic and artistic; they are characters in virtue of which anything meets the requirements of an enjoyable perception. "Art" does not create the forms; it is their selection and organization in such ways as to enhance, prolong and purify the perceptual experience. It is not by accident that some objects and situations afford marked perceptual satisfactions; they do so because of their structural properties and relations. An artist may work with a minimum of analytic recognition of these structures or "forms;" he may select them chiefly by a kind of sympathetic vibration. But they may also be discriminatively ascertained; and an artist may utilize his deliberate awareness of them to create works of art that are more formal and abstract than those to which the public is accustomed. Tendency to composition in terms of the formal characters marks much contemporary art, in poetry, painting, music, even sculpture and architecture. At their worst, these products are "scientific" rather than artistic; technical exercises, and of a new kind of pedantry. At their best, they assist in ushering in new modes of art and by education of the organs of perception in new modes of consummatory objects, they enlarge and enrich the world of human vision. But they do this, not by discarding altogether connection with the real world, but by a highly funded and generalized representation of the formal sources of ordinary emotional experience.

Thus we reach a conclusion regarding the relations of instrumental and fine art which is precisely the opposite of that intended by selective aestheticians; namely, that fine art consciously undertaken as such is peculiarly instrumental in quality. It is a device in experimentation carried on for the sake of education. It exists for a specialized use, use being a new training of modes of perception. The creators of such works of art are entitled, when successful, to the gratitude that we give to inventors of microscopes and microphones; in the end, they open new objects to be observed and enjoyed. This is a genuine service; but only an age of combined confusion and conceit will arrogate to works that perform this special utility the exclusive name of fine art.

Art is great in proportion as it is universal, that is, in proportion as the uniformities of nature which it reveals and utilizes are extensive and profound—provided, however, that they are freshly applied in concrete objects or situations. The only objects, insights, perceptions, which remain perennially unwithered and unstaled are those which sharpen our vision for new and unforeseen embodiments of the truth they convey. The "magic" of poetry—and pregnant experience has poetic quality—is precisely the revelation of meaning in the old effected by its presentation of the new. It radiates the light that never was on sea or land but that is henceforth an abiding illumination of objects.

20

From *Art as Experience* (1934)

This section closes with a reading from *Art as Experience*, Dewey's naturalistic account of the aesthetic dimension of human experience. Wide-ranging and highly resourceful, the book remains of interest to both artists and educators. In the final chapter, "Art and Civilization," Dewey returns to his leading idea—that art is at bottom not an object or event, but rather a quality that permeates experience. This aesthetic quality enriches the direct meaning of experience and is often enhanced by firsthand encounters with the arts. According to Dewey, this quality can also be present in countless forms in everyday experience. This includes both play and work when they are directly meaningful and fulfilling. The arts are additionally expressions of culture, and their health and vitality depend on their accessibility and connection to people's everyday lives and activities. Every civilization, Dewey observes, creates its own unique means of celebrating and transmitting its particular customs and values. For this reason the arts inevitably atrophy, and their shared meaning diminishes, when they are consigned to museums or other peripheral settings.

Art and Civilization

Art is a quality that permeates an experience; it is not, save by a figure of speech, the experience itself. Esthetic experience is always more than esthetic. In it a body of matters and meanings, not in themselves esthetic, *become* esthetic as they enter into an ordered rhythmic movement toward consummation. The material itself is widely human. So we return to the theme of the first chapter. The material of esthetic experience in being human—human in connection with the nature of which it is a part—is social. Esthetic experience is a manifestation, a record and celebration of the life of a civilization, a means of promoting its development, and is also the ultimate judgment upon the quality of a civilization. For while it is produced and is enjoyed by individuals, those individuals are what they are in the content of their experience because of the cultures in which they participate.

The Magna Carta is held up as the great political stabilizer of Anglo-Saxon civilization. Even so, it has operated in the meaning given it in imagination rather than by its literal contents. There are transient and there are enduring elements in a civilization. The enduring forces are not separate; they are functions of a multitude of passing incidents as the latter are organized into the meanings that form minds. Art is the great force in effecting this consolidation. The individuals who have minds pass away one by one. The works in which meanings have received objective expression endure. They become part of the environment, and interaction with this phase of the environment is the axis of continuity in the life of civilization. The ordinances of religion and the power of law are efficacious as they are clothed with a pomp, a dignity and majesty that are the work of imagination. If social customs are more than uniform external modes of action, it is because they are saturated with story and transmitted meaning. Every art in some manner is a medium of this transmission while its products are no inconsiderable part of the saturating matter.

"The glory that was Greece and the grandeur that was Rome" for most of us, probably for all but the historical student, sum up those civilizations; glory and grandeur are esthetic. For all but the antiquarian, ancient Egypt is its monuments, temples and literature. Continuity of culture in passage from one civilization to another as well as within the culture, is conditioned by art more than by any other one thing. Troy lives for us only in poetry and in the objects of art that have been recovered from its ruins. Minoan civilization is today its products of art. Pagan gods and pagan rites are past and gone and yet endure in the incense, lights, robes, and holidays of the present. If letters devised for the purpose, presumably, of facilitating commercial transactions, had not developed into literature, they would still be technical equipments, and we ourselves might live amid hardly a higher culture than that of our savage ancestors. Apart from rite and ceremony, from pantomime and dance and the drama that developed from them, from dance, song and accompanying instrumental music, from the utensils and articles of daily living that were formed on patterns and stamped with insignia of community life that were akin to those manifested in the other arts, the incidents of the far past would now be sunk in oblivion.

It is out of the question to do more than suggest in bare outline the function of the arts in older civilizations. But the arts by which primitive folk commemorated and transmitted their customs and institutions, arts that were communal, are the sources out of which all fine arts have developed. The patterns that were characteristic of weapons, rugs and blankets, baskets and jars, were marks of tribal union. Today the anthropologist relies upon the pattern carved on a club, or painted on a bowl to determine its origin. Rite and ceremony as well as legend bound the living and the dead in a common partnership. They were esthetic but they were more than esthetic. The rites of mourning expressed more than grief; the war and harvest dance were more than a gathering of energy for tasks to be performed; magic was more than a way of commanding forces of nature to do the bidding of man; feasts were more than a satisfaction of hunger. Each of these communal modes of activity united the practical, the social, and the educative in an integrated whole having esthetic form. They introduced social values into experience in the way that was most impressive. They connected things that were overtly important and overtly done with the substantial life of the community. Art was *in* them, for these activities conformed to the needs and conditions of the most intense, most readily grasped and longest remembered experience. But they were more than just art, although the esthetic strand was ubiquitous.

In Athens, which we regard as the home par excellence of epic and lyric poetry, of the arts of drama, architecture and sculpture, the idea of art for art's sake would not, as I have already remarked, have been understood. Plato's harshness toward Homer and Hesiod seems strained. But they were the moral teachers of the people. His attacks upon the poets are like those which some critics of the present day bring against portions of Christian scriptures because of evil moral influence attributed to them. Plato's demand of censorship of poetry and music is a tribute to the social and even political influence exercised by those arts. Drama was enacted on holy-days; attendance was of the nature of an act of civic worship. Architecture in all its significant forms was public, not domestic, much less devoted to industry, banking, or commerce.

The decay of art in the Alexandrian period, its degeneracy into poor imitations of archaic models, is a sign of the general loss of civic consciousness that accompanied the eclipse of city-states and the rise of a conglomerate imperialism. Theories about art and the cultivation of grammar and rhetoric took the place of creation. And theories about art gave evidence of the great social change that had taken place. Instead of connecting arts with an expression of the life of the community, the beauty of nature and of art was regarded as an echo and reminder of some supernal reality that had its being outside social life, and indeed outside the cosmos itself—the ultimate source of all subsequent theories that treat art as something imported into experience from without.

As the Church developed, the arts were again brought into connection with human life and became a bond of union among men. Through its services and sacraments, the Church revived and adapted in impressive form what was most moving in all prior rites and ceremonies.

The Church, even more than the Roman Empire, served as the focus of unity amid the disintegration that followed the fall of Rome. The historian of intellectual life will emphasize the dogmas of the Church; the historian of political institutions, the development of law and authority by means of the ecclesiastic institution. But the influence that counted in the daily life of the mass of the people and that gave them a sense of unity was constituted, it is safe to surmise, by sacraments, by song and pictures, by rite and ceremony, all having an esthetic strand, more than by any other one thing. Sculpture, painting, music, letters were found in the place where worship was performed. These objects and acts were much more than works of art to the worshipers who gathered in the temple. They were in all probability much less works of art to them than they are today to believers and unbelievers. But because of the esthetic strand, religious teachings were the more readily conveyed and their effect was the more lasting. By the art in them, they were changed from doctrines into living experiences.

That the Church was fully conscious of this extra-esthetic effect of art is evident in the care it took to regulate the arts. Thus in 787 A.D., the Second Council of Nicaea officially ordained the following:

"The substance of religious scenes is not left to the initiative of artists; it derives from the principles laid down by the Catholic Church and religious tradition. . . . The art alone belongs to the painter; its organization and arrangement belongs to the clergy."[1] The censorship desired by Plato held full sway.

From *Art as Experience* | 277

There is a statement of Machiavelli that has always seemed to me symbolic of the spirit of the Renascence. He said that when he was through with the business of the day, he retired into his study and lost himself in absorption of the classic literature of antiquity. This statement is doubly symbolic. On the one hand, ancient culture would not be lived. It could only be studied. As [George] Santayana has well said, Greek civilization is now an ideal to be admired, not one to be realized. On the other hand, knowledge of Greek art, especially of architecture and sculpture, revolutionized the practice of the arts, including painting. The sense of naturalistic shapes of objects and of their setting in the natural landscape was recovered; in the Roman school painting was almost an attempt to produce the feelings occasioned by sculpture, while the Florentine school developed the peculiar values inherent in line. The change affected both esthetic form and substance. The lack of perspective, the flat and profile quality of Church art, its use of gold, and a multitude of other traits were not due to mere lack of technical skill. They were organically connected with the particular interactions in human experience that were desired as the consequence of art. The secular experiences that were emerging at the time of the Renascence and that fed upon antique culture involved of necessity the production of effects demanding new form in art. The extension of substance from Biblical subjects and the lives of saints to portrayal of scenes of Greek mythology and then to spectacles of contemporary life that were socially impressive inevitably ensued.

These remarks are intended merely to be a bare illustration of the fact that every culture has its own collective individuality. Like the individuality of the person from whom a work of art issues, this collective individuality leaves its indelible imprint upon the art that is produced. Such phrases as the art of the South Sea islands, of the North American Indian, of the Negro, Chinese, Cretan, Egyptian, Greek, Hellenistic, Byzantine, Moslem, Gothic, Renascence, have a veridical significance. The undeniable fact of the collective cultural origin and import of works illustrates the fact, previously mentioned, that art is a strain in experience rather than an entity in itself. A problem has been made out of the fact, however, by a recent school of thought. It is contended that since we cannot actually reproduce the experience of a people remote in time and foreign in culture, we cannot have a genuine appreciation of the art it produced. Even of Greek art it is asserted that the Hellenic attitude toward life and the world was so different from ours that the artistic product of Greek culture must esthetically be a sealed book to us.

In part an answer to this contention has already been given. It is doubtless true that the total experience of the Greeks in presence of, say, Greek architecture, statuary, and painting is far from being identical with ours. Features of their culture were transient; they do not now exist, and these features were embodied in their experience of their works of art. But experience is a matter of the interaction of the artistic product with the self. It is not therefore twice alike for different persons even today. It changes with the same person at different times as he brings something different to a work. But there is no reason why, in order to be esthetic, these experiences should be identical. So far as in each case there is an ordered movement of the matter of the experience to a fulfillment, there is a dominant esthetic quality. *Au fond*, the esthetic quality is the same for Greek, Chinese and American.

This answer does not, however, cover the whole ground. For it does not apply to the total human effect of the art of a culture. The question, while wrongly framed with respect to the distinctively esthetic, suggests the question of what the art of another people may mean for our total experience. The contention of [Hippolyte] Taine and his school that we must understand art in terms of "race, milieu and time" touches the question, but hardly more than touches it. For such understanding may be purely intellectual, and so on the level of the geographical, anthropological and historical information with which it is accompanied. It leaves open the question of the significance of foreign art for the experience characteristic of present civilization.

The nature of the problem is suggested by Mr. [T. E.] Hulme's theory of the basic difference between Byzantine and Moslem art on one side and Greek and Renascence art on the other. The latter, he says, is vital and naturalistic. The former is geometric. This difference he goes on to explain is not connected with differences in technical capacity. The gulf is made by a fundamental difference of attitude, of desire and purpose. We are now habituated to one mode of satisfaction and we take our own attitude of desire and purpose to be so inherent in all human nature as to give the measure of all works of art, as constituting the demand which all works of art meet and should satisfy. *We* have desires that are rooted in longing for an increase of experienced vitality through delightful intercourse with the forms and movements of "nature." Byzantine art, and some other forms of Oriental art, spring from an experience that has no delight in nature and no striving after vitality. They "express a feeling of separation in the face of outside nature." This attitude characterizes objects as unlike as the Egyptian pyramid and the Byzantine mosaic. The difference between such art and that which is characteristic of the Western world is not to be explained by interest in abstractions. It manifests the idea of separation, of disharmony, of man and nature.[2]

Mr. Hulme sums up by saying that "art cannot be understood by itself, but must be taken as one element in a general process of adjustment between man and the outside world." Irrespective of the truth of Mr. Hulme's explanation of the characteristic difference between much of Oriental and Occidental art (it hardly applies in any case to Chinese art), his way of stating the matter puts, to my mind, the general problem in its proper context and suggests the solution. Just because art, speaking from the standpoint of the influence of collective culture upon creation and enjoyment of works of art, is expressive of a deep-seated attitude of adjustment, of an underlying idea and ideal of generic human attitude, the art characteristic of a civilization is the means for entering sympathetically into the deepest elements in the experience of remote and foreign civilizations. By this fact is explained also the human import of their arts for ourselves. They effect a broadening and deepening of our own experience, rendering it less local and provincial as far as we grasp, by their means, the attitudes basic in other forms of experience. Unless we arrive at the attitudes expressed in the art of another civilization, its products are either of concern to the "esthete" alone, or else they do not impress us esthetically. Chinese art then seems "queer," because of its unwonted schemes of perspective; Byzantine art, stiff and awkward; Negro art, grotesque.

In the reference to Byzantine art, I put the term nature in quotation marks. I did so because the word "nature" has a special meaning in esthetic literature, indicated especially by the use of the adjective "naturalistic." But "nature" also has a meaning in which it includes the whole scheme of things—in which it has the force of the imaginative and emotional word "universe." In experience, human relations, institutions, and traditions are as much a part of the nature in which and by which we live as is the physical world. Nature in this meaning is not "outside." It is in us and we are in and of it. But there are multitudes of ways of participating in it, and these ways are characteristic not only of various experiences of the same individual, but of attitudes of aspiration, need and achievement that belong to civilizations in their collective aspect. Works of art are means by which we enter, through imagination and the emotions they evoke, into other forms of relationship and participation than our own.

The art of the late nineteenth century was characterized by "naturalism" in its restricted sense. The productions most characteristic of the early twentieth century were marked by the influence of Egyptian, Byzantine, Persian, Chinese, Japanese, and Negro art. This influence is marked in painting, sculpture, music, and literature. The effect of "primitive" and early medieval art is a part of the same general movement. The eighteenth century idealized the noble savage and the civilization of remote peoples. But aside from Chinoiseries and some phases of romantic literature, the *sense* of what is back of the arts of foreign people did not affect the actual art produced. Seen in perspective, the so-called pre-Raphaelite art of England is the most typically Victorian of all the painting of the period. But in recent decades, beginning in the nineties, the influence of the arts of distant cultures has entered intrinsically into artistic creation.

For many persons, the effect is doubtless superficial, merely providing a type of objects enjoyable in part because of their individual novelty, and in part because of an added decorative quality. But the idea that would account for the production of contemporary works by mere desire for the unusual, or eccentric or even charm is more superficial than this kind of enjoyment. The moving force is genuine participation, in some degree and phase, in the type of experience of which primitive, Oriental, and early medieval objects of art are the expression. Where the works are merely imitative of foreign works, they are transient and trivial. But at their best they bring about an organic blending of attitudes characteristic of the experience of our own age with that of remote peoples. For the new features are not mere decorative additions but enter into the *structure* of works of art and thus occasion a wider and fuller experience. Their enduring effect upon those who perceive and enjoy will be an expansion of *their* sympathies, imagination, and sense.

This new movement in art illustrates the effect of all genuine acquaintance with art created by other peoples. We understand it in the degree in which we make it a part of our own attitudes, not just by collective information concerning the conditions under which it was produced. We accomplish this result when, to borrow a term from [Henri] Bergson, we install ourselves in modes of apprehending nature that at first are strange to us. To some degree we become artists ourselves as we undertake this integration, and, by bringing it to pass, our own experience is re-oriented. Barriers are dissolved, limiting prejudices melt away, when we enter into the spirit of Negro or Polynesian art. This insensible melting is far more efficacious than the change effected by reasoning, because it enters directly into attitude.

The possibility of the occurrence of genuine communication is a broad problem of which the one just dealt with is one species. It is a fact that it takes place, but the nature of community of experience is one of the most serious problems of philosophy—so serious that some thinkers deny the fact. The existence of communication is so disparate to our physical separation from one another and to the inner mental lives of individuals that it is not surprising that supernatural force has been ascribed to language and that communion has been given sacramental value.

Moreover, events that are familiar and customary are those we are least likely to reflect upon; we take them for granted. They are also, because of their closeness to us, through gesture and pantomime, the most difficult to observe. Communication through speech, oral and written, is the familiar and constant feature of social life. We tend, accordingly, to regard it as just one phenomenon among others of what we must in any case accept without question. We pass over the fact that it is the foundation and source of all activities and relations that are distinctive of internal union of human beings with one another. A vast number of our contacts with one another are external and mechanical. There is a "field" in which they take place, a field defined and perpetuated by legal and political institutions. But the consciousness of this field does not enter our conjoint action as its integral and controlling force. Relations of nations to one another, relations of investors and laborers, of producers and consumers, are interactions that are only to a slight degree forms of communicative intercourse. There are interactions between the parties involved, but they are so external and partial that we undergo their consequences without integrating them into an experience.

We hear speech, but it is almost as if we were listening to a babel of tongues. Meaning and value do not come home to us. There is in such cases no communication and none of the result of community of experience that issues only when language in its full import breaks down physical isolation and external contact. Art is a more universal mode of language than is the speech that exists in a multitude of mutually unintelligible forms. The language of art has to be acquired. But the language of art is not affected by the accidents of history that mark off different modes of human speech. The power of music in particular to merge different individualities in a common surrender, loyalty and inspiration, a power utilized in religion and in warfare alike, testifies to the relative universality of the language of art. The differences between English, French and German speech create barriers that are submerged when art speaks.

Philosophically speaking, the problem with which we are confronted is the relation of the discrete and the continuous. Both of them are stubborn facts and yet they have to meet and blend in any human association that rises above the level of brute intercourse. In order to justify continuity, historians have often resorted to a falsely named "genetic" method, wherein there is no genuine genesis, because everything is resolved into what went before. But Egyptian civilization and art were not just a preparation for Greek, nor were Greek thought and art mere reedited versions of the civilizations from which they so freely borrowed. Each culture has its own individuality and has a pattern that binds its parts together.

Nevertheless, when the art of another culture enters into attitudes that determine our experience genuine continuity is effected. Our own experience does not thereby lose its individuality but it takes unto itself and weds elements that expand its significance. A community and continuity that do not exist physically are created. The attempt to establish continuity by methods which resolve one set of events and one of institutions into those which preceded it in time is doomed to defeat. Only an expansion of experience that absorbs into itself the values experienced because of life-attitudes, other than those resulting from our own human environment, dissolves the effect of discontinuity.

The problem in question is not unlike that we daily undergo in the effort to understand another person with whom we habitually associate. All friendship is a solution of the problem. Friendship and intimate affection are not the result of information about another person even though knowledge may further their formation. But it does so only as it becomes an integral part of sympathy through the imagination. It is when the desires and aims, the interests and modes of response of another become an expansion of our own being that we understand him. We learn to see with his eyes, hear with his ears, and their results give true instruction, for they are built into our own structure. I find that even the dictionary avoids defining the term "civilization." It defines civilization as the state of being civilized and "civilized" as "being in a state of civilization." However, the verb "to civilize" is defined as "to instruct in the arts of life and thus to raise in the scale of civilization." Instruction in the arts of life is something other than conveying information about them. It is a matter of communication and participation in values of life by means of the imagination, and works of art are the most intimate and energetic means of aiding individuals to share in the arts of living. Civilization is uncivil because human beings are divided into non-communicating sects, races, nations, classes and cliques.

∽

The brief sketch of some historical phases of the connection of art with community life set forth earlier in this chapter suggests contrast with present conditions. It is hardly enough to say that the absence of obvious organic connection of the arts with other forms of culture is explained by the complexity of modern life, by its many specializations, and by the simultaneous existence of many diverse centres of culture in different nations that exchange their products but that do not form parts of an inclusive social whole. These things are real enough, and their effect upon the status of art in relation to civilization may be readily discovered. But the significant fact is widespread disruption.

We inherit much from the cultures of the past. The influence of Greek science and philosophy, of Roman law, of religion having a Jewish source, upon our present institutions, beliefs and ways of thinking and feeling is too familiar to need more than mention. Into the operation of these factors two forces have been injected that are distinctly late in origin and that constitute the "modern" in the present epoch. These two forces are natural science and its application in industry and commerce through machinery and the use of non-human modes of energy. In consequence, the question of the place and role of art in contemporary civilization demands notice of its relations to science and to the social consequences of machine industry. The isolation of art that now exists is not to be viewed as an isolated phenomenon. It is one manifestation of the incoherence of our civilization produced by new forces, so new that the attitudes belonging to them and the consequences issuing from them have not been incorporated and digested into integral elements of experience.

Science has brought with it a radically novel conception of physical nature and of our relation to it. This new conception stands as yet side by side with the conception of the world and man that is a heritage from the past, especially from that Christian tradition through which the typically European social imagination has been formed. The things of the physical world and those of the moral realm have fallen apart, while the Greek tradition and that of the medieval age held them in intimate union—although a union accomplished by different means in the two periods. The opposition that now exists between the spiritual and ideal elements of our historic heritage and the structure of physical nature that is disclosed by science, is the ultimate source of the dualisms formulated by philosophy since Descartes and Locke. These formulations in turn reflect a conflict that is everywhere active in modern civilization. From one point of view the problem of recovering an organic place for art in civilization is like the problem of reorganizing our heritage from the past and the insights of present knowledge into a coherent and integrated imaginative union.

The problem is so acute and so widely influential that any solution that can be proposed is an anticipation that can at best be realized only by the course of events. Scientific method as now practiced is too new to be naturalized in experience. It will be a long time before it so sinks into the subsoil of mind as to become an integral part of corporate belief and attitude. Till that happens, both method and conclusions will remain the possession of specialized experts, and will exercise their general influence only by way of external and more or less disintegrating impact upon beliefs, and by equally external practical application. But even now it is possible to exaggerate the harmful effect exercised by science upon imagination. It is true that physical science strips its objects of the qualities that give the objects and scenes of ordinary experience all their poignancy and preciousness, leaving the world, as far as scientific rendering of it is concerned, without the traits that have always constituted its immediate value. But the world of immediate experience in which art operates, remains just what it was. Nor can the fact that physical science presents us with objects that are wholly indifferent to human desire and aspiration be used to indicate that the death of poetry is imminent. Men have always been aware that there is much in the scene in which their lives are set that is hostile to human purpose. At no time would the masses of the disinherited have been surprised at the declaration that the world about them is indifferent to their hopes.

The fact that science tends to show that man is a part of nature has an effect that is favorable rather than unfavorable to art when its intrinsic significance is realized and when its meaning is no longer interpreted by contrast with beliefs that come to us from the past. For the closer man is brought to the physical world, the clearer it becomes that his impulsions and ideas are enacted by nature within him. Humanity in its vital operations has always acted upon this principle. Science gives this action intellectual support. The sense of relation between nature and man in some form has always been the actuating spirit of art.

Moreover, resistance and conflict have always been factors in generating art; and they are, as we have seen, a necessary part of artistic form. Neither a world wholly obdurate and sullen in the face of man nor one so congenial to his wishes that it gratifies all desires is a world in which art can arise. The fairy tales that relate situations of this sort would cease to please if they ceased to be fairy tales. Friction is as necessary to generate esthetic energy as it is to supply the energy that drives machinery. When older beliefs have lost their grip on imagination—and their hold was always there rather than upon reason—the disclosure by science of the resistance that environment offers to man will furnish new materials for fine art. Even now we owe to science a liberation of the human spirit. It has aroused a more avid curiosity, and has greatly quickened in a few at least alertness of observation with respect to things of whose existence we were not before even aware. Scientific method tends to generate a respect for experience, and even though this new reverence is still confined to the few, it contains the promise of a new kind of experiences that will demand expression.

Who can foresee what will happen when the experimental outlook has once become thoroughly acclimatized in a common culture? The attainment of perspective with reference to the future is a most difficult task. We are given to taking features that are most prominent and most troublesome at a given time as if they were the clews [clues] to the future. So we think of the future effect of science in terms derived from the present situation in which it occupies a position of conflict and disruption with reference to great traditions of the western world, as if these terms defined its place necessarily and forever. But to judge justly, we have to see science as things will be when the experimental attitude is thoroughly naturalized. And art in particular will always be distracted or else soft and overrefined when it lacks familiar things for its material.

So far, the effect of science as far as painting, poetry, and the novel are concerned, has been to diversify their materials and forms rather than to create an organic synthesis. I doubt if there were at any time any large number of persons who "saw life steadily and saw it whole." And, at the very worst, it is something to have been freed from syntheses of the imagination that went contrary to the grain of things. Possession of a quickened sense of the value for esthetic experience of a multitude of things formerly shut out, is some compensation amid the miscellany of present objects of art. The bathing beaches, street corners, flowers and fruits, babies and bankers of contemporary painting are after all something more than mere diffuse and disconnected objects. For they are the fruits of a new vision.[3]

I suppose that at all times a great deal of the "art" that has been produced has been trivial and anecdotal. The hand of time has winnowed much of this away, while in an exhibition today we are faced with it *en masse*. Nevertheless, the extension of painting and the other arts to include matter that was once regarded as either too common or too out of the way to deserve artistic recognition is a permanent gain. This extension is not directly the effect of the rise of science. But it is a product of the same conditions that led to the revolution in scientific procedure.

Such diffuseness and incoherence as exist in art today are the manifestation of the disruption of consensus of beliefs. Greater integration in the matter and form of the arts depends consequently upon a general change in culture in the direction of attitudes that are taken for granted in the basis of civilization and that form the subsoil of conscious beliefs and efforts. One thing is sure; the unity cannot be attained by preaching the need of returning to the past. Science is here, and a new integration must take account of it and include it.

The most direct and pervasive presence of science in present civilization is found in its applications in industry. Here we find a more serious problem regarding the relation of art to present civilization and its outlook than in the case of science itself. The divorce of useful and fine art signifies even more than does the departure of science from the traditions of the past. The difference between them was not instituted in modern times. It goes as far back as the Greeks when the useful arts were carried on by slaves and "base mechanics" and shared in the low esteem in which the latter were held. Architects, builders, sculptors, painters, musical performers were artisans. Only those who worked in the medium of words were esteemed artists, since their activities did not involve the use of hands, tools and physical materials. But mass production by mechanical means has given the old separation between the useful and fine a decidedly new turn. The split is reenforced by the greater importance that now attaches to industry and trade in the whole organization of society.

The mechanical stands at the pole opposite to that of the esthetic, and production of goods is now mechanical. The liberty of choice allowed to the craftsman who worked by hand has almost vanished with the general use of the machine. Production of objects enjoyed in direct experience by those who possess, to some extent, the capacity to produce useful commodities expressing individual values, has become a specialized matter apart from the general run of production. This fact is probably the most important factor in the status of art in present civilization. There are, however, certain considerations that should deter one from concluding that industrial conditions render impossible an integration of art in civilization. I am not able to agree with those who think that effective and economical adaptation of the parts of an object to one another with respect to use automatically results in "beauty" or esthetic effect. Every well-constructed object and machine has form, but there is esthetic form only when the object having this external form fits into a larger experience. Interaction of the material of this experience with the utensil or machine cannot be left out of account. But adequate objective relationship of parts with respect to most efficient use at least brings about a condition that is *favorable* to esthetic enjoyment. It strips away the adventitious and superfluous. There is something clean in the esthetic sense about a piece of machinery that has a logical structure that fits it for its work, and the polish of steel and copper that is essential to good performance is intrinsically pleasing in perception. If one compares the commercial products of the present with those of even twenty years ago, one is struck by the great gain in form and color. The change from the old wooden Pullman cars with their silly encumbering ornamentations to the steel cars of the present is typical of what I mean. The external architecture of city apartments remains box-like but internally there is hardly less than an esthetic revolution brought about by better adaptation to need.

A more important consideration is that industrial surroundings work to create that larger experience into which particular products fit in such a way that they get esthetic quality. Naturally, this remark does not refer to the destruction of the natural beauties of the landscape by ugly factories and their begrimed surroundings, nor to the city slums that have followed in the wake of machine production. I mean that the habits of the eye as a medium of perception are being slowly altered in being accustomed to the shapes that are typical of industrial products and to the objects that belong to urban as distinct from rural life. The colors and planes to which the organism habitually responds develop new material for interest. The running brook, the greensward, the forms associated with a rural environment, are losing their place as the primary material of experience. Part at least of the change of attitude of the last score of years to "modernistic" figures in painting is the result of this change. Even the objects of the natural landscape come to be "apperceived" in terms of the spatial relations characteristic of objects the design of which is due to mechanical modes of production; buildings, furnishings, wares. Into an experience saturated with these values, objects having their own internal functional adaptations will fit in a way that yields esthetic results.

But since the organism hungers naturally for satisfaction in the material of experience, and since the surroundings which man has made, under the influence of modern industry, afford less fulfillment and more repulsion than at any previous time, there is only too evidently a problem that is still unsolved. The hunger of the organism for satisfaction through the eye is hardly less than its urgent impulsion for food. Indeed many a peasant has given more care to the cultivation of a flower plot than to producing vegetables for food. There must be forces at work that affect the mechanical means of production that are extraneous to the operation of machinery itself. These forces are found, of course, in the economic system of production for private gain.

The labor and employment problem of which we are so acutely aware cannot be solved by mere changes in wage, hours of work and sanitary conditions. No permanent solution is possible save in a radical social alteration, which effects the degree and kind of participation the worker has in the production and social disposition of the wares he produces. Only such a change will seriously modify the content of experience into which creation of objects made for use enters. And this modification of the nature of experience is the finally determining element in the esthetic quality of the experience of things produced. The idea that the basic problem can be solved merely by increase of hours of leisure is absurd. Such an idea merely retains the old dualistic division between labor and leisure.

The important matter is a change that will reduce the force of external pressure and will increase that of a sense of freedom and personal interest in the operations of production. Oligarchical control from the outside of the processes and the products of work is the chief force in preventing the worker from having that intimate interest in what he does and makes that is an essential prerequisite of esthetic satisfaction. There is nothing in the nature of machine production *per se* that is an insuperable obstacle in the way of workers' consciousness of the meaning of what they do and enjoyment of the satisfactions of companionship and of useful work well done. The psychological conditions resulting from private control of the labor of other men for the sake of private gain, rather than any fixed psychological or economic law, are the forces that suppress and limit esthetic quality in the experience that accompanies processes of production.

As long as art is the beauty parlor of civilization, neither art nor civilization is secure. Why is the architecture of our large cities so unworthy of a fine civilization? It is not from lack of materials nor from lack of technical capacity. And yet it is not merely slums but the apartments of the well-to-do that are esthetically repellent, because they are so destitute of imagination. Their character is determined by an economic system in which land is used—and kept out of use—for the sake of gain, because of profit derived from rental and sale. Until land is freed from this economic burden, beautiful buildings may occasionally be erected, but there is little hope for the rise of general architectural construction worthy of a noble civilization. The restriction placed on building affects indirectly a large number of allied arts, while the social forces that affect the buildings in which we subsist and wherein we do our work operate upon all the arts.

Auguste Comte said that the great problem of our time is the organization of the proletariat into the social system. The remark is even truer now than when it was made. The task is impossible of achievement by any revolution that stops short of affecting the imagination and emotions of man. The values that lead to production and intelligent enjoyment of art have to be incorporated into the system of social relationships. It seems to me that much of the discussion of proletarian art is aside from the point because it confuses the personal and deliberate intent of an artist with the place and operation of art in society. What is true is that art itself is not secure under modern conditions until the mass of men and women who do the useful work of the world have the opportunity to be free in conducting the processes of production and are richly endowed in capacity for enjoying the fruits of collective work. That the material for art should be drawn from all sources whatever and that the products of art should be accessible to all is a demand by the side of which the personal political intent of the artist is insignificant.

The moral office and human function of art can be intelligently discussed only in the context of culture. A particular work of art may have a definite effect upon a particular person or upon a number of persons. The social effect of the novels of Dickens or of Sinclair Lewis is far from negligible.

But a less conscious and more massed constant adjustment of experience proceeds from the total environment that is created by the collective art of a time. Just as physical life cannot exist without the support of a physical environment, so moral life cannot go on without the support of a moral environment. Even technological arts, in their sum total, do something more than provide a number of separate conveniences and facilities. They shape collective occupations and thus determine direction of interest and attention, and hence affect desire and purpose.

The noblest man living in a desert absorbs something of its harshness and sterility, while the nostalgia of the mountain-bred man when cut off from his surroundings is proof how deeply environment has become part of his being. Neither the savage nor the civilized man is what he is by native constitution but by the culture in which he participates. The final measure of the quality of that culture is the arts which flourish. Compared with their influence things directly taught by word and precept are pale and ineffectual. Shelley did not exaggerate when he said that moral science only "arranges the elements that poetry has created," if we extend "poetry" to include all products of imaginative experience. The sum total of the effect of all reflective treatises on morals is insignificant in comparison with the influence of architecture, novel, drama, on life, becoming important when "intellectual" products formulate the tendencies of these arts and provide them with an intellectual base. An "inner" rational check is a sign of withdrawal from reality unless it is a reflection of substantial environing forces. The political and economic arts that may furnish security and competency are no warrants of a rich and abundant human life save as they are attended by the flourishing of the arts that determine culture.

Words furnish a record of what has happened and give direction by request and command to particular future actions. Literature conveys the meaning of the past that is significant in present experience and is prophetic of the larger movement of the future. Only imaginative vision elicits the possibilities that are interwoven within the texture of the actual. The first stirrings of dissatisfaction and the first intimations of a better future are always found in works of art. The impregnation of the characteristically new art of a period with a sense of different values than those that prevail is the reason why the conservative finds such art to be immoral and sordid, and is the reason why he resorts to the products of the past for esthetic satisfaction. Factual science may collect statistics and make charts. But its predictions are, as has been well said, but past history reversed. Change in the climate of the imagination is the precursor of the changes that affect more than the details of life.

⌒

The theories that attribute direct moral effect and intent to art fail because they do not take account of the collective civilization that is the context in which works of art are produced and enjoyed. I would not say that they tend to treat works of art as a kind of sublimated Aesop's fables. But they all tend to extract particular works, regarded as especially edifying, from their milieu and to think of the moral function of art in terms of a strictly personal relation between the selected works and a particular individual. Their whole conception of morals is so individualistic that they miss a sense of the *way* in which art exercises its humane function.

Matthew Arnold's dictum that "poetry is criticism of life" is a case in point. It suggests to the reader a moral intent on the part of the poet and a moral judgment on the part of the reader. It fails to see or at all events to state *how* poetry is a criticism of life; namely, not directly, but by disclosure, through imaginative vision addressed to imaginative experience (not to set judgment) of possibilities that contrast with actual conditions. A sense of possibilities that are unrealized and that might be realized are when they are put in contrast with actual conditions, the most penetrating "criticism" of the latter that can be made. It is by a sense of possibilities opening before us that we become aware of constrictions that hem us in and of burdens that oppress.

Mr. [Heathcote William] Garrod, a follower of Matthew Arnold in more senses than one, has wittily said that what we resent in didactic poetry is not that it teaches, but that it does not teach, its incompetency. He added words to the effect that poetry teaches as friends and life teach, by being, and not by express intent. He says in another place, "Poetical values are, after all, values in a human life. You cannot mark them off from other values, as though the nature of man were built in bulkheads." I do not think that what Keats has said in one of his letters can be surpassed as to the way in which poetry acts. He asks what would be the result if every man spun from his imaginative experience "an airy Citadel" like the web the spider spins, "filling the air with a beautiful circuiting." For, he says, "man should not dispute or assert, but whisper results to his neighbour, and thus, by every germ of spirit sucking the sap from mould ethereal, every human being might become great, and Humanity instead of being a wide heath of Furze and Briars with here and there a remote Pine or Oak, would become a grand democracy of Forest Trees!"

It is by way of communication that art becomes the incomparable organ of instruction, but the way is so remote from that usually associated with the idea of education, it is a way that lifts art so far above what we are accustomed to think of as instruction, that we are repelled by any suggestion of teaching and learning in connection with art. But our revolt is in fact a reflection upon education that proceeds by methods so literal as to exclude the imagination and one not touching the desires and emotions of men. Shelley said, "The imagination is the great instrument of moral good, and poetry administers to the effect by acting upon the cause." Hence it is, he goes on to say, "a poet would do ill to embody his own conceptions of right and wrong, which are usually those of his own time and place, in his poetical creations. . . . By the assumption of this inferior office . . . he would resign participation in the cause"—the imagination. It is the lesser poets who "have frequently affected a moral aim, and the effect of their poetry is diminished in exact proportion as they compel us to advert to this purpose." But the power of imaginative projection is so great that he calls poets "the founders of civil society."

The problem of the relation of art and morals is too often treated as if the problem existed only on the side of art. It is virtually assumed that morals are satisfactory in idea if not in fact, and that the only question is whether and in what ways art should conform to a moral system already developed. But Shelley's statement goes to the heart of the matter. Imagination is the chief instrument of the good. It is more or less a commonplace to say that a person's ideas and treatment of his fellows are dependent upon his power to put himself imaginatively in their place. But the primacy of the imagination extends far beyond the scope of direct personal relationships. Except where "ideal" is used in conventional deference or as a name for a sentimental reverie, the ideal factors in every moral outlook and human loyalty are imaginative. The historic alliance of religion and art has its roots in this common quality. Hence it is that art is more moral than moralities. For the latter either are, or tend to become, consecrations of the *status quo*, reflections of custom, re-enforcements of the established order. The moral prophets of humanity have always been poets even though they spoke in free verse or by parable. Uniformly, however, their vision of possibilities has soon been converted into a proclamation of facts that already exist and hardened into semi-political institutions. Their imaginative presentation of ideals that should command thought and desire have been treated as rules of policy. Art has been the means of keeping alive the sense of purposes that outrun evidence and of meanings that transcend indurated habit.

Morals are assigned a special compartment in theory and practice because they reflect the divisions embodied in economic and political institutions. Wherever social divisions and barriers exist, practices and ideas that correspond to them fix metes and bounds, so that liberal action is placed under restraint. Creative intelligence is looked upon with distrust; the innovations that are the essence of individuality are feared, and generous impulse is put under bonds not to disturb the peace. Were art an acknowledged power in human association and not treated as the pleasuring of an idle moment or as a means of ostentatious display, and were morals understood to be identical with every aspect of value that is shared in experience, the "problem" of the relation of art and morals would not exist.

The idea and the practice of morality are saturated with conceptions that stem from praise and blame, reward and punishment. Mankind is divided into sheep and goats, the vicious and virtuous, the law-abiding and criminal, the good and bad. To be beyond good and evil is an impossibility for man, and yet as long as the good signifies only that which is lauded and rewarded, and the evil that which is currently condemned or outlawed, the ideal factors of morality are always and everywhere beyond good and evil. Because art is wholly innocent of ideas derived from praise and blame, it is looked upon with the eye of suspicion by the guardians of custom, or only the art that is itself so old and "classic" as to receive conventional praise is grudgingly admitted, provided, as with, say, the case of Shakespeare, signs of regard for conventional morality can be ingeniously extracted from his work. Yet this indifference to praise and blame because of preoccupation with imaginative experience constitutes the heart of the moral potency of art. From it proceeds the liberating and uniting power of art.

Shelley said, "The great secret of morals is love, or *a going out of our nature* and the identification of ourselves with the beautiful which exists in thought, action, or person, not our own. A man to be greatly good must imagine intensely and comprehensively." What is true of the individual is true of the whole system of morals in thought and action. While perception of the union of the possible with the actual in a work of art is itself a great good, the good does not terminate with the immediate and particular occasion in which it is had. The union that is presented in perception persists in the remaking of impulsion and thought. The first intimations of wide and large redirections of desire and purpose are of necessity imaginative. Art is a mode of prediction not found in charts and statistics, and it insinuates possibilities of human relations not to be found in rule and precept, admonition and administration.

> But Art, wherein man speaks in no wise to man,
> Only to mankind—Art may tell a truth
> Obliquely, do the deed shall breed the thought.
> (Robert Browning, "The Ring and the Book")

Notes

1. Quoted from [Walter] Lippmann's *A Preface to Morals*, p. 98. The text of the chapter from which the passage is cited gives examples of the specific rules by which the painter's work was regulated. The distinction between "art" and "substance" is similar to that drawn by some adherents of a proletarian dictatorship of art between technique or craft that belongs to the artist and subject-matter dictated by the needs of the "party line" in furthering the cause. A double standard is set up. There is literature that is good or bad as mere literature, and literature that is good or bad according to its bearing upon economic and political revolution.

2. T. E. Hulme, *Speculations*, pp. 83–87, *passim*.

3. Mr. Lippmann has written as follows: "One goes to a museum and comes out with the feeling that one has beheld an odd assortment of nude bodies, copper kettles, oranges, tomatoes, and zinnias, babies, street corners and bathing beaches, bankers and fashionable ladies. 1 do not say that this person or that may not find a picture immensely significant to him. But the general impression for anyone, I think, is of a chaos of anecdotes, perceptions, fantasies and little commentaries which may be all well enough in their way, but are not sustaining and could readily be dispensed with." *A Preface to Morals*, pp. 103–104.

VIII

VOCATIONAL EDUCATION AND POLICY

21

Some Dangers in the Present Movement for Industrial Education (1913)

Raising equity issues related to differentiated curriculum, Dewey authored an opinion piece for the journal *American Teacher* on what was then called "industrial education." Initially titled "An Undemocratic Proposal," it was later revised and reprinted in the *Child Labor Bulletin* as "Some Dangers in the Present Movement for Industrial Education." The article aptly demonstrates Dewey's engagement with everyday affairs as a "public intellectual." Revealing as well, his normally reserved demeanor is infused with a palpable sense of anger and frustration. The piece was prompted by a proposal in Illinois calling for the complete separation of "industrial education" from general education, including the establishment of an independent state commission to "oversee all forms of industrial education." Dewey views this "undemocratic proposal" as a rejection of the kind of unified education *through* vocations conceived and developed at the Lab School in Chicago. Such reinvigoration of general education through hands-on activities would seemingly cease under the new proposal. Meanwhile, "industrial education" would be stripped of its "scientific and social bearings," and prepare students of the "'laboring classes'" only for a limited job market with limited growth potential. How, Dewey asks, can this not significantly reinforce class and racial/ethnic divisions both in and out of school?

∽

There is no greater need at the present time than a closer understanding and working agreement between those interested on general philanthropic and social grounds in the prevention of child labor and those interested in educational reform. It is not enough to keep children out of the factory and the shop till they have reached a certain age. Every success in raising the age level for labor of children should be accompanied by steps in a constructive educational policy so that youth, when they finally leave school, shall have a general education which fits them not only to find a better paying job, but a line of occupation suited to their own capacities and one in which there is a future for growth. Professional educators, on the other hand, need to awaken from the lethargy through which they have permitted noneducational associations to take the lead in measures for the amelioration of the condition of children. They should recognize their opportunities and their responsibilities and take an aggressive part in the formation and execution of all legislative and administrative measures concerned with the welfare of children.

The problems of vocational guidance and industrial education are by no means solved, and without intelligent cooperation of educators and reformers the newly awakened enthusiasm on these matters will result in hasty and superficial action. Thus it is absurd to talk about "vocations" in connection with the labor of children under sixteen at least, but the phrase is likely to have, with some people, an influence which it would not have were the ordinary words "finding jobs" substituted for the high sounding "vocational guidance." To encourage children under sixteen to leave school by assisting them to find jobs is a mischievous enterprise. There are nineteen chances out of twenty that any work they can get into will prove a blind alley both industrially and economically. Enthusiasm for vocational guidance should exhibit itself first in encouraging children to stay in school till they have an education which will fit them for work where there are genuine openings ahead; secondly, in guiding public opinion and activity to modify the regular school work so that it shall have a more genuine connection with social opportunities; thirdly, to provide supplementary agencies so that children when they do leave to go to work shall continue under some educational supervision that will counteract the tendency of almost any trade at the present time to arrest their further growth. Only as a last resort in desperate individual cases should agencies for vocational guidance act as labor placing bureaus.

Industrial Education Dangers

The kindred question of industrial education is fraught with consequences for the future of democracy. Its right development will do more to make public education truly democratic than any other one agency now under consideration. Its wrong treatment will as surely accentuate all undemocratic tendencies in our present situation, by fostering and strengthening class divisions in school and out. It is better to suffer a while longer from the ills of our present lack of system till the truly democratic lines of advance become apparent, rather than separate industrial education sharply from general education, and thereby use it to mark off to the interests of employers a separate class of laborers.

These general considerations have a particular application to the scheme of industrial education which has been proposed for adoption by the next legislature of the State of Illinois—one of the leading industrial states of the Union, and containing its second largest city. This scheme proposes a separate State Commission of Vocational Education, wherever the community may wish to develop any form of industrial education. In other words, the entire school system of the state as a whole and of such communities of the state as may desire to do something definite in the direction of industrial education is split into two for the education of all above fourteen years of age. Since whatever a state like Illinois may do in such a matter is sure to have influence in other states in this formative period, educators all over the country should be aroused to help ward off what, without exaggeration, may be termed the greatest evil now threatening the interests of democracy in education.

The statement of the scheme ought to be enough to condemn it. The least reflection shows fundamentally bad features associated with it. First, it divides and duplicates the administrative educational machinery. How many communities have such an excess of public interest in education that they can afford to cut it into two parts? How many have such a surplusage of money and other resources that they can afford to maintain a double system of schools, with the waste of funds and the friction therein involved? Second, the scheme tends to paralyze one of the most vital movements now operating for the improvement of existing general education. The old-time general, academic education is beginning to be vitalized by the introduction of manual, industrial and social activities; it is beginning to recognize its responsibility to train all the youth for useful citizenship, including a calling in which each may render useful service to society and make an honest and decent living. Everywhere the existing school system is beginning to be alive to the need of supplementary agencies to help it fulfill this purpose, and is taking tentative but positive and continuous steps toward it. The City of Chicago in this same State of Illinois probably ranks behind no other city of the country in the extent and wisdom of the steps already taken, steps which will of necessity be followed by others just as fast as those already taken demonstrate their efficiency.

These two movements within the established American public school system, the proposed scheme, if adopted, will surely arrest. General education will be left with all its academic vices and its remoteness from the urgent realities of contemporary life untouched, and with the chief forces working for reform removed. Increasing recognition of its public and social responsibilities will be blasted. It is inconceivable that those who have loved and served our American common school system will, whatever the defects of this system, stand idly by and see such a blow aimed at it. Were anything needed to increase the force of the blow, it is the fact that the bill provides that all funds for industrial education raised by the local community be duplicated by the state, although the funds contributed by the state for general school purposes are hardly more than five per cent of the amount raised by local taxation.

Thirdly, the segregation will work disastrously for the true interests of the pupils who attend the so-called vocational schools. Ex-Superintendent [Edwin G.] Cooley of Chicago, who is understood to be responsible for the proposed bill in its present form, has written a valuable report on "Vocational Education in Europe." He quite rightly holds in high esteem the work and opinions of Superintendent [Georg] Kerschensteiner of Munich. It is noteworthy that this leading European authority insists upon all technical and trade work being taught in its general scientific and social bearings. Although working in a country definitely based on class distinctions (and where naturally the schools are based on class lines), the one thing Superintendent Kerschensteiner has stood for has been that industrial training shall be primarily not for the sake of industries, but for the sake of citizenship, and that it be conducted therefore on a purely educational basis and not in behalf of interested manufacturers. Mr. Cooley's own report summarizes Mr. Kerschensteiner's views as follows:

> If the boy is to become an efficient workman he must comprehend his *work in all of its relations to science, to art, and to society in general*. . . . The young workman who understands his trade in *its scientific relations, its historical, economic and social bearings*, will take a higher view of his trade, of his powers and duties as a citizen, and as a member of society.

Whatever may be the views of manufacturers anxious to secure the aid of the state in providing them with a somewhat better grade of laborers to exploit, the quotations state the point of view which is self-evident to those who approach the matter of industrial education from the side of education, and of a progressive society. It is truly extraordinary that just at a time when even partisan politics are taking a definitely progressive turn, such a reactionary measure as the institution of trade and commercial schools under separate auspices should be proposed. It is not necessary to argue concerning the personal motives of the bankers and manufacturers who have been drawn into the support of the measure. Doubtless many of them have the most public spirited of intentions. But no one experienced in education can doubt what would be the actual effect of a system of schools conducted wholly separate from the regular public schools, with a totally different curriculum, and with teachers and pupils responsible to a totally independent and separate school administration. Whatever were the original motives and intentions, such schools would not and could not give their pupils a knowledge of industry or any particular occupation in relation to "science, art and society in general." To attempt this would involve duplicating existing schools, in addition to providing proper industrial training. And it is self-evident that the economical and effective way to accomplish this move is to expand and supplement the present school system. Not being able to effect this complete duplication, these new schools would simply aim at increased efficiency in certain narrow lines. Those who believe in the continued separate existence of what they are pleased to call the "lower classes" or the "laboring classes" would naturally rejoice to have schools in which these "classes" would be segregated. And some employers of labor would doubtless rejoice to have schools supported by public taxation supply them with additional food for their mills. All others should be united against every proposition, in whatever form advanced, to separate training of employees from training for citizenship, training of intelligence and character from training for narrow industrial efficiency. That the evil forces at work are not local is seen in the attempt to get the recent national convention on industrial education in Philadelphia to commit itself in favor of the Illinois scheme.

The only serious danger is that a number of sympathetic and otherwise intelligent persons should be misled, and on the basis of a justified enthusiastic support of the principle of industrial education (with whatever supplementary agencies that may be found necessary) jump to the support of this scheme, not realizing what is really involved in it. Such persons should first inform themselves as to what is actually being done already in this direction in the more progressive public schools, and should then devote their spare energies to backing up and furthering these undertakings, and to creating a public opinion that will affect the more backward and conservative public school systems. The problem is a difficult one, but many intelligent, though unadvertised, attempts are already making for its solution; and its difficulty is no reason for permanently handicapping the interests of both common school education and a democratic society by abruptly going back upon what, with all its defects, has been the chief agency in keeping alive a spirit of democracy among us—the American public school system.

22

Learning to Earn: The Place of Vocational Education in a Comprehensive Scheme of Public Education (1917)

At the annual meeting of the Public Education Association in New York City, Dewey gave a talk entitled "Learning to Earn: The Place of Vocational Education in a Comprehensive Scheme of Public Education." It was another commentary very much of its historical moment. Dewey's remarks appeared soon after in the journal *School and Society*, and again much later in Joseph Ratner's *Education Today* (1940). Dewey begins with the observation that grade-school education has always had a significant vocational dimension, be it the popular education provided to the day laborer and craftsman or the cultural education deemed best for churchman and academic. The problem, he says, is that the "learning for earning" of too many students only prepares them to "fill other people's pockets." At that time, just one in sixteen students entered high school and one in a thousand attended college. Under these circumstances, Dewey argues, elementary education is essentially a scheme of workplace education. The limited academic content most students encounter in school—the three Rs and a "smattering" of other subjects—becomes a de facto economic tool to meet the needs of industry rather than the interests and potentials of individual students. Any significant enrichment of this curriculum, like that found in elite private schools, is considered appropriate only for the children of politicians and business leaders. Moreover, they alone are provided an understanding of the workings of the economy and the dynamics of the job market, part of what Dewey calls "industrial intelligence." Yet such intelligence is absolutely critical to the democratic and economic prospects of those pursuing vocational careers.

～

The title assigned and announced, "Learning to Earn," has a pleasant jingling sound. The "Earn" part of it is attractive also. It is, however, objectionable to some persons to see earning brought into close connection with learning. Since words frequently hide facts from us, we inquire at the beginning what the practice has been in this respect in the past. Contrary to the general opinion, popular education has always been rather largely vocational. The objection to it is not that it is vocational or industrial, but that it serves a poor, one may say an evil, ideal of industry and is therefore socially inefficient. So-called cultural education has always been reserved for a small limited class as a luxury. Even at that it has been very largely an education for vocations, especially for those vocations which happened to be esteemed as indicating social superiority or which were useful to the ruling powers of the given period. Our higher education, the education of the universities, began definitely as vocational education. The universities furnished training for the priesthood, for medicine and the law. This training also covered what was needed by the clerks, secretaries, scribes, etc., who have always had a large part of the administering of government affairs in their hands. Some portions of this original professional training ceased to be vocationally useful and then became the staple of a cultural and disciplinary education. For it will be found true as a general principle, that whenever any study which was originally utilitarian in purpose becomes useless because of a change in conditions, it is retained as a necessary educational ornament (as useless buttons are retained on the sleeves of men's coats) or else because it is so useless that it must be fine for mental discipline. Even to-day it will be found that a considerable part of what is regarded in collegiate education as purely cultural is really a preparation for some learned pursuit or for the profession of teaching the same subjects in the future, or a preparation for the profession of being a gentleman at large. Those who object most bitterly to any form of vocational training will often be found to be those whose own monopoly of present vocational training is threatened. What concerns us more directly, however, is the fact that elementary education, the education of the masses, has been not only "Learning for Earning," but a badly conceived learning, an education where the ability of the learner to add to the earnings of others rather than to his own earnings has been the main factor in selecting materials of study and fixing methods. You are doubtless weary hearing the statistics of our school morbidity and mortality rehearsed: the fact that of the school population only one in nine goes through the eighth grade, one in sixteen enters the high school, and only one in a thousand goes to college. We don't, however, ask often enough what these figures mean. If we did ask, we should see that they prove that our present scheme of elementary education is in the first place a scheme of vocational education and in the second place a poor one.

Reading, writing, figuring, with a little geography and a smattering of other things, are what the great mass of those who leave our schools leave with. A few get something more. These things, when nothing else is added on to them, are pretty nearly pure economic tools. They came into the schools when the better-to-do classes discovered that under the conditions an elementary ability to read, write and figure was practically indispensable for salesmen and shop workers. He who is poorly acquainted with the history of the efforts to improve elementary education in our large cities does not know that the chief protest against progress is likely to come from successful business men. They have clamored for the three R's as the essential and exclusive material of primary education—knowing well enough that their own children would be able to get the things they protest against. Thus they have attacked as fads and frills every enrichment of the curriculum which did not lend itself to narrow economic ends. Let us stick to business, to the essentials, has been their plea, and by business they meant enough of the routine skill in letters and figures to make those leaving the elementary school at about the fifth or sixth grade useful in *their* business, irrespective of whether pupils left school with an equipment for advance and with the ambition to try to secure better social and economic conditions for their children than they had themselves enjoyed. Nothing in the history of education is more touching than to hear some successful leaders denounce as undemocratic the attempt to give all the children at public expense the fuller education which their own children enjoy as a matter of course.

Of late years, the situation has changed somewhat. The more intelligent employers have awakened to the fact that the mere rudiments of the three R's are not a good industrial training, while others of the community have awakened to the fact that it is a dangerously inadequate industrial education from the standpoint of the community. Hence there has arisen a demand for vocational and industrial education as if this were an entirely new thing; while, in fact, it is a demand that the present industrial education be so modified as to be efficient under the conditions of present machine industry, rapid transportation and a competitive market.

I have made these bald statements because they indicate to my mind the real issue at the present time concerning industrial education in public education. It isn't whether it shall be introduced in order to supplant or supplement a liberal and generous education already supposed to exist—that is pure romance. The issue is what sort of an industrial education there shall be and whose interests shall be primarily considered in its development. Now, I quite understand that I am here to speak from the educational standpoint and that [labor leader] Mr. Samuel Gompers who is to follow is quite competent to take care of the question from the standpoint of the workers affected by the issue. But to understand the *educational* issue is to see what difference is made in the schools themselves according as we take the *improving* of economic conditions to be the purpose of vocational training, or take its purpose to be supplying a better grade of labor for the present scheme, or helping on the United States in a competitive struggle for world commerce. I know that those who have the latter ends chiefly in view always make much of the increased happiness of the industrial worker himself as a product to result from better industrial education. But after all, there is a great difference between the happiness which means merely contentment with a station and the happiness which comes from the struggle of a well-equipped person to better his station. Which sort of happiness is to be our aim? I know, also, that stress is laid upon ability which is to proceed from a better industrial education to increase earnings. Well and good. But, does this mean simply that laborers are to have their skill to add to the profits of employers so increased, by avoiding waste, getting more out of their machines and materials, that they will have some share in it as an incidental by-product, or does it mean that increase in the industrial intelligence and power of the worker for his own personal advancement is to be the main factor?

I have said that the way these questions are answered makes all the difference in the world as to the educational scheme itself. Let me now point out some of the particular educational differences which will be made according as one or other idea of industry in education prevails. In the first place, as to administration, those who wish, whether they wish it knowingly or unknowingly, an education which will enable employees to fit better into the existing economic scheme will strive for a dual or divided system of administration. That is to say, they will attempt to have a separate system of funds, of supervisory authorities, and, as far as possible, of schools to carry on industrial education. If they don't go so far as this, they will at least constantly harp on the difference between a liberal or cultural and a money-earning education, and will endeavor to narrow the latter down to those forms of industrial skill which will enable the future workers to fall docilely into the subordinate ranks of the industrial army.

In the second place, the conception that the primary object of industrial education is merely to prepare more skilled workers for the present system, instead of developing human beings who are equipped to reconstruct that scheme, will strive to identify it with trade education—that is, with training for certain specific callings. It assumes that the needs of industrial education are met if girls are trained to be skilled in millinery, cooking and garment-making, and boys to be plumbers, electric wirers, etc. In short, it will proceed on a basis not far removed from that of the so-called prevocational work on the Ettinger plan in this city.

In the third place, the curriculum on this narrow trade plan will neglect as useless for its ends the topics in history and civics which make future workers aware of their rightful claims as citizens in a democracy, alert to the fact that the present economic struggle is but the present-day phase taken by the age-long battle for human liberties. So far as it takes in civic and social studies at all, it will emphasize those things which emphasize duties to the established order and a blind patriotism which accounts it a great privilege to defend things in which the workers themselves have little or no share. The studies which fit the individual for the reasonable enjoyment of leisure time, which develop good taste in reading and appreciation of the arts, will be passed over as good for those who belong by wealth to the leisure class, but quite useless in the training of skilled employees.

In the fourth place, so far as the method and spirit of its work is concerned, it will emphasize all that is most routine and automatic in our present system. Drill to secure skill in the performance of tasks under the direction of others will be its chief reliance. It will insist that the limits of time and the pressure for immediate results are so great that there is no room for understanding the scientific facts and principles or the social bearings of what is done. Such an enlarged education would develop personal intelligence and thereby develop also an intellectual ambition and initiative which might be fatal to contentment in routine subordinate clerical and shop jobs.

Finally, so far as such a training concerns itself with what is called vocational guidance, it will conceive guidance as a method of placement—a method of finding jobs. It will measure its achievements by the number of children taking out working papers for whom it succeeds in finding places, instead of by the number whom it succeeds in keeping in school till they become equipped to seek and find their own congenial occupations.

The other idea of industrial education aims at preparing every individual to render service of a useful sort to the community, while at the same time it equips him to secure by his own initiative whatever place his natural capacities fit him for. It will proceed in an opposite way in every respect. Instead of trying to split schools into two kinds, one of a trade type for children whom it is assumed are to be employees and one of a liberal type for the children of the well-to-do, it will aim at such a reorganization of existing schools as will give all pupils a genuine respect for useful work, an ability to render service, and a contempt for social parasites whether they are called tramps or leaders of "society." Instead of assuming that the problem is to add vocational training to an existing cultural elementary education, it will recognize frankly that the traditional elementary education is largely vocational, but that the vocations which it has in mind are too exclusively clerical, and too much of a kind which implies merely ability to take positions in which to carry out the plans of others. It will indeed make much of developing motor and manual skill, but not of a routine or automatic type. It will rather utilize active and manual pursuits as the means of developing constructive, inventive and creative power of mind. It will select the materials and the technique of the trades not for the sake of producing skilled workers for hire in definite trades, but for the sake of securing industrial intelligence—a knowledge of the conditions and processes of present manufacturing, transportation and commerce—so that the individual may be able to make his own choices and his own adjustments, and be master, so far as in him lies, of his own economic fate. It will be recognized that, for this purpose, a broad acquaintance with science and skill in the laboratory control of materials and processes is more important than skill in trade operations. It will remember that the future employee is a consumer as well as a producer, that the whole tendency of society, so far as it is intelligent and wholesome, is to an increase of the hours of leisure, and that an education which does nothing to enable individuals to consume wisely and to utilize leisure wisely is a fraud on democracy. So far as method is concerned, such a conception of industrial education will prize freedom more than docility;

initiative more than automatic skill; insight and understanding more than capacity to recite lessons or to execute tasks under the direction of others.

The theme is an endless one. But it seemed to me that the best thing which I, from my standpoint, could do, is to point out that the real issue is not the question whether an industrial education is to be added on to a more or less mythical cultural elementary education, but what sort of an industrial education we are to have. The movement for vocational educations conceals within itself two mighty and opposing forces, one which would utilize the public schools primarily to turn out more efficient laborers in the present economic regime, with certain incidental advantages to themselves, the other which would utilize all the resources of public education to equip individuals to control their own future economic careers, and thus help on such a reorganization of industry as will change it from a feudalistic to a democratic order.

At the present moment, the first bill appropriating federal funds for industrial education in schools below the grade of the college of agriculture and mechanic arts has been passed by the two houses of Congress. So far as provisions for the representation of employers and employed is concerned, the act is a fair one. So far as the interests of education is concerned, the representation of educators is scandalously inadequate. As passed, the original bill, which safeguarded unified control on the part of the states which take advantage of federal financial aid, has been changed so as to make a dual scheme optional with each state. I do not say these things to cast any discredit on the act. I refer to them only to indicate that the passage of the bill illustrates the whole situation in which we find ourselves. It settles no problem; it merely symbolizes the inauguration of a conflict between irreconcilably opposed educational and industrial ideals. Nothing is so necessary as that public-spirited representatives of the public educational interest, such as are gathered here to-night, shall perceive the nature of the issue and throw their weights in municipal, state and federal educational matters upon the side of education rather than of training, on that of democratic rather than that of feudal control of industry.

IX
THE PROFESSION OF TEACHING

23

My Pedagogic Creed (1897)

This final section of readings features *My Pedagogic Creed*, composed for a popular publication called the *School Journal*. Given the nature of the piece, Dewey does not provide detailed arguments for his statements of belief on the psychological and social aspects of teaching and learning, what he calls the "two sides" of the educational equation. However, the reading selections included in this book provide many of the omitted arguments. The *Creed's* five sections contain a number of Dewey's better-known statements on education, many of which he would return to and augment over the years. One enduring idea from Article Two, *What the School Is*, is essential for understanding Dewey's educational philosophy. It reads, "I believe that education is a process of living and not a preparation for future living." Education, in other words, is not like depositing money in a bank and leaving it there untouched for (possible) later withdrawal. If there is no direct "payoff" in the learning process itself, no immediate sense of personal growth and enrichment, any learning that does occur, if not used immediately, will likely be lost in the vault forever. In short, one can only prepare for the future by living fully in the present.

∽

Article One. What Education Is

I believe that all education proceeds by the participation of the individual in the social consciousness of the race. This process begins unconsciously almost at birth, and is continually shaping the individual's powers, saturating his consciousness, forming his habits, training his ideas, and arousing his feelings and emotions. Through this unconscious education the individual gradually comes to share in the intellectual and moral resources which humanity has succeeded in getting together. He becomes an inheritor of the funded capital of civilization. The most formal and technical education in the world cannot safely depart from this general process. It can only organize it; or differentiate it in some particular direction.

I believe that the only true education comes through the stimulation of the child's powers by the demands of the social situations in which he finds himself. Through these demands he is stimulated to act as a member of a unity, to emerge from his original narrowness of action and feeling and to conceive of himself from the standpoint of the welfare of the group to which he belongs. Through the responses which others make to his own activities he comes to know what these mean in social terms. The value which they have is reflected back into them. For instance, through the response which is made to the child's instinctive babblings the child comes to know what those babblings mean; they are transformed into articulate language and thus the child is introduced into the consolidated wealth of ideas and emotions which are now summed up in language.

I believe that this educational process has two sides—one psychological and one sociological; and that neither can be subordinated to the other or neglected without evil results following. Of these two sides, the psychological is the basis. The child's own instincts and powers furnish the material and give the starting point for all education. Save as the efforts of the educator connect with some activity which the child is carrying on of his own initiative independent of the educator, education becomes reduced to a pressure from without. It may, indeed, give certain external results but cannot truly be called educative. Without insight into the psychological structure and activities of the individual, the educative process will, therefore, be haphazard and arbitrary. If it chances to coincide with the child's activity it will get a leverage; if it does not, it will result in friction, or disintegration, or arrest of the child nature.

I believe that knowledge of social conditions, of the present state of civilization, is necessary in order properly to interpret the child's powers. The child has his own instincts and tendencies, but we do not know what these mean until we can translate them into their social equivalents. We must be able to carry them back into a social past and see them as the inheritance of previous race activities. We must also be able to project them into the future to see what their outcome and end will be. In the illustration just used, it is the ability to see in the child's babblings the promise and potency of a future social intercourse and conversation which enables one to deal in the proper way with that instinct.

I believe that the psychological and social sides are organically related and that education cannot be regarded as a compromise between the two, or a superimposition of one upon the other. We are told that the psychological definition of education is barren and formal—that it gives us only the idea of a development of all the mental powers without giving us any idea of the use to which these powers are put. On the other hand, it is urged that the social definition of education, as getting adjusted to civilization, makes of it a forced and external process, and results in subordinating the freedom of the individual to a preconceived social and political status.

I believe each of these objections is true when urged against one side isolated from the other. In order to know what a power really is we must know what its end, use, or function is; and this we cannot know save as we conceive of the individual as active in social relationships. But, on the other hand, the only possible adjustment which we can give to the child under existing conditions, is that which arises through putting him in complete possession of all his powers. With the advent of democracy and modern industrial conditions, it is impossible to foretell definitely just what civilization will be twenty years from now. Hence it is impossible to prepare the child for any precise set of conditions. To prepare him for the future life means to give him command of himself; it means so to train him that he will have the full and ready use of all his capacities; that his eye and ear and hand may be tools ready to command, that his judgment may be capable of grasping the conditions under which it has to work, and the executive forces be trained to act economically and efficiently. It is impossible to reach this sort of adjustment save as constant regard is had to the individual's own powers, tastes, and interests—say, that is, as education is continually converted into psychological terms.

In sum, I believe that the individual who is to be educated is a social individual and that society is an organic union of individuals. If we eliminate the social factor from the child we are left only with an abstraction; if we eliminate the individual factor from society, we are left only with an inert and lifeless mass. Education, therefore, must begin with a psychological insight into the child's capacities, interests, and habits. It must be controlled at every point by reference to these same considerations.

These powers, interests, and habits must be continually interpreted—we must know what they mean. They must be translated into terms of their social equivalents—into terms of what they are capable of in the way of social service.

Article Two. What the School Is

I believe that the school is primarily a social institution. Education being a social process, the school is simply that form of community life in which all those agencies are concentrated that will be most effective in bringing the child to share in the inherited resources of the race, and to use his own powers for social ends.

I believe that education, therefore, is a process of living and not a preparation for future living.

I believe that the school must represent present life—life as real and vital to the child as that which he carries on in the home, in the neighborhood, or on the playground.

I believe that education which does not occur through forms of life, forms that are worth living for their own sake, is always a poor substitute for the genuine reality and tends to cramp and to deaden.

I believe that the school, as an institution, should simplify existing social life; should reduce it, as it were, to an embryonic form. Existing life is so complex that the child cannot be brought into contact with it without either confusion or distraction; he is either overwhelmed by multiplicity of activities which are going on, so that he loses his own power of orderly reaction, or he is so stimulated by these various activities that his powers are prematurely called into play and he becomes either unduly specialized or else disintegrated.

I believe that, as such simplified social life, the school life should grow gradually out of the home life; that it should take up and continue the activities with which the child is already familiar in the home.

I believe that it should exhibit these activities to the child, and reproduce them in such ways that the child will gradually learn the meaning of them, and be capable of playing his own part in relation to them.

I believe that this is a psychological necessity, because it is the only way of securing continuity in the child's growth, the only way of giving a background of past experience to the new ideas given in school.

I believe it is also a social necessity because the home is the form of social life in which the child has been nurtured and in connection with which he has had his moral training. It is the business of the school to deepen and extend his sense of the values bound up in his home life.

I believe that much of present education fails because it neglects this fundamental principle of the school as a form of community life. It conceives the school as a place where certain information is to be given, where certain lessons are to be learned, or where certain habits are to be formed. The value of these is conceived as lying largely in the remote future; the child must do these things for the sake of something else he is to do; they are mere preparation. As a result they do not become a part of the life experience of the child and so are not truly educative.

I believe that moral education centres about this conception of the school as a mode of social life, that the best and deepest moral training is precisely that which one gets through having to enter into proper relations with others in a unity of work and thought. The present educational systems, so far as they destroy or neglect this unity, render it difficult or impossible to get any genuine, regular moral training.

I believe that the child should be stimulated and controlled in his work through the life of the community.

I believe that under existing conditions far too much of the stimulus and control proceeds from the teacher, because of neglect of the idea of the school as a form of social life.

I believe that the teacher's place and work in the school is to be interpreted from this same basis. The teacher is not in the school to impose certain ideas or to form certain habits in the child, but is there as a member of the community to select the influences which shall affect the child and to assist him in properly responding to these influences.

I believe that the discipline of the school should proceed from the life of the school as a whole and not directly from the teacher.

I believe that the teacher's business is simply to determine on the basis of larger experience and riper wisdom, how the discipline of life shall come to the child.

I believe that all questions of the grading of the child and his promotion should be determined by reference to the same standard. Examinations are of use only so far as they test the child's fitness for social life and reveal the place in which he can be of the most service and where he can receive the most help.

Article Three. The Subject-Matter of Education

I believe that the social life of the child is the basis of concentration, or correlation, in all his training or growth. The social life gives the unconscious unity and the background of all his efforts and of all his attainments.

I believe that the subject-matter of the school curriculum should mark a gradual differentiation out of the primitive unconscious unity of social life.

I believe that we violate the child's nature and render difficult the best ethical results, by introducing the child too abruptly to a number of special studies, of reading, writing, geography, etc., out of relation to this social life.

I believe, therefore, that the true centre of correlation of the school subjects is not science, nor literature, nor history, nor geography, but the child's own social activities.

I believe that education cannot be unified in the study of science, or so-called nature study, because apart from human activity, nature itself is not a unity; nature in itself is a number of diverse objects in space and time, and to attempt to make it the centre of work by itself, is to introduce a principle of radiation rather than one of concentration.

I believe that literature is the reflex expression and interpretation of social experience; that hence it must follow upon and not precede such experience. It, therefore, cannot be made the basis, although it may be made the summary of unification.

I believe once more that history is of educative value in so far as it presents phases of social life and growth. It must be controlled by reference to social life. When taken simply as history it is thrown into the distant past and becomes dead and inert. Taken as the record of man's social life and progress it becomes full of meaning. I believe, however, that it cannot be so taken excepting as the child is also introduced directly into social life.

I believe accordingly that the primary basis of education is in the child's powers at work along the same general constructive lines as those which have brought civilization into being. I believe that the only way to make the child conscious of his social heritage is to enable him to perform those fundamental types of activity which make civilization what it is.

I believe, therefore, in the so-called expressive or constructive activities as the centre of correlation.

I believe that this gives the standard for the place of cooking, sewing, manual training, etc., in the school.

I believe that they are not special studies which are to be introduced over and above a lot of others in the way of relaxation or relief, or as additional accomplishments. I believe rather that they represent, as types, fundamental forms of social activity; and that it is possible and desirable that the child's introduction into the more formal subjects of the curriculum be through the medium of these activities.

I believe that the study of science is educational in so far as it brings out the materials and processes which make social life what it is.

I believe that one of the greatest difficulties in the present teaching of science is that the material is presented in purely objective form, or is treated as a new peculiar kind of experience which the child can add to that which he has already had. In reality, science is of value because it gives the ability to interpret and control the experience already had. It should be introduced, not as so much new subject-matter, but as showing the factors already involved in previous experience and as furnishing tools by which that experience can be more easily and effectively regulated.

I believe that at present we lose much of the value of literature and language studies because of our elimination of the social element. Language is almost always treated in the books of pedagogy simply as the expression of thought. It is true that language is a logical instrument, but it is fundamentally and primarily a social instrument. Language is the device for communication; it is the tool through which one individual comes to share the ideas and feelings of others. When treated simply as a way of getting individual information, or as a means of showing off what one has learned, it loses its social motive and end.

I believe that there is, therefore, no succession of studies in the ideal school curriculum. If education is life, all life has, from the outset, a scientific aspect; an aspect of art and culture and an aspect of communication. It cannot, therefore, be true that the proper studies for one grade are mere reading and writing, and that at a later grade, reading, or literature, or science, may be introduced. The progress is not in the succession of studies but in the development of new attitudes towards, and new interests in, experience.

I believe finally, that education must be conceived as a continuing reconstruction of experience; that the process and the goal of education are one and the same thing.

I believe that to set up any end outside of education, as furnishing its goal and standard, is to deprive the educational process of much of its meaning and tends to make us rely upon false and external stimuli in dealing with the child.

Article Four. The Nature of Method

I believe that the question of method is ultimately reducible to the question of the order of development of the child's powers and interests. The law for presenting and treating material is the law implicit within the child's own nature. Because this is so I believe the following statements are of supreme importance as determining the spirit in which education is carried on:

1. I believe that the active side precedes the passive in the development of the child nature; that expression comes before conscious impression; that the muscular development precedes the sensory; that movements come before conscious sensations; I believe that consciousness is essentially motor or impulsive; that conscious states tend to project themselves in action.

I believe that the neglect of this principle is the cause of a large part of the waste of time and strength in school work. The child is thrown into a passive, receptive or absorbing attitude. The conditions are such that he is not permitted to follow the law of his nature; the result is friction and waste.

I believe that ideas (intellectual and rational processes) also result from action and devolve for the sake of the better control of action. What we term reason is primarily the law of orderly or effective action. To attempt to develop the reasoning powers, the powers of judgment, without reference to the selection and arrangement of means in action, is the fundamental fallacy in our present methods of dealing with this matter. As a result we present the child with arbitrary symbols. Symbols are a necessity in mental development, but they have their place as tools for economizing effort; presented by themselves they are a mass of meaningless and arbitrary ideas imposed from without.

2. I believe that the image is the great instrument of instruction. What a child gets out of any subject presented to him is simply the images which he himself forms with regard to it.

I believe that if nine-tenths of the energy at present directed towards making the child learn certain things, were spent in seeing to it that the child was forming proper images, the work of instruction would be indefinitely facilitated.

I believe that much of the time and attention now given to the preparation and presentation of lessons might be more wisely and profitably expended in training the child's power of imagery and in seeing to it that he was continually forming definite, vivid, and growing images of the various subjects with which he comes in contact in his experience.

3. I believe that interests are the signs and symptoms of growing power. I believe that they represent dawning capacities. Accordingly the constant and careful observation of interests is of the utmost importance for the educator.

I believe that these interests are to be observed as showing the state of development which the child has reached.

I believe that they prophesy the stage upon which he is about to enter.

I believe that only through the continual and sympathetic observation of childhood's interests can the adult enter into the child's life and see what it is ready for, and upon what material it could work most readily and fruitfully.

I believe that these interests are neither to be humored nor repressed. To repress interest is to substitute the adult for the child, and so to weaken intellectual curiosity and alertness, to suppress initiative, and to deaden interest. To humor the interests is to substitute the transient for the permanent. The interest is always the sign of some power below; the important thing is to discover this power. To humor the interest is to fail to penetrate below the surface and its sure result is to substitute caprice and whim for genuine interest.

4. I believe that the emotions are the reflex of actions.

I believe that to endeavor to stimulate or arouse the emotions apart from their corresponding activities, is to introduce an unhealthy and morbid state of mind.

I believe that if we can only secure right habits of action and thought, with reference to the good, the true, and the beautiful, the emotions will for the most part take care of themselves.

I believe that next to deadness and dullness, formalism and routine, our education is threatened with no greater evil than sentimentalism.

I believe that this sentimentalism is the necessary result of the attempt to divorce feeling from action.

Article Five. The School and Social Progress

I believe that education is the fundamental method of social progress and reform.

I believe that all reforms which rest simply upon the enactment of law, or the threatening of certain penalties, or upon changes in mechanical or outward arrangements, are transitory and futile.

I believe that education is a regulation of the process of coming to share in the social consciousness; and that the adjustment of individual activity on the basis of this social consciousness is the only sure method of social reconstruction.

I believe that this conception has due regard for both the individualistic and socialistic ideals. It is duly individual because it recognizes the formation of a certain character as the only genuine basis of right living. It is socialistic because it recognizes that this right character is not to be formed by merely individual precept, example, or exhortation, but rather by the influence of a certain form of institutional or community life upon the individual, and that the social organism through the school, as its organ, may determine ethical results.

I believe that in the ideal school we have the reconciliation of the individualistic and the institutional ideals.

I believe that the community's duty to education is, therefore, its paramount moral duty. By law and punishment, by social agitation and discussion, society can regulate and form itself in a more or less haphazard and chance way. But through education society can formulate its own purposes, can organize its own means and resources, and thus shape itself with definiteness and economy in the direction in which it wishes to move.

I believe that when society once recognizes the possibilities in this direction, and the obligations which these possibilities impose, it is impossible to conceive of the resources of time, attention, and money which will be put at the disposal of the educator.

I believe it is the business of every one interested in education to insist upon the school as the primary and most effective interest of social progress and reform in order that society may be awakened to realize what the school stands for, and aroused to the necessity of endowing the educator with sufficient equipment properly to perform his task.

I believe that education thus conceived marks the most perfect and intimate union of science and art conceivable in human experience.

I believe that the art of thus giving shape to human powers and adapting them to social service, is the supreme art; one calling into its service the best of artists; that no insight, sympathy, tact, executive power is too great for such service.

I believe that with the growth of psychological science, giving added insight into individual structure and laws of growth; and with growth of social science, adding to our knowledge of the right organization of individuals, all scientific resources can be utilized for the purposes of education.

I believe that when science and art thus join hands the most commanding motive for human action will be reached; the most genuine springs of human conduct aroused and the best service that human nature is capable of guaranteed.

I believe, finally, that the teacher is engaged, not simply in the training of individuals, but in the formation of the proper social life.

I believe that every teacher should realize the dignity of his calling; that he is a social servant set apart for the maintenance of proper social order and the securing of the right social growth.

I believe that in this way the teacher always is the prophet of the true God and the usherer in of the true kingdom of God.

24

Toward a National System of Education (1935)

"Toward a National System of Education" is the second piece in this reader initially published in the topical journal *Social Frontier*. Dewey opens by asserting that education in the US is too chaotic to be considered a system. This is understandable, he adds, given the gradual, impromptu development of the nation by geographic regions. Further, these regions were comprised of individual localities that made their own provisions for educating their children. (Recall that the Constitution, specifically the Tenth Amendment, allows for local control of schools, with oversight by individual states, not the federal government.) What, then, would constitute a national system of education and how would it differ from a nationalistic system? The former system, Dewey opines, corresponds with a shared spirit and sense of purpose leading to a distinctive "working unity in life." This working unity must derive from the interests of the people and grow from the bottom up. A nationalistic system, on the contrary, is imposed and maintained by the government in a top-down fashion. Here, the schools are controlled by the power structure in service of the welfare and interests of the nation-state and prevailing socioeconomic arrangements. (Dewey clearly associates this system with authoritarianism.) To develop a genuinely national system of education, however, teachers must be empowered to use their professional knowledge and expertise as valued contributors in school decision-making, especially with respect to curricular materials and instructional methods. With inclusive, collaborative forums for democratic debate and discussion, this professional knowledge and expertise can foster a bottom-up national system of education imbued with a common purpose and "working unity in life." Such a system, Dewey claims, is necessary to counter control by monied interests whose goals for education often promote disunity (e.g., class and racial/ethnic divisions) and that lie outside the realm of public schooling.

∾

From the standpoint of any European country, except Great Britain, the American public school system is a chaos rather than a system. The British system, from the continental standpoint, is even more chaotic than ours, because public education there is superimposed upon schools carried on by religious bodies. Until the arrival of Hitler, there was a good deal of provincial educational autonomy in Germany; the larger divisions of the U.S.S.R. exercise considerable autonomy though of course within the limits of the proletarian-communist scheme. But there is no other country where local control and differentiation are carried as far as in this country.

The historical causes for our peculiar difference are fairly evident. Regions developed in the country before the nation, and localities before regions. Settlers had no choice save to go without schools or themselves to form a school for their own locality, the latter often not being even a village but a collection of farm-homesteads scattered over a considerable territory. The district school and the little red schoolhouse were the answer. As settlers moved westward and out to the frontier, the same conditions prevailed; in addition they naturally followed the precedent with which they were familiar.

Some degree of centralization has followed, by townships, by counties, and by states—but always with the limitation suggested by the word "some." The movement never extended to the nation. The "Office of Education" in Washington is the expression and record of the limitation of the movement. I do not propose to discuss the concrete matter of changing the Office into a Cabinet Department, but rather to say something about a few general principles that seem to me to lie at the basis of a genuinely national system of education.

In the first place, there is a fundamental difference between a national and a nationalistic system, and we must face the issue of whether we can have one without growing sooner or later into the other. By a nationalistic system, I mean one in which the school system is controlled by the Government in power in the interest of what it takes to be the welfare of its own particular national state, and of the social-economic system the Government is concerned to maintain. The school systems of Japan,

Italy, the U.S.S.R., and now Germany, define better what is meant by "nationalistic" education than will any abstract descriptions.

A national system in its distinction from a nationalistic one is not so easy to define. Roughly speaking, it is an educational system that corresponds to the spirit, the temper, the dominant habits and purposes that hold the people of a country together, so far as they *are* held together in a working unity of life. These terms are all vague, but the vagueness lies in the nature of the situation. In spite of the vagueness, it may be readily demarcated from a nationalistic system. The latter is imposed by government and maintained by government, though not of necessity in opposition to the will of the people. A national system is an outgrowth from the people. It develops from below, rather than is imposed from above. The government intervenes by legislation and administratively, but it follows rather than precedes the more spontaneous and voluntary efforts of the people.

That we do not have a nationalistic system of education in this country is too obvious to require argument. Because of the historic conditions already mentioned, we have a national system only partially and somewhat amorphously. That, as time has passed, local and regional interests have tended to merge, while local boundaries have lost force in comparison with the concerns of the country as a whole, is clear in every field. The educational system could not escape this influence. Unification in economic directions has increased the importance of unity in the ideas and policies that affect national policies. Nevertheless, it was practically inevitable in so large a country and in one with so short a history that the intellectual and moral unification of the different regions of the country should lag behind economic unification.

Some undoubted advantages have accrued to offset the disadvantages of our local and dispersive system. The schools have been closer to the local communities; in many cases local responsibility has been stimulated. There has been, along with great unevenness, a stimulus to experimentation such as a closed centralized system does not afford. Meetings of teachers, emulation, and the spread of ideas by social osmosis, have had to play the part taken by ministries of education in other countries. Mechanical uniformity has not been allowed to exclude wholesome diversity.

Yet the necessity in a time of great changes, like the present, of direction in the interest of the people as a whole (unless we are to sink into deeper chaos) is a fact that cannot be escaped. It would however be a great mistake, in my opinion, to think that this urgent need settles the way in which the need should be satisfied. It rather presents a problem.

The easy conversion in Europe of centralized systems into agencies of a dominant political regime is a warning. Moreover, local interests and jealousies are still so strong in this country that an administrative national system could not be brought about in this country except through something approaching class coercion of a Fascist variety or a great amount of dangerous propaganda—or both. On the other hand, as I have already said, unless we are to drift into a worse situation than that in which we now find ourselves, a strong unified intelligence and purpose must be built up in support of policies that have a definite trend toward a socialized cooperative democracy. The schools cannot remain outside this task.

Here are the two horns of our dilemma. As far as I can see, the surest as well as safest way out is for teachers themselves to work actively to establish the autonomy of education, rather than to share in *direct* attempts to establish a national system. By autonomy I do not mean, of course, something separate. Autonomy means rather the right of teachers to determine the subject-matter and methods employed in the schools. This is a right they are far from now having. Part of the confusion and the social irresponsibility of public education at present springs from the fact that it is controlled in such large measure by interests that are concerned chiefly with ends that lie outside of the educative field. If the teaching profession can educate itself and the public to the need of throwing off this incubus, genuinely educative forces will be released to do their work. In consequence, the freedom and impetus that result will enable the schools, without a centralized system, to develop a system of truly national education—by which I mean one animated by policies and methods that will help create that common purpose without which the nation cannot achieve unified movement.

What is urged is far from indoctrination in the sense of inculcation of fixed beliefs. In the first place, this end could not be accomplished without first indoctrinating teachers into a single body of beliefs, and nothing but Fascist or Communist coercion can bring about even a semblance of such unification. In the second place, any unification of the national will effected by such a method will have no firm and enduring roots. Dr. [John H.] Randall has recently made the following pertinent remarks regarding the use of the method of intelligence in education:

> It is implied that because intelligence does not attain final truth, it reaches no conclusion at all. . . . The futile debate about "indoctrination" in education illustrates this strange

delusion. If you stimulate inquiry and educate, this leaves the student free to adopt any opinion or conclusion he wishes! Therefore it is necessary to "indoctrinate" him with the ends you have decided upon. As though, inquiry never discovered anything, and investigation never reached conclusions that force themselves upon the mind of the investigator! . . . Inquiry is meaningless unless you discover ideas that put other ideas at a disadvantage.

The bearing of these remarks upon my theme is that they point to the need of concentration and clarification of the methods of free mutual discussion and communication among teachers—methods that are responsible for whatever advances have been made in public education in the past. I do not say this is the final step in the development of a national education, but it is the first step. Moreover, concentration and clarification involve a good deal. They involve cutting out repetition of conventionalities, of hullabaloo, and settling down to basic issues of the relation of education to social direction. If this can be accomplished, I think the process of self-education of teachers will educate also the public, and take us on the sure road to the now distant goal of a truly national education.

25

To Those Who Aspire to the Profession of Teaching (1938)

In our final reading, "To Those Who Aspire to the Profession of Teaching," Dewey talks openly and honestly about the challenges and rewards of a career in teaching. This unique piece was included in a book of essays entitled *My Vocation*. Each essay was written by a prominent American figure describing their personal "calling" or vocation. As one might expect, Dewey warns of some misguided reasons for pursuing the profession of teaching; for example, the desire for material wealth or the political indoctrination of youth. He also notes the kind of personality traits likely to make for an ineffective or unsatisfied teacher. When describing the genuine call to teach, however, Dewey's remarks acquire a more personal tone and appeal repeatedly to a word he is not often associated with: "love." They also resonate strongly with prominent themes from literary Romanticism, invoking favorite authors from Dewey's youth. Dewey first talks about a love of contact with young people—of relationships that embody an appreciation for the virtues of youth and that keep teachers' own youth alive. Dewey additionally mentions a love of knowledge and of the sharing of knowledge, as well as a love of particular subject matter. Most notably, perhaps, Dewey echoes the Romantics in espousing a love of "arousing in others the same intellectual interests and enthusiasms which the teacher [themself] experienced." Or as English poet William Wordsworth puts it in *The Prelude*, "What we have loved, others will love, and we will teach them how."

There are three questions which I should want answered if I were a young man or woman thinking of choosing an occupation. I should want to know first what opportunities the vocation offers, opportunities for cultural development, intellectual, moral, social, and its material rewards along with its opportunities for usefulness and for personal growth. In the second place I should want to know what special demands it makes so that I could measure my personal qualifications against those which are required for genuine success in that calling. And thirdly, I should want to know something of the discouragements and "outs," the difficulties connected with the vocation I had in mind.

It does not require any long argument to show that teaching is pre-eminent among the callings in its opportunities for moral and spiritual service. It has always ranked with the ministry in that respect. Without drawing any invidious comparisons there are certain traits in the profession of education that are especially appealing at the present time. In the first place, it deals with the young, with those whose minds are plastic and whose characters are forming. Horace Mann said, "Where anything is growing one former is worth a thousand reformers." One who deals with the young does not have the obstacles to overcome that one has to meet who is dealing with adults. Educational work is moreover free from sectarian divisions and other divisions which depend upon dogma. The teacher can meet all pupils on a common ground. This fact adds to the ready approach afforded by the youthful mind. Again all modern psychology increasingly emphasizes the formative character of the earlier years of life. In very many cases, the adjustments which are made *then* are those which control the activities of adult life, normal adjustments to others being the foundation of a normal life in the later years, and failures in sane and wise social and personal adaptations being the chief source of later unhappiness and morbid states. The teacher shares with the parent the opportunity to have a direct part in promoting the mental and moral life which is healthy and balanced. The teacher has not only the advantage of dealing with a greater number of children, but also is in a condition to judge more wisely and impartially because of not being involved in emotional ways as the parent is.

The opportunities for intellectual development are so obvious that they hardly need extended exposition. All of the so-called learned professions bring those who pursue them in intimate contact with books, studies, ideas. They stimulate the desire for increased knowledge and wider intellectual contacts. No one can be really successful in performing the duties and meeting these demands who does not retain his intellectual curiosity intact throughout his entire career. It would not, therefore, be just to claim that there is anything unique in the opportunities for intellectual growth furnished by the vocation of teaching. But there are opportunities in it sufficiently great and varied so as to furnish something for every taste. Since literature and science and the arts are taught in the schools, the continued pursuit of learning in some or all of these fields is made desirable. This further study is not a side line but something which fits directly into the demands and opportunities of the vocation.

The social opportunities of teaching, in the narrower sense of the word "social" differ widely in different sections and places, so that no unqualified statement can be made. It is said, and probably with a great deal of truth, that in the large cities teachers are not as much looked up to as they once were; that in some places they are classed almost as household servants. These conditions, however, are exceptional. In general, the profession ranks high in the esteem of the public, and teachers are welcomed because of their calling as well as for their own sake.

The material or pecuniary rewards of the calling are not the chief reason for going into it. There are no financial prizes equaling those to be obtained in business, the law, or even, if we take the exceptional physician as the measure, in medicine. On the other hand, there are not the great disparities and risks which exist in most other callings. The rewards, if not great, are reasonably sure. Until the depression they were, moreover, pretty steadily increasing. If we include vacation periods as part of the material reward of teaching, the profession ranks high. There is no other calling which allows such a prolonged period for travel, for study, and recreation as does the educational. To many temperaments, this phase of teaching counterbalances all the material drawbacks.

The personal qualifications which are needed are indicated in a general way by the opportunities which the vocation presents, since from the standpoint of the individual who is thinking of going into the profession, these are demands made upon him. Good health is, under usual conditions, a prerequisite for success in all callings. One special feature of it may, however, be emphasized in connection with teaching. Those persons who are peculiarly subject to nervous strain and worry should not go into teaching. It is not good for them nor for the pupils who come under their charge. One of the most depressing phases of the vocation is the number of care-worn teachers one sees, with anxiety depicted on the lines of their faces, reflected in their strained high-pitched voices and sharp manners. While contact with the young is a privilege for some temperaments, it is a tax on others, and a tax which they do not bear up under very well. And in some schools, there are too many pupils to a teacher, too many subjects to teach, and adjustments to pupils are made in a mechanical rather than a human way. Human nature reacts against such unnatural conditions.

This point of nervous balance and all-round health connects slowly with the next point. Those who go into teaching ought to have a natural love of contact with the young. There are those who are bored by contact with children and even with youth. They can be more useful in other professions. Their contacts soon become perfunctory and mechanical, and children even if they are not able to express the matter in words, are conscious of the lack of spontaneous response, and no amount of learning or even of acquired pedagogical skill makes up for the deficiency. Only those who have it in themselves to stay young indefinitely and to retain a lively sympathy with the spirit of youth should remain long in the teaching profession.

The point which I would emphasize next is a natural love of communicating knowledge along with a love of knowledge itself. There are scholars who have the latter in a marked degree but who lack enthusiasm for imparting it. To the "natural-born" teacher learning is incomplete unless it is shared. He or she is not contented with it in and for its own sake. He or she wants to use it to stir up the minds of others. Nothing is so satisfactory as to see another mind get the spark of an idea and kindle into a glow because of it. One of the finest teachers I have ever known said to me, "I have never known a first-class teacher who did not have something of the preacher about him"—or her. And he went on to explain that what he meant was love of arousing in others the same intellectual interests and enthusiasms which the teacher himself experienced.

Finally, the teacher should combine an active and keen interest in some one branch of knowledge with interest and skill in following the reactions of the minds of others. I would not say that a teacher ought to strive to be a high-class scholar in all the subjects he or she has to teach. But I would say that a teacher ought to have an unusual love and aptitude in some one subject; history, mathematics, literature, science, a fine art, or whatever. The teacher will then have the *feel* for genuine information and insight in all subjects; will not sink down to the level of the conventional and perfunctory teacher who merely "hears" recitations, and will communicate by unconscious contagion love of learning to others.

The teacher is distinguished from the scholar, no matter how good the latter, by interest in watching the movements of the minds of others, by being sensitive to all the signs of response they exhibit; their quality of response or lack of it, to subject-matter presented. A personal sympathy is a great thing in a teacher. It does its best work, however, when it is in sympathy with the *mental* movements of others, is alive to perplexities and problems, discerning of their causes, having the mental tact to put the finger on the cause of failure, quick to see every sign of promise and to nourish it to maturity. I have often been asked how it was that some teachers who have never studied the art of teaching are still extraordinarily good teachers. The explanation is simple. They have a quick, sure and unflagging sympathy with the operations and process of the minds they are in contact with. Their own minds move in harmony with those of others, appreciating their difficulties, entering into their problems, sharing their intellectual victories.

I am not interested in putting any obstacles in the way of those who think of becoming teachers by dwelling on the obstacles it presents. To an active and energetic character, these will prove only stimuli to greater effort. But few things are more disastrous than the round peg in the square hole, than a person in work to which he or she is not suited. Those who go into the profession of teaching should then realize in advance that for some temperaments it is too safe, too protected, a calling. There is not enough stimulus from competition with their equals to call out their best energies. There are those to whom the young are inferiors; they tend to teach down to them from above, and to acquire a manner which is either tyrannical or patronizing. Such persons should refrain from teaching. There are communities in which political influences operate with great strength. Would-be teachers should ask themselves whether they have the strength of character to sustain their integrity against these influences; whether they can play their part with others without becoming timeservers, chairwarmers, place-holders. The so-called educator who is little more than a cheap politician looking out for his own interests is a sorry spectacle. In fact, every one can call up in his own experience the hard places he is likely to run into and ask whether he has the force to meet and overcome the difficulties which arise.

For those who are fitted for the work, the calling of the teacher combines three rewards, each intense and unique. Love of knowledge; sympathy with growth, intellectual and moral; interest in the improvement of society through improving the individuals who compose it.

Reader Bibliography

Addams, Jane. *Jane Addams on Education.* Edited by Ellen Condliffe Lagemann. New York: Teachers College Press, 1985.

Counts, George, S. *Dare the Schools Build a New Social Order?* New York: John Day, 1932.

Danforth, Scot. "Disability in the Family: John and Alice Dewey Raising Their Son, Sabino." *Teachers College Record* 120, no. 2 (February 2008): 1–30.

———. "John Dewey's Contributions to an Educational Philosophy of Intellectual Disability." *Educational Theory* 58, no. 1 (2008): 45–62.

Dewey, John. "The Reflex Arc Concept in Psychology," 1896 (*EW 5:* 96–109).

———. *My Pedagogic Creed,* 1897 (*EW 5:* 84–95).

———. "Ethical Principles Underlying Education," 1897 (*EW 5:* 54–83).

———. *The Child and the Curriculum,* 1902 (*MW 2:* 272–91).

———. "Education, Direct and Indirect," 1904 (*MW 3:* 240–48).

———. "The Relation of Theory to Practice in Education," 1904 (*MW 3:* 249–72).

———. *Moral Principles in Education,* 1909 (*MW 4:* 265–91).

———. "Address to National Negro Conference," 1909 (*MW 4:* 156–57).

———. "Some Dangers in the Present Movement for Industrial Education," 1913 (*MW 7:* 98–103).

———. *Democracy and Education,* 1916 (*MW 9*).

———. "Method in Science Teaching," 1916 (*MW 10:* 130–36).

———. "Learning to Earn: The Place of Vocational Education in a Comprehensive Scheme of Public Education," 1917 (*MW 10:* 144–50).

———. "The Classroom Teacher," 1922 (*MW 15:* 180–89).

———. *Human Nature and Conduct,* 1922 (MW 14).

———. "Individuality in Education," 1922 (*MW 15:* 170–79).

———. *Experience and Nature,* 1925 (*LW 1*).

———. "Experience, Nature and Art," 1925 (*LW 1:* 226–94).

———. "Individuality and Experience," 1926 (*LW 2:* 55–61).

———. *The Sources of a Science of Education,* 1929 (*LW 5:* 1–40).

———. "The Way Out of Educational Confusion," 1931 (*LW 6:* 75–89).
———. *How We Think* (rev. ed.), 1933 (*LW 8:* 105–352).
———. "The Need for a Philosophy of Education," 1934 (*LW 9:* 194–204).
———. *Art as Experience*, 1934 (*LW 10*).
———. "Toward a National System of Education," 1935 (*LW 11:* 356–59).
———. "Education and Social Change," 1937 (*LW 11:* 408–17).
———. "Democracy and Education in the World of Today," 1938 (*LW 13:* 294–303).
———. *Experience and Education*, 1938 (*LW 13:* 5–62).
———. "To Those Who Aspire to the Profession of Teaching," 1938 (*LW 13:* 342–346).
———. "I Believe," 1939 (*LW 14:* 91–92).
Jackson, Philip W. *John Dewey and the Lessons of Art*. New Haven: Yale University Press, 1998.
Lockheart, Earl Granger, comp. *My Vocation, by Eminent Americans: Or What Eminent Americans Think of Their Callings*. New York: H.W. Wilson, 1938.
McLellan, James A., and John Dewey. "What Psychology Can Do for the Teacher." In *The Psychology of Number and Its Applications to Methods of Teaching Arithmetic*. New York: Appleton, 1895.
Mead, George Herbert. *Mind, Self, and Society*. Chicago: University of Chicago Press, 1934.
Ratner, Joseph, ed. *Education Today*. New York: G.P. Punam's Sons, 1940.
Society for Ethical Culture. January 12, 2024, https://www.ethical.nyc/about/.
Skrtic, Thomas M. "A Political Economy of Learning Disabilities." *Learning Disability Quarterly* 28 (Spring 2005): 149–55.
Thorndike, E. L. "The Nature, Purposes, and General Methods of Measurements of Educational Products." In the *Seventeenth Yearbook of the National Society for the Study of Education*, vol. 2, edited by G. M. Whipple. Bloomington, IL: Public School Publishing, 1918.
Wordsworth, William. *The Prelude*. In *The Poetical Works of William Wordsworth*, edited by Thomas Hutchinson and Ernest de Selincourt. Oxford: Oxford University Press, 1969.

Selective Annotated Bibliography

Archambault, Reginald D., ed. *John Dewey on Education: Selected Writings*. New York: Modern Library, 1964.

> Though antiquated, Archambault's compilation of Dewey's writings on education is thoughtfully arranged and sufficiently comprehensive. It includes an excellent introduction as well. The book is somewhat heavier on philosophical themes and issues than this reader.

Boisvert, Raymond D. *John Dewey: Rethinking Our Time*. Albany: State University of New York Press, 1998.

> Boisvert provides an excellent overview of central themes in Dewey's philosophy. The book is accessible to nonspecialists and features an abundance of informative examples. Boisvert makes a strong case throughout for the enduring relevance of Dewey in "rethinking our time."

Boyles, Deron. *John Dewey's Imaginative Vision of Teaching: Combining Theory and Practice*. Gorham, ME: Meyers Education Press, 2020.

> Boyles writes for a broad audience in integrating Dewey's philosophy of education with critical issues in education policy and practice. The book is very scholarly yet accessible to undergraduate students. Highly recommended.

Breault, Donna Adair, and Rick Breault, eds. *Experiencing Dewey: Insights for Today's Classroom*. 2nd ed. New York: Routledge, 2014.

> This distinctive volume provides a selection of brief essays inspired by favorite quotations from Dewey. These quotations, organized around

six themes, were chosen by contributors for having an enduring impact on their teaching practice. Essays emphasize critical issues in education today.

Cuffaro, Harriet K. *Experimenting with the World: John Dewey and the Early Childhood Classroom*. New York: Teachers College Press, 1995.

Cuffaro explains the pedagogical value of Deweyan hands-on learning and explores its relevance for early childhood education. Instructive examples appear throughout. This is another well-written and very accessible book.

Dewey, John, and Evelyn Dewey. *Schools of To-Morrow*. 1915. MW 8: 205–404.

In this fascinating book, Dewey and daughter Evelyn chronicle the diverse forms of progressive education proliferating at the height of industrialization. Rather than presenting model schools for readers to emulate, the book is a thought piece on possible futures of the progressive movement.

Fishman, Stephen M., and Lucille McCarthy. *John Dewey and the Challenge of Classroom Practice*. New York: Teachers College Press, 1998.

Fishman and McCarthy draw on a wealth of classroom teaching experience to investigate the relationship between theory and practice in Dewey's vision of human learning. The authors also reflect critically on the results of their own Deweyan classroom experiments.

Fishman, Stephen M., and Lucille McCarthy. *John Dewey and the Philosophy and Practice of Hope*. Urbana: University of Illinois Press, 2007.

In their second coauthored book, Fishman and McCarthy reflect on what happens when Dewey's "philosophy of hope" encounters the complex realities of contemporary education policy and practice. Here again, the authors draw liberally on their own classroom-based research.

Frank, Jeff. *Teaching in the Now: John Dewey on the Educational Present*. West Lafayette, IN: Purdue University Press, 2019.

Frank's important book investigates Dewey's core belief that educators must attend thoughtfully to the present moment in the classroom, making it as meaningful and engaging as possible. Only then will students be adequately prepared for life's future challenges.

Garrison, James W. *Dewey and Erōs: Wisdom and Desire in the Art of Teaching.* New York: Teachers College Press, 1997.

> An instant classic, Garrison's book is a wellspring of insight and inspiration. Viewing Dewey through the lens of ancient philosophy, Garrison reveals the vital roles of wisdom and "passionate desire" in the art of teaching. Highly recommended.

Granger, David A. *John Dewey, Albert Barnes, and the Continuity of Art and Life: Revisioning the Arts and Education.* New York: Peter Lang, 2023.

> Granger tells the story of Dewey's personal and professional relationship with art collector and educator Albert C. Barnes. After comparing and contrasting their thinking about the arts, the book offers a Deweyan vision of the arts and education inspired by historical and contemporary developments in the artworld.

Greene, Maxine. *Releasing the Imagination: Essays on Education, the Arts, and Social Change.* San Francisco: Jossey-Bass, 1995.

> Greene's impassioned collection of essays draws on Dewey in exploring the many possible points of intersection between the arts, education, and social change. The common denominator for integrating these elements for the greater good, Greene argues, is imagination.

Hansen, David T., ed. *John Dewey and Our Educational Prospect: A Critical Engagement with Dewey's Democracy and Education.* Albany: State University of New York Press, 2006.

> This well-rounded set of critical essays stages a spirited encounter between Dewey's *Democracy and Education* and an array of contemporary educational issues and problems. With contributions from many well-known authors, the book is highly engaging throughout.

Hein, George E. *Progressive Museum Practice: John Dewey and Democracy.* Walnut Creek, CA: Left Coast Press, 2012.

> Hein's invaluable book examines an assortment of unique museums designed to serve the social good and informed by the progressive movement. Hein concludes, appropriately, with a Deweyan vision of progressive museum practice for the twenty-first century.

Jackson, Philip W. *John Dewey and the Lessons of Art.* New Haven: Yale University Press, 1998.

> In this highly readable book, Jackson identifies an array of educational lessons embedded in Dewey's thinking about the arts. The engaging commentary features illuminating examples drawn from diverse art forms and genres.

Johnson, James Scott. *Deweyan Inquiry: From Education Theory to Practice.* Albany: State University of New York Press, 2009.

> Johnson's book provides a wide-ranging overview of Dewey's theory of inquiry. This includes examination of different forms of inquiry and their relationships to educational theory and practice.

Martin, Jay. *The Education of John Dewey: A Biography.* New York: Columbia University Press, 2002.

> There are a number of quality biographies of Dewey currently in print. Martin's contribution was selected for its emphasis on the many important women in Dewey's life. This includes both family members and colleagues, all of whom contributed significantly to his personal and professional growth.

Mayhew, Katherine Camp, and Anna Camp Edwards. *The Dewey School: The Laboratory School of the University of Chicago 1896–1903.* New Brunswick, NJ: Transaction Publishers, 1936/2007.

> Mayhew and Edwards's classic text documents the early years of the Deweys' Chicago Laboratory School through the eyes of two former teachers and administrators. This richly detailed insider's view of the school provides a captivating window on a pivotal era of educational reform.

Noddings, Nel. *Philosophy of Education.* 4th ed. Boulder, CO: Westview Press, 2015.

> Noddings's popular textbook in philosophy of education contains a thought-provoking chapter geared to first-time readers of Dewey. The book is both appreciative and critical of Dewey's views on several issues germane to education policy and practice today.

Phillips, D. C. *A Companion to John Dewey's Democracy and Education.* Chicago: University of Chicago Press, 2016.

Phillips shares the story of his fifty-year relationship with Dewey's challenging but invaluable book. The wisdom and critique he provides, tinged with humor and personal anecdotes, is a worthy companion to *Democracy and Education* for both veterans and newcomers to Dewey.

Quay, John, and Jayson Seaman. *John Dewey and Education Outdoors: Making Sense of the "Educational Situation" through More Than a Century of Progressive Reforms*. Leiden, Netherlands: Brill Academic Publishers, 2013.

This unique book underscores the importance of the "educational situation" in Dewey's account of human learning. Following Dewey's lead, the authors consider the myriad possibilities of the outdoors as ideal sites for place-based education.

Rosenblatt, Louise M. *The Reader, the Text, the Poem: The Transactional Theory of the Literary Work*. Carbondale: Southern Illinois University Press, 1994.

In this classic text, Rosenblatt develops a theory of reading based on Dewey's transactional view of experience. Her approach allows for multiple interpretations of texts while also providing a justification for responsible reading.

Schubert, William H. *Love, Justice, and Education: John Dewey and the Utopians*. Charlotte, NC: Information Age Publishing, 2010.

Schubert's imaginative book looks at Dewey's ideal vision for education from the standpoint of a group of alien Utopians. This thought experiment allows Schubert to explore Dewey's ideal from an outsider's perspective. In doing so, he highlights the critical roles of love, empathy, and social justice in any substantive educational reform.

Seigfried, Charlene Haddock. *Pragmatism and Feminism: Reweaving the Social Fabric*. Chicago: University of Chicago Press, 1996.

This important book investigates multiple areas of intersection between American pragmatist philosophy and modern feminism. The crucial point of convergence, according to Seigfried, is the liberatory potential of everyday experience.

Simpson, Douglas J. *John Dewey*. New York: Peter Lang, 2006.

Simpson's eminently readable book offers a spirited case for the critical relevance of Dewey for education policy and practice today.

To make this a reality, he argues, we must replace dogmatic attitudes with genuine reflective thinking.

Simpson, Douglas J., Michael J. B. Jackson, and Judy C. Aycock. *John Dewey and the Art of Teaching: Toward Reflective and Imaginative Practice*. Thousand Oaks, CA: Sage Publications, 2005.

This useful book ponders the art of teaching through a host of different life and work roles. The result is a multifaced view of teaching and learning suffused with the democratic values embedded in Dewey's philosophy of education.

Simpson, Douglas J., and Sam F. Stack Jr., eds. *Teachers, Leaders, and Schools: Essays by John Dewey*. Carbondale: Southern Illinois University Press, 2010.

In this reader, Simpson and Stack have carefully assembled a selection of Dewey's writings of interest to teachers, administrators, and policymakers. Each set of readings begins with an essay that links the material in that section with current issues in education.

Tanner, Laurel N. *Dewey's Laboratory School: Lessons for Today*. New York: Teachers College Press, 1997.

Tanner's analysis of the policies and practices of the Laboratory School transports the reader back in time to the earliest days of the school. This engagingly written book also looks at how schools today might work toward genuine Deweyan reforms.

Index

Addams, Jane: and Hull House, 9; influence on Dewey, 2
Aristotle: on habit, 219; on ideal ends, 250–51
Arnold, Matthew: on poetry as criticism of life, 291
art, xvii, xxiv, 9, 12, 13, 14, 21, 23, 127, 132, 226, 241–42, 244, Section VII passim, 300, 319, 322–23; and aesthetics/esthetics, xvii, 12, 140, 226, 265, 267–71, 273–79, 285, 286–290; and instrumentality, 266–94 passim, 294n1; and science, xviii, 163, 166, 322–23; and teaching as an art, 75–76, 81–82, 163, 166–69
activism and social change, 2, 6–7, 9–10, 13, 15n2, 195–204, 238–39, 288, 297–98, 303–9 passim, 321, 322

Baldwin, William: on subject matter in education, 18
Barnard, Henry: and free public schooling, 209
Barnes, Albert C.: and the Barnes Foundation, 257; relationship with Dewey, 13
Bergson, Henri: on intuition, 252; on new modes of apprehending nature, 280

Browning, Robert: "The Ring and the Book," on possibility, 294
Butler, Nicholas Murray: Columbia president, supporter of Dewey's travels, 12

Carlyle, Thomas: on consciousness, 253
Cizek, Franz: and the Child Art Movement, 258, 261
Coleridge, Samuel Taylor: *Aids to Reflection*, influence on Dewey, 3, 4, 5
Comte, Auguste: on the proletariat, 289
Counts, George S.: *Dare the Schools Build a New Social Order?*, on schooling and social change, 195
Crothers, Samuel McChord: on originality, 188
culture, xvii, xix, 6, 10, 14, 15n2, 22, 58, 88, 106, 125, 181, 185, 205, 209, 227, 230, 247, 265, 269, 273–94 passim, 319

Danforth, Scot: on Dewey and disability, 206
Darwin, Charles, xxii; *Origin of Species*, 3; evolution and Dewey's naturalism, 3, 4, 5–6, 8, 11, 30, 31, 177, 239, 251

democracy, xvii–xviii, 3, 7, 12, 13, 91, 123, 134, 195, 202–4, 205, 206–15, 298, 299, 302, 307, 308, 315, 328
Descartes, Rene: dualism of, 284; and science born from doubting, 131
Dewey, Alice Chipman: influence on Dewey, 2, 6, 7, 9, 10, 13, 206
Dewey, Archibald, 1
Dewey, Lucinia Rich, 1, 2
Dewey, Sabino: disability of, 13, 206
Dickens, Charles: social influence of, 289
disability, xvii, 205–6

empiricism, xviii, 3, 4, 5, 22, 24, 84n1, 86, 90
experience, xvii–xxv passim, 3, 4, 6, 8–9, 10, 12, 14–15, 20, 24, 51, 63, 80–81; aesthetic or consummatory, xvii, 12, 267, 268, 271, 273–74, 285; and the arts, Section VII; and curriculum, 105–21; and education, 85–102; educative and mis-educative, xviii, 12, 35, 40, 85, 86, 87–93 passim, 98–100, 106, 129, 154, 176, 178–79, 202, 227, 314, 317, 318, 328; and individuality, 257–63; as practical, 145–62; and shared experience, 7, 11, 105, 123, 281, 293, and subject matter, 123–35
expression, xvii, xviii–xix, 9, 29, 62, 139, 149, 176, 187, 190, 208, 229, 230, 232, 246, 318, 319, 320, 326; and art, 257, 258, 267–68, 273–80 passim, 285

fact, xix, 8, 14, 19–32 passim, 44, 47–63 passim, 70–71, 106–10, 113–17, 123, 130, 170, 228, 240, 244
freedom, xix, 7, 82, 85, 91, 96, 97, 173, 177, 181, 189–90, 193, 209, 213, 238–39, 259–263 passim, 308, 315, 328

Garrod, Heathcote William: on didactic poetry, 291
Gompers, Samuel: as labor leader, 306
Grant, Roberta Lowitz, 16n12
grades and grading, 33, 77, 99, 225, 317

Hall, G. Stanley: and experimental psychology, influence on Dewey, 4
habit, xvii, xix, xx, xxi, xxiv, 8, 9, 40, 52, 60–63 passim, 67, 86, 91–92, 124–25, 147, 152–53, 157, Section VI passim, 263, 287, 293, 314–17 passim, 321, 327; as character, xix, 21, 22, 80, 130, 179, 201, 208, 209, 223, 242, 244, 322, 332; as democratic, xvii, 13, 123, 195; and Dewey as a writer, 14–15, 15n2; as will, 21, 30, 112, 141, 176, 182, 208, 212, 237, 244, 267, and freewill, 238, 243
Hamilton, Alexander: on economic independence, 212
Harper, William Rainey: Chicago president, fallout with Dewey, 10
Harris, William Torrey: on the treatment of educational subject-matter, 162n5
Hesiod: Plato on, 275
Hegel, G. W. F.: idealism of, xx; influence on Dewey, 4–6
Homer: Plato on, 275
Hulme, T. E.: on art and culture, 278–79
Huxley, Julian: on life, 140
Huxley, T. H.: *Elements of Physiology*, influence on Dewey, 3, 5

idealism, xx, 4–5, 6, 11

imagination, xx, xxi, xxiii, 8, 29, 41, 53, 71, 81, 82, 178, 230–31, 249, 252, 260, 263, 273–92 passim
impulse, xviii, xix, xx, 9, 19, 28, 29, 113–14, 128, 154, 173, 222, 233, 237, 241, 246–49, 252–254; as instinct, 314–15
individuality, xx–xxi, 11, 75–76, 109, 175–77, 185–94 passim, 215, 219, 237, 248, 257–63, 277, 282, 293
inquiry, xix, xxii, xxiii, xxiv, xxv, 11, 16n9, 25, 26, 32, 44, 47– 63 passim, 68, 71, 72, 81, 105, 129, 131–32, 138–39, 148, 155, 163, 164, 190, 221, 329
intelligence, xxi, 20, 27, 77, 97, 137, 148, 195, 196, 204, 208, 213, 233–39 passim, 249, 254, 293, 301, 307, 328; and industrial intelligence, 304, 306, 308; and I.Q., 77, 195, 205–6; and science, xxiv, 67, 68; and social intelligence, 219, 232

James, William: on consciousness, 253
Jefferson, Thomas: agrarianism of, 212
Johns Hopkins University: and Dewey's graduate education, 4, 5–6

Kant, Immanuel: influence on Dewey, 3, 4, 5; on ethics, 11; idealism of, 226, 251
Keats, John: on poetry and humanity, 291–92
Kirkpatrick, Clifford: on intelligence tests, 77
knowledge, xviii, xxi, xxii, xxiii, 10, 16n9, 20, 30, 54, 58, 61, 63, 67–69, 108, 120–21, 123, 125–133, 138, 139–40, 153, 171, 180–81, 240, 266–67, 325, 331, 334; as belief, 11, 44, 46, 47; and knowing, xxi, 4, 127, 131, 132, 252–53

language, xvii, xxi–xxii, 11, 225, 233, 281–82, 314, 319
Lewis, Sinclair: social influence of, 289
Lincoln, Abraham: on democracy, 88
Lippman, Walter: on art, 294n1, 294n3
Locke, John: dualism of, 284

Machiavelli, Niccolo: and antiquity, 277
Mann, Horace: as proponent of public schooling, 197, 209–10, 211, 332
Marsh, James: as popularizer of Coleridge, 3
Mead, George Herbert: social nature of mind and identity, influence on Dewey, 16n7
means and ends, xxii, 12, 26, 27, 32, 62, 67, 132, 176, 190, 193, 198, 208, 231, 259, 260, 262, 267, 269–70, 316, 328–29
mind, xx, xxi, xxii, xxiii, 4, 5, 6, 14, 16n7, 21–22, 25, 31–32, 41–45 passim, 52, 54, 58, 67, 107, 109, 113–14, 118–20, 128, 139, 151–57 passim, 176, 185, 190–91, 251, 274, 332, 334–35; and body, xviii, xix, xxiii, 4, 28, 95, 127, 221, 265
Montessori, Maria: on isolation and individuality, 191
morals and ethics, xxiii, 11, 12, 21, 27, 37, 39–40, 61, 78, 90, 92, 147–48, 162n6, 165, 201, 206, 214, Section VI passim, 314, 317, 327, 332; and art, 275, 283, 289, 294n1; and science, 21, 235, 239–40, 290, 322–23
Morris, G. S.: as proponent of Hegel, influence on Dewey, 4, 6, 16n10
Mussolini, Benito: on political liberty, 206

naturalism, xxii, 3, 5, 6, 8, 12; in art, 280
new psychology (constructivism), xix, xxiii, xxv, 4–5, 6, 7, 8, 10, 11, 16n9, 19, 32, 98, 100, 106, 110, 123, 177, 178, 206, 224, 232, 233, 249, 308, 318; and the Chicago Laboratory School, 7–11 passim, 15n6, 16n9, 33–34, 105–21 passim, 297

old psychology (faculty psychology), xxiii, 4, 8, 9, 30, 222

Parker, Francis: progressive demonstration school of, 10, 33
pedagogy, xxiii, 7, 11, 16n11, 25, 27–28, 30, 37, 119, 148, 153, 188, 319
perception, xxiii–xxiv, 29, 43, 47, 70, 206, 251, 259, 265, 267, 269–72, 280, 287, 293–94; vs. recognition, xxiii, 29, 52, 78, 159, 177, 271
philosophy, xxiv, 3–7 passim, 86, 88–89, 173–82 passim, 233, 251, 281, 284
Plato: as educational theorist, 79; and censorship of Homer and Hesiod, 275, 276
progressive education, 10, 16n11, 33, 85, 87–91, 95, 174, 177, 195, 198, 221, 302; and
progressivism, 2, 13, 221, 301

Rivera, Diego and Frida Kahlo: and the Dewey Commission, 14
Russeau, Jean-Jacques: on natural development, 175; on consciousness, 253

Santayana, George: on Greek civilization, 277

science, xxiv, 2, 3, 4, 6, 11, 21, 22, 59–60, 67–73, 90, 115, 116, 131–33, 153, 157, 163–172, 235, 239–40, 300, 308, 318–19; and art, xviii, 163, 166, 322–23, instrumentality of, 266–94 passim, 294n1; and hypothesis testing, 32, 55, 60–63 passim
Shelley, Percy Bysshe: on imaginative experience and morality, 290, 292, 293
situations, xix, xx, xxiv, 14, 41, 85, 87, 96–99, 105, 120, 124, 138, 159, 219, 222–23, 244; as problematic, 8–9, 49–57 passim, 134, 141, 170, 233, 254
Skrtic, Thomas: on Dewey and disability, 206
Socrates: on ignorance and wisdom, 131
Spencer, Herbert: on evolution, 251
Stalin, Joseph: and Leon Trotsky, 14
Starr, Ellen Gates: and Hull House, 9

Taine, Hippolyte: on art and culture, 278
Tennyson, Alfred Lord: "Ulysses," 102n1
theory and practice, xxiii, 7, 11, 109, 120, 139, Section IV passim, 187, 260, 293
testing, xxii, xxiii, 33, 35, 37, 75, 77, 149, 180, 195, 205, 317
Thorndike, E. L.: methods of and bigotry, 84n1
Torrey, H. A. P.: influence on Dewey, 3
Trotsky, Leon: and the Dewey Commission, 14
truth, xxii, xxiv–xxv, 11, 14, 38, 45, 48, 63n1, 106, 108, 110, 116, 120, 131, 272, 294, 328

University of Chicago: Laboratory School of, 7, 8–9, 10, 11, 15n6, 16n9, 33, 105, 297
University of Michigan: and Dewey's first academic appointment, 6, 7
University of Tokyo: and Dewey invited lecturer, 13
University of Vermont: and Dewey's undergraduate education, 1, 3–4

values and evaluation, xix, xxii, xxiv, xxv, 11, 19, 44, 93–94, 98, 99, 145, 179–80, 185, 186, 208–9, 227; and art, 273–94 passim

Wells, H. G.: on life, 140
Wordsworth, William: on the child as father of the man, 31; *The Prelude*, on love, 331

Young, Ella Flagg: on teachers and supervisors, 83; *Scientific Method in Education*, influence on Dewey, 162n4